"Past efforts to relate literature to contemporary religious discourse have been frustrated because the relevant texts have been inaccessible. Jeffrey Barbeau's anthology not only furnishes the ready access readers have needed, it also provides a chronology and a historical overview of the religious strife, dissenting factions, and theological quarrels. Surveying the developments from the advent of Methodism to the Oxford Movement, Barbeau's anthology enriches our understanding of the history and the literature of the period."

—FREDERICK BURWICK, Professor Emeritus of English, University of California, Los Angeles

"An outstanding anthology. We should be grateful to Barbeau for his judicious and illuminating selection of texts. The book constitutes a most discriminating guide to the religion of this momentous period of thought in the English-speaking world."

—DOUGLAS HEDLEY, Professor of the Philosophy of Religion, University of Cambridge

"*Religion in Romantic England* provides source materials essential to any student or scholar interested not only in religion but also in literary, political, and cultural developments. Selections from Wilberforce, Paley, Bentham, Law, Wesley, Wollstonecraft, Burke, Paine, Barbauld, Coleridge, Hemans, Keble, and a score more create a rich, full picture. Barbeau's introduction provides excellent, highly informative context. No student or scholar of the Romantic Age should be without this volume, and every college and research library should have it on its shelves and in its digital resources."

—JAMES ENGELL, Gurney Professor of English and Professor of Comparative Literature, Harvard University

DOCUMENTS OF
ANGLOPHONE CHRISTIANITY

GENERAL EDITORS

Roger Lundin
Arthur F. Holmes Professor of Faith and Learning
Wheaton College
requiescat in pace

Debora Shuger
Professor of English
University of California, Los Angeles

ALSO AVAILABLE IN
THE DOCUMENTS OF ANGLOPHONE CHRISTIANITY
SERIES

Religion in Early Stuart England, 1603–1638: An Anthology of Primary Sources
Edited by Debora Shuger

Religion in Tudor England: An Anthology of Primary Sources
Edited by Ethan H. Shagan and Debora Shuger

Religion in Enlightenment England: An Anthology of Primary Sources
Edited by Jayne Elizabeth Lewis

Religion in Romantic England
An Anthology of Primary Sources

Jeffrey W. Barbeau, editor

BAYLOR UNIVERSITY PRESS

Cover Design by Pam Poll

Library of Congress Cataloging-in-Publication Data

Names: Barbeau, Jeffrey W., editor.
Title: Religion in romantic England : an anthology of primary sources /
Jeffrey W. Barbeau, editor.
Other titles: Documents of Anglophone Christianity.
Description: Waco, Texas : Baylor University Press, [2018] | Series:
Documents of Anglophone Christianity | Includes bibliographical references.
Identifiers: LCCN 2017033803 | ISBN 9781481307222 (printed case :
alk. paper)
Subjects: LCSH: England—Church history—18th century—Sources. |
England—Church history—19th century—Sources.
Classification: LCC BR758 .R3835 2017 | DDC 274.2/081—dc23

Printed in the United States of America on acid-free paper.

for Aimee

TABLE OF CONTENTS

Acknowledgments   xv

Introduction   xvii

Historical Timeline   xxxvii

Abbreviations for Works Commonly Cited   xxxix

I. DIVINITY

William Jones: Trinity in Unity   3
"A letter to the common people in answer to some popular arguments
against the Trinity"
1767

Joseph Priestley: One God   9
An appeal to the serious and candid professors of Christianity
1770

William Hazlitt: Mission of Jesus   15
Human authority, in matters of faith, repugnant to Christianity
1774

Thomas Scott: Faith in Christ   21
The force of truth
1779

Samuel Horsley: Antiquity   27
A charge, delivered to the clergy of the archdeaconry of St Albans
1783

Percy Bysshe Shelley: Atheism   33
The necessity of atheism
1811

Renn Dickson Hampden: Mystery   38
"Knowledge of God through Christ"
1828

II. FAITH

George Whitefield: Repentance   46
"The Good Shepherd: a farewell sermon"
1769

Augustus Toplady: Predestination   51
More work for Mr. Wesley
1771

John Fletcher: Free Grace   57
The first part of an equal check to pharisaism and antinomianism
1774

Joseph Milner: Salvation in Christ   62
"An affectionate address to seamen"
1797

Southwood Smith: Divine Government   68
Illustrations of the divine government
1816

Edward Copleston: Fatalism   74
An enquiry into the doctrines of necessity and predestination
1821

Julius Charles Hare: Light and Darkness   79
"The children of light"
1828

III. CANON

Sarah Trimmer: Two Books   88
An easy introduction to the knowledge of nature, and reading the Holy Scriptures
1780

Herbert Marsh: Prayer Books   94
An inquiry into the consequences of neglecting to give the Prayer Book with the Bible
1812

Isaac Milner: Bible Societies   100
Strictures on some of the publications of the Rev. Herbert Marsh
1813

Peter Gandolphy: Rule of Faith   104
A defence of the ancient faith
1813

Edward Hawkins: Scripture and Tradition   109
A dissertation upon the use and importance of unauthoritative tradition
1819

Mary Anne Schimmelpenninck: Spiritual Interpretation   114
Biblical fragments
1821

Edward Irving: Living Word   119
For the oracles of God . . . For judgment to come
1823

Connop Thirlwall: Biblical Inspiration   125
"Introduction by the translator"
1825

IV. DOUBT

George Horne: Miracles   133
Letters on infidelity
1784

William Wilberforce: Unbelief   138
A practical view of the prevailing religious system of professed Christians
1797

Robert Hall: Infidelity   143
Modern infidelity
1800

William Paley: Evil   149
Natural theology
1802

Richard Whately: Miracles and Testimony   155
Historic doubts relative to Napoleon Buonaparte
1819

Jeremy Bentham: Pain and the Afterlife   162
Analysis of the influence of natural religion on the temporal happiness of mankind
1822

Hugh James Rose: Faith and Reason   167
The state of the Protestant religion in Germany
1825

V. ENTHUSIASM

William Law: Spiritual Life   176
An humble, earnest, and affectionate address to the clergy
1761

William Warburton: Divine Grace   182
The doctrine of grace
1762

William Romaine: Spirit and Conscience   187
The walk of faith
1771

John Foster: Evangelical Intellect   192
"On the aversion of men of taste to evangelical religion"
1805

Leigh Hunt: Dangers of Methodism   199
"An attempt to show the folly and danger of Methodism"
1808

Hannah More: Heart Religion   206
Practical piety
1811

Joanna Southcott: Prophecies   212
Prophecies announcing the birth of the Prince of Peace
1814

Joseph John Gurney: Pure Christianity   218
Sermons and prayers
1832

VI. PSALMS

Charles Wesley: Family Hymns   227
Hymns for the use of families
1767

John Newton and William Cowper: Light Revealed   243
Olney hymns
1779

William Wordsworth: English Church   253
Ecclesiastical sketches
1822

James Montgomery: Christian Hymnody   266
The Christian psalmist
1825

John Keble: Nature's Praise   274
The Christian year
1827

Felicia Hemans: Divine Mysteries   286
Records of woman
1828

VII. MORALS

Henry Venn: Marriage   297
The complete duty of man
1763

Soame Jenyns: Christian Virtue   303
A view of the internal evidence of the Christian religion
1776

Thomas Clarkson: Slavery   309
An essay on the slavery and commerce of the human species
1786

John Wesley: Holy Living   314
"The more excellent way"
1787

Mary Wollstonecraft: Creation   320
Original stories from real life
1788

Adam Clarke: Tobacco   325
A dissertation on the use and abuse of tobacco
1797

Robert Malthus: Chastity   331
An essay on the principle of population
1803

VIII. NATION

Samuel Palmer: English Dissent   339
The Protestant dissenter's catechism
1772

William Stevens: Spiritual Authority   347
A treatise on the nature and constitution of the Christian church
1773

George Dyer: Religious Subscription   352
An inquiry into the nature of subscription to the Thirty-Nine Articles
1789

Edmund Burke: Established Church   359
  Reflections on the revolution in France
    1790

Thomas Paine: Toleration   366
  Rights of man
    1791

Anna Letitia Barbauld: National Repentance   370
  Sins of government, sins of the nation
    1793

Samuel Taylor Coleridge: The Christian Church   376
  On the constitution of the church and state
    1830

IX. PAPACY

Charles Butler: Catholic Relief   385
  An address to the Protestants of Great Britain and Ireland
    1813

John Milner: Papal Authority   390
  The end of religious controversy
    1818

Joseph Blanco White: Catholic Tyranny   396
  The poor man's preservative against popery
    1825

William Poynter: Christian Obedience   404
  Declaration of the Catholic bishops
    1826

Thomas Hartwell Horne: Rome   411
  Romanism contradictory to the Bible
    1827

Thomas Arnold: Irish Catholicism   415
  The Christian duty of granting the claims of the Roman Catholics
    1829

X. OUTSIDERS

Joseph White: Christianity and Islam   425
  A comparison of Mahometism and Christianity
    1784

William Knox: Native Americans   430
  "Of the Indians in the colonies"
    1789

William Carey: Missionary Call   436
    An enquiry into the obligations of Christians
      1792

Thomas Coke: Methodism in Africa   443
    An interesting narrative of a mission
      1812

William Carus Wilson: Heathen Cruelty   449
    The children's friend
      1826

Reginald Heber: Missions in India   455
    Narrative of a journey through the upper provinces of India
      1828

Francis Henry Goldsmid: Jewish Emancipation   460
    Remarks on civil disabilities of the British Jews
      1830

ACKNOWLEDGMENTS

While preparing this anthology, I repeatedly noticed the many debts that authors owe to those around them. My experience has been no different. I am honored that the general editors of the Documents of Anglophone Christianity series, Debora Shuger and Roger Lundin, kindly invited me to collaborate with them on this project. Debora's meticulous feedback and gracious assistance cannot be overstated. Roger shared the journey with me not only through numerous conversations over meals or coffee, but also by team-teaching a course on transatlantic Romanticism. Roger unexpectedly passed away not long after I completed the first draft of this volume. I will miss his friendship enormously. Several other members of the Wheaton College community deserve my thanks, including Susanne Calhoun, Alyssa Lehr Evans, Rhett Austin, Amy Hughes, Gillian Mrva, and Adebola Fabiku. Insights at crucial stages came from Stuart Andrews, Timothy Larsen, Jayne Lewis, and Timothy Whelan. Carey Newman embraced the vision of this series enthusiastically; he and other members of Baylor University Press, including Diane Smith and Cade Jarrell, have devoted themselves to its completion. An almost invisible connection exists between scholarship and family: Elizabeth, Rebekah, Benjamin, Samuel, Jacob, Aaron, and Nathanael have provided me with endless encouragement and delight. My wife Aimee deserves my deepest gratitude for her unflagging support, advice, and friendship. I dedicate this volume to her as a symbol of my appreciation and love.

INTRODUCTION

Pray now, what do you mean by romantic? . . . perhaps you mean that the ideas which I
am expressing associate in your mind with all the fantastic images of romance and that you
cannot help thinking of enchanted castles, of giants and windmills, of fairy revels,
and journeys to the moon.

John Foster (1805)[1]

The Baptist minister John Foster (1770–1843) had no idea that the epithet "romantic" would, by the middle of the nineteenth century, designate one of the most thoughtful, meditative, and sometimes scandalous eras of English literature. The idea of an "English Romantic School," as scholars have time and time again emphasized, did not even emerge until Hippolyte Taine's *Histoire de la littérature Anglaise* (1862–1867; Eng. trans. 1871–1872) brought the term into wider use in the last decades of the nineteenth century.[2] When Foster used the label in 1805, however, he recognized that it already signified much more than tales of wizards, castles, and witches. In the public mind, the romantic individual was overwhelmed by an excess of imagination:

> Imagination may be indulged till it usurp an entire ascendency over the mind, and then every subject presented to that mind will excite imagination, instead of understanding . . . imagination will throw its colors where the intellectual faculty ought to draw its lines; imagination will accumulate metaphors, where reason ought to deduce arguments; images will take the place of thoughts, and scenes of disquisitions. The whole mind may become at length something like a hemisphere of cloud-scenery, filled with an ever-moving train of changing, melting

---

[1]   John Foster, "On the application of the epithet romantic," in *Essays in a series of letters to a friend,* 2 vols. (London: Longman, 1805), 2:11–12.

[2]   Jane Moore and John Strachan, *Key concepts in Romantic literature* (New York: Palgrave Macmillan, 2010), 7.

forms, of every color, mingled with rainbows, meteors, and an occasional gleam of pure sunlight . . .[3]

The romantic, so Foster thought, experiences far more than amorous feelings or rapturous attachments to another person: the romantic distorts real life and imagines individual destiny where such egoism can only be attributed to self-delusion.

The religious aspect of Romanticism may be detected in Foster's description. His epithet belongs to a wider public disputation over allegedly enthusiastic ministers who claimed inspiration by the divine Spirit, professed inner witness of divine adoption as God's children, and admonished people in churches and town squares alike to distrust their heritage or baptism as little more than nominal signs of faith. "Who hath not heard of the wondrous powers of the imagination, when raised and inflamed by fanaticism?," William Warburton wrote. "And tho' we be ignorant of its utmost force, yet we know enough of it to convince us that this faculty of the mind, the nurse and parent of enthusiasm, is able to put on every form of preternatural semblance."[4] On the other hand, the caricature of the Romantic as a dewy-eyed spiritualist ignores other religious developments. Robert Southey, close friend of William Wordsworth and S. T. Coleridge, *was* one of the leading English Romantic poets, yet his view of Wesley was largely critical. Southey thought that Wesley's Methodism had brought a spiritual revolution to England—unlike France—but Southey also deplored the movement's alleged superstition and extravagant abandonment of reason. The label "Romantic," in such a light, is undoubtedly complicated and artificial.

Modern readers might be tempted to make sharp distinctions between religion and other spheres of life. In the Romantic age, which for the purposes of this volume is bounded by the advance of Methodism during the late 1750s and the advent of the Oxford Movement in the early 1830s, no such separation between religious and secular life existed. Recent scholarship highlights the blurred lines that confound inflexible boundaries: "Theological debate was almost inseparable from philosophical, scientific, medical, historical, and political thought in the eighteenth and nineteenth centuries."[5] Religion was the currency of the times, and the reader who chooses to ignore it invariably misunderstands the period. The newcomer might read William Blake's widely anthologized *There is no natural religion* (1788) and presume that his protest marks the decline of religious life in England: "Man has no notion of moral fitness but from education . . . he is only a natural organ subject to sense."[6] Yet Blake's objection marks not the absence of religion but rather a stinging critique of rationalism: "He who sees the infinite in all things sees God. He who sees the *ratio* only sees himself." Gerald Cragg's history of early modern Christianity in England makes a similar point: "It is too easily assumed that during

[3]   Foster, "On the application of the epithet romantic," 15–16.
[4]   William Warburton, *The doctrine of grace; or, The office and operations of the Holy Spirit vindicated from the insults of infidelity, and the abuses of fanaticism*, 3rd ed. (London: A. Millar and J. and R. Tonson, 1763), 11–12.
[5]   Mark Knight and Emma Mason, *Nineteenth-century religion and literature: an introduction* (Oxford: Oxford University Press, 2006), 3.
[6]   William Blake, *There is no natural religion* (ca. 1794/1795), The Blake Archive (electronic edition accessed May 13, 2015); cf. idem, *Selected poetry*, ed. Michael Mason, Oxford World Classics (Oxford: Oxford University Press, 1994).

the period with which we have been concerned the religious life of Christendom was largely moribund. The facts do not support the assumption."[7] Constructions of religion in England during the Romantic era, no less than before, suffer under the commonplace belief that faith meekly fell silent under the protests of skepticism. Romantic religion, on such a view, only denominates another step along the winding road to modern secularity.[8]

In fact, the opposite is much closer to reality. Religion saturated Romantic society. The predominant belief in England was Christianity, and the Church of England enjoyed considerable prestige, rights, and advantages. The English Reformation and its aftermath brought sharp lines of division to religious life in England. Conformists followed the doctrinal and liturgical standards of the Church of England.[9] The monarch was the head of the church, so naturally the government enforced matters of doctrine and practice. Religious beliefs had concrete political consequences. The Clarendon Code established a series of measures enforcing religious conformity throughout the land. The Act of Uniformity (1662), for example, required all ministers to follow the Book of Common Prayer, while the Five Mile Act (1665) prohibited nonconformist ministers from approaching within five miles of any town or city. The Toleration Act of 1689 did allow nonconformists (also known as dissenters) the liberty to worship, but only upon taking oaths of supremacy and allegiance to the king. Moreover, various legal restrictions ("disabilities") remained in effect. Despite such disabilities, the Church of England failed to keep pace. While the total number of Anglican communicants increased significantly between 1760 and 1832, the church's growth rate failed to match the growth of the population as a whole. Dissenting membership, on the other hand, enjoyed rapid expansion, particularly among the many new groups that formed at the end of the eighteenth century. Between 1760 and 1832, immigration, industrialization, and interdenominational competition shifted the composition of English Christianity.[10] Yet, as Jayne Lewis observes in the previous volume in this series, credal pluralism did not amount to universal toleration.[11]

While clearly defined parties *within* Anglicanism are difficult to distinguish in this time, the public would have discerned (even if they would not necessarily have been able to name) significant differences between high church (or what was sometimes called "orthodox") and evangelical Anglicans.[12] High church orthodoxy represented less a theological than a political stance. Strong loyalist tendencies, political conservatism, and external

---

[7]   Gerald R. Cragg, *The church and the Age of Reason, 1648–1789,* The Penguin history of the church 4 (London: Penguin, 1990), 281.

[8]   Timothy Larsen addresses problematic assumptions that plague treatments of Victorian religion in *Crisis of doubt: honest faith in nineteenth-century England* (Oxford: Oxford University Press, 2006).

[9]   For more on conformity, see Jayne Lewis, ed., *Religion in Enlightenment England* (Waco, Tex.: Baylor University Press, 2017); cf. Mark Canuel, *Religion, toleration, and British writing, 1790–1830* (Cambridge: Cambridge University Press, 2002)

[10]   Alan D. Gilbert, *Religion and society in industrial England: church, chapel and social change, 1740–1914* (London: Longman, 1976), 23–48.

[11]   Lewis maintains that conformity is one of the chief characteristics of enlightened Christianity. Romantics, more often, were preoccupied with the relationship between unity and diversity.

[12]   On the challenges of defining church parties in the period, see Peter Nockles, "Church parties in the pre-tractarian Church of England 1750–1833: The 'orthodox'—some problems of definition and identity," in *The Church of England c. 1689–c. 1833: from toleration to tractarianism,* ed. John Walsh et al. (Cambridge: Cambridge University Press, 1993), 334–59.

uniformity characterized high churchmanship. They opposed the seventeenth-century latitudinarian commitment to reason in favor of tradition and commitment to the monarchy and episcopacy.[13] High church Anglicans observed the maliciously antireligious tendencies of the French Revolution and thought that the visible, sanctifying presence of the church was the key to strengthening and upholding the nation. They believed in the antiquity of the church and its apostolic heritage, cherished the legacy of Archbishop William Laud (1573–1645), and discovered new heroes in William Stephens and Edmund Burke. When some churchmen attempted to eliminate subscription to the Thirty-Nine Articles for ordinands to the Church of England (the so-called Feathers Tavern Petition of 1772), explicitly undermining the historical standards of Anglican belief, Stevens countered that the authority of the visible (national) church was an essential component for the responsible management of the household of God. The church, Stevens claimed, requires "stewards" whose inalterable task is the provision of spiritual nourishment, namely, the preaching of the Word and the administration of sacraments. No such power has been granted to "private Christians," who "must themselves expect them from the hands of God's ministers."[14] So, too, Edmund Burke, who, writing against the radical proponents of the French Revolution, proclaimed the English church's steadfast uniformity even in periods of crisis and change: "So tenacious are we of the old ecclesiastical modes and fashions of institution that very little alteration has been made in them since the fourteenth or fifteenth century . . . never entirely nor at once to depart from antiquity."[15] Around the turn of the century, supporters of Stephens and Burke clustered together in groups of like-minded intellectuals such as the Club of Nobody's Friends (a regular gathering in honor of Stevens) and the London-based Hackney Phalanx, and in the *British Critic* they published conservative theological and political opinions for wider distribution. High church Anglicans believed that the well-being of the nation required wide public support for the existing structures and societies of the Church of England, including the Society for Promoting Christian Knowledge (S.P.C.K.) and the Society for the Propagation of the Gospel in Foreign Parts (S.P.G.).[16] They rejected the proliferation of sects and interdenominational societies that might sap the resources and energy of English Christians, and

[13]   The complicated nature of pre-Tractarian high churchmanship may be illustrated by the relationship between the Oxford Movement and the Noetics at Oriel College, Oxford. Although their theological ideas were conducive to high churchmanship, Noetics such as Richard Whately, Edward Hawkins, and Edward Copleston cultivated a relatively liberal agenda through broadminded rational inquiry. Oriel Noetics mentored John Henry Newman, John Keble, and E. B. Pusey in the 1820s, but soon came into conflict with these young intellectuals as the latter repurposed the critical logic and disciplined rhetoric they had learned in the Oriel common room to promote high church ritualism and renewed attention to the sacramental life. On the Noetics, see Peter Nockles, "Oriel and religion, 1800–1833" and "A house divided: Oriel in the era of the Oxford Movement, 1833–1860," in *Oriel College: a history*, ed. Jeremy Catto (Oxford: Oxford University Press, 2013), 291–370.

[14]   William Stevens, *A treatise on the nature and constitution of the Christian church*, new ed. (London: F. and C. Rivington, 1799), 23.

[15]   Edmund Burke, *Reflections on the revolution in France, and on the proceedings in certain societies in London relative to that event*, 2nd ed. (London: J. Dodsley, 1790), 148.

[16]   Thus, when members of the evangelical British and Foreign Bible Society (B.F.B.S.) spread Bibles around England without accompanying Prayer Books, many high church Anglicans opposed the new Society for failing to support the visible unity of the church. William Wordsworth's brother Christopher was among those who wrote against the B.F.B.S. in *Reasons for declining to become a subscriber to the British and*

merely because small divisions reduce the church's mighty and overflowing river to little more than sectarian streams, "entirely wasted and dried up."[17] In an age of revolution and uncertainty, high church Anglicans believed that abiding truths and deeply rooted traditions alone—represented by the divinely established Church of England—could withstand the anxious hum and contentious clamor of the day.[18]

Evangelical Anglicans, not unlike high church Anglicans, remained loyal to the Thirty-Nine Articles, the authority of bishops, and the centrality of sacraments, but they prioritized a piety originating in the experience of conversion, or what some called "heart religion." As Anglicans, these evangelicals had received baptism as infants. Yet, each became convinced of their need for the inward experience of spiritual rebirth. John Wesley's experience of faith is particularly instructive. By the time he was in his mid-thirties, he had already served as a priest, a missionary, and a vocal evangelist working among the needy in orphanages and prisons—no slouch in matters of religious dedication. Still, this was not enough for the young minister. On May 24, 1738, after months of anxious waiting, Wesley finally experienced an evangelical conversion:

> In the evening, I went very unwillingly to a society in Aldersgate Street, where one was reading Luther's Preface to the Epistle to the Romans. About a quarter before nine, while he was describing the change which God works in the heart through faith in Christ, I felt my heart strangely warmed. I felt I did trust in Christ, Christ alone for salvation; and an assurance was given me that he had taken away *my* sins, even *mine*, and saved *me* from the law of sin and death.[19]

Eighteenth- and early nineteenth-century evangelicals looked to the English Reformers for inspiration. They emphasized justification by faith and the experience of new birth, but the priority they placed on individual renewal over church tradition and formality led (often quite controversially) to an openness to new methods of evangelism. Such practices highlighted their "low church" sensibilities: conversion and the experience of grace take priority over ceremony and church polity. David Bebbington defined the four leading characteristics of the movement (the so-called evangelical quadrilateral): *conversionism* ("the belief that lives need to be changed"), *activism* ("the expression of the gospel in effort"), *biblicism* ("a particular regard for the Bible"), and *crucicentrism* ("a stress on the sacrifice of Christ on the cross").[20] John Wesley's towering leadership of the evangelicals cannot be overstated, but other leaders include George Whitefield and Hannah More. Under the leadership of William Wilberforce and his circle (often known as the "Clapham Sect"), evangelical Anglicans led the campaign for broad social reform, fought to abolish

---

Foreign Bible Society, stated in a letter to a clergyman of the diocese of London (London: F. C. and J. Rivington, 1810).

[17] George Frederic Nott, *Religious enthusiasm considered, in eight sermons preached before the University of Oxford* (Oxford: Oxford University Press, 1803), 317–18.

[18] For more on high church developments in the period, see Kenneth Hylson-Smith, *High churchmanship in the Church of England: from the sixteenth century to the late twentieth century* (Edinburgh: T. and T. Clark, 1993); Peter Benedict Nockles, *The Oxford Movement in context: Anglican high churchmanship, 1760–1857* (Cambridge: Cambridge University Press, 1994).

[19] *John Wesley*, ed. Albert C. Outler (Oxford: Oxford University Press, 1964), 66.

[20] David Bebbington, *Evangelicalism in modern Britain: a history from the 1730s to the 1980s* (Grand Rapids: Baker, 1992), 2–3.

the slave system, and published in organs of the movement such as the *Christian Observer* (est. 1802). While high church Anglicanism tended to flourish among the upper classes of English society, evangelical Anglicans multiplied among the lower classes of industrial cities and increasingly mobile immigrant communities.[21]

However, not all eighteenth- and early nineteenth-century evangelicals were Anglicans. The complicated relationship between Methodism and the Church of England is a helpful case study. Early Methodists, following the example of John and Charles Wesley, were Anglicans through and through. When John Wesley ordained ministers for the work in America during the revolution, however, Charles protested the act as schism (John denied any such implication). High church Anglicans, likewise fearing schism, warned against evangelical preachers, who, traveling from town to town, teaching in public squares, and sharing cheap tracts, promised new life and the assurance of salvation:

> The minister, in his cottage visits, if he looks to the shelf will sometimes perceive peeping out between the Bible and Prayer Book one of these little tracts. He will upon inspection find it perhaps to contain no inconsiderable portion of sound doctrine and much practical Christianity worked up in a plain and familiar style well adapted to the lower class. In certain parts, however, the cloven foot will appear. The reader will be directed to consult his feelings whether the new birth has taken place. Or, a story will be told how long a sinner, groaning under the weight of his transgressions, attended his parish church without any good effect; but, accidentally putting his head into a conventicle, the discourse of the preacher went home to his heart and, after a few struggles, he was assured of salvation.[22]

The Anglican minister ought "always on the watch" for such evangelical literature—whether originating from Anglican or dissenting sources—for disorder and "enthusiasm" inevitably result from such evangelical incursions into the local parish.

While diverse forms of religion inflect the literature of the Romantic period, the pious "enthusiasm" associated with evangelicalism often overlaps with prominent themes in British Romantic literature. Thus, Wordsworth's inspired prophecy in *The prelude* impersonates the Methodist preacher, cast out of the church and into the public square:

> to the open fields I told
> A prophecy; poetic numbers came
> Spontaneously, and clothed in priestly robes
> My spirit, thus singled out, as it might seem
> For holy services; great hopes were mine.
> My own voice cheered me, and, far more, the mind's
> Internal echo of the imperfect sound.

---

[21]   Hylson-Smith, *High churchmanship in the Church of England*, xiv–xv.

[22]   Henry Handley Norris, *A manual for the parish priest: being a few hints on the pastoral care, to the younger clergy of the Church of England, from an elder brother* (London: F. C. and J. Rivington, 1815), 141–43; on the problem of evangelical identity, see Frances Knight, *The nineteenth-century church and English society* (Cambridge: Cambridge University Press, 1995), ch. 2.

> To both I listened, drawing from them both
> A cheerful confidence in things to come.[23]

Wordsworth takes up the mantle of the Christian minister, transforming the poet into a prophetic figure. Such claims to "inspired" language often instigated formidable opposition. Some Anglican clergy prohibited evangelical Anglicans from preaching in the parish church. Yet, despite the violent persecution that sometimes resulted from their gatherings, English evangelicals rose to positions of power in England during the Romantic age and established organizations that shaped the face of Christianity around the world. The London Missionary Society (est. 1795) and the British and Foreign Bible Society (est. 1804) offered interdenominational alternatives (or complements, some thought) to their Church of England counterparts.

While evangelicals shared a common piety, they were not unanimous in their theology: Methodists such as John Wesley and George Whitefield disputed publicly over divine election, predestination, and the freedom of the will, issues that had divided English Christians since the Reformation.[24] Moreover, although some evangelicals were dissenters, not all dissenters were evangelicals. Old Dissent had included varieties of Congregationalists, Baptists (including General and Particular Baptists, who differed over predestination), and Presbyterians, but dissent soon expanded into a broad umbrella covering old and new denominations, including assorted groups of Quakers, Unitarians, and Methodists. These groups differed widely on crucial matters of polity, doctrine, and religious practice. Some Old Dissenters embraced historic orthodoxy, but many English Presbyterians and General Baptists gradually took up Socinian beliefs in the eighteenth century. The English Unitarian dissent of Theophilus Lindsey, Richard Price, and Joseph Priestley found its theological roots in Socinian rationalism and biblical criticism, rejecting historically orthodox teachings on the full divinity of Jesus in favor of semi-Arian views that affirmed his divine vocation while objecting to any trinitarian teaching that distorted radical monotheism. Unitarian expansion, however, depended less on revival-style conversions (or de-conversions) than on the annexation of old Presbyterian and General Baptist congregations.[25] Quakers, for their part, shared an evangelical commitment to interiority and inward witness, but typically regarded the inner light as more authoritative than the Bible. Joseph John Gurney attempted a synthesis of Quaker and evangelical beliefs, but divided the Quaker community in the process.

---

[23]   William Wordsworth, *The prelude* (1805), in *Wordsworth's poetry and prose*, ed. Nicholas Halmi, A Norton Critical Edition (New York: W. W. Norton, 2014), 169 (book 1, lines 59–67); cf. Jasper Cragwall, *Lake Methodism: polite literature and popular religion in England, 1780–1830* (Columbus: The Ohio State University Press, 2013), 84–85.

[24]   Cf. previous volumes in this series, including Ethan H. Shagan and Debora Shuger, eds., *Religion in Tudor England* (2016); Debora Shuger, ed., *Religion in early Stuart England, 1603–1638* (2012); and Jayne Lewis, *Religion in Enlightenment England* (2017).

[25]   Gilbert explains the tepid outcome: "Once the original English Presbyterianism (the stock, however noble, upon which the initial growth of Unitarianism had depended) virtually disappeared in the second quarter of the nineteenth century, the Unitarian movement followed a growth pattern comparable with that of the Society of Friends" (*Religion and society in industrial England*, 41). On the intersection of the religious and political dimensions of dissenting religion, see Daniel E. White, *Early Romanticism and religious dissent* (Cambridge: Cambridge University Press, 2006).

As in centuries past, dissenters continued to face real social and political consequences for their beliefs during the Romantic period. The nation's two universities, Oxford and Cambridge, for example, were open only to those who could subscribe to the Thirty-Nine Articles of Religion—a restriction that remained in force until 1871. Dissenters also were required to solemnize their marriages in Anglican churches, regardless of any ceremony previously performed by a minister of their own tradition.[26] In short, dissenters suffered restrictions in personal, professional, and political life, and often faced public scrutiny in times of national distress. During the Birmingham Riots of July 1791, the Unitarian Joseph Priestley suffered the loss of his laboratory, papers, and nearly his life, after mobs attacked chapels, homes, and businesses associated with dissenting ministers. However, the Romantic period also ushered in new opportunities for dissenters to voice their opinions publicly. Against accusations that they undermined (or, at least, compromised) the unity of the nation, dissenters successfully defended their right to meet and worship on the grounds of liberty of conscience. Baptists, Quakers, and Unitarians, among others, publicly organized and voiced their beliefs in ways that would have been improbable even a century earlier.

The category of dissent often denotes *Protestant* dissent, but numerous Roman Catholics lived in England during this period as well. The origins of anti-Catholicism lie in the English Reformation, when fears of Catholic conspiracies and foreign invasions gripped the nation. The Gunpowder Plot of 1605 came to symbolize the Roman Catholic menace, and apprehension of encroaching popery was a key factor in the lead-up to the English Civil War. The religious tests imposed on nonconformists in the seventeenth century were thus partly intended to safeguard the nation from Roman Catholicism. Indeed, after 1689 Protestant dissenters could hold political office, but Roman Catholics (along with Jews) remained disqualified. Anti-Catholic teaching was not limited to the political arena alone. As in past centuries, many English Christians identified the pope as none other than the Antichrist of 2 Thessalonians 2. Thomas Newton, whose *Dissertations on the prophecies* (1758) appeared in twenty editions by the end of the period, charged the pope with the deceptions predicted by the Apostle Paul:

> The apostasy produces him, and he again promotes the apostasy. He is properly "the man of sin," not only on account of the scandalous lives of many popes but by reason of their more scandalous doctrines and principles, dispensing with the most necessary duties and granting or rather selling pardons and indulgences to the most abominable crimes . . . he is the great adversary to God and man, excommunicating and anathematizing, persecuting and destroying by crusades

[26] The Clandestine Marriages Act of 1753 strengthened this requirement, though there were exemptions for Quakers and Jews (though not Roman Catholics). The protections afforded to wives made the act particularly important, since desertion without a legal marriage left these women with little redress. The Marriage Act of 1836 effectively allowed for civil marriages, but dissenting couples continued to marry in the parish church for many years until the practice gradually fell into disuse; see Owen Chadwick, *The Victorian Church*, 2nd ed., 2 vols. (London: Adam and Charles Black, 1970), 1:142–45; and Rebecca Probert, "The impact of the Marriage Act of 1753: was it really 'a most cruel law for the fair sex'?" *Eighteenth-Century Studies* 38 (2005): 247–62.

and inquisitions, by massacres and horrid executions, those sincere Christians who prefer the Word of God to all the authority of men.[27]

As English Catholics (who had sought religious freedom on the Continent) returned home during the French Revolution, however, gradually expanding political and religious liberties facilitated their contributions to government and society. The matter was not without debate and setbacks. In Ireland, where Anglo-Protestants owned most of the land but Catholics constituted a majority of the population, unrest threatened revolution. Some believed a constitutional union between Ireland and Great Britain could bring about Catholic emancipation, but even after the passage of the Acts of Union that created the United Kingdom of Great Britain and Ireland in 1800, emancipation failed to materialize (in part due to the opposition of George III). Voters rejected Catholic emancipation several times in general elections. However, the Sacramental Test Act in 1828 eliminated the Lord's Supper (according to the liturgy of the Church of England) as a requirement for holding government office. A year later, with the threat of revolution in Ireland looming, Roman Catholic emancipation was finally achieved.[28]

At least part of the challenge facing Roman Catholics can be attributed to the events of the French Revolution and its aftermath (1789–1815). Britain had only recently ended its costly War of American Independence (1775–1783) when chaos and war with France threatened the nation anew. Some greeted the events in France as heralding a new age, but by 1793 attitudes gradually changed even among many of the most ardent supporters. In 1789 the storming of the Bastille (a fortress in the heart of Paris) marked the commencement of the Revolution. Political unrest in France continued to unfold, shaking confidence in the British government in the process. The execution of Louis XVI in Paris (1793) and the Reign of Terror (1793–1794) cast a pall over England. Some such as Edmund Burke, whose *Reflections on the revolution in France* (1790) quickly became a lightning rod for debate, were horrified by the revolutionaries' attempt to jettison church and crown. Others such as Thomas Paine, whose response to Burke in *Rights of man* (1791–1792) fueled calls for radical reform, thought revolution abroad could affect significant change at home. Some even welcomed the possibility of revolution: Wordsworth exclaimed in youthful exuberance, "Bliss was it in that dawn to be alive, / But to be young was very heaven."[29] Dissenters, inspired by the possibility of concrete political transformation, sought a repeal of Corporation and Test Acts that limited nonconformist participation in political office. Reforming societies organized political unions to mobilize workers and members of the middle class. The British government attempted to suppress opposition through legislation, arrests, and charges of treason, but it was the ongoing war with France (begun in 1793) that gradually dulled the lustrous appeal of radical reform. Food shortages throughout the 1790s led to riots in 1794 and 1795, and market instability stemming from international trade deficits were felt across the nation. English efforts

---

[27] Thomas Newton, *Dissertations on the prophecies, which have remarkably been fulfilled, and at this time are fulfilling in the world*, 2 vols. (London: J. and R. Tonson, 1758), 2:374–75.

[28] Soon after, English Jews sought the same freedoms and political representation that had been attained by other Christian monotheists (Unitarians had already been granted relief in 1813). Jewish emancipation, however, was not realized until 1858.

[29] William Wordsworth, *The prelude* (1805), book 10, lines 692–93.

to stop Napoleon (emperor from 1804) stressed an already beleaguered people with high inflation, individual income taxation, and the ongoing need for military personnel. In the midst of such disorienting circumstances, many young Romantics grew up knowing nothing other than conflict and unrest. Some Christian ministers advocated for calm reflection; others for change. Several denounced the government, while others urged commitment to powers divinely ordained.[30]

The end of conflict brought new challenges. Even after the Congress of Vienna (1814–1815) and the defeat of Napoleon at Waterloo (June 1815), Britain found itself in mixed social and economic circumstances. On one hand, the wars with France had required England to become less dependent on foreign trade. Agricultural change shifted with the political fortunes of the nation: large tracts of land in rural areas, for example, were gradually enclosed in order to sustain higher yields of wheat (modernizing church revenues in the process).[31] Industrialization in the cities brought suffering and the rise of the urban working class. In the face of child labor, disease, and limited access to education, denominations formed new societies to address social hardship. Working-class children, for example, desperately needed education. Churches responded by creating parish schools and infant schools, Sunday schools and charity schools. Beginning in 1780 Robert Raikes had established the Sunday school movement with the confidence that churches, better than any other institution, could protect the well-being of children. By some estimates, fewer than 10 percent of eligible children were regularly attending schools in England and Wales at the turn of the century, yet those who received an education often did so through the churches. Nearly 200 charity schools were actively educating poor children in London by 1800; and, beyond London, more than 2,300 Sunday schools could be found across the nation. By 1833 the Sunday schools were responsible for 1.5 million students.[32]

Reformers also questioned the moral complacency of the nation: British participation in the transatlantic slave trade and enslavement of Africans in the Americas and West Indies was a national moral quandary. Until the slave trade was abolished in 1808, English vessels transported enslaved Africans across the Atlantic to labor in Caribbean and North American plantations. In cities that served as major slaving ports, such as Bristol and Liverpool, abolitionists agitated against the social and spiritual depravity of the slave system. Many evangelicals were among the most vocal abolitionists. John Wesley's *Thoughts upon slavery* (1774), a revised edition of the noted Quaker abolitionist Anthony Benezet's *Some historical account of Guinea* (1772), called for captains of slave ships, buyers of enslaved Africans, and all those who held slaves to free their fellow humans and end their participation in an immoral institution—a call based on the religious mandate to

---

[30]   Richard Brown, *Revolution, radicalism and reform: England, 1780–1846* (Cambridge: Cambridge University Press, 2000), 12–27; Michael Ferber, *Romanticism: a very short introduction* (Oxford: Oxford University Press, 2010), 94–98; Boyd Hilton, *A mad, bad, and dangerous people?: England, 1783–1846* (Oxford: Oxford University Press, 2008), 57–109.

[31]   Land enclosure profited the Church of England, but also contributed to the eventuality of tithe reform (enacted in 1836); see Eric J. Evans, *The contentious tithe: the tithe problem and English agriculture, 1750–1850* (London: Routledge, 1976), ch. 5.

[32]   Eric Hopkins, *Childhood transformed: working-class children in nineteenth-century England* (Manchester: Manchester University Press, 1994); F. M. L. Thompson, *The rise of respectable society: a social history of Victorian Britain, 1830–1900* (Cambridge, Mass.: Harvard University Press, 1988); Marilyn Gaull, *English Romanticism: the human context* (New York: W. W. Norton, 1988).

love one's neighbor. A few slaveholders denounced violent treatment of the slaves while still defending their right to "employ" slaves on their plantations, but many worried that even a modest religious education could lead to insurrections.[33] Long after the abolition of the slave trade, largely effected by the activism of Christians, slavery continued to profit the nation substantially. Indeed, when slaveholding was finally prohibited in the empire by the Slavery Abolition Act 1833, the government distributed a massive compensation sum of £20 million to 46,000 British slaveholders.[34] Slavery and the slave trade were abolished, but slaveholding families prospered in the act.

Revolution, economic depression, and various social ills inspired the formation of new religious organizations to spread the gospel. Two organizations had firmly established reputations (as previously noted)—the Society for Promoting Christian Knowledge (1698) and the Society for the Propagation of the Gospel in Foreign Parts (1701)—but these bodies primarily focused their attention on Anglican interests. During the Romantic period, several new missionary organizations emerged in quick succession and refashioned the religious landscape through competition for public support, including the Baptist Missionary Society (1792), the London Missionary Society (1795), the Church Missionary Society (1799), and the Wesleyan Methodist Missionary Society (1813). Such groups were often interdenominational in character, maximizing the effort to elicit charitable support of English Christians. The organizers of the London Missionary Society (L.M.S.), for example, were lay and ordained leaders from Anglican, Presbyterian, Wesleyan, and other denominations, but their missionaries established churches with a congregational church polity in order "to prevent, if possible, any cause of future dissension."

Missionary societies had a common goal: to share the gospel with people in every region of the world. Missionary letters and memoirs provide a snapshot of English attitudes towards other religions at the time. Missionary reports, for example, often testified to the cruelty they discovered among "heathen" religious and cultural practices. Yet many of those same works also condemn—in equally strong language—rife immorality at home. Two historically orthodox if ostensibly contrary claims were widely held: (1) All humans are depraved and require correction and renovation. (2) All people, however depraved and immoral, are created in the divine image. Christopher Smart's "Moderation" (1771), for example, asserts the *imago Dei* as the shared bond of all humanity:

[33] The Society for the Propagation of the Gospel in Foreign Parts (S.P.G.) owned slaves in the Barbados after receiving a substantial charitable bequest upon the death of plantation owner Christopher Codrington in 1710. For more on the concern that religious education might lead to rebellion, see William Knox, *Three tracts respecting the conversion and instruction of the free Indians and Negroe [sic] slaves in the colonies*, new ed. (London: J. Debrett, 1789), 26–28.

[34] The current value of £20 million in compensation is difficult to estimate. In comparison to the increase in national debt, the amount equals £11 billion today; in relation to the size of the British economy, the total compensation to slaveholders may have been closer to £65 billion (Nick Draper, "'Possessing slaves': ownership, compensation and metropolitan society in Britain at the time of Emancipation 1834–40," *History Workshop Journal* 64 [2007]: 79; on the benefits received by the slaveholding family of William Gladstone, see Roland Quinault, "Gladstone and slavery," *The Historical Journal* 52 [2009]: 363–83).

Tho' I my party long have chose,
　And claim Christ Jesus on my side,
Yet will I not my peace oppose,
　By pique,[35] by prejudice, or pride. . . .

And yet I will my thoughts suppress,
　And keep my tongue from censure clear;
The Jew, the Turk, the heathen bless,
　And hold the plough and persevere.[36]

Not many English Christians could so easily "bless" their heathen neighbors, but most all shared Smart's belief in God's universal, creative work: "There's God in every man most sure." This common humanity provided the foundation for the medical, educational, and evangelistic labors of missionaries and mission societies. The expansion of Christianity around the world proved to be one of the lasting contributions of the Romantic period.

By the early 1830s, a new era in English religious life began to emerge. The issues that had captivated the nation, amalgamating religious, social, political, and intellectual facets of life, had passed. Rather unexpectedly, the Church of England witnessed its own revival: "Anglican expansion, negligible before about 1830, began to gather pace in the 1830s, and the period between this revival and the First World War saw a phase of continuous increase of Anglican churches, of Anglican clergy, and of participation by laymen in the institutions of the Church."[37] What shifted the religious landscape? There are no simple answers. In a move that worried traditionalists, the 1832 Reform Act brought wider political representation to the nation, limiting the power of a few wealthy individuals and expanding the electorate in major cities.[38] The rise of the Oxford Movement (1833–1845), in part stimulated by anxieties over secularization of the temporal sphere, fostered greater commitment to the authority of the Church of England, ancient Christian beliefs and practices, and, eventually, a pronounced Anglo-Catholic spirit.[39] Evangelicals—Anglican and dissenter alike—continued to play a prominent role in English Christianity, but new voices urged theological liberalism in what became known as the broad church movement associated with theologians such as F. D. Maurice and A. P. Stanley.[40] Victorian religion, however, built on the spirituality of the Romantic generation. The energetic expansion and improvement of church buildings in the Victorian period, for example, depended on

---

[35]　That is, animosity between people, parties, or countries.

[36]　Christopher Smart, "Moderation," in *Hymns for the amusement of children* (London: T. Carnan, 1771). Notably, English readers witnessed the rise of a growing body of literature related to Islam in the eighteenth century, including several influential English editions of the *Arabian nights*, histories of Islam in the Middle East, and George Sale's English translation of the Qur'an (1734); see Humberto Garcia, *Islam and the English Enlightenment, 1670–1840* (Baltimore: The Johns Hopkins University Press, 2012).

[37]　Gilbert, *Religion and society in industrial England*, 29.

[38]　Chadwick, *The Victorian Church*, 1:24–47.

[39]　The leaders of the Oxford Movement were commonly called Tractarians for their association with the publication of ninety pamphlets that appeared between 1833 and 1841 as *Tracts for the times*.

[40]　Cf. Tod E. Jones, *The broad church: a biography of a movement* (Lanham, Md.: Lexington, 2003).

the Romantic revival of Gothic art and architecture.[41] Romantic religion was the incubator for Victorian faith no less than for the Victorian crisis of doubt. The public preoccupation with church controversies, mid-century debates about doctrine, anxiety over church membership and weekly attendance, prominent articulations of disbelief, public battles over biblical authority and inspiration, the scandal over Darwinism, and so many debates about subscription, regeneration, church, and society belong to a new age yet emerge from the beliefs, practices, contests, doctrines, and developments of the Romantic era.

Romanticism *and* religion. The two belong together. This anthology, the first of its kind, attends to the ways English Christianity has shaped (and been shaped by) the social, cultural, political, ecclesial, and broader religious life of the nation between 1760 and 1832. Not all (or even most) individuals included in this anthology are properly "Romantics." The nineteenth-century theologies associated with the term—whether the German Protestant liberalism of Friedrich Schleiermacher, the French Catholicism of Félicité Lamennais, the American Congregationalism of Horace Bushnell, or even the post-Unitarian Anglicanism of S. T. Coleridge in England—should not be confused with the period.[42] While characteristic features of Romantic religion may be found in many of the writings in this volume—the emphasis on experience, interiority, imagination, organicism, nature, and history are all prominent themes—no single aspect encompasses the whole. William Law, William Romaine, Hannah More, and J. C. Hare each appeal to individual interiority in their religious musings, but in consistently different ways. So too nature could alternately serve the preaching of George Whitefield, the moral lessons of Mary Wollstonecraft, the embodied prophecies of a Joanna Southcott, or the liturgical poetics of John Keble, but each writer takes up the created order for unique ends. Even history, which so many of these authors recall in their quest for religious order, could be used by Joseph Priestley to counter historic orthodoxies even as Hugh James Rose defended the same orthodoxies on historical grounds. Location has proven something of a challenge. Most of the authors included in this volume were born in England, but several were raised in Scotland, Ireland, or further abroad. Some selections reflect religious life in England, while others describe foreign mission fields. Yet all these writings belong to the breadth of what might still be denominated "Romantic religion" in England. Throughout, I have selected works that will help students and scholars alike better to understand the many ways that English Christians taught, preached, collaborated, defended, participated, argued, practiced, hoped, and imagined their own faith. No one is more aware than I am of the many selections that could have been included, but what follows will introduce

---

[41]   David W. Bebbington notes this Romantic preference at mid-century: not only the Anglo-Catholics of the 1840s, but also the "Scottish Presbyterians and English Nonconformists who wanted striking new buildings turned to Dissenting Gothic instead of to classical architecture" (*The dominance of evangelicalism: the age of Spurgeon and Moody* [Leicester: InterVarsity, 2005], 143).

[42]   For more on Christian theology and Romanticism, see James C. Livingston, *Modern Christian thought: the Enlightenment and the nineteenth century*, 2nd ed., vol. 1 (Upper Saddle River, N.J.: Prentice Hall, 1997), chs. 4 and 6; cf. Warren Breckman, *European Romanticism: a brief history with documents* (Boston: Bedford/St. Martin's, 2008).

readers to major themes and controversies during this fascinating period of English religious history.

Part I ("Divinity") takes readers to the heart of Christianity by focusing on competing claims about God. New forms of religious dissent challenged not only the belief in the Trinity and the full divinity of Jesus Christ, but also undermined fundamental assumptions about the relationship between God and the world. Critics appealed to reason to invalidate historic Christian doctrine, while apologists looked to Scripture and the apostolic witness of the early church. Of course, inquiry into the nature and existence of God has spanned through the ages, as Anna Laetitia Barbauld's lines on "The Unknown God" underscore: "Yet still, where'er presumptuous man / His Maker's essence strives to scan / . . . Ah! still *that altar* stands."[43] Yet, in the Romantic period, Christian theologians began to question the authority of the Bible and the meaningfulness of traditional creeds. Unitarians such as Joseph Priestley, who emerged as a prominent voice during this era, drew on the Reformation tradition of *sola Scriptura* to counter trinitarian doctrine (the belief that one God could also be three divine persons). Defenders of the Trinity, for their part, maintained that Scripture allows for no other belief. Against Priestley's radical monotheism, William Jones highlights the longstanding Christian commitment to trinitarianism despite the alleged advantages that abandoning such ancient language would afford: "The Socinians objected it to us long ago that the doctrines of the Trinity and Incarnation prevent the conversion of Mahometans, Jews and pagans . . . Were we to alter the Christian faith into what Jews, Turks, and pagans believe, then we should gain them all; for then we should be agreed; that is, we should cease to be Christians as well as they."[44] Thomas Scott, among the most influential evangelical writers of the period, associated his own conversion to the intellectual and spiritual rewards of trinitarian doctrine. The intense conflict over the nature—and, at moments, even the existence—of God shaped the religious character of the period.

Part II ("Faith") turns to the question the jailor asks Paul and Silas: "What must I do to be saved?" The answer, "Believe on the Lord Jesus Christ" (Acts 16:30-31), remained the same eighteen centuries later. Selections in this part present two aspects of this claim. On one hand, faith involves acts of repentance and humble obedience. On the other hand, faith involves trust that it is God who accomplishes salvation. These two aspects, which reside at the heart of the Protestant understanding of salvation, were among the most popular topics for preachers in the Romantic period. George Whitefield, for example, offers a classic call for repentance in a charming sermon on the humble sheep who depend on God for life and direction in everyday affairs. Joseph Milner, by contrast, confronts mariners about to set sail on a dangerous voyage abroad with their need to repent for sin, reject immorality, and discover new life in Christ. J. C. Hare, alternately, calls listeners to discover the full meaning of walking as "children of light" through an appeal to the all-encompassing work of divine love. The initiative ascribed to divine grace in this Protestant model of salvation raised longstanding questions about whether human freedom

---

[43]   *The works of Anna Laetitia Barbauld*, 2 vols. (London: Longman, 1825), 1:229.

[44]   William Jones, "A letter to the common people in answer to some popular arguments against the Trinity," in *The Catholic doctrine of the Trinity*, 3rd ed., in *The theological, philosophical and miscellaneous works of the Rev. William Jones*, 12 vols. (London: F. and C. Rivington, 1801), 1:182.

and divine sovereignty are compatible: questions, that is, about predestination. While most preachers invoked the need to repent, not everyone believed that all were equally capable of such an act. Western Christians since Augustine affirmed the need for divine grace, but some thought that original sin had so completely damaged the individual that every aspect of repentance required divine assistance. According to some Calvinists, such as Augustus Toplady, God only extends his gracious help to those he predetermined as his own. Others likewise denied the compatibility of divine sovereignty and human freedom, but on philosophical rather than theological grounds. The Unitarian Southwood Smith, for instance, regarded human freedom as an illusion based on the mind's responses to pain or pleasure. By contrast, various prominent theologians such as Edward Copleston and the Methodist John Fletcher (like John Wesley) believed that denying human freedom made God a capricious tyrant, stripping humanity of moral responsibility in the process.

Part III ("Canon") focuses on the most important book in Romantic England: the Bible. Long before Coleridge declared that the Bible is "the lever by which the moral and intellectual character of Europe has been raised to its present comparative height," the Bible was preached from the pulpit, explicated through commentaries, rewritten in verse, sung from pews, questioned by critics, denied by skeptics, and distributed by believers. The Bible was the basis of education, and children across the nation learned their letters (no less than their history) from its pages. No book commanded more attention, praise, wonder, and respect. Human reason and attentiveness to nature could demonstrate God's existence, but the Bible alone reveals the redemption of the world through the Incarnation and atoning work of Christ and the promise of final peace and reconciliation. However, in what amounts to a revival of Reformation debates between Protestants and Roman Catholics, English Christians in the Romantic era clashed over the role of church traditions in biblical interpretation. Roman Catholics argued that church traditions not only clarified the meaning of the Bible but also constituted an independent record of divine revelation passed on by the apostles from Jesus Christ. The Church of England embraced early Christian creeds as guides to biblical interpretation, but some thought that interdenominational efforts to spread the gospel through Bible distribution risked leading readers into heresy. Particularly after the formation of the interdenominational British and Foreign Bible Society (1804), which pledged to produce inexpensive Bibles free of partisan doctrinal glosses that might favor one denomination over another, many Church of England clergy feared the worst. Herbert Marsh, a noted University of Cambridge biblical scholar, thought the absence of interpretive aids such as the creeds and catechism of the Book of Common Prayer might lead to an epidemic of misreading. Critics attacked Marsh for denying the Bible's sufficiency in matters of salvation—a tenet of the Thirty-Nine Articles of the Church of England—and wondered whether a too forceful advocacy for church traditions gave credence to Roman Catholic claims that the Bible was not, whatever Protestants might say to the contrary, either self-interpreting or self-authenticating. Disputes over the sufficiency of the Bible reemerged, in part, from the rise of biblical criticism. Although there had been a long history of biblical criticism in England, new theories of biblical composition, inspiration, and canonical authority (particularly surfacing in publications from Germany) challenged English Christians to rethink their doctrinal commitments. Still, even as controversy fomented uncertainties, other influential voices such as Edward Irving and Mary Anne Schimmelpenninck retained the ancient allegiance to biblical authority and its centrality to spiritual, devotional, and ethical life.

In Part IV ("Doubt"), allegations of an insurmountable conflict between faith and reason found expression in debates over the credibility of biblical miracles, the justice of God in allowing suffering, and the singularity of the revelation of God in Christ. In many circles, the Enlightenment had made reason appear unassailable, even in matters of religion. Through the powers of the human mind and the precision of the natural sciences, the vastness of the universe could be understood, the depths of the human person divulged, and the truths of religion and morality discerned. Time-honored confidence in the coordinate testimony of Scripture, the authority of the church, and human reason in matters of belief—Richard Hooker's classic Anglican triad—gradually faded. The greatest challenge came from the Scottish philosopher David Hume (1711–1776). In works such as the *Dialogues concerning natural religion* (1779), Hume's withering skepticism undermined both the new religious rationalism and traditional religious dogma. In his "Essay upon Miracles" (1748), Hume questioned the authenticity of biblical miracles and hence their value as a sure basis for Christian belief. Cragg describes the immensity of Hume's undertaking: "He demolished all the traditional certainties: God and the soul, nature and matter, causation and miracles. This did not mean that discussion of these subjects ceased or that reasonable belief came abruptly to an end. It meant that a new beginning had to be made."[45] Apologists—writers who championed Christian doctrine as the only true description of reality—rose to the challenge in a full-scale response. William Wilberforce, the famed abolitionist, believed that only two options exist in the modern world: Christianity or absolute skepticism. The latter, he warned, would lead to moral collapse and social deterioration. Richard Whately defended Scripture history by subjecting Hume's essay in a remarkable *reductio ad absurdum* that used the philosopher's reasoning to prove the nonexistence of Napoleon Bonaparte.

Part V ("Enthusiasm") features the rise of evangelical Christianity during the period. The movement inspired a new language of spiritual awareness, contributed to the elevation and empowerment of the commoner, and facilitated a fresh interest in human interiority, nature, and community through its emphases on conversion, biblical authority, the cross of Christ, and social activism. Although many denominations belonged to the evangelical revival, Methodists were among its most vocal representatives. John and Charles Wesley directed lay preachers equipped with Bibles and hymns to canvass the nation; they sent missionaries abroad to share the good news, encourage repentance for sin, and teach doctrines of "inner witness" and spiritual perfection. Opponents of evangelical enthusiasm decried the tendency of itinerant preachers to enter (uninvited) into parishes served by existing Church of England ministers, drawing people from the pews and into town squares, speaking directly to bustling crowds that gathered to witness the spectacle, and promoting peculiar standards of faith and practice. Interest in "heart religion" was fairly widespread, but often it was the fringe that captured the limelight. Joanna Southcott, whose visionary prophecies enthralled the press, claimed direct revelation from God for her apocalyptic interpretations and promoted the belief that she bore the promised messiah in her womb. Against such extravagant claims, critics such as William Warburton

---

[45]   Cragg, *The church and the Age of Reason, 1648–1789*, 168.

questioned the notion that divine inspiration was to be found outside the Bible, and Leigh Hunt, who wrote one of the finest attacks on Methodism in the period, charged enthusiasts with believing that the divine personally addressed them in the most commonplace accidents of everyday life: "In short, he cannot take a beefsteak or a walk, he cannot stumble upon a stone or a dinner, he cannot speak, look, or move without interesting the divine being most actively in his behalf; the whole order of nature is disturbed to indulge their little finger." Evangelical revival—a source of new life to some and dangerous enthusiasm to others—challenged a mechanistic view of the world through a new emphasis on the work of the Spirit in the heart.

Part VI ("Psalms") is devoted to the religious poetry of the era. The late eighteenth century saw the emergence of some of the greatest hymn writers in English history. Leaders of the evangelical revival used hymns to bring a sense of community to large groups gathered for preaching and solidarity to small bands of believers assembled for prayer and mutual instruction in Christian doctrine. As James Montgomery explains, hymns allow even an illiterate disciple to "sing with gladness and refreshment" of the most profound religious ideas. John Newton and William Cowper's *Olney hymns* (1779) provide a virtual snapshot of the revival in their hymns of grace and love transforming the sinful life. Charles Wesley composed more than nine thousand poems and hymns during his lifetime: some doctrinal, others centering on family life, including heartrending prayers related to the birth and death of his child. Yet not all lyrics were hymns: some poets wrote formal prayers in verse that could be used in private devotions. John Keble's *The Christian year* (1828) was one of the most popular devotionals of the times—a work that could be found at the bedside of many English Christians during the nineteenth century. Others wrote political verse with overt religious themes. William Wordsworth's *Ecclesiastical sketches* (1822), seldom anthologized in collections of Romantic poetry, includes remarkable sonnets tracing the history of Christianity in England. Whether in emotive hymns, encomiums in verse, or lyric expositions of spirituality, the Romantics used carefully fashioned poetry to express their beliefs about God and the world.

Part VII ("Morals") reveals the myriad ways that Christians encouraged reform of individual and social practices through reflection on the meaning of faithful living in the world. Personal piety and acts of service went hand in hand for many English Christians. Although caricatured as prudish regulators of conduct, Christians frequently advocated the moral life in order to advance society as a whole. Lessons on the right ordering of marriage and family, such as Henry Venn's advice in *The complete duty of man* (1763), sprang from an earnest effort to apply biblical wisdom to contemporary society. While some aspects of his advice will undoubtedly appear dated, his rejection of tyrannical dominion and his admonishment to mutual fidelity and affection calls husbands to a higher moral standard than might otherwise have been expected of a man in that time. Similarly, when Soame Jenyns argues that valor, patriotism, and friendship are "no virtues at all," he does so from a belief that the Christian practice of humility, forgiveness, and charity are higher values because based on a concern for others. John Wesley taught that all people were called not only to be saved or justified but also to be sanctified and perfected in holiness and love. Such a claim requires substance, and the English minister thought it his duty to provide concrete advice in how to progress in the Christian life. Thus Wesley, along with other ministers such as Adam Clarke, could recommend the right use of an individual's time and money. Rather than wasting away resources on fruitless pleasures, these ministers urged self-restraint, devotion to the poor, and concern for the welfare of others. Clarke condemned the use of tobacco for its negative impact on individual health, family income, and community. And, when Robert Malthus urged population control through chastity and delayed marriages to prevent mass starvation, he thought his economic advice aligned perfectly with biblical morality. Christians argued that the abolition of slavery, the foremost social issue of the day, was at heart a moral issue founded on respect for the dignity of all human beings. In sum, these writings reveal a self-conscious commitment to morality for the good of society.

The next two parts explore the intersection between the churches and the political life of the nation. The selections in Part VIII ("Nation") relate to the role of the Christian church vis-à-vis the state, to religious and political dissent, and to the idea of toleration. The French Revolution, more than any other event in the period, challenged the authority of the Church of England. Some believed that ecclesiastical authority depended on political allegiance to the monarchy: the Church of England must necessarily support government interests at home and abroad. Robert Holmes, for one, pleads for national repentance on such grounds: "suffer 'the word of exhortation' . . . suffer it, for our country's sake." The language of Holmes, at times, totters at the edge of an Hobbesian submission to the power of the state, but the influence of Edmund Burke, who theorized an organic union of church and state, proved far stronger.[46] On the other hand, some wrote in direct opposition to any association of church and state that enhanced the privileged status of the Church of England. George Dyer, for example, thought English universities ought not be closed to those who could not subscribe to the Articles of Religion. In Dyer's view, the state wrongfully denied the privileges of citizenship to dissenting Catholics, Jews, and Deists, no less than nonconforming Protestants, by requiring subscription to religious claims that had little to do with the well-being of the nation. In Thomas Paine's view, if the inherent dignity of every person as a bearer of the divine image could be affirmed, then toleration for all people would necessarily develop. Others decried the hypocrisy of a nation that claimed to represent Christian interests while slaughtering innocents abroad, and offered stinging critiques of English exceptionalism. Submission. Allegiance. Dissent. Questions surrounding the relationship between the church and state pervade the literature of the Romantic era.

Part IX ("Papacy") turns to English anxieties regarding the bishop of Rome and debate over Roman Catholic emancipation, which captured national headlines during the 1820s. The French Revolution brought new immigration from France, including thousands of English Catholics seeking protection from the violent anti-Catholicism of the revolutionaries. The crisis in France led to change at home. The Catholic Relief Act of 1791 allowed for political, religious, and economic mitigation, provided Catholics denied that the pope "has any civil jurisdiction, power, superiority, or preeminence, directly or indirectly, within this realm." The Relief Act meant that Roman Catholic churches could once again operate openly and educational institutions such as St. Edmund's College in Ware, Hertfordshire, could be established (English Catholic priests had previously trained at Douai in France until the Revolution forced its closure in 1793). Most Catholic recusants,

[46] Nockles, *The Oxford Movement in context*, 45–103.

as they were sometimes called, argued for civil and religious liberties along the same lines as Protestant dissenters, but a closer examination of Catholic writings on emancipation reveals sharp divisions among Catholics about how to achieve their common goal. Some, such as Charles Butler, sought emancipation by pursuing gradual political gains and accepting Protestant demands that they reject papal claims to temporal authority. Others, such as John Milner, took a more aggressive stance that refused any language that might discredit Roman Catholic teaching. By the 1820s, with political momentum increasingly favoring Catholic emancipation, sermons and pamphlets brought old anxieties to the surface. Convert writers such as Blanco White, who was raised in Spain and experienced life in a Catholic nation firsthand, warned of political encroachment, doctrinal impurity, and moral decline. Others, such as Thomas Hartwell Horne, advised against conciliation on biblical grounds. Toleration, in the end, won the day. Emancipation was finally achieved with the passage of a second Roman Catholic Relief Act in 1829 (notably, another two decades passed before a similar measure emancipated English Jews).

The final part ("Outsiders") documents the beliefs and attitudes held by English Christians towards members of other cultures, places, or religions. To be sure, religious "outsiders" were present in England since at least the sixteenth century, but the proliferation of travel literature and commerce abroad led to a new awareness of religious and cultural diversity. Christian missionaries followed wherever the nation exerted its power. Many believed that the symbiotic relationship enjoyed between the churches and the British Empire was a necessary evil, as a representative letter from Robert Southey to William Wilberforce indicates: "No man can abhor all schemes of conquest & aggression more deeply than I do; but it is an act of humanity, & even a duty, to assume the guardianship of those who are palpably in a state of moral & intellectual infancy. The rights of savages are of infinitely little importance when compared with the temporal & eternal advantages of them & their posterity."[47] The rise of numerous missionary societies, especially the formation of the interdenominational London Missionary Society in 1795, brought the English reading public into contact with worldwide religious diversity. In travel narratives, memoirs, letters from missionaries, and reports of their activities overseas, English Christians across denominational lines attempted to describe the religious, social, and cultural practices of "non-believers." Some wrote scathing critiques of non-Christian religions. Joseph White warned readers that Islam fosters violence that cannot be reconciled with Christian faith. William Carus Wilson, one of the most widely read tract writers in the period, told similarly frightening stories of neglect and cruelty in distant lands. William Knox, who owned slaves in Georgia, developed a detailed proposal for the civilization and eventual conversion of Native Americans. Others offered very different perspectives. William Carey, one of the most famous English missionaries, challenged his contemporaries to cast aside fear for the religious other and renounce the comforts of home in order to share the good news with those who had never heard the gospel. Thomas Coke, often called the Father of Methodist Missions, praised the work of former slaves in the colonies who courageously founded Methodist churches in Sierra Leone. All the

---

[47] Letter, 2280. Robert Southey to William Wilberforce, 14 July 1813, in *The collected letters of Robert Southey, part four: 1810–1815*, ed. Ian Packer and Lynda Pratt, Romantic Circles, https://www.rc.umd .edu (accessed July 5, 2015); cf. Letter, 2270.

while, religious pluralism existed in England, and with the recognition of political liberty for Roman Catholics came appeals for emancipation of other minorities who contributed to the welfare of the nation.

Across these seven crucial decades, men and women of vastly different creeds, denominations, and cultures reinvigorated the English nation with new patterns of reflection on God, the human, the community, and the world. The Romantic era cannot be regarded as uniform in any sense of the word, but the authors in these most fascinating times share a common interest in the religious dimensions of topics as diverse as revolution, the individual self, reason, history, and tradition. Looking back through the centuries, these authors located resources for reflection in the past and experimented with new possibilities for the future. In the process, they participated in one of the great eras of literature, theology, and history.

⪼﹏⪻

Each selection in this volume is preceded by an introduction and list of sources consulted. Whenever possible, I have used the earliest available edition of a work, except when additions and corrections in later editions have historical significance. Consistent with the editorial practice of this series, I have silently modernized all texts in matters of punctuation, capitalization, and spelling; eliminated the ubiquitous penchant for italicization; and expanded contractions (even in poetry, except when expanding would change poetic meter). All rhymes in poetry are true ones: thus, for example, love, above, move, and approve all rhyme in British English. Wherever possible, I have defined potentially confusing words, though readers should remain mindful that some words may be used in multiple senses, such as "want," which may mean either "lack" or "to desire." Ellipses indicate that some material, usually less than a page, has been omitted. Longer omissions are noted by a dagger ‡ on a new line. Everything in square brackets [ ] is an editorial addition, whether in the text or in the notes. Authors in this era commonly included numerous footnotes, many of which I have removed silently. Eighteenth- and nineteenth-century authors drew freely (and often from memory) on the Authorized "King James" Bible: citations that the original author included in the main text are marked in parentheses ( ); or, when an author provided a reference at the bottom of the page, I have moved the reference into the text with braces { }. I have identified many additional references to the Bible in square brackets [ ].

HISTORICAL TIMELINE

1760   Accession of George III (October)

1772   Feathers Tavern Petition seeks abolition of subscription to Thirty-Nine Articles

1775   Commencement of American War of Independence

1776   Thomas Paine, *Common sense*

1778   Catholic Relief Act removes some restrictions upon declaration of oath

1779   John Newton, "Amazing Grace"
        David Hume, *Dialogues concerning natural religion*

1780   Robert Raikes Sunday school movement

1783   Treaty of Paris ends American War of Independence

1784   John Wesley ordains ministers for America

1789   French Revolution begins (July)

1790   Edmund Burke, *Reflections on the revolution in France*

1791   Birmingham Riots target Joseph Priestley
        Death of John Wesley
        Roman Catholic Relief Act permits practice of law and religion

1792   Mary Wollstonecraft, *Vindication of the rights of woman*

1793   Execution of Louis XVI (January)
        France declares war on England and Holland (February)
        Reign of Terror begins (September)
        William Carey departs for India

1794   Reign of Terror ends (July)

1795   Formation of London Missionary Society

1798   Wordsworth and Coleridge, *Lyrical ballads*

1799   Napoleon, First Consul

1800   Acts of Union create the United Kingdom of Great Britain and Ireland

1801   Birth of John Henry Newman
        Napoleon signs Concordat with Pope Pius VII

1802   Napoleon proclaimed First Consul for life
1803   England declares war on France (May)
1804   Formation of British and Foreign Bible Society
       Napoleon declared emperor
1807   Abolition of the slave trade (March)
1808   Formation of interdenominational Lancastrian Society (British and Foreign
       School Society from 1814)
1810   End of reign of George III
1811   Appointment of Prince Regent
       Church of England forms the National Society on Andrew Bell's monitorial
       system of education
       Percy Bysshe Shelley dismissed from University of Oxford
       Hannah More, *Practical piety*
1812   Places of Religious Worship Act repeals restraints on dissenters
       United States declares war on Great Britain
1813   Doctrine of the Trinity Act grants toleration to Unitarians
       Robert Southey named Poet Laureate
1814   Joanna Southcott alleges divinely ordained pregnancy
       Thomas Coke dies at sea while traveling to India and Ceylon
       Napoleon abdicates (April) and exiled to Elba (May)
       Treaty of Ghent ends war between Great Britain and United States (December)
1815   Napoleon escapes Elba and returns to power in France (March)
       Napoleon defeated at Battle of Waterloo (June)
1819   Peterloo Massacre (August)
1820   Death of George III
       Accession of George IV
1821   Death of John Keats in Rome (February)
       Napoleon dies in exile on St. Helena (May)
1822   Edward Irving begins preaching in London
       Shelley drowns in Gulf of Spezia (Italy) (July)
1824   Robert Southey, *Book of the church*
1825   S. T. Coleridge, *Aids to reflection*
1827   Founding of the University of London
       John Keble, *The Christian year*
1828   Sacramental Test Act ends requirement that all government officials receive the
       Lord's Supper in the Church of England in order to hold office
       Thomas Arnold named headmaster at Rugby
1829   Roman Catholic Relief Act emancipates Roman Catholics to sit in Parliament
1830   F. H. Goldsmid, *Remarks on civil disabilities of the British Jews*
       Death of George IV
       Accession of William IV
1832   Passage of Reform Bill (May)

ABBREVIATIONS FOR
WORKS COMMONLY CITED

Bebbington	Bebbington, David. *Evangelicalism in modern Britain: a history from the 1730s to the 1980s.* Grand Rapids: Baker, 1992.
BDE	*Biographical dictionary of evangelicals.* Edited by Timothy Larsen. Downers Grove, Ill.: InterVarsity, 2003.
Cragg	Cragg, Gerald R. *The church and the Age of Reason, 1648–1789.* The Penguin History of the Church 4. London: Penguin, 1990.
ECL	*Encyclopedia of Christian literature.* Edited by George Thomas Kurian and James D. Smith III. 2 vols. Lanham, Md.: Scarecrow, 2010.
Hylson-Smith	Hylson-Smith, Kenneth. *High churchmanship in the Church of England: from the sixteenth century to the late twentieth century.* Edinburgh: T. and T. Clark, 1993.
NCE	*New Catholic encyclopedia.* Edited by Bernard L. Marthaler. 2nd ed. Washington, D.C.: Catholic University of America, 2002.
Nockles	Nockles, Peter Benedict. *The Oxford Movement in context: Anglican high churchmanship, 1760–1857.* Cambridge: Cambridge University Press, 1994.
OCEL	*Oxford companion to English literature.* Edited by Dinah Birch. 7th ed. Oxford: Oxford University Press, 2009.
OED	*Oxford English dictionary.* 20 vols. 2nd ed. Oxford: Oxford University Press, 1989.
ODCC	*Oxford dictionary of the Christian church.* Edited by F. L. Cross and E. A. Livingstone. 3rd ed. Oxford: Oxford University Press, 1997.
ODNB	*Oxford dictionary of national biography.* Edited by H. C. G. Matthew and Brian Harrison. Oxford: Oxford University Press, 2004.
RCBEC	Gregory, Jeremy, and John Stevenson. *The Routledge companion to Britain in the eighteenth century, 1688–1820.* London: Routledge, 2007.
VC	Chadwick, Owen. *The Victorian church.* 2 vols. 2nd ed. London: Adam and Charles Black, 1970, 1972.

I

DIVINITY

The existence and character of the Deity is . . . the most interesting of all human speculations.

William Paley, *Natural theology* (1802)

WILLIAM JONES
(1726–1800)
Trinity in Unity

One of the formative theological debates in early Christianity centered on the divinity of Jesus Christ. Against the teachings of Arius (d. 336)—who is said to have had followers who allegedly rallied in the streets, shouting of Jesus Christ, "There was a time when he was not!"—the Council of Nicaea (325) affirmed the full divinity of the Son. Occasional controversy continued over the centuries, but a fresh wave of polemics emerged in England in the latter half of the eighteenth century. The Socinians, who took their name from a sixteenth-century theologian who challenged the divinity of Christ, were precursors to modern Unitarians (a name that became increasingly common during the Romantic period). As dissenters, they eschewed church traditions and relied on rationalist biblical criticism to affirm a Christian monotheism divested of all traces of Hellenization and superstition.

William Jones of Nayland—a vocal apologist for the doctrine of the Trinity, and a precursor to the Oxford Movement—was born at Lowick, Northampton, and educated at Charterhouse. Jones was a descendant of the regicide Colonel John Jones, and it is said that he grieved each year on January 30 in commemoration of the regrettable act of his forebear. While a student at University College, Oxford (B.A., 1749), Jones established a lifelong friendship with George Horne and later served as Horne's chaplain when the latter became bishop of Norwich. The two men found intellectual companionship in the writings of John Hutchinson, who believed that the unpointed Hebrew Bible opened new avenues for biblical interpretation and an understanding of the natural sciences. Ordained priest in 1751, Jones served as rector at Pluckley, Kent, from 1765. A little more than a decade later, Jones assumed the perpetual curacy of Nayland, Suffolk, from which he took the name "Jones of Nayland." Against the agitation and irreligion associated with the French Revolution, Jones inaugurated the Society for the Reformation of Principles in 1792. One result of this short-lived society was the formation of the conservative journal *British Critic*. Jones and others in his circle (such as William Stevens) worked to extend the high church traditions of the English Nonjurors. Among his several writings are scientific treatises marked by Hutchinsonian principles (biblically oriented, anti-Newtonian views of natural science), which earned Jones election to the Royal Society in 1775. His many works of divinity defend high church dogma and challenge anti-Trinitarian dissent.

Unlike Jones' *A short way to truth* (1792), which appeals to examples of triads in nature to defend the Trinity, *The Catholic doctrine of the Trinity* (1756) contends for the biblical foundations of the doctrine. John Henry Newman noted that Jones' "admirable work" helped to solidify his own commitment to "that fundamental truth of religion" (*Apologia*, 26). The following selection comes from "A letter to the common people in answer to some popular arguments against the Trinity," which Jones appended to the third edition in 1767. While the letter addresses a number of common arguments against the Trinity, he directs much of the work against the Cuckfield controversialist William Hopkins (1706–1786), who appealed to the "common sense" of ministers of the Church of England against the historic confession of the full divinity of Christ.

SOURCES: G. M. Ditchfield, "Reverend William Jones 'of Nayland' (1726–1800): some new light on his years in Kent," *Notes & Queries* 40 (1993): 337–42; Hylson-Smith; John Henry Newman, *Apologia pro vita sua* (New York: Penguin, 1994); Nockles; *ODCC*; *ODNB*; *RCBEC*; B. W. Young, *Religion and Enlightenment in eighteenth-century England* (Oxford: Clarendon, 1998).

WILLIAM JONES
"A letter to the common people in answer to some popular arguments against the Trinity"
1767

Men and Brethren,

As Christians and members of the Church of England, you have been taught that the true God, whom you are bound to believe and worship, is a "Trinity in Unity."[1] In the name of these three persons, the Father, the Son, and the Holy Ghost, you have been baptized; and in the Litany are directed to pray to this "holy, blessed, and glorious Trinity, three persons and one God," that he would "have mercy upon us miserable sinners."[2]

From the first propagation of the gospel there has been a sort of men in the Christian church who had too high an opinion of their own knowledge and wisdom to submit quietly to this doctrine. They pretended it was contrary to their reason and common sense, and impossible in the nature of things that the true God should be made manifest in the flesh for the salvation of the world; and hence they argued that the Incarnation must either have been a delusion, a fact brought to pass only in show and appearance; or that the person incarnate must have been some created being, far inferior in power and dignity to the divine nature itself.

About three hundred years after the death of Christ, when paganism, or the worship of idols, was losing its influence in the Roman Empire, this heresy, being come to its full growth, did immediately supply the place of it and prospered to such a degree that it overspread the greatest part of the East and ended at last in the imposture of the false prophet Mahomet, whose doctrine was readily embraced wherever Arianism prevailed, and nowhere else among Christians; and his disciples do at this day most zealously deny that Trinity which you worship.[3]

---

[1]   [Ed. From the Athanasian Creed.]

[2]   [Ed. The Litany, or General Supplication, of the Book of Common Prayer.]

[3]   [Ed. Jones links Muhammad (570–632) to Arianism due to the Islamic belief that Jesus was not fully divine, but only a revered prophet. Fourth-century Arians claimed that Jesus was the first creation of the Father and an instrument of the creation of the world.]

When the teachers of the church found themselves disturbed, and their people corrupted more and more by the daily increase of this heresy, upwards of three hundred Christian bishops, many of whom had been tortured and maimed in the heathen persecutions, assembled together at the city of Nice in Bithynia;[4] and one Arius, a principal promoter of this wickedness, was summoned to appear before them. His doctrine and writings were condemned; the faith which these holy men had brought with them to the council was declared and is now preserved in the Nicene Creed, which form we make use of in the Church because it comprehends the sense of our faith in a few words. But we do not rest our belief upon the authority of any human form, because the doctrine therein expressed is secured by the unquestionable authority of the Old and New Testaments.

‡

I. You know, my dear brethren, that *pride* is a very prevailing passion in human nature; and unless we are very much upon our guard and are fortified with the true principles of Christian humility, we are all of us in danger of being ensnared by it. Men are proud of their clothes and proud of their riches and proud of their titles; but, above all, they are proud of their understanding. Some men are endued with a strength of mind which enables them to bear up with cheerfulness under the common trials of sickness and losses and disappointments; while, perhaps, the same men cannot endure the thought of being cheated and imposed upon, because it is a reflection upon their understanding. Our adversaries, therefore, hoping to make the stronger impression, apply themselves first of all to your pride and inform you that this doctrine of the Trinity is "imposed upon your consciences by Church authority."[5] . . . Let us put it to the trial and begin with the first article of the Creed: "I believe in God the Father Almighty."[6] How is this article imposed? Does the Church determine by her own authority whether there is a God or not? And so for the rest. Does the Church determine whether there is a Christ or an Holy Ghost? Whether there will be a "resurrection of the dead" and a "life everlasting"? Certainly the Church neither does nor can pretend to determine any of these things for us because where anything is determined by authority, such authority must be superior to what it determines—to suppose which, in this case, would be equally false and presumptuous. Therefore the truth of the matter is this: that the Church does only declare that faith which it has received; and instead of her imposing, this faith is imposed upon the Church by the uncontrollable authority of God in the Holy Scripture to which every private Christian is referred for the proper evidence of any particular doctrine, and for that of the Trinity amongst the rest. . . .

II. But "the gospel," they say, "was designed for persons of all capacities," and unless "all persons of common sense" are qualified to understand what the Lord requires of

---

4   [Ed. In 325 Emperor Constantine convened the Christian bishops at Nice (or Nicaea) in order to address (and ultimately condemn) the doctrines of Arius and his followers. The gathering became known as the first ecumenical council of Christianity.]

5   [Ed. Jones refers to the full title of Hopkins' *An appeal to the common sense of all Christian people, more particularly the members of the Church of England, with regard to an important point of faith and practice, imposed upon their consciences, by church authority* (1753). Subsequent references will be drawn from the 2nd ed. (London: A. Millar, 1754).]

6   [Ed. Jones draws attention in this paragraph to key phrases from the Nicene Creed.]

them, we must "charge Almighty God with dealing unfairly with his creatures."[7] Now if the gospel be so easy that nothing but bare common sense is wanted for the understanding of it, why do these authors write so many books to help you to understand it in the Arian sense? If you are able, as they flatter you, to instruct yourselves out of the gospel, then their practice is a contradiction to their principle, and their labor is superfluous by their own confession. My brethren, we do not argue in this manner; we know that you have sense and ability to understand the merits of a cause and are ready to hear reason when it is plainly represented to you. But if you were able to make all things intelligible to your own selves, we should neither preach to you nor write books for you.

‡

III. They tell you, moreover, that people of all sorts have a "right to judge for themselves in matters of religion."[8] As this principle very nearly affects the peace of the Christian world and the salvation of individuals, I would advise you to inquire strictly into the meaning of these terms, and to consider how far they may be justified, and how far they are to be condemned. "Right" is a pleasing thing, and "liberty" is an old temptation; but if any Christian doth so assert his right against an human law, as to depart from his obedience and subjection to the divine law, such a right will do him no good when he has got it because it will not protect him under his religious mistakes against the superior judgment of God; so far from it, that it is probably one of the chief mistakes he will have to answer for.

When they assert that you are to "judge" for yourselves, they must mean either that you are to judge of truth by its proper evidence or that by a certain prerogative of conscience you are to *guess* for yourselves what is right or wrong without any evidence at all. If only the former of these senses is intended, they say no more than we all say, and what the Church hath said ever since the Reformation. If the latter is also allowed and unlearned people have a right to follow their conscience (that is, their *inclination*) without any evidence, or with some false and partial representation of it, then it will follow that the difference between good and evil is not real, but imaginary; that truth and falsehood, like temporary fashions, are not the objects of reason, but of fancy; which doctrines, if admitted in their full latitude, would turn all reason and religion upside down; and I think they have done it in part already.

‡

IV. To prejudice your minds against the Athanasian Creed,[9] they inform you that the doctrine of the Trinity, as there set forth, is "not expressed in the words of Scripture; there are no such propositions to be found in the declarations of Christ and his apostles."[10] By this it is meant that you do not find any such expressions as "Trinity in Unity," "not three

---

[7]   [Ed. Hopkins, *An appeal to the common sense of all Christian people*, 2.]

[8]   [Ed. Hopkins, *An appeal to the common sense of all Christian people*, 133.]

[9]   [Ed. The Athanasian Creed, used predominantly in the West, was incorrectly attributed to Athanasius, the fourth-century bishop of Alexandria. Trinitarian controversy in England during this period led some to call for its removal from the Book of Common Prayer because of its controversial authorship, date, and provenance.]

[10]   [Ed. Hopkins, *An appeal to the common sense of all Christian people*, 5.]

eternals, but one eternal,"[11] and such like. The best course you can take upon this occasion is to argue with them upon their own principles, which generally stop a man's mouth sooner than any other. Ask them, where they find it asserted in the words of Scripture, "Almighty God is one supreme intelligent Being or Person?"[12] Ask them, in what chapter or verse Christ or his apostles did ever declare that "the Holy Spirit" is "first Minister in the government" of the Church; and where it is said that he has "angels for his assistants"?[13] Ask them, again, where they meet with the proposition "the worship of Christ is inferior or mediatorial"?[14] And you might ask them twenty more such questions, which they can never answer upon their own principles, so that they have employed an argument to corrupt you which returns upon themselves, and with this disadvantage on their side . . . they have departed from the *sense* as well as the *words* of Scripture—but the Church, if besides the words of Scripture it uses others, does still retain such a sense as the words of Scripture will clearly justify.

TEXT: William Jones, "A letter to the common people in answer to some popular arguments against the Trinity," in *The Catholic doctrine of the Trinity*, 3rd ed., in *The theological, philosophical and miscellaneous works of the Rev. William Jones*, 12 vols. (London: F. and C. Rivington, 1801), 1:149–61.

[11]   [Ed. These are phrases from the Athanasian Creed.]

[12]   [Ed. Hopkins repeats, throughout the *Appeal*, that he writes in order that readers might "be fully satisfied who the person is whom St. Paul describes by the Name of God, and you will soon be convinced that he is one, supreme, intelligent agent or person, the Lord of heaven and earth, as distinguished from Christ, and consequently is the Father only, and not Father, Son, and Holy Ghost" (28).]

[13]   [Ed. Hopkins, *An appeal to the common sense of all Christian people*, 115.]

[14]   [Ed. Hopkins, *An appeal to the common sense of all Christian people*, 115.]

JOSEPH PRIESTLEY
(1733–1804)
One God

Among the critics of Trinitarian doctrine in the eighteenth century, none proved more influential than the dissenting minister and scientist Joseph Priestley. By all accounts, Priestley was a precocious child. As a dissenter, he could not attend either of the two major universities in England, but instead studied at the liberal dissenting college, Daventry Academy (1751). Priestley accepted a call to ministry at the Presbyterian church at Needham Market, Suffolk, in 1755. He later served at Nantwich, where he also opened a school. In 1761 Priestley joined Warrington Academy. He restructured the curriculum, placing greater emphasis on history and the natural sciences. Priestley's scientific achievements include the isolation and identification of oxygen in 1774. While serving as minister of Mill Hill Chapel, Leeds, Priestley embraced Socinian anti-Trinitarianism. During this time, he challenged major doctrines of the historic Christian faith, including the divinity of Christ, his atonement for original sin, and biblical inspiration. This doctrinal shift not only shaped the future of his ministry and writings, but also ended his relationship with his family.

Philosophically, Priestley was a materialist and a necessitarian. Among his most important works (from over 150 volumes) was *An history of the corruptions of Christianity* (2 vols., 1782), which argues that early church Trinitarian doctrine represented a compromise position between Jewish-Christian monotheism and Hellenistic polytheism. After the publication of the follow-up to that volume, *An history of early opinions concerning Jesus Christ* (1786), Priestley became involved in protracted controversy with Samuel Horsley and several other defenders of traditional Christian doctrine. In 1791 Priestley helped to found English Unitarianism with Theophilus Lindsey. The same year, he nearly lost his life in the Birmingham Riots. Incensed by Priestley's controversial claims, the violent mob attempted to rid the city of religious and political dissenters, destroying his home, laboratory, library, and papers in the process. Priestley spent the last decade of his life in Pennsylvania, where he befriended George Washington and Thomas Jefferson.

Priestley's *An appeal to the serious and candid professors of Christianity* (1770) was published by "A lover of the gospel." The pseudonym reminds one of Priestley's buoyant optimism. Priestley's *Appeal*, originally directed at Calvinistic Methodists, tackles six major topics of Christian disputation: (1) the use of reason in matters of religion, (2) the power of the individual to do the will of God, (3) original sin, (4) election and reprobation, (5) the divinity of Christ, and (6) atonement for sin by the death of Christ. When Christians assess the truth of revelation by the right use of reason, Priestley asserts, they discover the favor of God, the goodness of the human person, and their own happiness in the face of temptation and evil. The following selection lays out Priestley's basic teachings about human reason and Jesus Christ. Priestley encourages the use of reason not to the exclusion of the Bible, but in concert with the Scriptures. Jesus Christ, the Second Adam, provides the ideal pattern for all people to imitate. The *Appeal* challenges the common assertion that Socinianism offers little more than cold rationalism. Rather, as Cragg notes, Priestley's "confidence is reminiscent of a warm, bright morning in spring" (172).

SOURCES: Stuart Andrews, *Unitarian radicalism: political rhetoric, 1770–1814* (New York: Palgrave Macmillan, 2003); Cragg; *OCEL*; *ODCC*; *ODNB*; *RCBEC*; Kathryn J. Ready, "Dissenting heads and hearts: Joseph Priestley, Anna Barbauld, and conflicting attitudes towards devotion within rational dissent," *Journal of Religious History* 34 (2010): 174–90; Isabel Rivers and David L. Wykes, eds., *Joseph Priestley, scientist, philosopher, and theologian* (Oxford: Oxford University Press, 2008).

JOSEPH PRIESTLEY
An appeal to the serious and candid professors of Christianity
1770

Be not backward or afraid, my brethren, to make use of your reason in matters of religion or where the Scriptures are concerned. They both of them proceed from the same God and Father of us all, who is the giver of every good and every perfect gift [Jas 1:17]. They cannot, therefore, be contrary to one another, but must mutually illustrate and enforce each other. Besides, how can we distinguish one scheme of religion from another, so as to give the preference to that which is the most deserving of it, but by the help of our reason and understanding? What would you yourselves say to a Mahometan[1] whom you would persuade to abandon the imposture of Mahomet and embrace Christianity but bid him use his reason and judge, by the help of it, of the manifest difference between the two religions and the great superiority of yours to his? Does not God himself appeal to the reason of man when he condescends to ask us, "Whether his ways be not equal? (Ezek 18:29). Does not the apostle exhort us that "in understanding we be men" (1 Cor 14:20)? Are we not expressly commanded to "prove all things, and then hold fast that which is good" (1 Thess 5:21)? Also, when we are commanded to "search the Scriptures" (John 5:39), more must be meant than merely *reading* them or *receiving implicitly* the interpretations of others. "Searching" must imply an earnest endeavor to find out for ourselves and to understand the truths contained in the Scriptures; and what faculty can we employ for this purpose but that which is commonly called reason, whereby we are capable of thinking, reflecting, comparing, and judging of things?

Distrust, therefore, all those who decry human reason and who require you to abandon it wherever religion is concerned. When once they have gained this point with you, they can lead you whither they please and impose upon you every absurdity which their sinister views may make it expedient for them that you should embrace. . . . The papist, therefore, as might well be expected, is forward on all occasions to vilify human reason and to require men to abandon it; but true Protestants will not part with it. It is by the help of reason, in conjunction with the Scriptures, that we guard ourselves against the

---

[1]   [Ed. That is, a Muslim.]

gross delusions of the papists, who, after relinquishing reason, have been "made to believe a lie";[2] and by the diligent and continued use of the same power, let us endeavor to combat every remaining error, and trace out and reform every corruption of Christianity, till we hold the pure "truth as it is in Jesus" and "obey it in the love thereof."[3]

‡

If you ask who, then, is Jesus Christ, if he be not God, I answer in the words of Peter, addressed to the Jews after his resurrection and ascension: that "Jesus of Nazareth was a man approved of God by miracles and wonders and signs, which God did by him" (Acts 2:22). If you ask what is meant by "man" in this place, I answer that "man," if the word be used with any kind of propriety, must mean the same kind of being with yourselves. I say, moreover, with the author of the Epistle to the Hebrews that "it became him by whom are all things, and for whom are all things, to make this great captain of our salvation in all respects like unto us his brethren, that he might be made perfect through sufferings" (Heb 2:10, 17), "and that he might have a feeling of all our infirmities" (Heb 4:15). For this reason it was that our Savior and deliverer was not made of the nature of an angel, or like any super-angelic being, but was of "the seed of Abraham" (Heb 2:16): that is (exclusive of the divinity of the Father, which resided in him, and acted by him), a mere man, as other Jews, and as we ourselves also are.

Christ being made by the immediate hand of God and not born in the usual course of generation is no reason for his not being considered as a man. For then Adam must not have been a man. But in the ideas of Paul, both "the first and second Adam" (as Christ, on this account, is sometimes called) were equally men: "By man came death, by man came also the resurrection of the dead" (1 Cor 15:21). And, certainly, in the resurrection of a man—that is, of a person in all respects like ourselves—we have a more lively hope of our own resurrection; that of Christ being both a *proof* and a *pattern* of ours. We can, therefore, more firmly believe that "because he lives, we," who are the same that he was and who shall undergo the same change by death that he did, "shall live also" (John 14:19).

Till this great corruption of Christianity be removed, it will be in vain to preach the gospel to Jews or Mahometans, or, indeed, to any people who retain the use of the reason and understanding that God has given them. For how is it possible that *three* persons—Father, Son, and Holy Ghost—should be separately, each of them, possessed of all divine perfections so as to be *true*, *very*, and *eternal* God, and yet that there should be but *one* *God*—a truth which is so clearly and fully revealed that it is not possible for men to refuse their assent to it; or else it would, no doubt, have been long ago expunged from our Creed as utterly irreconcilable with the more favorite doctrine of a Trinity, a term which is not to be found in the Scriptures. Things *above* our reason may, for anything that we know to

---

2   [Ed. The quote may indicate that Priestley writes with Jeremy Taylor's *The real presence and spiritual of Christ in the blessed sacrament* (1654) at hand; the same wording, which incorporates 2 Thess 2:11, appears in section 10 (on transubstantiation) of Taylor's work.]

3   [Ed. Priestley may be quoting from Isaac Watts' sermon on Christian morality, where the phrase "truth as it is in Jesus" appears, or perhaps simply providing a paraphrase of Eph 4:15. The latter quote, "obey it in the love thereof," alters Rom 6:12: ". . . that ye should obey it in the lusts thereof."]

the contrary, be true; but things expressly *contrary* to our reason, as that *three* should be *one* and *one three*, can never appear to us to be so.

With the Jews, the doctrine of the divine unity is, and indeed justly, considered as the most fundamental principle of all religion. "Hear, O Israel, the Lord our God is one Lord" (Deut 6:4; Mark 12:29). To preach the doctrine of the Trinity to the Jews can appear to them in no other light than an attempt to seduce them into *idolatry*, a thing which they dare not entertain the most distant thought of.

The great creed of the Mahometans is that "There is one God, and Mahomet is his prophet."[4] Now, that Mahomet is not the prophet of God, it is to be hoped they may, in time, be made to believe; but we must not expect that they will so easily give up their faith in the unity of God. To make the gospel what it was originally, "glad tidings of great joy" [Luke 2:10], and as at last it certainly will be to all the nations of the world, we must free it from this most absurd and impious doctrine, and also from many other corruptions which have been introduced into it. It can no otherwise appear worthy of God and favorable to the virtue and happiness of mankind.

. . . It is often said that Christ speaks of his *humanity* only, whenever he represents himself as inferior to the Father and dependent upon him. But the Scriptures themselves are far from furnishing the least hint of any such method of interpretation, though, according to the Trinitarians, it is absolutely necessary to the true understanding of them.

. . . Could our Lord say with truth and without an unworthy prevarication that "the Father is the only true God" (John 17:3), if any other person not implied in the term "Father" was as much the true God as himself? Now the term "Father," being appropriated to what is called the first person in the Godhead, cannot comprehend the "Son," who is called the second. This key, therefore, is of no service in this case, and our Lord, by expressing himself as he has done, could not but lead his hearers into what is called a dangerous mistake.

When our Lord said that "his Father was greater than he" [John 14:28], did he make any reserve, and secretly mean not his whole self but only part, and the inferior part of himself, the other part being equal in power and glory with the Father? How mean the prevarication, and how unworthy of our Lord!

When our Lord said that the time of the Day of Judgment was not known to himself, the Son, but "to the Father only" [Matt 24:36], could he mean that his *humanity* only did not know it, but that his *divinity* (which is supposed to be intimately united with his humanity) was as well acquainted with it as the Father himself? If the human nature of Christ had been incapable of having that knowledge communicated to it, the declaration would have been needless. But as that was not the case, his hearers must necessarily understand him as speaking of himself in his highest capacity, as he certainly must do, if at all, when he speaks of himself as the *Son* corresponding to the *Father*.

If Christ had not satisfied the Jews that he did not mean to make himself equal with God, would they not have produced it against him at his trial when he was condemned as a blasphemer because he confessed that he was the Christ only; and yet no Jew expected anything more than a man for their Messiah, and our Savior nowhere intimates that they were mistaken in that expectation. It is plain that Martha considered our Lord as a

---

4   [Ed. The *shahada* is one of the five pillars of Islam.]

different person from God, and dependent upon God when she said to him, "I know that even now, whatsoever thou wilt ask of God, God will give it thee" [John 11:22].

‡

The sound knowledge of Christianity is not of importance as a matter of speculation merely—though abstract truths, especially truths that relate to God and the maxims of his moral government, are not without their utility and obligation—but the truths that I here contend for nearly affect the sentiments of our hearts and our conduct in life, as, indeed, has been shown in many respects already. Considering God as possessed of the character in which some divines represent him, it is impossible, while human nature is what it is, that he should appear in an amiable or respectable light. Such a God may, indeed, be the object of *dread* and *terror* to his creatures, but by no means of their *love* or *reverence*. And what is obedience without love? It cannot be that of the heart, which, however, is the only thing that is of any real value in religion. Also, how can a man love his fellow-creatures in general, when he considers the greatest part of them as the objects of the divine abhorrence and doomed by him to an everlasting destruction, in which he believes that he himself must forever rejoice? And what can remain of virtue when these two great sources of it—the love of God and of mankind—are thus grossly corrupted? Lastly, how must the genuine spirit of *mercy* and *forgiveness*, which so eminently distinguishes the gospel of Christ, be debased, when God himself (whose conduct in this very respect is particularly proposed to our imitation) is considered as never forgiving sin without some previous atonement, satisfaction, or intercession.

TEXT: [Joseph Priestley,] *An appeal to the serious and candid professors of Christianity* (Birmingham: Pearson and Rollason, 1784), 4–5, 14–17, 21–22.

WILLIAM HAZLITT
(1737–1820)
Mission of Jesus

Although his son is better known among readers of British Romanticism, William Hazlitt Sr. was a Unitarian minister of considerable importance during the eighteenth century. As with many other dissenters, Hazlitt's Presbyterian family encouraged independence of mind and political dissent. Hazlitt received his B.A. and M.A. from Glasgow University, where he studied under Adam Smith. He ministered as chaplain to Sir Conyers Joscelyn in Hertfordshire and later served various Presbyterian meetinghouses in Wisbech and Gloucestershire. Following his marriage in 1766, Hazlitt began publishing: he contributed to Priestley's *Theological repository* under the pseudonyms Philalethes and Rationalis, and he wrote newspaper articles critical of the British treatment of American prisoners of war. In 1783 Hazlitt moved his family to the United States, where he associated with leading ministers in Philadelphia and Boston. He continued to publish periodical literature, prepared for the press an American edition of Priestley's *An appeal to the serious and candid professors of Christianity* (1784), and helped establish the first Unitarian church in Boston (King's Chapel). In 1786 Hazlitt returned to England, where he served as headmaster of his son William's school while continuing to publish.

Hazlitt's *Human authority, in matters of faith, repugnant to Christianity* (1774) argues that the only guide to truth is Jesus Christ. The subtitle describes the work as two discourses on Matthew 23:8: ". . . for one is your master, even Christ; and all ye are brethren." The tract reminds readers that Hazlitt and other Socinian radicals held the life and witness of Jesus in the highest esteem. Christological dissent meant not the overthrow of Christ, but the toppling of competing sources of religious authority. Hazlitt calls Christians to reject the authority of catechisms, articles, and confessions, for if "we have only one master, away with all other masters" (52). True Christianity requires devotion to Jesus Christ, rather than submission to the authority of the church.

SOURCES: *ODNB*; Duncan Wu, "The journalism of William Hazlitt (1737–1820)," *Review of English Studies* 57 (2006): 221–46; idem, "'Polemical divinity': William Hazlitt at the University of Glasgow," *Romanticism* 6 (2000): 163–77; idem, "William Hazlitt (1737–1820), the priestley circle, and the theological repository: a brief survey and bibliography," *Review of English Studies* 56 (2005): 758–66.

WILLIAM HAZLITT
Human authority, in matters of faith, repugnant to Christianity
1774

Hence, then, it will clearly appear that Jesus Christ was the anointed messenger of God and fully commissioned by him to point out the way of salvation to man. For he taught us no doctrines that are contrary to our reason, but such as rather illuminate and perfect our reason in the highest degree; and, he established these very doctrines, not, as ignorance or malice have falsely asserted, by attempting to extinguish the light of reason within us, but by the most solemn appeals to this primary law of God to man. What a wonderful contrast do we discover between him and all his pretended delegates or vicegerents and coadjutors upon earth! How proud are they? How humble was he! Without professing the least portion of his spirit, they have lorded it over God's heritage with rod and iron. But, he—though the way to truth and the life [John 14:6], though he spoke as never man spoke, and though God was always with him and always taught him—did not yet require an implicit faith from any of his followers. He knew, on the contrary, that one divine law is best enforced and recommended by another divine law; and he, therefore, submitted all his claims to the decisions of reason. He drew up no inexplicable systems of faith for us to subscribe or to acquiesce in, in the room of works. The point that he labored was to make men good, and not what the fashion of the times had received as orthodox. In short, he never addressed himself to the Jews in the imperative tone of modern priests: "swallow down this mystery, and the other mystery; believe, though your own reason demonstrates the contrary, that three are no more than one and that one is as many as three, else you shall have no peace in the other world, and I will give you as much trouble as I can in this." No; he challenged them to examine his own pretensions, according to those very Scriptures in which they themselves believed. "Search the Scriptures," says he, "for they be they that testify to me" [John 5:39]. He challenged them to accuse him, if they could, of any single transgression of the divine laws. "Which of you convinceth me of sin?" [John 8:46]. He challenged them to convict him of any falsehood or to fix upon him any expressions or declarations that were contrary to the most indubitable perfections of God. "And if I say the truth, why do ye not believe me?" [John 8:46]. He challenged them to show that any one of his miracles could be effected by any other power than that of omnipotence. "And, if I do not the works of my Father, believe me not" [John 10:37]. And he challenged them to produce any arguments why God would be with him in all that he did if he had not come to do the will of God and had not received his commission immediately from God. "The works which I do, in my Father's name, bear witness of me. A kingdom divided against itself cannot stand. And, if Satan cast out Satan, his kingdom cannot stand. But if I by the Spirit of God overwhelm the works of darkness, then is the kingdom of God come unto you" [John 5:36; Matt 12:25-26, 28].

All this, we must see, was sound reasoning and demonstrably proved that Jesus was the Son of God with power, that he came not of himself, that he spoke not of himself, that he did nothing of himself, but that whatever he did was by the power of the Highest. His holiness, his wisdom, his humility, his self-denial, and his innumerable astonishing miracles did all proclaim him to be the well-beloved of the Father, full of grace and truth [John 1:14]; and the importance of his doctrines and the benevolent scheme which he came to propose to the souls of men call up our most earnest attention to all that he did and taught and suffered for us.

He was holy, harmless, undefiled, and separate from sinners; the spotless lamb of God, without blemish, without guile, without a single deflection from the ways of righteousness and truth. All this was fully characteristic of his heavenly origin. It is such a one as he whom we would naturally expect the Holy Majesty of the Universe and the Father of all Mercies to send into the world; one who could no more betray us by his example than by his precepts; one who was as amiable and lovely in his life as in his doctrines; one in whom virtue might be seen breathing celestial sweetness, displaying a thousand-thousand inexpressibly venerable charms; adorned with every grace, possessing every excellence and beauty, and superior in glory to the splendor of the sun and the brightness of the firmament.

But the wisdom of Jesus is another demonstrable proof of his divine mission. The people might well be astonished at his doctrines, for they were such as never had been taught before—such as infinitely surpassed all the systems of the ancient sages. He carried morality to its highest purity and perfection; nothing now can be added to what he has said upon it; and, after a trial of above seventeen hundred years, no exception can yet be made to a single precept he has given. Besides, he alone hath represented to us the perfections of the true God in their native dignity and glory; leading us to consider him as the one Spirit, and universal Father, the only omnipotent, the only author of every good, whose providence continually watcheth over the minutest works of his hand; and he being the best judge of human nature that ever appeared in our world, both in delivering those sublime and unparalleled doctrines universally and with an astonishing exactness, adapted his address to the various characters of his audience; frequently drawing them to condemn their impious conduct, according to their own principles; and afterwards, with irresistible force, in extempore parables abounding with innumerable beauties, and such as have never been equaled by any other son of man, beating down all the strongholds of iniquity that stood before him and majestically scattering the whole immense mass of darkness which covered the world. Now, upon what other conceivable foundation is such wisdom to be accounted for than by allowing him to have been a divine messenger? How is it possible to be accounted for that the reputed son of a poor carpenter—untrained in the schools, without any of the aids of philosophy—should have been the wisest of men and the only infallible teacher of righteousness and truth, unless he was taught of God and sent by him to be the light of men? Could he, without either any divine or human aids, have been so singularly happy as to have infinitely eclipsed in knowledge all the men who lived before and after him? Or would the God of all wisdom and grace have given *him only* an understanding to know the things that are excellent, had not he been under the constant influence of his good will and pleasure?

But the humility and self-denial of the blessed Jesus likewise demonstrably prove him to have been our heavenly-appointed master or teacher. Had he come to establish some favorite scheme of his own, he would certainly have aimed at as much power and authority as he could prudently assume. He would have availed himself of the friendship of this world, and would have let no fair opportunity escape of fanning the fire of popular prejudices in his favor. But he was meek and lowly of heart, and he came not to be ministered unto, but to minister [Matt 20:28]. He sought not honor from men, but that which cometh from God only. Instead of aiming at temporal dominions, grasping at the scepter of universal empire, or climbing the summit of transient greatness, he cheerfully offered himself to be the servant of all. He declared, in the most unequivocal language, that his kingdom was not of this world [John 18:36]; and, that if we would stand candidates for his favor or finally enter into the joy of our Lord, we must deny ourselves and take up our cross daily to follow him [Acts 9:23]; and he died as he lived, gloriously avowing the same sentiments, maintaining the same dignity, expressing the same contempt for all earthly possessions, discovering the same generous benevolence to man, and reposing the same unlimited confidence in his God and Father.

Now, could all this have possibly happened unless God had sent him? Did any person ever yet espouse a cause that promised and aimed at nothing but poverty, contempt, and sufferings, and die in the same without reluctance, unless he had full evidence, clear and irresistible evidence, that this cause was the cause of God? The supposition is ridiculous and a contradiction to itself. This argument alone, therefore, sufficiently proves that Jesus had his authority from above, that the God of all wisdom inspired and taught him, and that he was divinely appointed to be our master in religion.

But, besides the holiness, the wisdom, the humility, and self-denial of our Lord, God also bore witness to him by a successive train of the most stupendous miracles—miracles which mere human art or power can no more accomplish than we can arrest the sun in its course or create another sun or another world. The tempestuous ocean was instantly becalmed; lunatics were restored to their right mind; the deaf, the dumb, the lame, and the blind lost all their complaints and the sick all their diseases in a moment; and the dead were raised to life only by his word or touch; and these things were not done in a corner nor transacted in darkness, but in the face of day and amidst thousands of spectators, and under the inspection, too, of determined enemies.

But last of all, God gave his omnipotent sanction to all his claims by making him victorious over death and the grave the third day after his crucifixion and, shortly after, carrying him up visibly into heaven to give him the government of thrones and dominions and principalities and powers. Hence, then, it is demonstrable that he was his well-beloved Son, in whom he was well-pleased [Matt 3:17]; that he could have taught us nothing but the will of the most high God, since the most high God was always with him; and that he had, therefore, the most unquestionable authority for assuming and exercising the sublime office of instructing all the children of men in the way of salvation.

TEXT: [William Hazlitt,] *Human authority, in matters of faith, repugnant to Christianity* (London: J. Johnson, 1774), 10–18.

THOMAS SCOTT
(1747–1821)
Faith in Christ

The conversion narrative, one of the most widespread literary forms in the period, provides powerful examples of theological reflection. Thomas Scott's *The force of truth* (1779) shaped evangelical thinking on God and faith for many decades. Indeed, none other than John Henry Newman heaped praise on Scott for his "bold unworldliness and vigorous independence of mind" and named Scott's influence on his spiritual formation as deeper "than any other, and to whom (humanly speaking) I almost owe my soul" (*Apologia*, 26).

The tenth of thirteen children, Thomas Scott was born to a Lincolnshire farmer's family. At fifteen, Scott was briefly apprenticed to a surgeon, but he was dismissed for apparent misconduct and returned home to the family farm. He worked as a farm laborer there for nine years before learning that his father intended to give the property to Scott's brother, at which point Scott left home to pursue his education. In 1772 the bishop of Lincoln ordained Scott despite some reservations. Although he had previously held numerous doubts about Trinitarian belief, in 1777 Scott experienced a profound conversion that settled him squarely within the bounds of historic Christian orthodoxy. Scott succeeded the noted hymn writer John Newton at Olney in 1781. After a short time there—largely unsuccessful, he thought—Scott took a position at the Lock Hospital for reformed prostitutes in London, where his working-class background helped him relate to those he served. Over the next two decades he authored numerous theological works and biblical commentaries, in addition to training missionaries for the Church Missionary Society. From 1801 until his death in 1821, Scott served as rector of Aston Sandford, Buckinghamshire.

Scott's spiritual autobiography, *The force of truth* (1779), explores his transformation from rationalist Socinianism to evangelical Trinitarianism. Scott's violent reaction to the Trinitarian claims of the Athanasian Creed provides a central moment of crisis in the narrative: "My disbelief of the doctrine of a Trinity of *coequal* persons in the unity of the Godhead and my pretensions to candor both combined to excite my hatred to this creed" (37). In turn, Scott felt increasingly weighed down by his having subscribed to the Articles of Religion: "Subscription to articles which I did not believe—paid as a price for church preferment—I looked upon as an impious lie, a heinous guilt, that could never truly be repented of without throwing back the wages of iniquity" (38). In fact, much of Scott's story recounts the careful study he made of the doctrines he once doubted. *The force of truth*, then, is both an evangelical narrative of inner transformation from selfish ambition and pride to humble acceptance of biblical truth and an exposition of Trinitarian theological principles.

SOURCES: *BDE*; Bebbington; D. Bruce Hindmarsh, "The Olney autobiographers: English conversion narrative in the mid-eighteenth century," *Journal of Ecclesiastical History* 49 (1998): 61–84; John E. Marshall, *Thomas Scott (1747–1821) and The force of truth (1779)* (London: Evangelical Library, 1979); John Henry Newman, *Apologia pro vita sua* (London: Penguin, 1994); *ODCC*; *ODNB*.

THOMAS SCOTT
The force of truth
1779

At this period,[1] though I was the slave of sin, yet, as my conscience was not pacified nor my principles greatly corrupted, there seemed some hope concerning me. But at length Satan took a very effectual method of silencing my convictions, that I might sleep securely in my sins; and justly was I given over to a strong delusion to believe a lie, when I held the truth that I did know in unrighteousness. A Socinian comment on the Scriptures came in my way, and I greedily drank the poison because it quieted my fears and flattered my abominable pride. The whole system coincided exactly with my inclinations and the state of my mind, and approved itself to me. In reading this exposition, sin seemed to lose its native ugliness and to appear a very small and tolerable evil; man's imperfect obedience seemed to shine with an almost divine excellency; and God appeared so entirely and necessarily merciful that he could not make any of his creatures miserable without contradicting his natural propensity. These things influenced my mind so powerfully that I concluded that, notwithstanding a few little blemishes, I was, upon the whole, a very worthy creature. Then further—the mysteries of the gospel being explained away or brought down to the level of man's comprehension by such proud and corrupt (though specious) reasonings—by acceding to these sentiments, I was, in my own opinion, in point of understanding and discernment exalted to a superiority above the general run of mankind, and amused myself with looking down with contempt upon such as were weak enough to believe the orthodox doctrines. Thus I generally soothed my conscience; and if at any time I was uneasy at the apprehension that I did not thoroughly deserve and was not entirely fit for heaven, the same book afforded me a soft pillow on which to lull myself to sleep. It argued—and I thought proved—that there were no *eternal* torments, and insinuated that there were no torments except for notorious sinners, and that such as should fall just short of heaven would sink into their original nothing. With this welcome scheme I silenced all my fears and told my accusing conscience that if I fell short of heaven, I should be annihilated and never be sensible of my loss.

---

[1]   [Ed. Scott refers to the years following his sixteenth birthday.]

23

‡

The doctrine of a Trinity of coequal persons in the Unity of the Godhead had been hitherto no part of my creed. I had long been accustomed to despise this great mystery of godliness; I had quarreled with the Articles of the established Church about this doctrine; I had been very positive and open in my declarations against it; and my unhumbled reason still retained objections to it. But about June 1777 I began to be troubled with doubts about it and to suspect the truth of Dr. Clark's hypothesis.[2] I had just read Mr. Lindsey's *Apology* and *Sequel*.[3] Before I saw them, I had made a jest of those who thought of confuting him on the orthodox scheme and was not without thoughts of maintaining Dr. Clark's system against him. But when I understood that he claimed Dr. Clark as a Socinian, I was surprised and engaged in much anxious consideration of the subject. The more I studied, the more I was dissatisfied. Many things now first occurred to me as strong objections against my own sentiments on that head; and being perplexed and unable to make out a scheme for myself, I easily perceived that I was not qualified to dispute with another person. My pride and my convictions struggled hard for the victory. I was very unwilling to become a Trinitarian in the strict sense of the word, though in my own sense I had for some time pretended to be one; and yet, the more I considered it, the more I was dissatisfied with all other systems . . . After much meditation upon the subject, together with a careful examination of all the Scriptures which I then understood to relate thereto, accompanied with hearty prayer for divine teaching, I was at length constrained to renounce as utterly indefensible all my former sentiments and to accede to that doctrine which I had so long despised. I saw, and I could no longer avoid seeing, that the offices and works attributed in Scripture to the Son and Holy Ghost are such as none but the infinite God could perform; that it is a contradiction to believe the real and consequently infinite satisfaction to divine justice made by the death of Christ, without believing him to be very God of very God; nor could the Holy Ghost give spiritual life unto and dwell in the hearts of all believers at the same time, to suit his work of convincing, enlightening, teaching, strengthening, sanctifying, and comforting to the several cases of every individual, were he not the omniscient, omnipresent, infinite God. And being assured from reason as well as from Scripture that there is not and cannot be more gods than one, I was driven from my reasonings and constrained to submit my natural understanding to divine revelation; and allowing that the incomprehensible God alone can fully know the unsearchable mysteries of his own divine nature and the manner of his own existence, to adopt the doctrine of a "Trinity in Unity" in order to preserve consistency in my own scheme. But it was a considerable time before I was disentangled from my embarrassments on this subject.

‡

Thus, I trust, the old building that I had purposed to repair was pulled down to the ground, and the foundation of the new building of God laid aright; old things were

---

2   [Ed. Samuel Clarke (1675–1729) drew fire among some Church of England clergy for his unorthodox Trinitarian views in *Scripture-doctrine of the Trinity* (1712). In short, Scott's attraction to Clarke's views drew him closer to Unitarianism.]

3   [Ed. Theophilus Lindsey (1723–1808) defended English Unitarian theology in his *Apology* (1774) and *Sequel to the "Apology"* (1776).]

passed away, behold all things were become new [2 Cor 5:17]. What things were gain to me, those I have counted loss for Christ [Phil 3:7]. My boasted reason I discover to be a blind guide, until humbled, enlightened, and sanctified by the Spirit of God; my former wisdom I now know to have been foolishness, and that, when I thought I knew much, I knew nothing as I ought to know. Since this period, everything I have experienced in my own heart, everything I have heard and read, everything I observe around me confirms and establishes me in the assured belief of those truths which I have received; nor do I in general any more doubt their being from God than I doubt whether the sun shines when I see its light and am warmed with its refreshing beams. I see the powerful effects of them continually amongst those to whom I preach. I experience the power of them daily in my own soul; and, whilst by meditating on and rejoicing in the cross of Christ, I find the world crucified unto me, and I unto the world. By preaching Jesus Christ and him crucified [1 Cor 2:2], I see notoriously immoral persons influenced to deny ungodliness and worldly lusts, and to live soberly, righteously, and godly in this present world, being an example to such as before they were a scandal to.

And now by this change, the consequences of which I so much dreaded, what have I lost even in respect of this present world? Indeed I have lost some degree of favor and escape not pity, censure, scorn, and opposition; but the Lord is introducing me to a new and far more desirable acquaintance, even to that of those whom the Holy Ghost hath denominated the excellent of the earth [Ps 16:3]; nay the Lord the Spirit condescends to be my Comforter. In general, I enjoy an established peace of conscience through the blood of sprinkling and continual application to the heavenly Advocate; with a sweet content, and that peace of God which passeth all understanding, in casting all my cares upon him who careth for me [Phil 4:7; 1 Pet 5:7]. And I am not left utterly without experience of that joy which is unspeakable and full of glory [1 Pet 1:8]. These the world could not give me were I in favor with it; of these it cannot deprive me by its frowns. My desire henceforth, God knoweth, is to live to his glory, and by my whole conduct and conversation to adorn the doctrine of God my Savior [Titus 2:10], and to show forth his praise, who hath called me out of darkness into his marvelous light [1 Pet 2:9]; to be in some way or other useful to his believing people; and to invite poor sinners who are walking in vain shadow and disquieting themselves in vain to taste and see how gracious the Lord is, and how blessed they are, who put their trust in him [Ps 39:6; 34:8; 2:12].

> Now would I tell to sinners round,
> What a dear Savior I have found;
> Would point to his redeeming blood,
> And cry, behold the way to God![4]

Thus hath the Lord led me, a poor blind sinner, in a way that I knew not; he hath made darkness light before me, crooked things straight, and hard things easy; and hath brought me to a place of which I little thought when I set out; and having done these things for me—I believe, yea I am undoubtingly sure—he will never leave me nor forsake

---

[4]   [Ed. These verses, with slight alterations, derive from the Moravian hymn writer John Cennick's (1718–1755) "Jesus, My All, to Heaven Is Gone."]

me [Isa 42:16; Deut 31:6]. To him be the glory of his undeserved, long resisted grace; to me be the shame, not only of all my other sins, but also of my proud and perverse opposition to his purposes of love towards me. But all this was permitted that, my high spirit and stout heart being at length humbled and subdued, I might remember and be confounded and never open my mouth more because of my shame, now that the Lord is pacified to me for all that I have done.

TEXT: Thomas Scott, *The force of truth: an authentic narrative* (Boston: J. Belcher and S. T. Armstrong, 1814), 12–14, 95–99, 118–22.

SAMUEL HORSLEY
(1733–1806)
Antiquity

If Joseph Priestley was the greatest Unitarian of the age, Samuel Horsley was Unitarianism's chief antagonist. Horsley was born at St. Martin's Place, London. His father, a minister, came from a dissenting family but moved to a conformist position shortly before his son's birth. In 1751 Horsley proceeded to Trinity Hall, Cambridge, intending on a legal career. He entered the Middle Temple in 1755. Horsley changed course, however, and was successively ordained deacon and priest in 1758. The following year, Horsley's father vacated his position as rector at Newington Butts on the outskirts of London in order that his son might take his place. In time, it became clear that Horsley's interest in the church was chiefly intellectual rather than pastoral. He moved to London, pursued experimental science and classical history, and was elected fellow of the Royal Society (1767), devoting much of the next decade to service in that body. Robert Lowth, bishop of London, made Horsley his domestic chaplain in 1771, prebendary of St. Paul's in 1777, and archdeacon of St. Asaph in 1781. In 1788, already a national figure for his defense of Christianity against Unitarianism, Horsley was consecrated bishop of St. David's. Following a rousing sermon against the spirit of revolution before the House of Lords, he was translated to Rochester (1793). Horsley spent his final years as bishop of St. Asaph (1802).

Horsley was a prolific author, whose writings reflect his scientific interests, stalwart advocacy for high church and establishment principles, and defense of the besieged Test and Corporation Acts. But Horsley's most famous publications—including his episcopal address, *A charge, delivered to the clergy of the archdeaconry of St Albans* (1783)—defend the doctrine of the Trinity against the assertions of Joseph Priestley. Horsley, who was disinclined to participate in public dispute, contends that Priestley's *An history of the corruptions of Christianity* (2 vols., 1782) misrepresents the history of dogma. Priestley had maintained that the earliest Christians were strict Unitarians, and the second generation, under the influence of a Platonic philosophy of the Logos, divinized Christ. By contrast, Horsley, in the following selection, claims that Priestley incorrectly reads early church writings and fails to recognize the significance of the fact that even pagan religions held triadic principles. Far from speculation or an absurdity, Trinitarian doctrine faithfully conveys the teachings of the earliest Christians. Horsley's writings solidified Trinitarian support in England, revived high church interest in apostolic authority, and convinced a few to abandon Socinianism. Indeed, they led the formerly Unitarian poet Samuel Taylor Coleridge to declare, "No Trinity, no God."

SOURCES: Jeffrey W. Barbeau, *Coleridge, the Bible, and religion*, Nineteenth-Century Major Lives and Letters (New York: Palgrave Macmillan, 2008); Hylson-Smith; F. C. Mather, *High church prophet: Bishop Samuel Horsley (1733–1806) and the Caroline tradition in the later Georgian church* (Oxford: Clarendon, 1992); Nockles; *ODCC*; *ODNB*; B. W. Young, *Religion and Enlightenment in eighteenth-century England: theological debate from Locke to Burke* (Oxford: Clarendon, 1998).

SAMUEL HORSLEY

A charge, delivered to the clergy of the archdeaconry of St Albans
1783

The notion therefore of a Trinity, more or less removed from the purity of the Christian faith, is found to have been a leading principle in all the ancient schools of philosophy and in the religions of almost all nations; and traces of an early popular belief of it appear even in the abominable rites of idolatrous worship. If reason was insufficient for this great discovery, what could be the means of information but what the Platonists themselves assign, Θεοπαραδοτος Θεολογια, "a theology delivered from the gods," i.e., a revelation. This is the account which Platonists, who were no Christians, have given of the origin of their master's doctrine. But from what revelation could they derive their information, who lived before the Christian and had no light from the Mosaic? For whatever some of the early Fathers may have imagined, there is no evidence that Plato or Pythagoras were at all acquainted with the Mosaic writings;[1] not to insist that the worship of a trinity is traced to an earlier age than that of Plato or of Pythagoras or even of Moses. Their information could be only drawn from traditions founded upon earlier revelations: from scattered fragments of the ancient patriarchal creed; that creed, which was universal before the defection of the first idolaters, which the corruptions of idolatry, gross and enormous as they were, could never totally obliterate. Thus the doctrine of the Trinity is rather confirmed than discredited by the suffrage of the heathen sages, since the resemblance of the Christian faith and the pagan philosophy in this article, when fairly interpreted, appears to be nothing less than the consent of the latest and the earliest revelations.

‡

The reasonableness of our faith will be best understood from the writings of the Fathers of the three first centuries. And among these, those wicked Platonists of the second age, who, in Dr. Priestley's judgment, sowed the seeds of the anti-Christian corruption, deserve particular attention for the great perspicuity with which in general they expound the faith

[1]   [Ed. Some early Christian apologists (such as Clement of Alexandria) believed that Greek philosophers had access to the Hebrew Scriptures and thereby reflected Jewish and Christian ideas about God.]

29

and the great ability with which they defend it. And as these corrupters brought with them into the church the language of their school (I say the language, for its opinions, except so far as they harmonized with the gospel, they had the ingenuity[2] to retract), the writings of the pagan philosophers, particularly the Platonists, will be of considerable use to the Christian student, as they will bring him more acquainted with a phraseology which is used even by the Christian Platonists; nor for this purpose only, but for some degree of light which they will throw upon the argument. The error of the later Platonists was that they warped the genuine doctrine of the original tradition, their Θεοπαραδοτος Θεολογια, to a form in which it might be in friendship with the popular idolatry. Their writings therefore are a mine in which the true metal is indeed mingled with a dross of heterogeneous substances, but yet the richness of the ore is such as may well repay the cost and trouble of the separation. Or if leisure should be wanting for a minute study of a subject, which may seem but of a secondary importance, it will at least be expedient—I had almost said it will be necessary—to know so much of the opinions of heathen antiquity as is to be learned from those authentic documents, which the industry of the indefatigable Cudworth hath collected and arranged with great judgment in his *Intellectual system.*[3]

The advantage to be expected from these deep researches is not any insight into the manner in which the three divine persons are united (a knowledge which is indeed too high for man, perhaps for angels; which in our present condition at least is not to be attained and ought not to be sought), but that just apprehension of the Scripture doctrine, which will show that it is not one of those things that "no miracles can prove"[4]—that will be the certain fruit of the studies recommended. They will lead us to see the Scripture doctrine in its true light: that it is an imperfect discovery, not a contradiction; that the catholic faith is not properly compared with the tale of Mahomet's journey to the third heaven, his conferences there while the pitcher of water fell, or even with the doctrine of transubstantiation; that even the Athanasian Creed is something very different from a set "of contradictions, the most direct which any person the most skilled in logic might draw up."[5] . . . In the opinions of the pagan Platonists we have in some degree an experimental proof that this abstruse doctrine cannot be the absurdity which it seems to those who misunderstand it. Would Plato, would Porphyry, would even Plotinus have believed the miracles of Mahomet or the doctrine of transubstantiation?[6] But they all believed a doctrine which so far at least resembles the Nicene as to be loaded with the same or greater objections. By everyone who will thus combine the studies of divinity and philosophy, the truth of Plato's observation, I am persuaded, will be soon experienced: that to those who apply themselves to these speculations with a humble disposition to be taught, rather than with the unphilosophical and irreligious habit of deciding hastily upon the first view

2   [Ed. Wisdom or perceptiveness.]

3   [Ed. The Cambridge Platonist Ralph Cudworth (1617–1688), fellow of Emmanuel College, Cambridge, was the author of a formidable work of philosophical theology, *The true intellectual system of the universe, wherein all the reason and philosophy of atheism is confuted, and its impossibility demonstrated* (1678).]

4   "They are things which no miracles can prove," says Dr. Priestley in his address to Mr. Gibbon, speaking of the doctrines of the Trinity and the atonement. [See Joseph Priestley, *An history of the corruptions of Christianity*, 2 vols. (Birmingham: J. Johnson, 1782), 2:461.—Ed.]

5   [Ed. Priestley, *An history of the corruptions*, 1:87.]

6   [Ed. Porphyry and Plotinus are third-century Neoplatonists.]

of difficulties, what at first appeared the most incredible will in the end seem the most evident and certain, and maxims which seemed at first indisputable will be discarded.

An extensive erudition in pagan as well as Christian antiquity, joined with a critical understanding of the sacred text, is that which hath so long enabled the clergy of the Church of England to take the lead among Protestants as the apologists of the apostolic faith and discipline, and to baffle the united strength of their adversaries of all denominations. God forbid that through an indolence, which would be unpardonable, we should ever lose the superiority which we have so long maintained. The acquisition of learning is indeed laborious, but the fruit is sweet. . . . It is a maxim of Dr. Priestley's that every man who in his conscience dissents from the established Church is obliged in conscience to be a declared dissenter. I honor the generosity of the sentiment . . . It ought much more to be the sentiment of everyone who stands with the received doctrine to be a declared churchman. If he would reap any solid advantage from the purity of his faith, he must be an open and avowed believer; lest if he confess not Christ his God and Savior before men, he should not be at last confessed before the angels of heaven [Matt 10:32]. If this confession be the general duty of every man who feels conviction, it is the particular duty of everyone who hath been called to the evangelist's office. He holds the authority of his commission for no other purpose, but to be a witness of the truth. A conviction that it is the truth, founded on a deep investigation of the subject, will supply him with firmness to persevere in the glorious attestation, unawed by the abilities of his antagonists, undaunted by obloquy, unmoved by ridicule, which seem to be the trials which God hath appointed, instead of persecution, in the present age, to prove the sincerity and patience of the faithful. The advocate of that sound form of words, which was originally delivered to the saints hath to expect that his opinions will be the open jest of the Unitarian party, that his sincerity will be called in question, or if "a bare *possibility* of his being in earnest"⁷ be charitably admitted, the misfortune of his education will be lamented, and his prejudices deplored. All this insult will not alarm nor discompose him. He will rather glory in the recollection that his adherence to the faith of the first ages hath provoked it. The conviction, which he will all the while enjoy, that his philosophy is Plato's and his creed St. John's, will alleviate the mortification he might otherwise feel in differing from Dr. Priestley; nor suffer him to think the evil insupportable, although the consequence of this dissent should be that he must share with the excellent bishop of Worcester in Dr. Priestley's "pity and indignation."⁸ . . . He will admit much more than a possibility that Dr. Priestley may be in earnest in all his misinterpretations of the Scriptures and the Fathers, and in all his misrepresentations of facts. Appearances to the contrary, however strong, he will refer to the fascinating power of prejudice and to the delusive practice of "looking through"⁹ authors, which the historian of religious opinions ought to have read. Though truth in these controversies can be only on one side, he will indulge (and he will avow the charitable opinion) that sincerity may be on both. And he will enjoy the reflection that by an equal sincerity—through the

---

7   [Ed. Priestley, *An history of the corruptions*, 2:471.]

8   [Ed. Priestley, *An history of the corruptions*, 2:471. Richard Hurd (1720–1808), bishop of Worcester, was "a stiff and orthodox prelate, high in royal favor," who engaged in controversies on miracles and religious history (Mather, 56).]

9   "I have taken a good deal of pains to read, or at least look carefully through, many of the most capital works of the ancient Christian writers." [Priestley, *An history of the corruptions*, 1:xvii.—Ed.]

power of that blood which was shed equally for all—both parties may at last find equal mercy. In the transport of this holy hope, he will anticipate that glorious consummation, when faith shall be absorbed in knowledge and the fire of controversy forever quenched; when the same generous zeal for God and truth—which too often, in this world of folly and confusion, sets those at widest variance whom the similitude of virtuous feelings should the most unite—shall be the cement of an indissoluble friendship; when the innumerable multitude of all nations, kindreds, and people (why should I not add of all sects and parties) assembled round the throne shall, like the first Christians, be of one soul and one mind, giving praise with one consent to him that sitteth on the throne and to the Lamb that was slain to redeem them by his blood [Rev 5:13].

TEXT: Samuel Horsley, *A charge, delivered to the clergy of the archdeaconry of St Albans*, 2nd ed. (London: J. Robson, 1783), 44–45, 67–74.

PERCY BYSSHE SHELLEY
(1792–1822)
Atheism

One of the greatest poets of his generation, Percy Bysshe Shelley epitomizes the radicalism of younger Romantics and the scandal of atheism in a time of "radical Enlightenment." Born near Horsham, Sussex, Shelley entered Eton in 1804. By the time he matriculated at University College, Oxford, Shelley had already published the Gothic romance *Zastrozzi* (1810) and, with his sister, *Original poetry by Victor and Cazire* (1810). Shelley's time at Oxford was brief. His growing and intense opposition to Christianity led to a singularly decisive event in his life: he was expelled from Oxford for his role in the publication of *The necessity of atheism* (1811), which he wrote with some assistance from Thomas Jefferson Hogg (1792–1862). The two young men moved to London. The same year, Shelley eloped with Harriet Westbrook, the daughter of a tavern owner—a move that severely strained Shelley's relationship with his father. Shelley's first major poem, *Queen Mab* (1813), was written and privately circulated around this time. The poem, which includes much of *The necessity of atheism*, demonstrates Shelley's early radicalism. His marriage to Harriet gradually faltered, and he later abandoned his wife and daughter, running away with Mary Wollstonecraft Godwin to France in 1814. The year 1816 brought accomplishment and tragedy in equal measure. Shelley composed his "Hymn to intellectual beauty" and "Mont Blanc" (Mary, too, wrote *Frankenstein* during this creative period), but he suffered anguish following the suicides of both Mary's half-sister Fanny Imlay and his first wife Harriet, who was found dead (and pregnant) in the Serpentine. The Shelleys, with Jane Clairmont, moved to Italy in 1818, where Shelley devoted himself to poetry, translated Plato's *Symposium* (1818), and wrote *Prometheus unbound* (1820). Shelley died at sea near Livorno, Tuscany, while sailing on the *Don Juan* to meet his friend Leigh Hunt.

The necessity of atheism (1811) was a collaborative project from its inception: Hogg likely did much of the research and wrote an early draft, while Shelley composed the final draft and arranged for its publication and distribution. Despite a rather noble advertisement in defense of inquiry ("As a love of truth is the only motive which actuates the author of this little tract . . ."), the young men undoubtedly intended to provoke public controversy: they sent the pamphlet under false names to bishops, clergy, and college heads. The work, viewed from one angle, stated little more than Locke, Hume, or any number of skeptics had previously intimated, but the treatise's brazen conclusion against the legitimacy of belief simply could not be tolerated at Oxford: "Every reflecting mind must allow that there is no proof of the existence of a deity."

Sources: James Bieri, *Percy Bysshe Shelley: a biography* (Baltimore: The Johns Hopkins University Press, 2008); Colin Jager, *Unquiet things: secularism in the Romantic age* (Philadelphia: University of Pennsylvania Press, 2015); F. L. Jones, "Hogg and the 'necessity of atheism,'" *Publications of the Modern Language Association of America* 52 (1937): 1423–26; *ODNB*; Martin Priestman, *Romantic atheism: poetry and freethought, 1780–1830* (Cambridge: Cambridge University Press, 1999); *RCBEC*; Michael Scrivener, *Radical Shelley: the philosophical anarchism and utopian thought of Percy Bysshe Shelley* (Princeton: Princeton University Press, 1982).

PERCY BYSSHE SHELLEY
The necessity of atheism
1811

A close examination of the validity of the proofs adduced to support any proposition has ever been allowed to be the only sure way of attaining truth, upon the advantages of which it is unnecessary to descant; our knowledge of the existence of a deity is a subject of such importance that it cannot be too minutely investigated; in consequence of this conviction, we proceed briefly and impartially to examine the proofs which have been adduced. It is necessary first to consider the nature of belief.

When a proposition is offered to the mind, it perceives the agreement or disagreement of the ideas of which it is composed. A perception of their agreement is termed belief. Many obstacles frequently prevent this perception from being immediate; these the mind attempts to remove in order that the perception may be distinct. The mind is active in the investigation in order to perfect the state of perception, which is passive. The investigation being confused with the perception has induced many falsely to imagine that the mind is active in belief—that belief is an act of volition, in consequence of which it may be regulated by the mind.[1] Pursuing, continuing this mistake they have attached a degree of criminality to disbelief of which in its nature it is incapable; it is equally so [i.e., incapable] of merit.

The strength of belief, like that of every other passion, is in proportion to the degrees of excitement.

The degrees of excitement are three.

The senses are the sources of all knowledge to the mind; consequently their evidence claims the strongest assent.

The decision of the mind, founded upon our own experience derived from these sources, claims the next degree.

The experience of others, which addresses itself to the former one, occupies the lowest degree.

---

[1]   [Ed. Cp. Thomas Aquinas, *Summa theologica* IIa.IIae, q. 4, art. 1, 8; *Quaestiones disputatae de veritate*, q. 14.1–2.]

Consequently no testimony can be admitted which is contrary to reason; reason is founded on the evidence of our senses.

Every proof may be referred to one of these three divisions; we are naturally led to consider what arguments we receive from each of them to convince us of the existence of a deity.

First: The evidence of the senses. If the Deity should appear to us, if he should convince our senses of his existence, this revelation would necessarily command belief. Those to whom the Deity has thus appeared have the strongest possible conviction of his existence.

Reason claims the second place. It is urged that man knows that whatever is must either have had a beginning or existed from all eternity; he also knows that whatever is not eternal must have had a cause. Where this is applied to the existence of the universe, it is necessary to prove that it was created. Until that is clearly demonstrated, we may reasonably suppose that it has endured from all eternity.[2] In a case where two propositions are diametrically opposite, the mind believes that which is less incomprehensible. It is easier to suppose that the universe has existed from all eternity than to conceive a being capable of creating it. If the mind sinks beneath the weight of one, is it an alleviation to increase the intolerability of the burden? The other argument, which is founded upon a man's knowledge of his own existence, stands thus: A man knows not only he now is, but that there was a time when he did not exist; consequently there must have been a cause. But what does this prove? We can only infer from effects causes exactly adequate to those effects. But there certainly is a generative power which is effected by particular instruments; we cannot prove that it is inherent in these instruments, nor is the contrary hypothesis capable of demonstration. We admit that the generative power is incomprehensible, but to suppose that the same effect is produced by an eternal, omniscient, almighty Being leaves the cause in the same obscurity, but renders it more incomprehensible.

The third and last degree of assent is claimed by testimony. It is required that it should not be contrary to reason. The testimony that the Deity convinces the senses of men of his existence can only be admitted by us if our mind considers it less probable that these men should have been deceived than that the Deity should have appeared to them. Our reason can never admit the testimony of men who not only declare that they were eyewitnesses of miracles but that the Deity was irrational: for he commanded that he should be believed; he proposed the highest rewards for faith—eternal punishments for disbelief. We can only command voluntary actions; belief is not an act of volition; the mind is even passive. From this it is evident that we have not sufficient testimony, or rather that testimony is insufficient to prove the being of a God. We have before shown that it cannot be deduced from reason. They who have been convinced by the evidence of the senses, they only can believe it.

From this it is evident that having no proofs from any of the three sources of conviction, the mind *cannot* believe the existence of a god. It is also evident that, as belief is a passion of the mind, no degree of criminality can be attached to disbelief; they only

---

[2]   [Ed. Shelley's *Queen Mab* adds: "We must prove design before we can infer a designer. The only idea which we can form of causation is derivable from the constant conjunction of objects and the consequent inference of one from the other" (307n5).]

are reprehensible who willingly neglect to remove the false medium through which their mind views the subject.

It is almost unnecessary to observe that the general knowledge of the deficiency of such proof, cannot be prejudicial to society. Truth has always been found to promote the best interests of mankind. Every reflecting mind must allow that there is no proof of the existence of a deity. Q.E.D.[3]

⟡⟡

TEXT: Percy Bysshe Shelley, *The necessity of atheism* (Worthing: E. and W. Phillips [1811]) in *The prose works of Percy Bysshe Shelley*, ed. Harry Buxton Forman, 4 vols. (London: Reeves and Turner, 1880), 1:305–9.

---

[3]   [Ed. *Q.E.D.*, an initialism for *quod erat demonstrandum*, means literally "which was to be demonstrated" and marks the end of a formal proof (*OED*).]

RENN DICKSON HAMPDEN
(1793–1868)
Mystery

Although Renn Dickson Hampden is frequently associated with Church of England controversies in the later 1830s, his major publications came a decade earlier and set the stage for oppositional voices among Oxford Tractarians such as John Henry Newman. When Hampden was five years old, he moved from his birthplace in Barbados to England, his father thinking this necessary to ensure a proper education for his child. Just over a decade later, Hampden matriculated at Oriel College, Oxford, where he received a double first in classics and mathematics. Oriel brought Hampden new connections—Thomas Arnold and Richard Whately became his close friends—and formative theological influences, in particular, the liberal theologians of Oriel's Noetic circle. In 1814 Hampden was elected a fellow. He served several parishes as curate, edited the *Christian remembrancer* between 1825 and 1826, and achieved some recognition for his *Essay on the philosophical evidence of Christianity* (1827), which reflects the sustained influence of inductive biblical scholarship, the analogical theology of Joseph Butler, and the moral philosophy of Dugald Stewart (in opposition to the Utilitarian, evidentiary theology of William Paley). In 1832 Hampden delivered the Oxford Bampton Lectures on *The scholastic philosophy, considered in its relations to Christian theology*. The 1830s, however, put an end to Hampden's scholarly life. A shy and sensitive individual, Hampden suffered immensely from controversy surrounding his 1836 appointment to Oxford's prestigious regius professorship of divinity. His public support for the abolition of subscription at Oxford left many dissatisfied with his selection. Critics argued that Hampden, a latitudinarian of questionable orthodoxy in the minds of many high church leaders, could not represent the theological interests of the Church of England. A firestorm of political and ecclesial debate ensued, including some forty-five books and pamphlets. The appointment stood. Yet Hampden once again encountered Tractarian opposition when he was named the bishop of Hereford in 1848. In point of fact, Hampden never strayed far from the church establishment in all his years in the episcopacy. He published on national political issues only rarely, devoted resources to church building and renovation throughout his diocese, and supported the conservative cause in disputes over both Roman Catholic encroachment in England and the controversial biblical criticism of *Essays and reviews* (1860).

Decades after the rise of Unitarianism in the late eighteenth century, questions about the divinity of Christ continued to attract attention, often with respect to the language of the Athanasian Creed. Against the skeptical objection that the Creed engages in speculative philosophy, Hampden's sermon "Knowledge of God through Christ" asserts that the doctrine of "Trinity in unity" encapsulates the biblical witness about the nature of God. Hampden argues that the Bible provides a progressive revelation of God. Presaging debates that would reemerge in John Henry Newman's Oxford Movement, Hampden claims that knowledge of sacred doctrine developed over time but never changed through distortion or falsehood. God is not, as some had asserted, unknown or nonexistent, but gradually revealed through the testimony of the Patriarchs and finally through apostolic witness to the life, death, and resurrection of Jesus Christ. According to Hampden, while the language of the Creed reflects fourth-century disputes, its theology depends on biblical revelation alone.

SOURCES: Jeremy Catto, ed., *Oriel College: a history* (Oxford: Oxford University Press, 2013); E. R. Fairweather, "'Apostolical tradition' and the defense of dogma: an episode in the Anglo-Catholic Revival," *Canadian Journal of Theology* 11 (1965): 277–89; *ODCC*; *ODNB*; Robert Pattison, *The great dissent: John Henry Newman and the liberal heresy* (New York: Oxford University Press, 1991); Bernard M. G. Reardon, *Religious thought in the Victorian Age: a survey from Coleridge to Gore*, 2nd ed. (London: Longman, 1995); Hamish F. G. Swanston, *Ideas of order: Anglicans and the renewal of theological method in the middle years of the nineteenth century* (Assen: Van Gorcum, 1974); *VC*.

RENN DICKSON HAMPDEN
"Knowledge of God through Christ"
1828

This character of the Christian religion is comprehensively touched in the words of our text: "no man hath seen God at any time; the only-begotten Son, which is in the bosom of the Father, he hath declared him" [John 1:18]. No one is able, from actual vision or absolute contemplation of the Deity as he is in his own nature, to describe to us what he is or set him forth to us as the direct object of our thoughts; but the Son of God—he who was with the Father from all eternity and knew all the divine counsel—he it is, who, by coming into the world, and by consummating in his appearance and by his teaching, all the previous events in the history of divine providence, has "declared" or made known to us the Deity by the transactions in which he was personally engaged, finally opening to mankind what it was intended that they should know of the nature and counsels of God.

Hence it is that the Christian religion has been progressive in its development. The scheme of it has been gradually unfolded. Abraham saw the day of Christ indeed, but it was at a distance [Heb 11:13]. At the time when he lived, much remained to be transacted of God's special interference in the affairs of the world; and consequently a very imperfect evidence of the divine Being was afforded to him compared with that manifested in the fullness of time when all was "finished" which God had it in his heart to perform. The same observation applies to the Patriarchs who preceded or followed that great father of the faithful. They all looked forward to the hope of redemption, but with various degrees of light and knowledge on the subject, according to the period at which they lived. And the voice of prophecy, in like manner, spoke in more express accents of the things pertaining to God, as the ways of God found their outlet in the course of human events. It gradually told of the light which should lighten the Gentiles, and of the glory which should be to the chosen people [Luke 2:32], until at length the only-begotten Son came forth from the bosom of the Father, full of grace and truth, and declared, or disclosed, the perfect being of God to mankind [John 1:14, 18].

Thus have we, my brethren, arrived at the knowledge of that sacred mystery, which we denote by the comprehensive expression of the Trinity. The doctrine of a "Trinity in

Unity"[1] is the ineffably sublime result of all that God is related to have done in our behalf in that narrative of his providences which we call the Bible. It is not a mere dogma, or formal declaration of some opinion concerning God, simply deduced from certain texts of Scripture—as the adversaries of the faith once delivered to the saints [Jude 1:3] are apt to assert—but it is a general fact clearly resulting from all those manifold occasions on which the Deity is manifested to us as we read the pages of the Bible. We discover it not in the books of Moses or in the Prophets or in the Scriptures of the New Testament, taken by themselves alone and independently of each other, but in the united views which they present of the Head of the kingdom of providence. Now indeed that we enjoy the full light, we can trace with more or less clearness, in each separate portion of Scripture, intimations of the doctrine of the Trinity. . . . But it is because we enjoy the full light, and reflect back on the past the rays emitted from the later dispensations of God, that we see these evidences of him in the first revelations. To us, the prophets of the Old Covenant speak the message of apostles and evangelists because we have learned their words in the school of apostles and evangelists. This, indeed, is a consideration which must be ever borne in mind when we bring any particular passage of the older Scriptures in testimony of the doctrine of the Trinity—that we do not rest or found the doctrine upon this or that passage, but that we adduce it only in confirmation of a truth which results from the whole tenor of Scripture; from taking a collective survey of the successive dispensations therein recorded; from viewing God, not only as the Creator and Governor of the world, but also as our Savior in the person of our Lord Jesus Christ and our Comforter and Sanctifier in the person of the Holy Ghost.

This is the firm and impregnable ground on which Christians should maintain the scriptural truth of a "Trinity in Unity." They should never suffer themselves to be entangled in mere verbal controversy with the heretical opposers of this doctrine. The clearest intellect as well as the soundest faith may be sometimes embarrassed by verbal difficulties, by objections to particular passages, by ingenious interpretations of particular texts, emptying them of that glory which they possess as vehicles of the doctrine of the Trinity; but there is no disturbing the faith or the sense of that Christian who points to the Bible as a whole containing this doctrine in it as a matter of fact—as a truth identified with and inseparable from the events which it records. Let it be conceded . . . that certain texts which appear to us plainly to speak of a Trinity may admit of a different interpretation; still, shall we admit the force of mere critical ingenuity to destroy the plain and indisputable evidence of facts? Shall we suffer ourselves to be compelled to deny a conviction resulting from what God is related by the sacred historians to have done in the administration of the affairs of the world, because a dexterous interpreter may avail himself of the ambiguities of language to weaken the application of certain passages to the point in question? . . .

To illustrate to you how just a ground on which to rest your belief in the mystery of the Trinity such an evidence is, I would suggest to you to consider the parallel case of any common fact which has occurred to your own observation or for which you have the testimony of a credible witness. Would you suffer your belief in a fact for which you have such certain evidence to be weakened by the ingenious reasonings of an objector who should

---

[1]   [Ed. From the Athanasian Creed.]

remark to you that he could not account for the fact from principles which you acknowl-edge no less than himself; that the witness who reports it to you might possibly have been deceived; that his words would admit of a construction which would leave the fact at least open to doubt; or that the fact is so strange and unaccountable that the mind is placed in the uncertainty of an equipoise between the improbability of the thing related and that of the falsehood of the witness; or who should urge any similar sophistical objections? In any familiar case, you would readily answer the objector that he might puzzle and perplex you, but that he could not destroy your conviction of the truth of the fact; he might raise a mist before your eyes, but still the fact itself would remain—obscured only, but not removed from its place; that its existence and reality, in short, are matters quite indepen-dent of any difficulties in regard to it which may be felt in your mind. Apply then the like decision of mind to the doctrine of the Trinity. Here is a fact, as I have already stated to you, which is the general result of the whole collection of Scripture-facts. You survey all the transactions in which the Bible reports to you the sovereign Author of the universe to have been engaged, and you are irresistibly led to form a notion of him as subsisting by a "Trinity in Unity." You acknowledge the Bible to be the true Word of God; you believe all the facts therein recorded to rest on the indisputable testimony of faithful witnesses. Consistently with this profession of belief in the authenticity of the Scripture-narrative, you believe the fact of a "Trinity in Unity." Hold then this sacred fact with a firm and unflinching conviction. There is no greater reason in the transcendent sacredness of the mystery involved in it that it should be rejected, though attested by the strongest evidence, than that any other fact should be implicitly believed, which has nothing but good testi-mony to establish it. Sophistry may weave its cobwebs round the sacred truth and wrap it from our sight in the folds of human mysticism, but it cannot expunge it from the stub-born record of the Bible. It may suffice to raise within you disquietude and searchings of heart, but it cannot say to the Bible that it shall not declare the truth; it cannot roll back the tide of past events in which the doctrine of the Trinity is involved.

It may be worthwhile to state that it is upon this view of the doctrine of the Trinity that the formulary of the Athanasian Creed is grounded. If that Creed were an expression of abstract opinions formed by human reason on an incomprehensible subject, then it would be both rash and profane in any church to exact a general conformity of declaration on a matter so precarious in its foundation. But that Creed, on the contrary, presupposes that the doctrine of the "Trinity in Unity" is a certain fact of Scripture. It simply notes and records what Scripture reveals, and it delivers no opinion whatever concerning the matters revealed and there specified. As a brief statement, it brings together points which are scattered throughout Scripture, collecting in one the rays that diverge from the various facts of the different dispensations of God. . . . Our Church humbly following Scripture, wishes all her members to make a true confession of what they learn from Scripture; and, therefore, as I conceive, appoints the doctrine of the Trinity as the most comprehensive declaration of Scripture-truths—as the doctrine in which all other doctrines ultimately center—to be confessed by her members with peculiar emphasis and distinctness on cer-tain occasions. . . .

You are now fully prepared, I should hope, to go along with me in the assertion that the doctrine of a "Trinity in Unity" is one which no person who has the Bible before him, and who is able to search and see whether these things are so, can hold it a matter of indifference whether he receives or rejects. What I have been endeavoring to impress on you is that if the Scriptures exist, this doctrine exists; that it is the very substance of our whole faith, and not a mere article of it; or rather that either this doctrine is, or Christianity is not; and that in the act of renouncing it, we depart into another system of faith and quit that which results from the records of Scripture. . . . This is the general rule by which our own conduct should be regulated, whether in action or in verbal profession of our faith. . . .

And let us labor to prove by our lives the saving efficacy of that pure profession of Christianity which we make in professing the doctrine of the Trinity. Our unalterable attachment to this sacred truth—our zeal in defending it—above all, our wisdom in understanding it—are best evinced not by our dexterity in adducing texts in proof of it, not by our readiness of argument in combating the objections of its opponents, not by our acuteness in distinguishing and guarding our notions from heretical imputations—not, I say, by all these modes of profession, however useful and indispensable in themselves to the maintenance of the doctrine—but, by still more vital and effectual means, by showing forth the love of the Father, almighty in constraining us to the obedience of dutiful children, the grace of our Lord Jesus Christ, almighty in rescuing us from the bonds of sin and death, the communion of the Holy Ghost, almighty in consecrating our hearts to the service and glory of that Godhead in which the Holy Three are One.

Text: Renn D. Hampden, *Parochial sermons illustrative of the importance of the revelation of God in Jesus Christ* (London: C. and J. Rivington, 1828), 25–42.

II

FAITH

Christianity is not a theory or a speculation but a life—not a philosophy of life, but a life and a living process.

S. T. Coleridge, *Aids to reflection* (1825)

GEORGE WHITEFIELD
(1714–1770)
Repentance

George Whitefield was a prominent evangelical and early member of the Oxford Methodists. Born in Gloucester, Whitefield entered Pembroke College, Oxford in 1732, met the Wesley brothers, and joined the meetings of the "Holy Club." Here Whitefield adopted severe ascetic practices including extended periods spent in prayer, fasting, and service. Whitefield was ordained deacon in 1736, traveled to Georgia in 1738, and returned to England only four months later to raise funds for English charity schools and an orphanage in Georgia. As with other Methodists, Whitefield found many Church of England pulpits closed to him, in part because he regularly denounced Anglican ministers for laziness, ignorance, and dereliction of their Christian duties, suggesting that "the reason why congregations have been so dead is because dead men preach to them."[1] Early Methodist practices of open-air preaching and outreach to populations neglected by the established church find their origin in Whitefield's innovative methods of evangelism. Although both were known as Methodists, Whitefield and John Wesley publicly disagreed over the Calvinist doctrine of predestination, leading to a break in their friendship in 1741. Despite this falling out, the two men otherwise shared broadly evangelical theological commitments. Whitefield's dramatic, sensational preaching garnered wide public interest in Britain; in America, it helped fuel the Great Awakening. Benjamin Franklin conducted an experiment during one American tour that led him to conclude that up to thirty thousand people could hear Whitefield preach at one time. Whitefield lived for many years in England leading the Calvinist Methodists at Moorfields Tabernacle and Tottenham Court Chapel, serving as personal chaplain to Lady Selena, Countess of Huntington, and traveling tirelessly. Some estimate that Whitefield preached fifteen thousand times during his lifetime. He died in Massachusetts, and his tomb became a pilgrimage site for evangelicals throughout the next century. To the displeasure of many of Whitefield's Calvinist followers, his funeral sermon was preached by John Wesley.

[1]   Sydney E. Ahlstrom, *A religious history of the American people* (New Haven: Yale University Press, 1972), 284.

Before departing for his final American preaching tour, Whitefield delivered "The good Shepherd: a farewell sermon," which relies on the commonplace comparison of the Christian to a humble sheep. The sermon weaves together prominent evangelical themes: appeals to repent of sin, challenges to pursue good works, and devotion to biblical wisdom. The sermon, preached at the Whitefield's Tabernacle on August 30, 1769, and taken down in shorthand by Joseph Gurney, calls listeners to respond to the good news of redemption in Christ and reveals the heart of a minister devoted to the task of evangelism.

SOURCES: Sydney E. Ahlstrom, *A religious history of the American people* (New Haven: Yale University Press, 1972); Bebbington; Robert E. Cray Jr., "Memorialization and enshrinement: George Whitefield and popular religious culture, 1770–1850," *Journal of the Early Republic* 10 (1990): 339–61; Mark A. Noll, *A history of Christianity in the United States and Canada* (Grand Rapids: Eerdmans, 1992); *ODCC*; *ODNB*; *RCBEC*; Harry S. Stout, *The divine dramatist: George Whitefield and the rise of modern evangelicalism* (Grand Rapids: Eerdmans, 1991).

GEORGE WHITEFIELD
"The Good Shepherd: a farewell sermon"
1769

"My sheep hear my voice, and they follow me" [John 10:27]. It is very remarkable, there are but two sorts of people mentioned in Scripture; it does not say the Baptists and Independents, nor the Methodists and Presbyterians; no, Jesus Christ divides the whole world into but two classes: sheep and goats. The Lord give us to see this morning to which of these classes we belong.

But, it is observable, believers are always compared to something that is good and profitable, and unbelievers are always described by something that is bad, and good for little or nothing.

If you ask me why Christ's people are called sheep, as God shall enable me, I will give you a short and, I hope it will be to you, an answer of peace. Sheep, you know, generally love to be together; we say a flock of sheep; we don't say a herd of sheep. Sheep are little creatures and Christ's people may be called sheep because they are little in the eyes of the world and they are yet less in their own eyes. O some people think, if the great men were on our side, if we had king, lords, and commons on our side—I mean if they were all true believers—O if we had all the kings upon the earth on our side! Suppose you had; alas! alas! do you think the church would go on the better? Why, if it was fashionable to be a Methodist at court, if it was fashionable to be a Methodist abroad, they would go with a Bible or a hymn-book instead of a novel. But religion never thrives under too much sunshine. "Not many mighty, not many noble are called, but God hath chosen the foolish things of the world to confound the wise, and God hath chosen the weak things of the world to confound the things which are mighty" [1 Cor 1:26–27]. Dr. Watts says, here and there I see a king, and here and there a great man in heaven, but their number is but small.[1]

Sheep are looked upon to be the most harmless, quiet creatures that God hath made. O may God, of his infinite mercy, give us to know that we are his sheep by our having this blessed temper infused into our hearts by the Holy Ghost. "Learn of me," saith our

[1]   [Ed. Whitefield refers to the English hymn writer Isaac Watts (1674–1748).]

blessed Lord. What to do, to work miracles? No. "Learn of me, for I am meek and lowly in heart" [Matt 11:29]. A very good man now living said once, if there is any one particular temper I desire more than another, it is the grace of meekness, quietly to bear bad treatment, to forget and to forgive; and at the same time that I am sensible I am injured, not to be overcome of evil, but to have grace given me to overcome evil with good. To the honor of Moses it is declared that he was the meekest man upon earth [Num 12:3]. Meekness is necessary for people in power; a man that is passionate is dangerous; every governor should have a warm temper, but a man of an unrelenting, unforgiving temper is no more fit for government than Phaeton to drive the chariot of the sun—he only sets the world on fire.[2]

You all know that sheep of all creatures in the world are the most apt to stray and be lost; Christ's people may justly, in that respect, be compared to sheep. Therefore, in the introduction to our morning service, we say, "We have erred and strayed from thy ways like lost sheep."[3] Turn out a horse or a dog and they will find their way home, but a sheep wanders about, he bleats here and there, as much as to say, "dear stranger, show me my way home again." Thus Christ's sheep are too apt to wander from the fold; having their eye off the Great Shepherd, they go into this field and that field, over this hedge and that, and often return home with the loss of their wool.

But at the same time sheep are the most useful creatures in the world: they manure the land and thereby prepare it for the feed; they clothe our bodies with wool; and there is not the least part of a sheep but is useful to man. O my brethren, God grant that you and I may, in this respect, answer the character of sheep. The world says because we preach faith we deny good works. This is the usual objection against the doctrine of imputed righteousness, but it is a slander, an impudent slander. It was a maxim in the first Reformers' time that, though the *Arminians* preached up good works, you must go to the *Calvinists* for them. Christ's sheep study to be useful and to clothe all they can. We should labor with our hands that we may have to give to all those that need.

Believers consider Christ's property in them.[4] He says, "My sheep." O blessed be God for that little, dear, great word "my." We are his by eternal election: "the sheep which thou hast given me," says Christ. They were given by God the Father to Christ Jesus in the covenant made between the Father and the Son from all eternity. They that are not led to see this, I wish them better heads; though, I believe, numbers that are against it have got better hearts. The Lord help us to bear with one another where there is an honest heart.

He calls them *my sheep*; they are his by purchase. O sinner, sinner, you are come this morning to hear a poor creature take his last farewell, but I want you to forget the creature that is preaching. I want to lead you farther than the Tabernacle.[5] Where do you want to lead us? Why, to Mount Calvary, there to see at what an expense of blood Christ purchased those whom he calls his own. He redeemed them with his own blood, so that they are not only his by eternal election, but also by actual redemption in time; and they were given to him by the Father, upon condition that he should redeem them by his

---

[2]   [Ed. In Greek mythology, Phaeton was the son of Helios. Ovid's *Metamorphoses* describes Phaeton's reckless effort to drive Helios' fiery chariot, setting the world aflame before Zeus' intervention left Phaeton dead.]

[3]   [Ed. Whitefield draws from the "General Confession" of the Book of Common Prayer.]

[4]   [Ed. Christ's ownership of them.]

[5]   [Ed. Whitefield founded the Tabernacle in Moorfields, London, in 1741.]

heart's blood. It was a hard bargain, but Christ was willing to strike the bargain that you and I might not be damned forever.

><><

TEXT: George Whitefield, "The Good Shepherd: a farewell sermon," in *Eighteen sermons, preached by the late Rev. George Whitefield*, ed. Joseph Gurney and Andrew Gifford (London: Joseph Gurney, 1771), 434–39.

AUGUSTUS TOPLADY
(1740–1778)
Predestination

Evangelical ministers commonly preached against the effects of sin. Every man, woman, and child, they contended, bears the guilt of original sin and inevitably commits actual sins through willful deeds contrary to the moral law. For those who lack the saving grace of Jesus Christ, sin results in eternal damnation. The marked emphasis on sin in their preaching brought many evangelicals into conflict with fellow clergymen of the Church of England (no less than with some dissenters, Deists, and outright skeptics). Yet, despite this shared concern, evangelical preachers often differed quite significantly within their own ranks over the Calvinist doctrines of election and predestation, that is, whether before all time God had elected some to salvation and ordained the rest to damnation.

Augustus Montague Toplady was an author, hymn writer, and devoted Calvinist minister. Toplady, whose father was from Ireland, attended Westminster School after his recently widowed mother settled in London. He later returned to Ireland and took the B.A. at Trinity College, Dublin, in 1760. While at Trinity, Toplady came under the influence of the Methodist itinerant preacher James Morris. Later, Toplady came to reject the teachings of John Wesley in favor of the Calvinism of George Whitefield, William Romaine, and the Baptist John Gill. Toplady was ordained a priest in the Church of England in 1764 and named vicar of Broad Hembury in Devonshire in 1768. During this period, Toplady wrote several hymns including "Rock of Ages," which was first published in 1775. He died of tuberculosis in 1778.

For many years of his life, Toplady engaged in public controversy over the doctrine associated with John Wesley, and, before that, with Arminianism, which maintained that God's election was based on divine foreknowledge of human responses to divine grace. In a series of combative works, including *The Church of England vindicated from the charge of Arminianism* (1769), *A letter to Mr. John Wesley relating to his pretended abridgement of Zanchius on Protestantism* (1771), *More work for Mr. Wesley* (1771), and *The historic proof of the doctrinal Calvinism of the Church of England* (1774), Toplady defended Calvinism against the dilution of Christian teaching that he perceived in Arminian Methodism.

Toplady, whose writings reflect the teachings of the Dutch Reformed Synod of Dort of 1618–1619, believed in the total depravity of fallen humans, unconditional election by God, limited redemption of the elect alone, the irresistibility of God's grace, and the perseverance of those converted by grace to final glorification.

John Wesley argued that Calvinism derogates from divine justice, since its doctrine of *double* predestination entails that many people—probably most people—have been preordained to perdition before they ever committed an actual sin; indeed, before Adam sinned. At a key moment of *The consequence proved* (1771), Wesley leveled a particularly memorable quip at his opponent: "The sum of all is this: one in twenty (suppose) of mankind are elected; nineteen in twenty are reprobated. The elect shall be saved, do what they will; the reprobate shall be damned, do what they can." Toplady's riposte in *More work for Mr. Wesley* (1771), from which the following selections are drawn, contends that the Wesleyan-Arminian effort to absolve God of injustice must logically lead to universal salvation. On this basis, Toplady turns Wesley's quip on its head: "Every man shall be saved, do what he will; no man shall be condemned, do what he can." The debate, of course, was far from over.

>∽⌒∾<

Sources: Bebbington; Oliver A. Beckerlegge, "Wesley and Toplady," *Epworth Review* 17, no. 2 (1990): 48–53; George Lawton, *Within the rock of ages: the life and work of Augustus Montague Toplady* (Cambridge: James Clarke, 1983); *ODCC*; *ODNB*.

AUGUSTUS TOPLADY
More work for Mr. Wesley
1771

Common justice commands me to acknowledge that no man has strove more to distinguish himself in this illaudable warfare than Mr. John Wesley; and, at the same time, stubborn fact constrains me to add that few warriors have acquitted themselves more contemptibly.

‡

To multiply instances would be endless. Let us apply the few that have been given. If the Scriptures are true, God did, from all eternity, choose an innumerable multitude of Adam's posterity to the certain attainment of grace and glory. This choice of them was in his Son. Being pre-considered as fallen, they were chosen under that character and federally[1] given to him to be redeemed by his blood and clothed with his righteousness. But this alone would not have sufficed. It was necessary that, as sinners, they should not only be redeemed from punishment and entitled to heaven, but endued, moreover, with an internal meetness[2] for that inheritance to which they should be entitled and redeemed. This internal meetness for heaven can only be wrought by the restoring agency of God the Holy Ghost, who graciously engaged and took upon himself, in the covenant of peace, to renew and "sanctify all the elect people of God,"[3] saying, "I will put my law in their minds, and write it upon their hearts" [Heb 10:16]. This, most certainly, was the view in which the decree of predestination was considered by the Apostle Peter when he thus wrote: "Elect, according to the foreknowledge of God the Father (according to his foreknowledge of the human Fall, which foreknowledge made it necessary that election should be decreed to take effect not independently [of] God the Son and God the Holy Ghost, but) through sanctification of the Spirit, unto obedience, and sprinkling of the

---

[1]   [Ed. On the basis of a covenant.]

[2]   [Ed. Fitness or suitability.]

[3]   [Ed. Toplady draws the phrase "sanctify all the elect . . ." from the Catechism of the Church of England.]

blood of Jesus Christ."[4] It appears from this golden passage: 1. That all the three divine persons are equally concerned in the salvation of sinners. The Father elected them, the Son shed his blood for them, the Spirit sanctifies them. 2. That the objects of election were considered in that eternal decree as fallen, else I cannot see how they could be chosen unto the sprinkling of the Messiah's blood and unto the sanctification of the Spirit. 3. That election, though productive of good works, is not founded upon them. On the contrary, they are one of the glorious ends to which the elect are chosen. Saints do not bear the root, but the root them.[5] "Elect—unto obedience." 4. That they who have been elected by God the Father shall be sprinkled by the Son or legally purified by his atonement in a way of pardon, and experience the Holy Spirit's sanctification in beginning, advancing, and perfecting the good work of grace on their souls. Whence, 5. the elect, the sprinkled and the sanctified, are made to obey the commandments of God and to imitate Christ as a pattern, at the same time that they trust in him as their propitiation. I said "made to obey." Here perhaps, the unblushing Mr. Wesley may ask, "Are the elect, then, mere machines?" I answer, No. They are made willing to obey in the day of God's power [Ps 110:3]. And, I believe, nobody ever yet heard of a willing machine. . . .

Prior to the taking of Jericho, it was revealed to Joshua that he should certainly be master of the place. Nay, so peremptory was the decree and so express the revelation of it that it was predicted as if it had already taken effect: "I have given into thy hand Jericho, and the king thereof, and the mighty men of valor" {Josh 6:2}. This assurance, than which nothing could be more absolute, did not tie up Joshua's hands from action and make him sit down without using the means which were no less appointed than the end. On the contrary, he took care to regulate the procession pursuant to God's command, and the event was accomplished accordingly. From fact, let us ascend to speculation. The doctrine, which stands this united test, is and must be true. Suppose it was infallibly revealed to an army or to any single individual that the former should certainly gain such a battle and the latter certainly win such a race. Would not the army be mad to say, "Then we will not fight a stroke?" Would not the racer be insane to add, "Nor will I move so much as one of my feet?" Now it is no less irrational to insinuate that the elect shall be saved without being spiritually and morally conformed to the image of Christ, than it would be to dream of gaining a battle without fighting or of winning a prize without contending. Would it not be absurd to affirm that Adam might have tilled and dressed the Garden of Eden whether he had been created or not? Equally illogical is Mr. Wesley's impudent slander that "the elect shall be saved do what they will," i.e., whether they are holy or not.

This writer passes with some for a man of profound learning. But, surely, either his head is not so well furnished as these good people suppose or his heart must be totally void of justice, candor, and truth. Either he is absolutely unacquainted with the first principles of reasoning or he offers up the knowledge he has as a whole burnt-sacrifice on the altar of malice, calumny, and falsehood.

---

4   [Ed. Toplady inserts the parenthetical interpolation of 1 Pet 1:2.]

5   [Ed. The claim recalls early modern controversies over justification and predestination. For example, in his *Exposition of the first epistle of St. John*, William Tyndale comments on the priority of faith over goodness, noting that "faith in Christ is root of all godly virtue, and the cause of keeping the commandments."]

Justice consists in rendering to every man his due. The supposed injustice, therefore, of preterition turns on this question, "Whether God is or is not a debtor to man?" I more than imagine that he is not a debtor to any man. He owes no man the least of all his favors, and, indeed, his blessings could not be called favors if man could claim them in a way of debt. Who hath prevented me (i.e., been beforehand with me in any good thing) that I should repay him {Job 41:11}? Even those whom he had made righteous are unable to earn or merit the smallest temporal or eternal benefit of his hands. "If thou be righteous, what givest thou him? Or, what receiveth he of thy hand" (Job 35:7)? Much less can the wicked (with whom alone reprobation has anything to do) lay their Maker under obligation to save them. If it be proved that he owes salvation to every rational being he has made, then, and then only, it will follow that God is unjust in not paying this debt of salvation to each of his reasonable creatures. But, on the contrary, if God, instead of being an universal debtor (as Arminianism supposes him to be), is himself the universal creditor—who beneficently lends every earthly and munificently bestows every celestial happiness according to the riches of his own free, sovereign unmerited bounty—what shadow of injustice can be fastened on his conduct for, in some cases, withholding what he does not owe? The objection, therefore (if it may be dignified by that name), being founded on a mistaken principle, evaporates into air.

. . . If God is indebted to some men, why not to all? And if he owes salvation to all men, why will he condemn any man at last? Should it be said, that "some men will not permit God to pay them their debt of salvation, and, by their own misbehavior, disqualify themselves from receiving it," I answer that to talk of man's not permitting God to be just is assuming a principle that cannot be allowed. God can never be overruled by man until man is superior to God. Not to add that the Arminian hypothesis of men being God's creditors rests (if it has anything to rest upon) on the natural claim to happiness, wherewith man is supposed to be invested in right of involuntary creatureship; he derives his existence from God, and therefore (says Arminianism) God is bound to make that existence happy. Admit but this and universal salvation comes in with a full tide. There can be none, no, not one, to whom the Judge will or can say at the final audit, "Depart from me, I know you not, ye workers of iniquity" [Matt 7:23]. For even those who live and die in their sins are certainly God's creatures; and if God owe salvation to all his creatures as such, even the workers of iniquity will and must be saved or God must cease to be just. Who sees not that the Arminian scheme, if probed to the bottom, opens by necessary consequence the flood-gates of practical licentiousness, and, with all its pretences to good works, is in reality but varnished antinomianism?[6] It says, in effect, "Every man shall be saved, do what he will; no man shall be condemned, do what he can. Let narrow-spirited Calvinists cease to do evil and learn to do well. Let gloomy predestinarians insist that without holiness no man shall see the Lord and fondly dream that sanctity and salvation are indissolubly connected. But let us, the liberal disciples of Arminius, act on a more expanded plan. Every son of Adam is God's creature and every creature of God is good.

---

[6] [Ed. *Antinomians* are those who believe they are free from the requirements of the moral law by virtue of divine grace.]

We are all endued with independent free will. Our Maker loves every man alike. His justice will not suffer him to reject any of us, especially seeing we are all redeemed, one as well as another. Let us, therefore, take our ease, eat, drink, and be merry, and tomorrow shall be as this day and much more abundant."

This is the true language of Arminianism, though not of all Arminians. It is the natural consequence of the scheme itself, though many who embrace the scheme are not aware of the consequence. You may say, "Oh, but no man shall actually be saved though salvation is his due, except he perform certain conditions." This is no better than a very thin evasion: a mere barrel thrown out for the amusement of the whale to keep him in play and make him lose sight of the ship. Permit me to ask: Is salvation due to a man who does not perform those conditions? If you say yes, you jump hand over head into what you yourself call antinomianism. If you say that "salvation is not due to a man unless he fulfills the conditions," it will follow: 1. That man's own performances are meritorious of salvation and bring God himself into debt; 2. That man, as a creature of God, is not entitled to salvation; and that God, as the creator of man, is not therefore bound to save the men he has created.

There is no possible alternative. Either God is obliged in justice to save mankind or he is not. If he be, it must be the works of men that lay him under the obligation. If he be not, then neither is he unjust in passing by some men. Nay, he might, had he so pleased, have passed by the whole of mankind without electing any one individual of the fallen race and yet have continued inviolably holy, just, and good.

TEXT: Augustus Toplady, *More work for Mr. John Wesley*, in *The works of Augustus Toplady, A.B.*, 6 vols. (London: The Proprietors, 1794), 5:360–61, 376–79, 388–91.

JOHN FLETCHER
(1729–1785)
Free Grace

John William Fletcher, originally named Jean Guillaume de la Fléchère, was born and educated in Switzerland. In 1746 he matriculated at Geneva University, where he studied classics after deciding against a clerical career. In 1750 he moved to England, joining the Methodists in 1753. Early in 1754 Fletcher experienced a conversion of faith and committed his life to ministry. Three years later, Fletcher was ordained deacon and priest in the Church of England, becoming curate at Madeley, Shropshire (vicar from 1760). His wife, Mary Bosanquet (1739–1815), received John Wesley's permission to preach under an "extraordinary call." Wesley discovered a kindred spirit in Fletcher. Intellectually his equal and known for his saintly piety, Fletcher developed Wesley's doctrine of Christian perfection through reference to "baptism in the Spirit," opposed Joseph Priestley's Unitarianism, and earned the respect of those familiar with his preaching and writing in England and abroad. Fletcher enthusiastically joined Wesley's side in his controversy with the Calvinists during the 1770s. Wesley hoped that, after his death, Fletcher would lead the Methodists, writing to Fletcher: "Who is he? *Thou art the man!*"[1] Fletcher, however, weathered Wesley's multiple proposals and, in the end, died several years before his elderly friend.

English Calvinists believed that Wesley's emphasis on free will, grace, and divine love diminished both the sovereignty of God and the utter sinfulness of humanity. In numerous writings and sermons, Wesley embraced the pejorative label "Arminian"—that is, a follower of the Dutch theologian Jacobus Arminius (1560–1609), who asserted that God elected those whom he foreknew would accept the offer of grace, rejecting only those whose refusal of the same offer he likewise foresaw—and even published a journal named *The Arminian Magazine*. Wesley argued that the Calvinist doctrine of predestination fails to account for the biblical notion of salvation on two decisive points. On one hand, the doctrine brands God a capricious tyrant, since God actively chooses that innumerable creatures be condemned to eternal damnation. Charles Wesley's *Hymns on*

---

[1] Richard P. Heitzenrater, *Wesley and the people called Methodists* (Nashville: Abingdon, 1995), 254.

God's everlasting love (1741), for instance, takes up this "hellish doctrine" in his "Horrible Decree":

> To limit thee, they dare,
> Blaspheme thee to thy face;
> Deny their fellow worms a share
> In thy redeeming grace.

The Calvinist doctrine not only charged God with grave injustice but also made mockery of human responsibility. If sinful people receive an assurance of salvation apart from their actions, then open licentiousness inevitably results. Fletcher emphasizes this second aspect of the controversy in the following selection from *The first part of an equal check to pharisaism and antinomianism* (1774–1775), where he argues that both Calvinists and Roman Catholics ignore the tension between faith and works. As the title indicates, Fletcher contrasts two types: antinomians vainly boast of election without works, while Pharisees vainly attempt to earn salvation through works. Fletcher associates the two types with the errors of Calvinists (antinomians) and Roman Catholics (Pharisees), respectively. Salvation depends, Fletcher declares, on the merits of Christ alone. Still, faith and works operate in union, just as the two oars of a boat or the process of respiration in the body.

✕✄

Sources: *BDE*; Richard P. Heitzenrater, *Wesley and the people called Methodists* (Nashville: Abingdon, 1995); *ODCC*; *ODNB*; Patrick Streiff, *Reluctant saint?: a theological biography of Fletcher of Madeley* (Peterborough: Epworth, 2001); John R. Tyson, *Assist me to proclaim: the life and hymns of Charles Wesley* (Grand Rapids: Eerdmans, 2007); Laurence W. Wood, *The meaning of Pentecost in early Methodism: rediscovering John Fletcher as Wesley's vindicator and designated successor* (Lanham, Md.: Scarecrow, 2002).

JOHN FLETCHER
The first part of an equal check to pharisaism and antinomianism
1774

See that sculler upon yonder river. The unwearied diligence and watchful skill with which he plies his two oars point out to us the work and wisdom of an experienced divine. What an even, gentle spring does the mutual effort of his oars give to his boat! Observe him: his right hand never rests but when the stream carries him too much to the left; he slacks not his left hand unless he is gone too much to the right; nor has he sooner recovered a just medium than he uses both oars again with mutual harmony. Suppose that for a constancy he employed but one—no matter which—what would be the consequence? He would only move in a circle; and if neither wind nor tide carried him along, after a hard day's work he would find himself in the very spot where he began his idle toil.

This illustration needs very little explaining. I shall just observe that the antinomian is like a sculler who uses only his right hand oar, and the Pharisee like him who plies only the oar in his left hand. One makes an endless bustle about *grace* and *faith*, the other about *charity* and *works*; but both, after all, find themselves exactly in the same case, with this single difference: that one has turned from truth to the right and the other to the left.

Not so the judicious, unbiased preacher who will safely enter the haven of eternal rest for which he and his hearers are bound. He makes an equal use of the doctrine of *faith* and that of *works*. If at any time he insists most upon faith, it is only when the stream carries his congregation upon the pharisaical shallows on the left hand. And if he lay a preponderating stress upon works, it is only when he sees unwary souls sucked into the antinomian whirlpool on the right hand. His skill consists in so avoiding one danger as not to run upon the other.

‡

Should you ask which is most necessary to salvation, *faith* or *works*, I beg leave to propose a similar question: Which is most essential to breathing, *inspiration* or *expiration*? If you reply that "the moment either is absolutely at an end, so is the other, and therefore both are equally important," I return exactly the same answer. If *humble faith* receives the breath of spiritual life, *obedient love* gratefully returns it and makes way for a fresh supply. When it does not, the Spirit is grieved; and if this want of cooperation is persisted in to the end of the day of salvation, the sin unto death is committed, the Spirit is quenched in his saving operation [1 Thess 5:19], the apostate dies the second death, and his corrupt soul is cast into the bottomless pit as a putrid corpse into the noisome grave [Rev 20:14-15].

Again, if faith has the advantage over works by giving them birth, works have the advantage over faith by perfecting it. "Seest thou," says St. James speaking of the father of the faithful, "how faith wrought with his works and by works was faith made perfect?" [Jas 2:22]. And if St. Paul affirms that works without faith are dead, St. James maintains that "faith without works is dead also" [Jas 2:17].

Once more: Christ is always the primary, original, properly meritorious cause of our justification and salvation. To dispute it is to renounce the faith and to plead for Antichrist.[1] And yet to deny that under this primary cause there are secondary, subordinate, instrumental causes of our justification (and consequently of our salvation) is to set the Bible aside and fly in the face of judicious Calvinists who cannot help maintaining it both from the pulpit and from the press. Now, if in the day of our conversion faith is the secondary, subordinate cause of our acceptance as penitent sinners, in the day of judgment works, even the works of faith, will be the secondary, subordinate cause of our acceptance as persevering saints. Let us therefore equally decry dead faith and dead works, equally recommend living faith and its important fruits.

‡

Error moves in a circle; extremes meet in one. A warm popish Pharisee and a zealous Protestant antinomian are nearer each other than they imagine. The one will tell you that by going to mass and confession he can get a fresh absolution from the priest for any sin that he shall commit. The other, whose mistake is still more pleasing to flesh and blood, assures you that he has already got an eternal absolution, so that "under every state and circumstance he can possibly be in, he is justified from all things, his sins are forever and forever canceled."

But, if they differ a little in the idea of their imaginary privileges, they have the honor of agreeing in the main point. For, although the one makes a great noise about faith and free grace, and the other about works and true charity, they exactly meet in narrow grace and despairing uncharitableness. The Pharisee in Jerusalem asserts that "out of the Jewish Church there can be no salvation,"[2] and his companions in self-election heartily say, "Amen!" The Pharisee in Rome declares that "there is no salvation out of the apostolic, Romish Church," and all the Catholic elect set their seal to the anti-Christian decree. And the antinomian in London insinuates (for he is ashamed to speak quite out in a Protestant country) that there is no salvation out of the Calvinistic predestinarian Church. Hence, if you oppose his principles in ever so rational and scriptural a manner, he supposes that

---

[1] [Ed. Fletcher's emphasis on works as an instrumental cause protects Wesleyan Arminianism from charges of Pelagianism (an historically unorthodox belief that the individual earns salvation through good works), since the instrumental cause only assists the principal ("efficient") cause.]

[2] [Ed. Fletcher plays on Cyprian of Carthage's famous declaration: *extra Ecclesiam nulla salus* ("outside the church there is no salvation") (*Epistle* 72.21).]

you are "quite dark," that all your holiness is "self-made," and all your "righteousness a cobweb spun by a poor spider out of its own bowels."[3] And if he allows you a chance for your salvation, it is only upon a supposition that you may yet repent of your opposition to his errors and turn Calvinist before you die. But might not an inquisitor be as charitable? Might he not hope that the poor heretic whom he has condemned to the flames may yet be saved if he cordially kisses a crucifix and says "Ave, Maria"[4] at the stake?

‡

What good has Calvinism done in England? Alas! very little. When a bow is bent beyond its proper degree of tension, does it not fly to pieces? When you violently pull a tree toward the west, if it recovers itself, does it not violently fly to the east? Has not this generally been the case with respect to all the truths of God which have been forced out of their scriptural place one way or another?

Text: [John William Fletcher,] *The first part of an equal check to pharisaism and antinomianism* (Shrewsbury: J. Eddowes, 1774), 2–6, 16–17, 19.

---

³   [Ed. Fletcher's memorable image echoes Robert South (1634–1716): "And as the spider draws all out of its own bowels, so the hypocrite weaves all his confidence out of his own inventions and imaginations" (*Sermons preached upon several occasions*, Sermon 44).]

⁴   [Ed. The Latin title ("Hail, Mary") of the prayer seeking for the intercession of the Virgin Mary.]

JOSEPH MILNER
(1744–1797)
Salvation in Christ

Joseph Milner, evangelical Anglican, educator, and church historian, received his early education from Leeds grammar school, whose headmaster John Moore noted the young man's talent in Greek and Latin, and helped to secure him a place at St. Catherine's, Cambridge, where Milner excelled in mathematics and classics (B.A., 1766). Ordained in the Church of England, Milner served as curate or vicar at several Yorkshire churches in the next decades. He influenced the formation of numerous students (including quite a number of evangelical missionaries) as headmaster of the grammar school at Hull. In 1769 Milner came in contact with several of the Countess of Huntingdon's Methodist students staying in Hull. He attended their services, applied his time to studying the doctrine of justification, and in 1770 experienced an evangelical conversion that changed his life and preaching. Milner's newfound evangelical faith disturbed a number of the city's merchants, but in time his popularity recovered, especially among the poor and working classes for whom he showed great concern.

Milner's legacy rests on his widely popular *History of the church of Christ* (1794–1809). Unlike other histories of the time, including J. L. Mosheim's *Ecclesiastical history* (which John Wesley abridged for Methodist preachers), Milner avoided the tendency to emphasize divisions, heresy, and error in the history of Christianity, instead emphasizing the unity of faith through the ages. The *History* drew extensively from the writings of the early church; it was the work that awakened John Henry Newman's appreciation for Christian antiquity. Other works by Milner included a response to the leading historian Edward Gibbon in 1781 and *Essays on several religious subjects* (1789).

Joseph Milner's sermons were collected and posthumously published as *Practical sermons* (4 vols., 1800–1830). As with other evangelical preachers of the day, Milner was not afraid to preach on the terrors of hell and the need for salvation through repentance for sin. In the following sermon, "An affectionate address to seamen," Milner delivers a classic evangelical call for repentance at the North Sea port of Hull, a prominent eighteenth-century center for imports and exports. After first addressing the barbarity to which people succumb in the face of danger, he rebukes the mariners for their tendency to immorality, describing their vulgar language and the common dissoluteness among those living far from home. Milner encourages the men to avoid waiting for perilous circumstances to overtake them, imploring them to surrender to the grace of God, find forgiveness through Christ, and live moral lives in accordance with the teachings of Christ.

SOURCES: *The Blackwell dictionary of evangelical biography, 1730–1860*, ed. D. M. Lewis (Oxford: Blackwell, 1995); Bebbington; Hylson-Smith; Nockles; *ODCC*; *ODNB*; J. D. Walsh, "Joseph Milner's evangelical church history," *Journal of Ecclesiastical History* 10 (1959): 174–87.

JOSEPH MILNER
"An affectionate address to seamen"
1797

You who may shortly be called hence by providence to the mighty waters, reflect how possible it is that you may be brought into imminent danger of your lives. Is not then a knowledge of certain peace with God in this life desirable? Blessed be God, it may be had. Jesus still lives and will forever live. Seek to be acquainted with his real gospel—that which Paul preached. The constant attendant of this gospel has ever been the reproach of the wicked from without, the consolations of God's Holy Spirit from within. Content not yourselves with the form, the outside of religion. Consider how much happier it is to be able with Paul to say, "I am God's, and my God will protect me," though you be despised by the men of this world, than to share with those who are respected and courted upon earth, though they live without God in the world [Eph 2:12]. The same Jesus will be yours and manifest to you the same blissful consolations, if you seek him.

If we look at the rest of the company in this ship,[1] whose voyage and wreck is here described, we see a true picture of natural men, unconverted, and deplorably regardless of every admonition to take care of their souls; men not to be moved by the most imminent peril to call upon God. On the contrary, see how the mariners act! "Under color as though they would have cast anchors out of the foreship, they let down the boat into the sea with an intent to flee out of the ship" [Acts 27:30]. What perfidy and cruelty is here! To leave the soldiers and prisoners who were their charge to perish in the storm! Paul, indeed, discovered the base design and prevented it. But we have another instance of hardened wickedness, which works with more deadly marks of desperate enmity against all goodness. It is the wickedness of the soldiers, I mean, who were for killing the prisoners, lest any should flee and make their escape. The humanity of their commander prevented it indeed; but that men, in such imminent peril of their lives themselves, should be capable of meditating such barbarity would be surprising indeed did not the fallen state of human nature, confirmed by the testimony of history in all ages, prove that nothing is too base and wicked for unconverted men to perpetrate.

---

[1]   [Ed. Milner refers to the shipwreck of Paul in Acts 27.]

Let me now look nearer home and ask you: O mariners! Are there not too many of you as void, as these men were, of the fear of God? As ungrateful to him for past preservations, as insensible of his kind providence, and living as much without real religion and regard for your immortal souls?

‡

O mariners, do not pretend to Christianity, to any sense of honor, generosity, or gratitude, if you live thus without regard to Christ. Do not pretend to any goodness of heart, if Christ's love has never yet melted your breasts. Every oath and curse is a spitting on his face; every act of lewdness is a nailing of his hands; every wanton breach of the Sabbath a scourging of his body; and a constant course of carelessness about an hereafter in your conduct is the same thing as saying, "O Jesus, thou needest not have died to obtain eternal redemption for us. We will have our portion in this life. We desire to have nothing to do either with thee or the heaven thou hast purchased." As men—as rational, accountable creatures—you ought to be moved with fear of hell, with desire of real happiness, with sense of favors received.

I address you with an affectionate concern for your souls, and beseech you to bear with me while I mention a few instances of wickedness, which I wish I could say were not too commonly practiced among you. Weigh and consider them well. There is no hope of your hearty repentance and amendment if you never be brought to serious consideration. How and why is this—that one cannot come within the sound of your voices in the haven of this town, but one's ear is struck with the constant repetition of oaths and curses? This horrible language is particularly heard when you are in a hurry or under the influence of anger for some little cross or untoward accident. Surely you will not think of excusing this by the force of habit? Consider that if you had any reverence for God in your hearts, you durst not affront him so basely. Why do not you pray earnestly and strive earnestly against it? The continuance of such a vile, ungrateful practice which you cannot pretend to be of any sort of service to you, evidently shows that you are living in open war against God and that dying thus you must feel his wrath forever. Alas! What shall I say? Is God who has been so kind in preserving you, hitherto, in so many perils, deserving of this vile usage from you? Is Satan so very good a master, and are the wages of eternal destruction, which he gives to all his slaves, so very pleasant that you should serve him with such zeal? If you had any feeling of your baseness, you would weep and howl for your horrid blasphemies and cry out. "O thou much injured Jesus! Wash out my oaths with thy blood and teach me to use my tongue for the future to thy praise and not to thy dishonor."

I am afraid there are too many, not only among mariners, but others also in this profane libidinous age, who have no idea of any great guilt, or perhaps any guilt at all, in fornication and whoredom. Hence they can live in sin without remorse or fear. But if Scripture is to be regarded at all, fornication as well as adultery are sins that incur the wrath of God. For it is written "marriage is honorable, and the bed undefiled; but whoremongers and adulterers God will judge" [Heb 13:4]. Light as whoremongers may make of this offense, the last chapter in the Bible ranks them with "dogs, and murderers, and idolaters, and liars" [Rev 22:15] who shall be shut out of heaven. Make a conscience then, I beseech you, of this sin and carry past transgressions to the throne of grace to be washed from them in the blood of Christ and taught to live soberly, as well as righteously, and godly in this present world.

I am afraid too many mariners, also, make little conscience of observing either private or public worship, even when they have opportunity. There is not a day but gives you opportunities of praying in secret, and surely you are answerable to God for every day's neglect of this duty. As to public worship, surely, when you have opportunity you should not let a trifle hinder you from attending it. Oh, if you had hearts at all sensible of the kindness of God in preserving you from so many dangers, and were impressed with any lively ideas of the providence of God, which you of all men have the greatest opportunities and occasions of being impressed with, you would gladly wait upon God in his house. You would pay your vows in the sight of all his people with thankful acknowledgments of past deliverances and listen to the sound of the blessed gospel of Christ, which alone can make you wise unto salvation.

Let me ask you also, O mariners, how have you fulfilled those resolutions which you made of amending your ways when you were in distress? You seemed in a storm to be near approaching to eternity. Then, perhaps, you cried to God and promised how good you would be for the future if he spared you. But did you not return immediately, when danger was over, to your old sins? Think of the aggravated baseness of this ingratitude.

In truth, it is no wonder you kept not those resolutions, not only because they were extorted from you by fear, but also because there is a reason why no resolutions whatever made by a man in his own strength have any power to turn him to God. The new creature in Christ is not the product of man's resolving. Those who are, indeed, born again, are, as the Scripture tells us, "born not of the will of man, but of God" [John 1:13]. Read the third chapter of St. John's Gospel carefully with prayer and be well assured from thence that if ever you be, indeed, saved from your sins and made good and holy, you must be born again [John 3:3]. Whether you have led moral or immoral lives in time past, this change is necessary to all who would enter the kingdom of heaven. Shake off that levity and carelessness of spirit, I beseech you, too common among persons of your profession, and begin to inquire what you shall do to be saved with the earnestness becoming men, who are sensible they have immortal souls, which must one day appear before God in judgment.[2]

Would you carry with you, in your hearts, to the seas, a God in Christ, a reconciled and a loving Father to you? Oh, be supremely concerned to seek his face. Consider, you are sinners by nature and in practice. It is no light thing that can take away your iniquities and reconcile you to God. The sole Physician of souls who can give you both repentance and remission of sins is he who is exalted for that end to be a Prince and a Savior. Implore him to look upon you, to create in you new and contrite hearts, that "worthily lamenting your sins, and acknowledging your wretchedness, you may obtain remission,"[3] perfect remission from the God of all mercy, through his well-beloved Son. If any of you are sensible that you have hitherto lived in sin and wickedness, and would gladly be guided into the way of salvation, I declare unto you that "Jesus is the way" [cf. John 14:6]. Through

2   [Ed. In this paragraph, Milner distinguishes between the effort to become worthy of God by grit and determination, and the godly faith that comes by trusting Christ alone for the new birth.]
3   [Ed. Collect for Ash Wednesday, Book of Common Prayer.]

him there is plenteous redemption. Yes, he whom you have pierced with your sins is good and gracious and of great mercy unto all them that call upon him. All things are now ready. Pardon is ready; sanctification is ready; the consolations of God's Holy Spirit are ready. They wait your acceptance. What you want is faith in Christ, to lay hold of him for holiness and happiness. The Lord draw you by his power; and whoever is willing to be saved from his sins and taught to live righteously, soberly, and godly, let him come to Christ and take of the water of life freely.

Thus far, O mariners, I have endeavored to exhort you. Some of you may be sailing hence very shortly, and perhaps you may never more have an opportunity of hearing the glad tidings of salvation. You will be answerable to God for the neglect of what I have said, if you do neglect it. Some of you may shortly be involved in imminent peril of your lives. If so, may you then think of what I have this day said to you—if not before.

I add no more but this: sin and wickedness will entail God's everlasting curse upon those who die in it. If you would escape it, seek to God by Jesus Christ to obtain pardon and holiness of heart and life.

TEXT: Joseph Milner, *Practical sermons*, 2 vols. (York: G. Peacock, 1809), 2:258–60, 264–69.

SOUTHWOOD SMITH
(1788–1861)
Divine Government

The attempt to reconcile the Calvinist doctrine of predestination with the goodness of God led some to examine the relationship between divine sovereignty and human freedom, among them the Unitarian minister (Thomas) Southwood Smith. Smith was born at Martock, Somerset, of Strict Baptist parents. After attending John Ryland's Baptist academy at Bristol, Smith had a brief career as a Baptist preacher. By age twenty, however, he had renounced Calvinism for Unitarianism and in 1808 published a work defending the doctrine of universal salvation (*The benevolence of God displayed in the revelation of a future state of perfect happiness*). In 1812 the Unitarian Fund in London sent Smith to Edinburgh, where, in addition to working as a preacher, Smith received his medical degree (1816). Smith and his young family moved to London in 1820, where the marriage rapidly dissolved; his wife and child moved to the continent shortly afterwards. Although occasionally preaching in Unitarian chapels, Smith spent the remainder of his career as a physician. His friends included leading intellectuals such as Jeremy Bentham. He helped to found the public health movement in Britain.

Smith's *Illustrations of the divine government* (1816) reflects the widespread influence of philosophical Necessitarianism on English Unitarianism. Joseph Priestley promoted Necessitarian doctrine after reading David Hartley's (ca. 1705–1757) *Observations on man, his frame, his duty, and his expectations* (1749), which relies on a complex variant of Newtonian science whereby neurological sensations are associated with mental processes and ideas. English Unitarians often relied on Hartley's deterministic views to develop theories of moral psychology and human freedom. In the following selection, Smith defends God's moral government of the world via a Necessitarian account of human freedom, whereby God works through a series of secondary causes that achieve the perfect accomplishment of the divine will. In several respects, Smith's position is akin to the Calvinist understanding of freedom as doing as one wills even when the possibility of willing otherwise is not an option (i.e., the freedom of one who voluntarily remains in a barred room). For Smith, the illusion of freedom stems from human consciousness of volitional acts associated with sensations of pleasure and pain. Free will, consequently, is only a state of mind predicated on the foreordained gifts and endowments provided by God for the well-being of the world.

SOURCES: John Richard Guy, *Compassion and the art of the possible: Dr. Southwood Smith as social reformer and public health pioneer* (Wisbech: Octavia Hill Society and Birthplace Museum Trust, 1997); *ODNB*; Robert Kiefer Webb, "Southwood Smith: the intellectual sources of public service," in *Doctors, politics and society*, ed. Dorothy Porter and Roy Porter (Amsterdam: Editions Rodopi, 1993), 46–80.

SOUTHWOOD SMITH
Illustrations of the divine government
1816

When the Deity is represented as appointing and controlling every event, it may seem difficult to conceive how this can be reconciled with the agency and accountability of man. A little consideration, however, will show that these truths are not incompatible with each other.

Though the sovereign Arbiter of events regulates and determines everything, yet he carries on the administration of the world by the *instrumentality* of other beings. Seldom does he act *directly*; seldom is he the *immediate* cause of anything. He has left the development of his vast plan to the operation of what are termed secondary causes, but these can act only so far and in such a manner as he has appointed.

The material world is governed by certain general laws, which are never interrupted except on occasions of supreme importance, foreseen and provided for from the beginning. These laws, though thus steady and invariable in their operation, bring about in every instant of time precisely that condition only of the material world which he appoints and which is necessary to carry on his purposes with regard to his animal and moral creation.

The animal and moral world he governs by laws equally fixed and invariable; but being of a nature different from that of the material world, they require to be governed by different laws. By different laws, therefore, they are governed. By laws admirably and exactly suited to its nature, each is guided to its destined end.

The material world being without sensation and thought is governed by a particular set of laws. The animal world possessing sensation and thought is governed by another set. By sensation and thought an animal is induced to act. Every animal possesses a fixed and determinate constitution according to which sensation and thought are excited in it in a particular, determinate manner. The great agent in inducing sensation and thought in the animal is the material world. A certain state of the material world will inevitably produce a certain sensation in an animal possessing a particular constitution; that sensation will produce a particular volition, and that volition will lead, certainly, to a particular action. It only requires, therefore, an exact knowledge of the constitution of the animal world to render its state at all times precisely what may be required. . . .

If we ascend in the scale of creation, we shall find that the principle of the divine administration is exactly the same. Man is endowed not only with the faculties of sensation and thought, but with the power of distinguishing between the rectitude and immorality of conduct. He is capable of understanding his obligations and the grounds of them. Certain actions appear to him to be good; others he regards as evil. The performance of the one is attended with a consciousness that he has acted right and excites the sensation of happiness; the performance of the other is attended with an inward conviction that he has acted wrong and produces misery. All this takes place in a fixed and invariable manner, according to certain laws which are termed *principles of his nature*, and the faculty on which this discrimination and feeling depends is termed his *moral nature*.

Now it is obvious that to a certain extent, a being thus endowed may be governed exactly in the same manner as a creature who possesses only an animal nature. In him, as well as in the mere animal, sensations will be excited by the external circumstances in which he is placed. In him, too, a particular sensation will excite a particular volition, but the exercise of this volition will be attended with a result which is never found in the animal: with a consciousness that he has acted well or ill, with a feeling of approbation or of disapprobation, with a sensation of happiness or misery arising purely from the action itself. This train of sensation becomes itself a new source of action, but it arises according to certain fixed laws and operates as steadily as any other principle of his nature or as any law of the material world. He, therefore, who perfectly understands *this* nature—who knows how every circumstance will affect this *moral* agent, and who has a sovereign control over events—can govern him with the same steadiness with which he regulates the animal or the material world; can make him at all times feel, and think, and act, as may be necessary to carry on the great designs of his administration without violating any principle of his nature. By adapting the particular situation in which he is placed to the particular state of his mind, he can excite whatever volition and secure whatever action he pleases. What is maintained, then, is that with respect to every individual in the world there is this exact adaptation of circumstances to his temper, his habits, his wants, so that while he is left to the full and free exercise of every faculty he possesses, he can feel and act only as the Sovereign of the universe appoints, because the circumstances which excite his sensations and volitions are determined by him. It is not just to suppose that the Deity exercises any such control over his creatures as to force them to act contrary to their will or to violate any principle of their nature. They always act and must act according to their will and in conformity to their nature, but, at the same time, he secures his own purpose by placing them in circumstances which so operate upon their nature as certainly to induce the conduct he requires.

Volition cannot arise, as is often imagined, at the pleasure of the mind. The term volition expresses that state of the mind which is immediately previous to the actions which are called voluntary; but that state is not induced by the mind itself, but by objects operating upon it. The circumstances in which a percipient being is placed excite sensations; and sensations, ideas. Sensations and ideas induce that peculiar condition of the mind which is termed pleasurable, or its opposite which is termed painful. The feeling of pleasure excites desire; that of pain aversion. Will is the result of this state of the mind. Prove to the mind that an object is desirable—that is, that it will induce pleasure—and you immediately excite in it the volition to possess it. Prove to it that an object will occasion pain, and you excite the volition to avoid it. Volition then, it is manifest, depends on the object, whatever it be, which the mind contemplates as desirable or otherwise. Take away the object, there is no volition. . . .

Volition being thus dependent on the circumstances in which an individual is placed, any given volition may be excited in him by a certain modification of his circumstances. We find that the tempers of different men are infinitely various; the Deity has made a corresponding variety in the situations in which he has placed them. To every individual, he has assigned his allotted work. To every intelligent and moral agent, he has given a certain part of his administration to carry on, and in order to qualify him for it, he has adjusted to the particular constitution of his nature every circumstance of his being, from the first instant of his existence to that which terminates his earthly career. If what is termed his natural disposition be such as would seem to render him incapable of performing it, the situation in which he is placed is adapted to it, and is such as to excite, to repress, or to modify it till it becomes exactly what is necessary to fit him for his work; so that every individual is strictly an instrument raised up and qualified by God to carry on the wise and benevolent purposes of his government.

Suppose it is his will to lead men to the discovery of the most interesting truths respecting the phenomena of nature and the laws by which the universe is governed. He endows an individual with a clear and capacious mind; he places him in circumstances favorable to the development of his intellectual faculties; he leads him to observe, to reflect, to investigate; he forms him to those habits of patient and profound inquiry which are necessary to elicit the truths to be disclosed and sufficient to secure him from every temptation to carelessness and dissipation. He raises up a Newton. Suppose—after having for wise though perhaps inscrutable reasons permitted the most low and degrading notions to prevail respecting his own character, government, and worship—he determines to lead back the minds of men to purer and nobler sentiments, and to overthrow those corrupt systems of religion which have prevailed for ages, and in the support of which the passions and interests of men are now engaged. He raises up an individual whose mind he enlightens; whose soul he fills with an ardent zeal for the purity of religion and the simplicity of its rites; whose spirit danger does but excite and suffering cannot subdue; who, though cities and empires arm against him, and one general cry of execration and menace follow him from land to land, goes on with undaunted courage to expose abuses, and to call in a louder and louder voice for reformation. It is the voice of a Luther, which makes corruption rage and superstition tremble. Suppose it is his will to save a people in love with liberty (and worthy because capable of enjoying it) from oppression, and to exhibit to the world an example of what the weak who are virtuous and united may effect against the strong who are corrupt and tyrannical. In the very season when he is needed he forms, and in the very station where his presence is necessary, he places a Washington. And suppose it is his will to pour the balm of consolation into the wounded heart, to visit the captive with solace, to extend mercy to the poor prisoner, to admit into his noisome cell the cheering beams of his sun and his refreshing breezes, he breathes the genuine spirit of philanthropy into some chosen bosom; he super-adds an energy which neither the frown of power, nor the menace of interest, nor the scorn of indifference can abate; which exhibits so strongly to the view of men the horrors of the dungeon, as to force them to suspend for awhile their business and their pleasures; to feel for the sufferings of others, and to learn the great lessons that the guilty are still their brethren; that it is better to reclaim than to destroy; that the punishment which is excessive is immoral; that that which does not aim to reform is unjust and that which does not actually do so, unwise. He gives to a suffering world the angel-spirit of a Howard.[1]

The bodily frame and the natural temper of an individual may seem, as has already been observed, ill-adapted to execute the work which the Deity has determined to perform by him. Yet no *force* is employed to induce him to do it. He is not *compelled* to act against his volition, but the circumstances in which he is placed are so adapted to his corporeal, his mental, and his moral constitution, as to excite the requisite volition.

TEXT: T. Southwood Smith, *Illustrations of the divine government, tending to shew that every thing is under the direction of infinite wisdom and goodness, and will terminate in the production of universal purity and happiness*, 2nd ed. (London: G. Smallfield, 1817), 35–44.

---

[1]   [Ed. John Howard (1726–1790), philanthropist and author of *The state of the prisons in England and Wales, with preliminary observations, and an account of some foreign prisons* (1777).]

EDWARD COPLESTON
(1776–1849)
Fatalism

Edward Copleston, bishop of Llandaff, was a moral philosopher and leading educator at Oriel College, Oxford. Copleston was born at Offwell, Devon, where his father was the local rector. He was educated at home until he matriculated at Corpus Christi College. Copleston quickly achieved success, won numerous awards, and was invited to be a fellow of Oriel College in 1795. By 1802 Copleston had completed the requirements for ordination. He was also named professor of poetry and, as treasurer, was responsible for the college's finances from 1806 to 1812. Copleston was elected provost of Oriel in 1814 and served the college in this capacity until 1828. In addition to writing several works in philosophy, economics, and theology, Copleston helped form the modern examination system at Oxford that remains largely in place today, promoted a revival of interest in the moral philosophy of Joseph Butler, and developed Oriel's tutorial system. Under his leadership, Oriel became the preeminent college at Oxford. Copleston was the center of the so-called Oriel "Noetics" (from the Greek *noesis* for "intellect" or "reason"). With fellow Noetics Edward Hawkins, Richard Whately, and R. D. Hampden, Copleston established Oriel's reputation for theological inquiry by advocating for closer scrutiny of Christian doctrine by reason and philosophy. Although Oriel became the launching pad for the Oxford Movement in the 1830s, Copleston was not a Tractarian (that is, a supporter of John Henry Newman and his collaborators), though Tractarian intellectual habits of rigorous logic and disciplined rhetoric owe much to the influence of the Noetics. In 1826 Copleston was appointed dean of Chester and then, concurrently, bishop of Llandaff and dean of St. Paul's from 1827. As bishop, Copleston supported Roman Catholic emancipation in 1829, opposed the Reform Bill in 1831, and favored government support for Church of England schools.

In *An enquiry into the doctrines of necessity and predestination* (1821), Copleston challenges the theology of Calvinism and its implications for individual conduct. Calvinists insisted on the priority of God's sovereignty, but many other Protestants believed that such an affirmation—while theologically sound, if rightly understood—risked leaving

74

humanity without any freedom at all. Copleston's *Enquiry* charges Calvinists with a form of philosophical Necessitarianism. He defends the compatibility of seemingly contrary beliefs such as divine providence and free will, questions the doctrine of predestination, and maintains the contingency of all events within the scope of divine foreknowledge. In the following selection, Copleston builds the philosophical foundation of his book by arguing that Calvinism is akin to fatalism. Where the fatalist sees no need for *religious* duty in this life, the convinced Calvinist will find no need for *moral* duty. If individuals' eternal destiny remains wholly unrelated to their actions, then they will be hard-pressed to see why they *should* pursue a life of high moral conduct.

SOURCES: Jeremy Catto, ed., *Oriel College: a history* (Oxford: Oxford University Press, 2013); William James Copleston, *Memoir of Edward Copleston* (London: Parker, 1851); Boyd Hilton, *The age of atonement: the influence of evangelicalism on social and economic thought, 1795–1865* (Oxford: Clarendon, 1988); Peter Nockles, "The making of a convert: John Henry Newman's Oriel and Littlemore experience," *Recusant History* 30 (2011): 461–83; *ODCC*; *ODNB*; Bernard M. G. Reardon, *Religious thought in the Victorian Age: a survey from Coleridge to Gore*, 2nd ed. (London: Longman, 1995); Richard Allen Soloway, "Episcopal perspectives and religious revivalism in England, 1784–1851," *Historical Magazine of the Protestant Episcopal Church* 40 (1971): 27–61; *VC*.

EDWARD COPLESTON
An enquiry into the doctrines of necessity and predestination
1821

Of the two grand motives then which actuate reasonable beings, hope and fear, the influence is always diminished in proportion to the opinion men have of the unalterable conditions under which they are placed. The nearest approach to that necessity which the laws of the material universe imply is to be found in the laws of civil society; and if these are such as to render exertion needless or fruitless, indolence uniformly takes [the] place of exertion when good is before them, and languor or despondency instead of manly endeavors to avert any apprehended evil. Such is universally admitted to be the effect of our own laws for the maintenance of the poor. The motive of *fear* is almost extinguished. And, on the other hand, from the absence of *hope*, the labor of slaves is well known to be less productive than that of freemen; and this precisely in proportion to the persuasion they have that they must always be slaves and that no prospect of emancipation lies before them. So, too, in the conduct of those who are condemned to death and to whom all the steps that lead to the final execution of their sentence assume the appearance of inevitable necessity. What stronger instinct is there in man than the love of life, and what incredible exertions have been often made to preserve it! Yet mark the conduct of him who is doomed to perish under sentence of the law: no struggle or resistance even to avoid that at which nature shudders—but a calm submission to decrees which he is convinced must take effect, however idly he may contend against them.

‡

Now this is precisely the point to which I was desirous of leading the whole question. For if *to discover the true relations of things* be one of the proper employments of our being, if in proportion to the exercise and improvement of our intellectual faculties we come to see these things more clearly and to think of them more justly, so that our progress in this knowledge is a kind of measure of our intellectual advancement, it would follow, *upon the hypothesis of fatalism*, that every step we advance in knowledge we recede from utility; and that in the same proportion as we grow wiser, we become less fit and less disposed to fulfill the purposes of our being. If fatalism represents the true relations of things, the path of error is then the path of utility and of happiness. Truth has a tendency to lead us away from both. And the Creator has formed us full of active powers and principles, and yet with a capacity and a disposition to draw nearer and nearer to that state, which, if we could ever actually reach it, would make all these faculties and principles implanted in us useless and would reduce us to absolute inactivity.

But again, man is not only an *active* being, he is also a *moral* agent. He is not only made for the pursuit of his own good by certain powerful internal springs of action, he is also furnished with a sense of right and wrong, a feeling that he *ought* to do some things and not to do others, without reference to his immediate pleasure, but because he would be justly blamable for doing otherwise. These two constitute the most essential principles of his nature. We have seen how the doctrine of necessity is incompatible with the one. Let us now briefly enquire how the other is affected by it, pursuing here the same method of investigation— that is, first taking a view of man as he actually *is* in respect of moral principles and then considering what he *would* be in the same respect if the doctrine of necessity were true.

Now it cannot be denied that in the habitual judgment of all mankind the moral quality of actions depends upon the freedom of the agent. Praise and blame, reward and punishment, uniformly imply that we think the party who is the object of them might have acted otherwise; and as soon as it is discovered that he acted under compulsion, we no longer measure the action by the standard of duty. It is in fact the first excuse which a culprit makes if he can, that his will had no share in the deed. The deed may, it is true, although proceeding from ignorance or from an extraneous power, still be culpable to a certain degree if that ignorance were not inevitable or if the person placed himself voluntarily in that state of subjection which deprived him of choice. But still our judgments in these matters all have respect to one principle—that man is not accountable for what was not in his own power. If there be a strict physical necessity, as if one man hurt another by being forced against him, although a momentary sense of anger may arise, yet it would be quite absurd to impute blame to the party so impelled; and no one consulting reason only ever does so. Further, if the necessity be *not absolute* or *physical* like this, but depending on *moral* causes almost equally powerful, we still acquit the agent of responsibility, as in the case of soldiers performing their military duty or the mere executioners of laws and decrees, however severe. And so with regard to good actions, as soon as it is found that they are not spontaneous—that some secret bias or impulse made it impossible for the person to withhold the good he has done—we even grudge the praise and admiration which his conduct may have before extorted from us. . . .

And not only does this judgment arise in the breast when we form an estimate of the conduct of *others*, but there is no palliative more frequently applied to an uneasy conscience, no surer advocate of crime and falsehood, no argument more apt to stifle the virtuous emotions and kindly feelings of our nature, than this plea of necessity. When this cause really and literally exists, the most solemn obligations—and instincts more sacred, if possible, even than they—have been known to yield. We turn from such cases with horror, but we pity rather than condemn the victim thus entangled, as it were, in the inevitable net of fate. But the invention of man when bent either upon some favorite object or willing to vindicate his crimes is ever busy in devising *pretended forms* of necessity to sanction a deviation from moral rectitude. And thus it is that evil of every kind public and private—cruel wars, oppressive government, unjust measures of state, dishonesty, deceit, rapine, and even murder—find a ready excuse. Men prove how valid and substantial the real plea is by grasping thus eagerly at its shadow and mere resemblance whenever the case will bear it. *Artificial difficulties* are misnamed *necessity*—and then, their "poverty but not their will consents"[1] to the most dreadful crimes. For the voice of all mankind does undoubtedly bear testimony to this rule—that in proportion as the case *approaches* to absolute necessity, in the same degree is the offense of the party extenuated and his responsibility abated.

‡

The generality of Calvinists, when charged with the *consequences* of their opinions, like the fatalists, answer that we ought to *address* mankind as if their doom were unsettled—as if God were willing that all should be saved—and as if much depended on themselves whether they should obtain salvation or not. And when further pressed with the *inconsistency* of these opinions, they reply that such exhortations are the *appointed means of perseverance.* Be it so. Then they are means, the efficacy of which is increased by turning our eyes away from the truth. For in proportion to the conviction we feel of the truth of the main doctrine, that is, the better we become acquainted, according to them, with the right interpretation of Scripture, and the more we meditate upon it, the weaker do these means become which are the appointed instruments of our salvation. . . .

In comparing the probable effects of fatalism and of Calvinism upon the conduct of men, an important distinction ought always to be made, which is however very generally overlooked. The doctrines rest indeed upon the same basis, but that of Calvinism is practically far more dangerous.

The fatalist acts in general as other men do. He is not likely to neglect urgent duties or to endure pain and privation for the sake of an abstract theory. His habits, his interests, his affections, his regard for character and for the opinion of the world, all keep him from being led astray by a speculative absurdity. But whatever security the Calvinist has of this kind is *weakened* by the very nature of his opinions. According to them he suffers *comparatively* nothing by yielding practically to their force; and their force is exerted in lessening the motives of a worldly nature which control the other. The instincts, the appetites, and the interests of the Calvinist may indeed rouse him to action, although in this respect their influence must be weaker than it is with the mere fatalist, while the worldly restraints upon vicious indulgence are almost entirely removed. . . .

The chief characteristic in fact of fatalism, taken apart from revelation, is its tendency to breed a disregard of *religious* duties, while Calvinism has the same tendency with respect to *moral* duties. The man who looks only to this life, and who believes all events to be already fixed and unalterable, has little inducement to betake himself to prayer or to the worship of the Deity—while he who looks chiefly to another life, and believes his destiny in that life to be fixed and unalterable, may naturally be careless and indifferent about his conduct here.

TEXT: Edward Copleston, *An enquiry into the doctrines of necessity and predestination*, 2nd ed. (London: John Murray, 1821), 12–13, 18–23, 26–30.

[1]   [Ed. William Shakespeare, *Romeo and Juliet*, 5.2.75.]

JULIUS CHARLES HARE
(1795–1855)
Light and Darkness

Theologian and archdeacon of Lewes, Julius Charles Hare emerged as a leading representative of the so-called broad church movement in England, a movement that promoted the
insights of German philosophy and the English philosophical theologian S. T. Coleridge.
Hare's parents eloped and moved to Italy, where he was born. They returned to England
when he was four, but travels abroad in 1804 brought the young Hare in contact with
key figures in the Romantic Movement such as Goethe and Schiller. He was educated at
Charterhouse, London, and matriculated as a pensioner at Trinity College, Cambridge
(1812). In 1818 Hare was elected a fellow of Trinity, where he briefly taught classics and
developed meaningful friendships with future broad church representatives John Sterling
and F. D. Maurice. Due to his knowledge of German language and literature, Hare served
as a consultant for Connop Thirlwall's translation of Schleiermacher in 1825 (see Part III).
He was ordained in 1826, appointed rector of Herstmonceux in 1832, and archdeacon of
Lewes in 1840. In publications such as *The victory of faith* (1840) and *The mission of the
Comforter* (1846), Hare defended a broad vision of the Church of England that challenged
the tendency to segment the church into rival parties.

Hare delivered his sermon "The children of light" at Cambridge on Advent Sunday
in 1828. The best-known of Hare's sermons, it signals the maturation of the Romantic
commitment to human interiority, reflection, and organic development—in effect, the
commencement of the English broad church movement. F. D. Maurice, who reviewed the
print edition in *The Athenaeum and literary chronicle* (1828), called "The children of light,"
"the most hopeful omen we have discovered of better things to come."[1] Hare's provoc-
ative oration disclaims those who cripple religion by the exclusive, tyrannical authority
of human intellection, including Jeremy Bentham and other Utilitarian philosophers.
True reason—the inner light of divine grace—is known and demonstrated to all creation
through the love of God and faith in Jesus Christ.

---

[1] Quoted in N. Merrill Distad, *Guessing at truth: the life of Julius Charles Hare (1795–1855)* (Shepherdstown: Patmos, 1979), 48.

SOURCES: Jeffrey W. Barbeau, *Sara Coleridge: her life and thought* (New York: Palgrave Macmillan, 2014); N. Merrill Distad, *Guessing at truth: the life of Julius Charles Hare (1795–1855)* (Shepherdstown: Patmos, 1979); Mary Louise McIntyre, "Julius Charles Hare on the Catholic revival: 'signs of hope,'" *Anglican and Episcopal History* 75 (2006): 224–44; *ODCC*; *ODNB*; Bernard M. G. Reardon, *Religious thought in the Victorian Age: a survey from Coleridge to Gore*, 2nd ed. (London: Longman, 1995); David A. Valone, "Theology, German historicism, and religious education at Cambridge: the controversies of Connop Thirlwall and Julius Hare, 1822–1834," *Anglican & Episcopal History* 78 (2009): 139–73.

JULIUS CHARLES HARE
"The children of light"
1828

Ye were sometimes darkness; but now are ye light in the Lord: walk as children of light.

Ephesians 5:8

"We were sometimes darkness; but now we are light." We are, most of us, only too ready to believe this; and many are not slow to say it. We are prone to believe that we *are light*; and we are not loth to confess that we *were darkness*. Indeed the assumption which vents itself in an exclamation of this sort is an easy and perpetual—I might almost say a natural and inevitable—delusion. All those impulses which lead us to action tend to make us view the present, whatever it may be, as the paramount object of human interest; and while we are hastening onward, we are careless about what we have left behind. Above all is this wont to be the case during the ardent and hopeful season of youth, when the mind, at least in those who have been endowed with a capacity of receiving speculative truth, yearns after it with impatient longing, and on catching sight of it, or of some phantom wearing its likeness, will rush forward to embrace it with the passionate fervor and prodigal devotedness of a first love. . . . One cannot expect, scarcely ought one to wish, that the brilliancy of the youthful eye should be dimmed by the lackluster discretion of age. Nor is it to be wondered at . . . that every fresh light . . . should so dazzle its unpracticed organs as to make it fancy that it has hitherto been wandering in darkness, and has only now at length suddenly come forth for the first time into the full noonday light and radiance of heaven. Doubtless the snake must often cheat itself with the vain belief that its slough has already been cast off. Doubtless that insect, in which philosophy has delighted to contemplate the symbol of the emancipated soul, must many a time fondly imagine that the term of its imprisonment is already arrived, that its shell is falling away, and that it is already rising out of the state, in which its doom was to creep and crawl about the earth, into a life of paradisiacal innocence and playfulness and freedom and joy.

‡

81

It is the frequency of this very delusion that has given our age its revolutionary character. We have asserted that *we are light* and that *we were darkness* with equal eagerness and vehemence. In so doing we have been emboldened by the exclusive dominion which, during the last half century, reason has usurped over all our other faculties. The absolute supremacy of reason, that is, of certain logical processes, in the concerns of mankind having once been acknowledged, reason, too, according to the usual fate of despots, became a tyrant. Nor was there any act of tyranny, however irrational, that she shrank from committing. Although in no operations (as in this place we know well) are errors more likely to occur or often more difficult to be detected, still reason is at once so headstrong and so heartless that no consideration for her own infirmity or for that of others will deter her from pursuing her course. . . . The boast of the age has been not merely that we are wiser than our ancestors, but that, while we are perfectly wise and clear-sighted, our ancestors were utterly ignorant and blind. Often too they who have reached one step higher on some one of the ladders of knowledge, dizzied by their elevation, have madly cut the ladder in sunder for the sake of breaking off all connection with those on whom they were scornfully looking down; forgetting that only by the help of that connection could they ever have mounted so high, and that the moment it is dissolved they must fall to the ground; forgetting that all human improvement must be gradual, that we can only advance step by step, that there is no absolute beginning upon earth, that the law of continuity cannot be infringed, that the chain of causes and effects cannot be broken; forgetting in fine that, if the earth were to be stripped of her heavenly mantle[1] and left naked in bare space, she would never be able by her own revolutionary energy to pass from darkness into light, and that all that her children can do for her is to kindle a feeble, flickering, distorting glare, no glimpse of which can be descried beyond a very narrow range.

If therefore we are indeed to pass from darkness into light, the light must have another, an unearthly, a superterraneous source. Now wherever an error or a folly has exercised a wide influence, we may be sure that it must have been the parody or caricature of some truth; and its extensive influence has mainly been owing to the likeness of this truth, which, however unconsciously, was discerned in it, notwithstanding the disfigurement. . . . Our dissatisfaction with our former selves is well-grounded. Indeed a dissatisfaction of the character described will never be found, except where there is ample reason for it. Only it would do better to express itself more meekly; nor ought it to stop short with the past; it ought to spread out its shade over the present to keep that from being quite scorched up. It ought to put off all resemblance to that sorrow of this world, which only worketh death, which would lead us to slay and to bury the past, and to trample on its grave; and it ought to put on the form of that godly sorrow, which worketh repentance unto salvation [2 Cor 7:10]. True again is it that we have been sitting in darkness; but so are we still. Unless a hand from above has burst through the darkness and scattered it, we must still be sitting in darkness. The blaze we may have lit up round about us sends forth no genuine genial light; it will soon have burnt itself out, and the darkness will then become deeper and more deeply felt than before. Nor is our longing for light a wrong feeling; nor are we wrong in our eager joy to welcome the faintest gleam of it. Our error lies in persisting to wait on the earthborn partial flame after we are aware or may and ought

---

[1]   [Ed. The earth's atmosphere.]

to be aware that it is nothing better; in fancying that the great object of life is already in our grasp, that the prize is already won; in counting that we have already apprehended, instead of forgetting the things hitherto attained, and pressing incessantly onward to the things which still lie and ever will lie before us [Phil 3:13-14].

‡

For this is in truth and in the fullest sense a transformation. The only way in which man can really pass from spiritual darkness into spiritual light is when his eyes are opened to behold the light of the gospel shining upon him—that light which in these days encompasses us all from our birth, but to which many continue blind for years (not a few, it is to be feared, all their lives)—when that true light, which lighteth every man who cometh into the world [John 1:9], bursts through the dark shroud which sin casts over it, and burns up into a pure and steady flame, and manifests its affinity to heaven. All other changes in man are merely of degree, from more to less or from less to more. We may improve the talents which have been committed to us, or we may waste them. We may extend our wanderings further and further on the sphere of human knowledge; but the utmost we can accomplish is to return from another quarter to the spot from which we started, having merely made the round of the globe without once setting foot out of or beyond it. Search as diligently, as curiously, as you may, with the most strenuous desire to glorify the works and the powers of man; the more thoroughgoing your search is, the more it will convince you that the only new element which has been grafted into nature since the creation is the religion of Christ—that this is the one sole absolute beginning since man was first cast on the waters of time, the one sole second birth of the world. So that it is not arbitrarily, but with sound reason, that even in our chronology we refer to the coming of our Lord as the epoch from which all subsequent events are to be dated. For that coming has given a new character to the history of the world, a new tone and spirit to the destinies of mankind.

‡

Let me suppose, however, that you have a righteous dread of such darkness. Let me suppose that you never have been or that, if you once were, you are now no longer under it. Let me suppose that, to the full extent of the apostle's meaning, you are indeed light in the Lord [Eph 5:8]. What follows? Is this enough? Are you already become masters in Christianity? Have you nothing more to do than to lie basking beneath the light and to let it shine upon you? What profits the light of day to the sluggard who slumbers in his bed? And what can the light of Christianity profit you, if, after staring at it idly for awhile, you throw yourselves back upon the couch of your former nature, and relapse into the drowsy torpor of your ancient habits, or try to lure back the dreamy excitements of the vices which have hitherto charmed you? What can it profit? What can it avail you? Nothing; yea, worse than nothing. It can only make your darkness visible. It can only serve to discover sights of woe.[2] It can only deepen your condemnation. When the gentle touch

---

[2]   [Ed. Hare draws from John Milton's *Paradise lost*: "yet from those flames / No light; but rather darkness visible / Served only to discover sights of woe" (1.62–64).]

of morning light draws back your eyelids, it admonishes you of the labors and the duties of the day, and summons you to arise and discharge them. A like admonition is conveyed by the gentle touch of the light of the gospel, when it draws back the lids of your souls, and enables you to behold the truth as it is in Christ Jesus. Accordingly an inference to this effect is drawn by St. Paul in our text. Having told the Ephesians that they, who had sometimes been darkness, had now become light in the Lord, he commands them to walk as children of light [Eph 5:8].

Walk as children of light. This is the simple and beautiful substance of your Christian duty. This is your bright privilege, which, if you use it according to the grace whereby you have received it, will be a prelude and foretaste of the bliss and glory of heaven. It is to light that all nations and languages have had recourse, whenever they wanted a symbol for anything excellent in glory; and if we were to search for an emblem of pure, unadulterated happiness, where could we find such an emblem, except in light? . . . Our thoughts and feeling should all be akin to light, and have something of the nature of light in them; and our actions should be like the action of light itself, and like the actions of all those powers and of all those beings which pertain to light, and may be said to form the family of light; while we should carefully abstain and shrink from all such works as pertain to darkness and are wrought by those who may be called the brood of darkness.

‡

Finally, the children of light will also be children of love. Indeed it is only another name for the same thing. For light is the most immediate outward agent and minister of God's love, the most powerful and rapid diffuser of his blessings through the whole universe of his creation. It blesses the earth, and makes her bring forth herbs and plants. It blesses the herbs and plants, and makes them bring forth their grain and their fruit. It blesses every living creature, and enables all to support and to enjoy their existence. Above all it blesses man, in his goings out and his comings in, in his body and in his soul, in his senses and in his imagination and in his affections, in his social intercourse with his brother, and in his solitary communion with his Maker. Merely blot out light from the earth, and joy will pass away from it, and health will pass away from it, and life will pass away from it, and it will sink back into a confused turmoiling chaos. In no way can the children of light so well prove that this is indeed their parentage as by becoming the instruments of God in shedding his blessings around them. Light illumines everything, the lowly valley as well as the lofty mountain; it fructifies everything, the humblest herb as well as the lordliest tree; and there is nothing hid from its heat. Nor does Christ, the original of whom light is the image, make any distinction between the high and the low, between the humble and the lordly. He comes to all, unless they drive him from their doors. He calls to all, unless they obstinately close their ears against him. He blesses all, unless they cast away his blessing. Nay, although they cast it away, he still perseveres in blessing them, even unto seven times, even unto seventy times seven [Matt 18:22]. Ye then who desire to be children of light, ye who would gladly enjoy the full glory and blessedness of that heavenly name, take heed to yourselves that ye walk as children of light in this respect more especially. No part of your duty is easier. You may find daily and hourly opportunity of practicing it. No part of your duty is more delightful. The joy you kindle in the heart of another cannot fail of shedding back its brightness on your own. No part of your duty is more godlike. They who attempted to become like God in knowledge fell in the Garden of Eden. They who strove to become like God in power were confounded on the plain of Shinar.[3] They who endeavor to become like God in love will feel his approving smile and his helping arm; every effort they make will bring them nearer to his presence, and they will find his renewed image grow more and more vivid within them until the time comes when they too shine forth as the sun in the kingdom of their Father [Matt 13:43]. That such may be our portion, may God in his infinite mercy grant to you who have been listening to my words, and to his servant who has been permitted to utter them before you, for the sake of his Son Jesus Christ, the Sun of Righteousness, to whom, with the Father and the Holy Ghost, be all honor and glory, world without end.

TEXT: Julius Charles Hare, "The children of light," in *The victory of faith, and other sermons* (Cambridge: J. and J. J. Deighton, 1840), 209–10, 213–17, 220–21, 232–34, 239–41.

[3]   [Ed. Hare refers to the efforts of those who built the Tower of Babel in the land of Shinar (Gen 11).]

III

CANON

*Let us strictly adhere to what our Lord has transmitted to us . . . that thereby the
unbelievers, in viewing us, may become enamored of the gospel, and may know that we are
truly pious by the love we bear the commandments of God.*

Teyoninhokarawen (a.k.a. John Norton), "Address to the six nations" (1805)

SARAH TRIMMER
(1741–1810)
Two Books

Christian faith springs from the revelation of God in Jesus Christ. Historically, Christians have believed that all knowledge of God's acts in the world—from creation to the promised eschaton—comes by way of two "books": nature and the Bible. Nature provides a general revelation of God's existence, while the Scriptures demonstrate the specific works of God for the salvation of men and women. The "two books tradition" of divine revelation can be discerned throughout the Romantic period.

Sarah Trimmer (née Kirby) was a widely read author and evangelical-Anglican educator. Born in Ipswich, Suffolk, to a lay theologian, architect, and artist who taught drawing to the future George III and Queen Charlotte, she attended Mrs. Justiner's School for Young Ladies in Ipswich. In 1762 Sarah married James Trimmer (1739–1792), a brick and tile maker, with whom she had twelve children. Like many other mothers of her day, Trimmer was responsible for their education. In response to her own felt need for better materials to assist with the moral formation of her children, Trimmer began publishing religious literature, including her six-volume *Sacred history selected from the Scriptures* (1782–1784). She established a charity school and a Sunday school in Old Brentford, which by 1788 had more than three hundred pupils. Many of Trimmer's publications aimed to assist children in these schools. Trimmer, whose training in art under her father proved a lasting influence, is credited with the popularization of pictorial literature for children, including various collections of prints from the Old and New Testaments. Unlike the *Sacred history*, which was written for children, Trimmer wrote her landmark commentary on the entire Bible (including the Apocrypha) for women *and* men who had "little leisure," but sought greater understanding of the Christian faith (*A help to the unlearned in the study of Holy Scripture: being an attempt to explain the Bible in a familiar way*, 1805).

Trimmer's earliest work, *An easy introduction to the knowledge of nature, and reading the Holy Scriptures, adapted to the capacities of children* (1780), reflects the tone and content of her writings for children. Inspired by Isaac Watts' *A treatise on the education of children and youth* (1753), most of the book takes the form of a conversation between a mother

88

and her two children about the world of nature, but concludes with a guide to reading the Bible. In the following selection, a mother instructs her children about the rational soul (the book of nature) before introducing the Bible (the book of God). The selection shows how some parents educated children to understand the relationship between general and special revelation.

SOURCES: *ODCC*; *ODNB*; *RCBEC*; Donelle Ruwe, "Guarding the British Bible from Rousseau: Sarah Trimmer, William Godwin, and the pedagogical periodical," *Children's Literature* 29 (2001): 1–17; Marion Ann Taylor and Heather E. Weir, eds., *Let her speak for herself: nineteenth-century women writing on women in Genesis* (Waco, Tex.: Baylor University Press, 2006); Heather E. Weir, "Helping the unlearned: Sarah Trimmer's commentary on the Bible," in *Recovering nineteenth-century women interpreters of the Bible*, ed. Christiana de Groot and Marion Ann Taylor (Atlanta: Society of Biblical Literature, 2007), 19–30; idem, "Reading nature before reading the Bible: Sarah Trimmer's natural theology," in *Breaking boundaries: female biblical interpreters who challenged the status quo*, ed. Nancy Calvert-Koyzis, and Heather E. Weir (New York: T. and T. Clark, 2010), 53–68; Doris M. Yarde, *The life and works of Sarah Trimmer, a lady of Brentford* (Bedfont: Hounslow and District History Society, 1971).

SARAH TRIMMER
An easy introduction to the knowledge of nature,
and reading the Holy Scriptures
1780

The rain will prevent our walking out today, so come and sit with me, Henry and Charlotte, and let us have a little conversation together. Did I not tell you, my dears, that we should find much to amuse and instruct us while we were taking our walks, if we would but pay attention to the different objects which should present themselves to our observation? And have you not really found the amusement and instruction I promised you? And yet, my dears, you have had but a very slight view of the wonders which the earth contains, nor have I said anything to you of the highest creatures in it—I mean *mankind*, that race of beings to which you yourselves belong. Yes, Henry, though you are now but a little boy, you are really one of mankind; and I hope, if you grow up to be quite a man, you will be a good one and live according to the dignity of your nature. It is a great honor, I assure you, to be a human creature, that is, one of mankind, as you will be convinced when I tell you what mankind are and what God has done for them.

Mankind, my dear children, are rational creatures. They have immortal souls and God designed them to be angels hereafter and to live happy forever and ever in heaven. You know we have taken notice in our walks of many different kinds of living creatures—sheep, oxen, horses, birds, fishes, insects, etc.—these are all called animals and brute creatures; and very wonderful they are in respect to their make and the various qualities belonging to them from the least to the biggest, whether they move about upon the land, fly in the air, or swim in the waters. But they are greatly inferior to mankind. In respect to their bodies, indeed, mankind are animals themselves and greatly resemble the inferior animals, for they have flesh, bones, blood, eyes, ears, feet, and the senses of seeing and hearing, and they move about from place to place. But mankind are more noble in their form than the inferior animals and by walking erect they have a more majestic appearance. They have also the faculty of speech by means of which they can converse together and make their thoughts and wishes known to each other in a great variety of languages, while the inferior animals are dumb. They can only utter a few sounds peculiar to their respective kinds to call their young and express their fears and sufferings when they are in danger or greatly hurt. Some particular kinds of birds, such as parrots and magpies, may, it is true, be taught to pronounce a few words without knowing the meaning of them; but no creatures in this world besides mankind have the faculty of speech so as to converse together. But, my dear children, the great difference betwixt mankind and the inferior animals consists in their having *immortal souls*. The soul is that part of a human creature which thinks. You wish me to describe the soul to you, Henry. This, my dear, I cannot do, any further than that it is of a spiritual nature and consequently invisible, for a spirit has not bodily parts and therefore cannot be seen with the eyes. But I am convinced that I have a soul by what passes within myself and that human creatures have souls by what I observe in other people. Do not each of you, Charlotte and Henry, find that there is something within you which thinks; that is, which contrives, resolves, recollects, and remembers? Are these things done by your bodies? Do you think with your eyes, your ears, your hands, your feet, or any part of you which can be seen? What can it be then that thinks? Your soul, to be sure.

‡

Well, my dear children, have you been reading the Book of Nature or have you in your morning walk passed over the works of God without examining any of them or bestowing a thought on their excellency? I judge not, by the collection which Henry has got in his little basket: plants, flowers, snail-shells, pebbles, and I know not what besides. Here are materials for study in abundance! And we will consider them all in the afternoon. But we have another book to talk about, so the Book of Nature must be laid aside for the present. Here, my dear children, is the Bible, God's best gift to mankind. I told you that the soul of man is immortal, and that God graciously designed mankind, when he created them, for eternal happiness in heaven. This sacred book instructs them what to do in order to obtain this happiness, for it cannot be thought reasonable that God should do so much for mankind without requiring something on their part, as he has made them capable of knowing the difference between right and wrong and has given them powers and faculties by means of which they can please and obey him.

Do not you, my dear children, wish to please that good and gracious Being who has given you life and bestowed so many other blessings upon you? Do not you wish to be admitted to his glorious presence in heaven and to dwell forever in that blessed place where there is nothing but joy and goodness? If you really have these wishes, you must read the Bible and practice the lessons it teaches.

There is not in the whole world such another book as the Bible, for it is really and truly the Book of God, the Holy Scriptures. Men indeed were the writers of it, but they were inspired, that is, God himself put into their minds what to write, and it is full of wisdom from beginning to end. This most excellent book, my dear children, was written for all sorts of people; it is calculated to inform the ignorant, to improve the wise, to comfort the afflicted, and to increase the joy of the happy; it contains precepts suited to people of all descriptions, from childhood to old age; it teaches the poor to be contented in a state of poverty, and instructs the rich how to make their riches a blessing to themselves and others; and, above all, it instructs every human creature how to think of God, how to pray to him, and how to thank him, and points out the means by which they may prepare themselves for the society of angels in heaven.

When you come to read the Bible, my dear children, you will be quite surprised to find what the greatest of all beings, who fills heaven and earth, who is the Creator of all things, has done for mankind, for those sinful creatures, who, as you will learn from the Scriptures, broke his commandments and forfeited all the blessings he graciously bestowed upon them. But I will not tell you in my own words what cannot be fully expressed but in the words of Scripture. You shall learn of God himself in his holy Word, what he has graciously done, and what he has been pleased to reveal. But remember, my dear children, that you are not to read the Bible either as a reading task or as a book of amusement, but as the Word of God.

Open the Bible and read the title page, Henry. You find, my dears, it is called the Holy Bible, which is in other words the Book of God. It consists, you see, of two principal parts, the Old Testament and the New Testament. The first of these contains what God was pleased to make known to mankind before the coming of our Lord Jesus Christ; the other gives us the history of our Savior's life and doctrine and of the preaching of his apostles. The Bible is here said to have been "translated out of the original tongues."[1] You know what translating is, Charlotte. The Bible was first written in Hebrew, Greek, and Latin;[2] and then it could only be read by the learned, but at length it was translated into English, which was a most happy thing for the nation. Do not you think, my dears, that it is a great blessing to have the Word of God in the language we all understand? . . . The Bible is a large volume. It was not all written by the same person, nor at the same time, but God inspired different people at different ages of the world to write the separate books of which it is composed; and these books are divided into chapters, and the chapters into verses. Here you see are the names of all the books as they follow one another in the Old Testament. Here are the books called Apocrypha, which are reckoned as making no part of the Bible because it is not known that the writers of them were inspired, but they are very pious good books. And here are the names of the books of the New Testament, as they follow one another. These figures show the number of chapters each book contains. Look here, my dear Henry, this is the beginning of the first book of the Bible, called Genesis in the Table of Contents. Here you see is chapter 1, and it is divided into verses; look down the left hand side of the page, and you will see the numbering of the verses from one to thirty-one. Now let us see how many chapters there are in the Book of Genesis. What says the Table of Contents? Genesis hath chapters fifty. Let us turn over and find the last chapter: fifty you see. Which is the second book of the Bible? Exodus. Well, is not Exodus immediately at the end of Genesis? And you will find all the rest of the books agreeing with the Table of Contents. Do not you think, Charlotte and Henry, you should be a long while reading through such a great book as the Bible? You would indeed, my dears; and a hard task you would find it, for a great part of the Scripture is too difficult

---

[1] [Ed. Trimmer refers to the full title of the Authorized or King James Bible (1611), "The Holy Bible, containing the Old and New Testaments translated out of the original tongues and with the former translations diligently compared and revised by his majesty's special command."]

[2] [Ed. The Bible was first written in Hebrew, Aramaic, and Greek. The fourth-century Latin Vulgate, largely produced by Jerome (ca. 345–420), was the canonical biblical text used in the West until the proliferation of vernacular Bibles during and after the Protestant Reformation.]

for children to understand. But it contains the most delightful and instructive histories in the world, and these I have got separated from the difficult parts of Scripture that you might have both the pleasure and benefit of reading them. Tomorrow you shall begin with some lessons from the Old Testament, which I will explain to you as you go on, and I trust it will please God of his infinite goodness to open your minds to understand the Scripture, and that he will graciously incline your hearts to do his holy will and obey his commandments that you may enjoy his blessing upon earth and dwell with him in heaven hereafter [Eph 6:3].

Text: [Sarah] Trimmer, *An easy introduction to the knowledge of nature, and reading the Holy Scriptures, adapted to the capacities of children*, 10th ed. (London: T. Longman and C. Rees, G. G. and J. Robinson, 1799), 128–31, 142–47.

HERBERT MARSH
(1757–1839)
Prayer Books

Leaders of the Protestant Reformation challenged the belief that church traditions, such as the Nicene Creed and various liturgical practices, belong to an oral apostolic tradition. The reliance on church traditions seemed to undermine the perspicuity and sufficiency of the Bible. Further, allegorical and spiritual readings of the biblical text were often used to substantiate teachings that arose long after the first century. Against the Protestants, the Roman Catholic Council of Trent (1546) declared that "all saving truth and rules of conduct . . . are contained in the written books and in the unwritten traditions." The council further maintained that these two vehicles of divine revelation ought to be received and venerated with an equal "feeling of piety and reverence." However, while some extreme Protestants rejected church traditions completely (in favor of the Bible or individual experience alone), others, including most Anglicans, accepted the first four ecumenical councils and theological writings of the patristic era as part of an inheritance that could help interpret Scripture (even though they avoided older, allegorical models of biblical interpretation). The next four readings all relate to a revival of interest in biblical authority during the early years of the nineteenth century. Political relief in the early 1790s brought Roman Catholic churches in England out of the shadows for the first time in more than two centuries, and the unexpected arrival of thousands of Catholics returning to England during the French Revolution stirred old prejudices. Suddenly, a seemingly innocuous decision, made by an interdenominational society, to publish copies of the Bible "without note or comment" set off a pamphlet war over the authority of Christian tradition vis-à-vis the biblical text and over the Church of England's claim to be the rightful interpreter of Scripture.

The biblical critic Herbert Marsh, bishop of Peterborough, helped disseminate German biblical scholarship in England at the close of the eighteenth century. Marsh's unique combination of scholarship and organizational ability have led some to regard him as "the foremost English bishop of his age" (*ODCC*). He was born at Faversham, Kent, to a local vicar and the daughter of a stonemason. Along with his cousin, the future radical William

Frend, Marsh attended King's School, Canterbury. He then studied mathematics and physics at St. John's College, Cambridge, where he was admitted as a foundress scholar in 1775. He was named a fellow of the college and ordained in 1780. Travel in Europe proved formative. Marsh met the biblical scholar Johann David Michaelis (1717–1791) in Göttingen and gained access to writings in Enlightenment biblical criticism. Marsh translated Michaelis' *Introduction to the New Testament* (4 vols., 1793–1801) and published his own hypothesis on the relationship between the New Testament Gospels, building on J. G. Eichhorn's work, in *Dissertation on the origin and composition of the three first canonical Gospels* (1801). In 1805 he provoked controversy in a series of sermons against the Calvinist doctrine of double predestination; two years later, he was named Lady Margaret professor of divinity at Cambridge, a post he maintained until his death. Marsh's leadership grew more conservative and insular in later years. Appointed bishop of Llandaff in 1816 and translated to Peterborough in 1819, he contended with prospective evangelical and Calvinist clergy before suffering from dementia in the final years of his episcopacy.

In 1811 Marsh publicly opposed the opening of a non-denominational Lancastrian school in Cambridge on the grounds that truly religious education ought to inculcate principles of the Church of England (his sermon helped to consolidate conservative efforts to form the National Society). When undergraduates proposed a Cambridge auxiliary of the British and Foreign Bible Society, Marsh wrote and distributed an *Address to the members of the senate of the University of Cambridge* (1811), which similarly argued that Bibles distributed in the region ought to inculcate solidarity with the established church. The following selection from *An inquiry into the consequences of neglecting to give the Prayer Book with the Bible* (1812) was Marsh's second foray into the debate. A decisive theological move against his evangelical opponents, it provoked disagreement far beyond Cambridge. Although Marsh maintained that the Bible is the final authority in matters of doctrine, his claim that the Book of Common Prayer was vital for the right interpretation of the Bible renewed fears of Roman Catholicism among those who held that Scripture is self-authenticating and self-interpreting. The controversy captured the interest of leading divines across England. Marsh's later theological treatise, *A comparative view of the churches of England and Rome* (1814), defended his position against charges of latent Catholicism.

Sources: Robert Kendall Braine, "The life and writings of Herbert Marsh (1757–1839)" (Ph.D. diss., University of Cambridge, 1989); Leslie Howsam, *Cheap Bibles: nineteenth-century publishing and the British and Foreign Bible Society* (Cambridge: Cambridge University Press, 1991); Nockles; *ODCC*; *ODNB*.

HERBERT MARSH

An inquiry into the consequences of neglecting to give the Prayer Book
with the Bible
1812

Whoever objects to the British and Foreign Bible Society is invariably asked, "Where is the harm of giving away a Bible?" I will answer therefore by saying, "None whatever." On the contrary, the more widely the Scriptures are disseminated, the greater in all respects must be the good produced.

Having answered this question and, as I hope, to the satisfaction of every member in the Society, I beg leave to ask in my turn, "Where is the harm of giving away a Prayer Book?" Of course I propose this question only to those members of the Society who are also members of the Church. For I have explicitly declared both in the sermon at St. Paul's[1] and in the *Address to the senate* that I have no desire to interfere either with the religious opinions or the religious conduct of the dissenters. . . . I am addressing myself to churchmen . . . And as the Liturgy is the book which distinguishes churchmen, I may certainly ask of them, "Where can be the harm, when we give away a Bible, of giving also a Prayer Book?" As I think no real churchman would say that there is, he cannot consistently object to those who recommend their joint distribution. Secondly, I ask the churchman whether it is not useful when we give away a Bible to give also the Book of Common Prayer—not as a corrective, a name lately given it by the Dean of Carlisle,[2] but as a proper companion for the Bible. Does it not contain devotional exercises composed in the true spirit of the Scriptures? Is it not the book which we hear constantly at church; and is it not equally designed for our meditations in the closet? The usefulness then of this book to every churchman, I think, no churchman can deny. . . . Thirdly, I ask the churchman whether it is not necessary when he gives Bibles to the poor (I do not mean among dissenters, as I have repeatedly declared) to provide them at the same time with a Prayer Book? Ought it not to be used by every churchman? And can he join in the service of the church without it? Can it therefore be a matter of indifference whether the poor of our

[1]   [Ed. Marsh's sermon on "National religion the foundation of national education" at St. Paul's Cathedral (June 13, 1811).]
[2]   [Ed. Isaac Milner, who was dean of Carlisle between 1791 and 1820.]

96

Establishment are provided with Prayer Books? Do we perform our duty, do we properly provide for their religious instruction, if we provide them only with the Bible and leave them unprovided with the Prayer Book? In this case, the rubric and the canons have very unnecessarily enforced the learning of the church catechism. When we further consider that there is at present hardly a town or even a village which is not visited by illiterate teachers[3] who expound the Bible with more confidence than the most profound theologian, it becomes doubly necessary, if we would preserve the poor of the Establishment in the religion of their fathers, to provide them with a safeguard against the delusions of false interpretation. And what better safeguard can we offer than the Book of Common Prayer, which contains the doctrines of the Bible according to its true exposition; in which those doctrines are applied throughout the prayers and collects to the best purposes of religion and are condensed in a manner which is intelligible to all in that excellent formulary, the church catechism? Under these circumstances, to leave the poor, who without assistance cannot understand the Scriptures, as the itinerant preachers themselves admit by their own practice, to leave, I say, the poor under such circumstances, to be tossed about by every wind of doctrine [Eph 4:14], which they must be unless provided with that authorized exposition[4] of the Scriptures which is contained in the Liturgy and which every honest churchman must believe to be the true one, is at least in my judgment (I speak with deference to the judgment of others) such a dereliction of our duty as churchmen that I little expected to hear clergymen within the precincts of the University reprehend a professor of divinity because he contended that the Prayer Book should be distributed with the Bible.

‡

I acknowledge that the arguments for the distribution of the Bible alone are so specious,[5] so popular, so apparently in the spirit of true Protestantism, while the arguments for the contrary lie so concealed from the public view and are now so confidently asserted to savor of popery that they are equally difficult to explain and dangerous to propose. Believing, however, as I do, that there is a fallacy in the arguments of those who oppose me, and conscious of the rectitude of my intentions, I tremble not at the obstacles which present themselves on every side. If it were now a question, as it was at the Reformation, whether the Bible should be distributed or not, men might justly exclaim to those who withheld it: can the Bible be injurious to the real interest of the church? But this is *not* the question, as everyone must know who argues against me. There were channels in abundance for the distribution of the Bible long before the existence of the modern Society . . . Here let me ask whether the Bible itself is not capable of perversion, whether the best of books may not be misapplied to the worst of purposes? Have we not inspired authority for answering this question in the affirmative? St. Peter himself, speaking of the Epistles of St Paul, said, "in which are some things hard to be understood, which they that are unlearned and unstable wrest as they do also the other Scriptures, unto their own destruction" [2 Pet

---

[3]   [Ed. Cf. William Kingsbury, *Apology for village preachers* (1798).]

[4]   [Ed. Marsh refers to the Book of Common Prayer, with its liturgies for prayer, Holy Communion, and the attached creeds.]

[5]   [Ed. That is, "attractive, or plausible, but wanting in genuineness or sincerity" (*OED*).]

3:16]. Would St. Peter, if he had lived in the present age, have thought this admonition less necessary than in the age of the apostles? Can churchmen therefore who know that one party wrests the Scriptures by the aid of false interpretation into authority for the rejection of the Trinity and the atonement, that another party wrests them into authority for the rejection of the sacraments, that other parties again on the authority of the same Bible prove other doctrines which are at variance with their own, think it unnecessary when they distribute Bibles to the poor, who are incapable without assistance of judging for themselves and who alone are the objects of gratuitous distribution, can churchmen, I say, under such circumstances think it unnecessary to accompany the Bible with the Liturgy in which the doctrines of the Trinity, the Atonement, the sacraments with the other doctrines of our Church are delivered as contained in the Bible? It is not the Bible itself but the perversion of it, the wresting of the Scriptures (as St. Peter expresses it) by the "unlearned and unstable" with which England now swarms, whence the danger proceeds. And this danger must increase in proportion as we neglect the means of counteracting it. But if we neglect to provide the poor of the Establishment with the Book of Common Prayer, as well as with the Bible, we certainly neglect the means of preventing their seduction from the established Church. The dissenters remain dissenters because they use not the Liturgy; and churchmen will become dissenters if they likewise neglect to use it with the Bible. Have the persons to whom Bibles are gratuitously distributed either the leisure or the inclination or the ability to weigh the arguments for religious opinions? Do they possess the knowledge and the judgment, which are necessary to direct men in the choice of their religion? Must they not learn it therefore from their instructors? And can there be a better instructor, in the opinion of churchmen, than the Book of Common Prayer?

‡

When our Reformers contended, and properly contended, for the Bible alone, they contended in opposition to those other sources of authority which were recognized by the Church of Rome. Without denying the validity of those other sources, such as tradition and the decrees of councils, they could never have secured to the Bible such an interpretation as they themselves believed to be true. For this purpose it was previously necessary to divest it of the glosses which perverted its real meaning. But did they stop here and leave the Bible without any interpretation? No. One of the first steps which were taken by Luther and Melanchthon[6] was to compose a confession of faith which in their opinion was founded on a true interpretation of the Bible. This confession was afterwards improved into the Confession of Augsburg,[7] which became and still remains the standard of Lutheran faith. Our own Reformers acted in the same manner. Though they asserted that the Bible alone contained all things which were necessary to salvation,[8] they did not leave the interpretation of it to mere chance. From a knowledge of former perversions they justly apprehended perversions of it in *future*. Nor was it possible, without devising some means of security, to prevent a relapse into those very errors which they sacrificed their

---

6   [Ed. Martin Luther (1483–1546) and his associate Philipp Melanchthon (1497–1560).]

7   [Ed. The Augsburg Confession (1530), chiefly the work of Melanchthon, established Lutheran doctrine.]

8   [Ed. A reference to the sixth article of the Thirty-Nine Articles of Religion (1563).]

lives to remove. They deemed it necessary, therefore, to employ that knowledge of the Scriptures, which they so eminently possessed, in composing a system of doctrines which are really founded on the Bible when rightly understood.

TEXT: Herbert Marsh, *An inquiry into the consequences of neglecting to give the Prayer Book with the Bible,* 4th ed. (London: Law and Gilbert, 1812), 3–5, 6–8, 13.

ISAAC MILNER
(1750–1820)
Bible Societies

Isaac Milner, dean of Carlisle, was a leading evangelical in the Church of England known for his large frame, full voice, and imposing intellect. Born in Mabgate, Leeds, Milner's education was temporarily halted when his father died in 1760. For several years, Milner was apprenticed as a weaver until his elder brother Joseph took a position as master of the grammar school at Hull. He attended Queen's College, Cambridge as a sizar. Fascinated by Newton's mechanical philosophy, Milner excelled in natural philosophy and chemistry. Despite various difficulties at his college, Milner took a B.A. in 1774. By 1780 Milner was an ordained priest, fellow of Queen's, college tutor, rector at St. Botolph, and fellow of the Royal Society for his work in mathematics. In 1782 Milner was awarded the Jacksonian professor of natural philosophy inaugural chair. Milner corresponded or collaborated with many leading scientists of the day, including Joseph Priestley, William Whewell, and Humphry Davy. In 1788 he was elected president of Queen's College, and in 1798 was named the Lucasian professor of mathematics. Through the influence of William Pitt, Milner was selected as dean of Carlisle (1791). By the turn of the century, Milner was one of the foremost evangelicals within the Church of England: he shaped religious life and attitudes across Cambridge, helped bring about the conversion of William Wilberforce in 1784–1785, and, with his brother Joseph, coauthored the massive *Ecclesiastical history of the Church of Christ* (7 vols., 1818).

Milner's *Strictures on some of the publications of the Rev. Herbert Marsh* (1813) responds to Marsh's *An inquiry into the consequences of neglecting to give the Prayer Book with the Bible* (1812) (see previous selection). Marsh's *Inquiry*, Milner objects, presumes that evangelical Anglicans lack devotion to the Prayer Book, overstates the dogmatic authority of the church, and echoes Roman Catholic derogations of biblical authority. According to Milner, if the poor cannot benefit from reading the Bible without the aid of church commentary, then the Protestant doctrine of Scripture runs aground.

SOURCES: L. J. M. Coleby, *Isaac Milner and the Jacksonian chair of natural philosophy* (London: Taylor and Francis, 1954); *ODCC*; *ODNB*; Simon Schaffer, "Machine philosophy: demonstration devices in Georgian mechanics," *Osiris* 9 (1994): 157–82.

ISAAC MILNER

Strictures on some of the publications of the Rev. Herbert Marsh
1813

It should constantly be remembered that the question before us is not what are the sentiments which Dr. Marsh *intended* to express, but, what are the sentiments which, upon a fair construction of the words, he *has actually expressed*. I do not hesitate to acknowledge that I *cannot* believe he used terms designedly to sanction popish doctrines; but, notwithstanding this concession, should it be the opinion of an impartial public that in *fact* he has brought forward arguments which savor of the Roman Catholic persuasion, then the least offensive conclusion to which a true Protestant can arrive must be that whoever pretends to great industry, deep penetration, and profound thought, unless these endowments are tempered with caution and discretion, must fail to become a judicious adviser and supporter of our ecclesiastical Establishment.

Throughout almost every page of Dr. Marsh's *Inquiry*, I perceive the influence of an opinion which I cannot but think very erroneous, although it may have proved abundantly sufficient to betray the author into much inconclusive reasoning.

Everywhere he takes it for granted that the poor and unlearned cannot understand the Bible. Now, whatever doubts may be raised on other points, this is notoriously a popish sentiment and is doubtless the foundation of a large portion of mischievous popish practice. I differ essentially from Dr. Marsh in this point, that the poor and unlearned have not judgment, have not ability, have not leisure, have not inclination for understanding the Holy Scriptures and the great fundamental truths contained in them. I believe they can understand them in all the essential points, that is, in all the points which concern the salvation of the soul, as well as the most learned professors of divinity. Nay, I believe that a number of poor, modest, simple-minded, unlearned inquirers after truth, would, on reading the Scriptures with devout care and application, and with a direct view to improve the heart and correct the practice, differ much less from one another in their ideas of the gospel than learned divines frequently do, who, leaning too much to their "own understanding" {Prov 3:5} and attainments become "spoiled through philosophy and vain deceit, after the traditions of men, after the rudiments of the world, and not after

Christ" {Col 2:8}. Indeed, if these things were not so, if the gospel were not peculiarly adapted to the circumstances of the poor, so as to be intelligible to their understandings in all things necessary to salvation,[1] I should be utterly at a loss to comprehend that memorable thanksgiving of our blessed Savior: "I thank thee, O Father, Lord of heaven and earth, because thou hast hid these things from the wise and prudent, and hast revealed them unto babes" {Matt 11:25}, as also that no less memorable answer which he returned to the disciples of John, "Go and show John again those things which ye do hear and see: the blind receive their sight and the poor have *the gospel preached unto them*" {Matt 11:4-5}.

Here I know not whether Dr. Marsh will allow (certainly most Christians will) that by the preaching of the gospel to the poor is to be understood those very things which through the inestimable blessing of Almighty God are delivered to us in the Sacred Oracles. Even if Dr. Marsh should think that the gospel as originally preached was contained in that document which he supposes to have once existed although it is now no more, the argument will be in no wise affected by that consideration.[2]

‡

Let any candid person pause, at the present moment, and contemplate the good which, beyond all controversy, has been done by the Bible Society already. Does it not stand demonstrated that thousands and ten thousands of Bibles are actually in the hands of poor persons, both of our own and of foreign countries, which would not have been there if the Bible Society had never existed? Does not this very consideration warm the best affections of every Christian—churchman, dissenter, Protestant, and even Roman Catholic, I would hope—with a grateful spirit of thanksgiving to that kind and bountiful providence whose blessed influence is the best preparation of the hearts of men {Prov 16:1}? Is it possible that any reader of the New Testament should be disposed to dwell on one part only of Gamaliel's dilemma, "If this counsel or this work be of men, it will come to naught," and to forget the other part, "but if it be of God, ye cannot overthrow it, lest haply ye be found even to fight against God?" The advice of this learned doctor was, "Refrain from these men, and let them alone" {Acts 5:38-39}.

Text: Isaac Milner, *Strictures on some of the publications of the Rev. Herbert Marsh* (London: T. Cadell and W. Davies, 1813), 334–36, 382–83.

[1]   [Ed. Milner intimates the sixth article, on Scripture, of the Thirty-Nine Articles of Religion (1563).]

[2]   [Ed. Milner refers to Marsh's hypothesis that the first three Gospels depend upon a document that was subsequently lost (see Marsh, *Dissertation on the origin and composition of the first three canonical Gospels* [1801]).]

PETER GANDOLPHY
(1779–1821)
Rule of Faith

When ministers of the Church of England, such as Herbert Marsh, advocated for distributing Prayer Books with Bibles, Roman Catholics heard echoes of their own opposition to Protestant translations of the Bible into vernacular English. English Protestants rejected the claim that the Roman church provides the only orthodox interpretation of Scripture. Some Catholics, among them the Roman Catholic priest Peter Gandolphy, welcomed the renewal of these arguments in the hope that the controversy would aid the Roman Catholic cause in England. Gandolphy was born in London and educated by English Jesuits at Liège Academy. He returned to England in 1794 and attended Stonyhurst College in Lancaster. Gandolphy taught humanities at Stonyhurst between 1801 and 1804, at which point he was ordained by Bishop John Douglass, vicar apostolic of the London district. His first parish was at the mission at Newport, Isle of Wight, where he served between 1804 and 1806. Gandolphy gained prominence in London for preaching at the Spanish Chapel in Manchester Square, where he ministered from 1806 and gained a number of converts. However, Douglass' successor in London, Bishop William Poynter (1762–1827), accused Gandolphy of heresy following the publication of his sermons and, especially, *A liturgy, or Book of Common Prayers and administration of sacraments* (1812). Poynter—a leading figure in the efforts towards Catholic emancipation in the 1810s and 1820s—believed that Gandolphy's work, modeled on the Church of England's Book of Common Prayer, capitulated to Protestantism. Poynter thought that Gandolphy's artful use of language—for example, referring to the Eucharist as the Lord's Supper—pressed sacred and technical terminology beyond legitimate theological boundaries. An appeal to Rome brought only minor corrections, but Poynter nonetheless forbade the sale of Gandolphy's books in London while awaiting a formal ruling from the Congregation of Propaganda in Rome. Gandolphy refused to stop the circulation of his books, claiming that the copyrights had passed to another some years earlier. Poynter suspended him for disobedience in 1816. After he received a formal apology, the bishop briefly allowed Gandolphy to return to preaching. In 1818, wearied by years of controversy, Gandolphy retired from the pulpit—the same year that the Congregation officially condemned his works.

Gandolphy's *A defence of the ancient faith* (1813) attempts to rebut common English stereotypes of Roman Catholics, explains Roman Catholic doctrine, and defends the Roman church against charges of idolatry, allegiance to a foreign power (the papacy), and confining salvation to Roman Catholics. The following selection draws upon the tenth sermon in the collection: "On the inadequacy of the Bible to be an exclusive rule of faith." Like earlier Catholic apologists, Gandolphy challenges Protestant claims for the sufficiency of the Bible: "My brethren, the principle to which I direct my observation is no other than the grand and fundamental maxim of the Protestant Reformation . . . that the Sacred Scriptures are divinely made the *single* and *exclusive* authority from which men are to learn their religion" (271). Gandolphy, who had previously penned *A congratulatory letter to the Rev. Herbert Marsh* (1812), explains that Christianity requires neither literacy nor learning, only an adequate teacher of faith: the Roman Catholic Church.

SOURCES: Philip Hughes, *The Catholic question, 1688–1829: a study in political history* (New York: Benziger, 1929); *ODCC*; *ODNB*.

PETER GANDOLPHY
A defence of the ancient faith
1813

My friends, in order to show that an acquaintance with letters is not essential to the knowledge of the Christian religion, I will engage by actual experiment to prove that if twenty persons of equal talents be produced—all ignorant of the art of reading, one excepted—within three days I will communicate to the unlettered nineteen a knowledge of all those necessary truths and mysteries of the Christian religion which the biblical student shall not acquire, from his Bible only, at the expiration of the twelvemonth—I will venture to add, at the end of his life, however protracted. In naming three days, I have greatly extended the time that would be essentially necessary. For where the heart is already disposed, a much shorter period would be sufficient. Reflect how few in the earlier ages of Christianity were ever taught to read; comparatively speaking, perhaps, not one in ten thousands. Besides, if essential to the knowledge of religion, would not the Scriptures themselves have particularly directed our attention to that object? Yet Jesus Christ sent Saul to Ananias (Acts 9:11), the angel referred Cornelius to the apostle (Acts 10:5), and Jesus has pronounced those exclusively blessed "who hear the Word of God and keep it" (Luke 11:28).

There may be many present whom I have had the happiness thoroughly to instruct in religion—yet, have I done it with books? You have heard me deliver from this pulpit instructions on all points of doctrine—yet I have read little from the Bible to you and believe I can say for myself that before I had read a chapter of the Bible I knew my religion. My friends, I will go as far to assert that if we had never found the use of letters or should ever be deprived of that noble discovery, the Christian religion would lose nothing essential to its existence, and the whole moral system of faith, as it is practiced and professed by Catholics, comprehending the administration of all the sacraments, might be handed down to posterity as inviolate and unchanged in every material point as it subsists at present. I am not so weak as to undervalue the discovery of letters—I have styled it a noble discovery and will allow it the precedence among human inventions. But if I praise in the same manner many other discoveries and inventions—for instance, the invention of a watch or a coach—does it follow that we could not dispense with these luxuries? How did our forefathers contrive? Thus the system of religion among Catholics is independent of the accidental inventions of man and suited to him in his natural state of existence. Nay, provided there be no moral obstacle in the individual, the full benefit of it may be reaped, however physically imperfect he may be. The newborn infant and expiring age are equally the object of its benedictions.

Returning then to the fundamental principle of Protestantism—namely, that the Bible, in print or manuscript, is the only rule of faith and basis of religion prescribed by God to men[1]—I must reject it on the ground that it would be charging the Deity with the folly and injustice of binding mankind to a religion unattainable to the far greater part, and which, in the course of possibilities, might be impracticable to all. Now to accuse God of imposing on men the obligation to an impossibility would be to place the divine Lawgiver in a situation where no human legislator would consent to be found. For surely none require to be told that a book is only useful to those who can read and purchase it; what kind of a help would it even be to you if through some awkward circumstance you had never received any education? And how many Protestants have there been and are still living who have never had this advantage? Were the Bible only the religion of Christians, I maintain that should they come into the world already endowed from their mother's wombs with the talent of reading—as birds are self-instructed to form their own nests, to swim, and fly—even then would they be insecure unless they were also born with a Bible in their hands already printed in that particular dialect and language they were afterwards to learn as they advanced towards manhood. Besides, what would be the course of proceeding should these Bibles be burnt in a general conflagration? Would all have money and means to procure others? And if unable, would they remain without religion? For the "Bible only" is said to [be] the "religion of Protestants."[2]

There is a society in this kingdom which, acting very consistently on this Protestant principle, most charitably printed at a great expense thousands and tens of thousands of copies of the Bible, translated we must suppose correctly into various languages, and, with a zeal that deserved a better success, sent them to nations which had them not. Unfortunately however, these nations had never been taught to read, at least in the language of these Bibles, and though they were born with good understandings like other men, it was the same as if pearls had been thrown to swine [Matt 7:6]. In which circumstance we have to account for an incongruity unobservable in the other works of the Deity. And thus, although the people were well disposed, the society have found it impossible to give their charitable zeal an effect.

How different was the termination of the labors of the apostles! How different is the success attending a Catholic missioner, acting on Catholic principles or in the name of the Catholic Church of Christ. As soon as he has contrived to render himself intelligible

---

[1]   [Ed. In a long footnote, Gandolphy alleges contradictions between major Protestant Reformers such as Martin Luther and John Calvin, while citing diverse English Protestant opinions on the need for a written or spiritual guide for interpreting the Bible, including remarks from Herbert Marsh, John Wesley, John Fletcher, and spiritualists such as Quakers and Swedenborgians.]

[2]   [Ed. The English theologian William Chillingworth (1602–1644) first penned the famous maxim "the Bible, I say, the Bible only is the religion of Protestants," in *The religion of Protestants: a safe way to salvation* (1638).]

to the natives, he announces himself an apostle or minister of that Church and calls upon them to say whether they will receive him in that character or not. He unfolds to them the grand motives of credibility together with the circumstance of the Fall and redemption of man. He pledges the unity, the sanctity, the catholicity, and the apostolicity of that Church in whose name he preaches. He speaks to them of the sacred and inspired Scriptures, encourages the more enlightened to qualify themselves for their perusal, and assures them that his whole doctrine will be confirmed by their testimony. In fine, he calls upon them to say if they will receive him in his apostolic character or not. If they consent, he immediately instructs them in all the truths and mysteries of the Christian religion as I instruct you. If they refuse, he attends to the directions of Jesus Christ to his apostles, and "whosoever shall not receive you, nor hear your words, going forth out of that house or city, shake the dust from your feet" (Matt 10:14.)

‡

But, my brethren, since you have urged this difficulty as an objection, permit me to retort and call upon you to say how, in the first instance, any people are to distinguish what a Bible is. We will suppose that a vessel freighted in part by the Bible Society is shipwrecked upon the African shore, and that a copy of the Bible together with a Common Prayer Book and Milton's *Paradise Lost* have fallen into the hands of some of the heathenish natives. We will moreover suppose either that they have been transcribed into the language of that country or that by the means of an English prisoner who had once lived amongst them some of these savages have been taught to read and understand these works. In these circumstances they would read and admire them, but how would they distinguish that one was more divine than another? The prayers and explanatory Articles of Religion would be preferred to the Epistles of St. Paul because more intelligible. The poetry of Milton would be considered more sublime than that of the inspired prophet; his history of man's Fall more complete, more connected and interesting than the Mosaic account. In short, if a comparison be made by the savage, it would be in favor of that work which is human, and nothing will he discover which can indicate to him that the Bible only contains the Word of God. But how wholly perplexed would he be were he to attempt to form his religion by it! No! Not a step can he advance unless he first calls in tradition to his assistance; unless he address himself to one who, being already instructed, is able to direct him. With the eunuch of Queen Candace he will exclaim, "how can I understand unless someone show me?" (Acts 8:31). Who then so proper as a minister of the gospel? *Behold, the Catholic rule of faith.*

TEXT: Peter Gandolphy, *A defence of the ancient faith . . .; or, A full exposition of the Christian religion in a series of controversial sermons*, 4 vols. (London: Keating, Brown and Keating, 1813), 1:276–88.

EDWARD HAWKINS
(1789–1882)
Scripture and Tradition

Edward Hawkins, provost of Oriel College, Oxford was born in Bath to a vicar and his wife. Hawkins graduated from St. John's College, Oxford with a double first in classics and mathematics. He was named a fellow of Oriel in 1813 and ordained three years later. In 1823 he became vicar of the University Church of St. Mary's. In 1828 Hawkins succeeded Edward Copleston as provost of Oriel College, Oxford, where he struggled to establish control of several rising fellows, and in 1830 ended up evicting Hurrell Froude, John Henry Newman, and Robert Wilberforce from their tutorships, which led many to believe that Oriel's preeminence would deteriorate under his leadership. In fact, his personal and theological influence on students and fellows proved especially important to major theological developments in the coming decades: he delivered the prestigious Bampton Lectures in 1840 (an expansion and subtle revision of his *Dissertation* sermon of 1819), wrote the university's condemnation of John Henry Newman's controversial *Tract 90*, and held the inaugural Dean Ireland chair as professor of the exegesis of Holy Scripture (1847–1861). In later years, after much disputation and confusion over high church teaching, Hawkins continued to advocate for the Church of England at Oriel.

The sermon *A dissertation upon the use and importance of unauthoritative tradition* (1819) proved to be one of Hawkins' lasting theological achievements, in large part because it influenced a young John Henry Newman, who gradually moved away from his early evangelical and Calvinistic tendencies. Thus, however unintentionally, the work contributed to the rise of the Oxford Movement. Newman later recalled that Hawkins' sermon taught him "that, if we would learn doctrine, we must have recourse to the formularies of the Church; for instance to the Catechism, and to the Creeds."[1] In the following selection, Hawkins argues that the traditions of the churches are a help to the study of the Bible and "*intended* to assist us" by God's own design. While Scripture gives necessary proofs of doctrine, traditions provide the systematic arrangement of truth.

---

[1]   John Henry Newman, *Apologia pro vita sua* (New York: Penguin, 1994), 30.

⌖

SOURCES: John William Burgon, "Edward Hawkins: the great provost," in *Lives of twelve good men* (New York: Scribner and Welford, 1891), 194–241; Hylson-Smith; John Henry Newman, *Apologia pro vita sua* (New York: Penguin, 1994); Nockles; Peter Nockles, "Oriel and the making of John Henry Newman— his mission as college tutor," *Recusant History* 29 (2009): 411–21; *ODCC*; *ODNB*; H. J. Schroeder, *Canons and decrees of the Council of Trent* (Rockford, Ill.: Tan Books, 1978); *VC*.

EDWARD HAWKINS
A dissertation upon the use and importance of unauthoritative tradition
1819

It may indeed be very possible for men of superior learning, industry, and capacity to make out from the Scriptures, without assistance, many or most of the doctrines of our faith, which they may then impart to others; and this, it may be said, would be analogous to the method by which the great and beneficial discoveries of human science have been often made by learned men and afterwards bestowed upon the rest of mankind. But the cases do not appear altogether parallel, because here the great mass of Christians, the ignorant quite as much as the learned, are so deeply interested in the truths of Christianity that we might expect the mode of acquiring them would originally be more level to their capacity. . . .

Let any man who is now convinced from Scripture of the truth of the Christian doctrines, but who has not perceived how easily they might of themselves have escaped his notice, consider only how many great truths there are in the world quite clear and confessed at present, yet originally overlooked or disbelieved. What can be more generally admitted now than the laws of motion? How easy to teach them even to a child, and yet how many ages passed away before they were thought of, although all the elements of these truths were present to the minds of all men from the first. Most readers will probably admit that the theory of population elucidated by Mr. Malthus[1] is a remarkable example to the same purpose. But to take a stronger instance, how striking and convincing is the argument by which Paley has proved the genuineness of St. Paul's Epistles,[2] and yet the materials of that argument lay unnoticed for many centuries in the hands of every Christian! . . . Just so the method of the Christian writings affords indeed the very strongest *proofs* of doctrines, interwoven by allusion, implication, and every indirect mode with the texture of the sacred books; but it is often the least adapted to the purpose of *teaching* those doctrines, which

[1]   [Ed. Thomas Robert Malthus (1766–1834), English economist, was the author of *An essay on the principle of population* (1798, 2nd ed., 1803) (see Part VII).]

[2]   [Ed. In *Horae Paulinae; or, The truth of the Scripture history of St Paul evinced* (1790), William Paley (1743–1805) defended the authenticity of Paul's Epistles by reference to the Book of Acts.]

was the end we should have expected them to have in view. And some of the doctrines themselves, like the argument of Paley, might have been undiscovered possibly till the present age had the only mode of acquiring a knowledge of them been the research of the learned, who should impart their discoveries to other men. Nay more, it is matter of fact that the difficulty which we have supposed is sometimes felt by learned and able, as well as sincere believers; by those, in short, who would naturally be the best qualified to elicit from Scripture the scheme of Christian doctrines. They indeed who can best appreciate the whole difficulty of such a task are perhaps the most likely to feel the perplexing thought: why should the divine Spirit have chosen by such means to convey to the whole Christian world the doctrines most important for the whole world to know and believe?

‡

Now exactly such an aid and guide may surely be found in *tradition*, the traditions conveyed from age to age by the church in general. They are allowed by the most orthodox divines to be "a good help" to the study of the Scriptures. Why may they not have been *intended* to assist us? Common experience and common practice seem to declare that some assistance of the kind is *needful* and *reasonable*. Why may not this assistance have been designed for us from the first—as from the first *in fact* almost every Christian has been by such aid introduced to Christianity? In a word, why may it not have been the general design of heaven that by early oral or traditional instruction the way should be prepared for the reception of the mysteries of faith; that the church should carry down the *system*, but the Scriptures should furnish all the *proofs* of the Christian doctrines; that tradition should supply the Christian with the *arrangement*, but the Bible with all the *substance* of divine truth? . . .

In the first place, this opinion is not in the least connected with the errors of the Romanists, since it claims *no independent authority* for the traditions conveyed to us by the church. Their error consisted in claiming an authority for tradition equal or even superior to that of the Scriptures themselves;[3] they did not allow the possibility of their traditions being either fallible or corrupted. But we, perceiving that tradition has often been corrupt and must be by its nature liable to corruption and therefore fallible, allow it no independent authority whatsoever.

We perceive that traditions may be contradictory to the Scriptures, and then we absolutely reject them; or they may be unsupported by the Scriptures, and then we allow them no further than as they coincide with the dictates of reason; or they may be supported by the sacred writings, and then we respect them as the original sentiments of the first believers, as derived indeed from the true and only authority. In this manner the outline of revealed truths which we have now exhibited to us in the Apostles' Creed has been of eminent service to Christians in tracing the system of their faith. . . .

Because the Romanist has raised tradition to a level with inspired authorities, the Protestant has often neglected, or denied, its natural use and value. That great errors

---

[3] According to the theory of the Romanists, tradition, or, as they define it, the unwritten word of God, is of equal authority with the written Word or the Scriptures; but in practice tradition often obtains with them an authority paramount to that of the Scriptures, as the bishop of Llandaff has shown in the *Comparative view of the churches of England and Rome* . . . [namely, Herbert Marsh's publication in 1814.—Ed.]

should produce their contraries has been indeed so constant an evil that every prudent person feels it necessary to guard his own mind against such an effect; and it is matter of notoriety that, when the papal error respecting tradition was first refuted, the wildest notions sprung up on all sides in the opposite extreme. Hooker is obliged to apologize even for the use of the word tradition, though it were only in respect of indifferent customs or ceremonies;[4] and even if history had been silent, it might have been inferred from our thirty-fourth article that there had previously existed very wide deviations on this subject from the plainest dictates of common sense. . . .[5]

And it will be allowed by thoughtful members of the English Church that it is a comparatively light and easy task to prove the important doctrines of our faith from Holy Writ when once we have received them in a definite form with that presumption, how low soever in their behalf, to which they are justly entitled even because they have been handed down to us through the medium of the church. With this guide before us, passages become often as clear as prophecies whose completion is known, which, like those before the event, would otherwise seem dark or contradictory. The parallel is more close than may at first sight appear: as the prophecies concerning the greatness of the Messiah's kingdom, apparently opposed to those which announced his humiliation and sufferings, were a stumbling block to the Jews (although to Christians the true sense of both appears exceedingly simple and evident), so likewise are there doctrines in the orthodox creed of Christianity which furnish a key to passages in the New Testament otherwise irreconcilable, and which indeed, to those who want or refuse this aid, are yet sources of perplexity and error.

‡

Every Christian who receives the doctrines of his faith becomes by the very nature of the case the keeper of the tradition so far as he knows the Christian doctrines; and it is not more his duty than his glorious privilege to assist in spreading wider the blessings which he has received. It were devoutly to be wished that every guardian, every master or mistress of a family, every mother felt how much was due from them in this particular; for thus it surely is that Christ would have every faithful servant of his both interested and engaged in the great work of spreading the elements of Christian truth; and thus also did he probably intend a great advantage to every succeeding period by providing instruments of instruction accommodated to all ages and all characters.

TEXT: Edward Hawkins, *A dissertation upon the use and importance of unauthoritative tradition, as an introduction to the Christian doctrines* (Oxford: W. Baxter, 1819), 8–12, 17–25, 46–47.

4   [Ed. Hawkins refers to the sixteenth-century defense of the Anglican *via media* in *Of the laws of ecclesiastical polity* by Richard Hooker (ca. 1554–1600).]

5   [Ed. The thirty-fourth of the Thirty-Nine Articles of the Church of England reads, in part, "It is not necessary that traditions and ceremonies be in all places one, or utterly alike; for at all times they have been diverse, and may be changed according to the diversity of countries, times, and men's manners, so that nothing be ordained against God's Word."]

MARY ANNE SCHIMMELPENNINCK
(1778–1856)
Spiritual Interpretation

Born in Birmingham, Mary Anne Schimmelpenninck (née Galton) was raised a Quaker. During her childhood, Joseph Priestley, Erasmus Darwin, and Richard Lovell Edgeworth, among others, visited her home in Staffordshire, where her family moved when she was still a young girl. Educated primarily by her mother, she developed a keen mind and curiosity for the world around her. According to her autobiography, her mother (and later, her father) guided her strict religious and intellectual development through biblical readings, Priestley's *Catechism* (1767), and Barbauld's *Hymns in prose for children* (1781); she also read widely in the classics. In 1806 she married a Dutch shipping tradesman, Lambert Schimmelpenninck. Now in Bristol, Schimmelpenninck was baptized by a Methodist minister. She became involved in education and local charities. Life in Bristol also led to contact with Hannah More, who encouraged Schimmelpenninck to publish her writings, which included works on aesthetics and biblical interpretation, including *Theory on the classification of beauty and deformity* (1815) and *An essay on the Psalms, and their spiritual application* (1825). After ten years as a Methodist, she joined an English Moravian congregation. In later years, she even considered a move to Roman Catholicism, but ultimately decided against it. She was buried at the Moravian chapel in Bristol after her death in 1856.

Schimmelpenninck's *Biblical fragments* (2 vols., 1821–1822) illustrates, more than any other work, the breadth and depth of her learning and exegetical insight. The composition, as she explains in the introduction, speaks to the needs of Christian parents and children alike. Part biblical commentary, part devotional, Schimmelpenninck's *Biblical fragments* provides lengthy explanations of numerous passages of Scripture in order to reveal the spiritual or typological meaning beneath the literal sense of the text. Deep devotion to Scripture, she holds, provides the best foundation for training a child to grow in love and service of God. In the following selection, Schimmelpenninck affirms the trustworthiness of Scripture and the authority of spiritual interpretation.

SOURCES: Natasha Duquette, "Anna Barbauld and Mary Anne Schimmelpenninck on the sublimity of Scripture," in *Sublimer aspects: interfaces between literature, aesthetics, and theology*, ed. Natasha Duquette (Newcastle Upon Tyne: Cambridge Scholars, 2007), 62–79; idem, "'Dauntless faith': contemplative sublimity and social action in Mary Anne Schimmelpenninck's aesthetics," *Christianity and Literature* 55 (2006): 513–38; *ODNB*; Marion Ann Taylor and Heather E. Weir, eds., *Let her speak for herself: nineteenth-century women writing on women in Genesis* (Waco, Tex.: Baylor University Press, 2006); Mona Wilson, *Jane Austen and some contemporaries* (London: Cresset, 1938); Lissa M. Wray Beal, "Mary Anne Schimmelpenninck: a nineteenth-century woman as Psalm reader," in *Recovering nineteenth-century women interpreters of the Bible*, ed. Christiana de Groot and Marion Ann Taylor (Atlanta: Society of Biblical Literature, 2007), 81–98.

MARY ANNE SCHIMMELPENNINCK
Biblical fragments
1821

How earnestly would the author say to every mother, "Consider well the grounds on which you believe the Bible to be the Word of God! Do you believe it with full purpose of heart and soul? If you do not, does it not behoove you to give no rest to your eyes nor slumber to your eyelids till you have investigated its truth?"

The Bible professes to be a revelation from God. If it be so, he cannot hold you guiltless for having neglected it for want of inquiry into its proofs.

And if it be of him, he has certainly afforded the means of ascertaining its truth to those who desire to do so.

There are two modes [that] present themselves before you: there is external evidence and internal evidence.

The first places before you the historic evidence on which the New Testament rests, which is within the full light of the records of history and is traceable from seventeen contemporary authors by an unbroken chain to this very time; and, if the divinity of the New Testament be once acknowledged, you must receive at the value that Testament assigns to them all the books of the Old.

The last mode of proof is internal evidence, by which you find that Scripture describes your disease as it truly is and lays down a remedy to be received by faith, which, when received, you actually find performs the cure it proposes. From doubt you find certainty; for restlessness, peace; from fear you are animated by love to God and man. A moral miracle has been wrought in you, and you are, therefore, sure the power is of God; for you have often before as cordially believed the systems of men, but they never wrought any cure upon you.

Such are the two avenues of evidence which equally center in the proof of Scripture. Have you followed them? If not, are you excusable for not having done so?

But perhaps you have and are convinced that Scripture is true.

If then you do believe it, be consistent; act as if you believed it.

If you are assured it is the everlasting rock of ages, make it your only foundation.

If it be the only infallible guide, follow it alone.

If it be alone given by inspiration, believe it implicitly, follow it implicitly, trust it implicitly.

How long will ye halt between two opinions? If the world be the Lord, follow it; but if Jehovah Jesus be the Lord, follow him.

‡

To return: spiritual interpretation is the grand means established by God to preserve scriptural truth from adulteration. That it is a means effectually answering this end will appear from this circumstance. Since the great doctrines of the Fall of man, the divinity and atonement of Christ, salvation of grace through faith, and the fruits and work of the Spirit rest by this means not upon mere insulated doctrinal and abstract texts which various critics may twist and bend to an infinite variety of contradictory theories; but in order to warp the truth they exhibit, they must (on the scheme of spiritual interpretation) be compelled not only to wrest and mistranslate abstract terms in the texts themselves, but they must also be compelled to make a correspondent alteration in the circumstances of the whole ritual of the Mosaic law, the denunciations and figures of prophecy, and the whole biography of the typical personages and prophetic figures by which those truths are prefigured throughout the whole of Scripture. Thus every page of the Bible must be in some respect altered before one fatal error can find legs to stand on. It is by this means that every part of the divine record is dovetailed into one solid mass and trenelled[1] down, as it were, on Christ the rock of ages, so that no storm, however furious, can ever more wash away any part of the lighthouse without tearing up the whole. Hence the literal sense of Scripture, even down to the most minute circumstantial detail, acquires dignity, importance, and sanctity by being the conveyance, by bearing witness to, and being the interpreter of that spiritual truth which is alone that living and eternal reality, without which the letter would be a mere dead, dry, and unavailing husk.

Again, the mode adopted by the Holy Spirit of couching eternal truths under sensible types is a necessary consequence of the fallen state of man. When man fell, his spiritual light departed. His spiritual senses became closed; and as spiritual truths are not objects of sense, it became necessary to clothe them in sensible types to manifest to him the invisible truths proposed to that faith which is alone the gift of God. It became necessary, when he had forgotten his native heavenly tongue, to have the language of the heavenly Canaan which he did not understand translated into a language of sensible objects which he did understand; and having first acquired accurate conceptions of those truths from sensible images, he was prepared by this key to unlock the doctrinal and abstract positions to which else he would not have affixed a definite sense. Accordingly, we find the Epistles, or doctrinal and abstract parts of Scripture, addressed to already established churches who were hence in possession of the key; whereas, in the infancy of the church, it was addressed in the parabolic language of the Old Testament, or that used by our Lord in the New, or by the plain matter of fact preached by the apostles in the Acts; but in all instances instruction by palpable figures or facts is given to the unlearned; and instruction by abstract position only to those already established. . . .

[1]   [Ed. Fastened.]

117

Hence, spiritual truths being at once the most foreign to temporal things, and yet the most necessary to be thoroughly understood, it follows that of all other books the Bible must the most abound in parabolic representation and typical[2] illustration.

‡

Though the Bible, like the external world, remains the same, yet does it present distinct faces of truth and yield different uses according to the various wants of those who search it; and as man grows in spiritual knowledge, in spiritual light and love, more extensive views of divine truth expand on every side—unexpected treasures of divine love are discovered, couched beneath even the most apparently barren Scripture ground—and fresh fountains of living water burst forth in sweet refreshing streams from every part of what once appeared a desert waste. Every apparently hard, rugged, and craggy rock of Christian doctrine is found, on proof, to constitute a bulwark of defense, or to offer a cavern of refuge or a shadow from the heat in a weary land; and every beautiful flower of Scripture eloquence is discovered, on its application to the heart, to be rich in healing virtues as well as refulgent with beauties. . . .

By this means not only different individuals and different centuries, but the very same individual at various periods may receive different lights on the very same passage of Scripture; and he may, at successive epochs of his spiritual life, discover very distinct strata of that divine truth which yet were from the beginning couched under one and the same figure. Indeed, nothing can well be more dissimilar in its aspect than the very same divine scheme viewed through the darkness of the natural human heart or seen by the light of the Spirit. Nor, indeed, can two views presenting the same outline be further removed in beauty than the Scripture scheme when viewed merely in the grey dawn of the Sun of Righteousness and viewed in its meridian beams. The Scripture might almost be compared to the tower of some venerable Gothic cathedral which, when beheld through the darkness of nature, seems to stand in fixed menace, a shapeless, dark, unlovely mass, frowning defiance through the gloom and only blackening the surrounding night; whilst, to the believer, it appears like the same building viewed by daylight in its just proportions; its venerable tower is seen firmly and solidly founded on the rock below, whilst its lofty pinnacles point to heaven above; but to the spiritually minded Christian, it is as when a beam of light from the Sun of Righteousness suddenly bursts forth, illuminating its venerable form. Then the whole of its rich tracery starts into light, and whilst the grand outline remains in equally majestic simplicity, each subordinate part is rich with varied ornament—each fretted molding is embellished with infinite variety, and yet every variety conduces to the one great whole; and even the least of its purfled canopies or ornamented pinnacles beams, encircled with living fire, and glows midst the surrounding flood of light in venerable and hallowed majesty, reflecting the glories of that sun that crowns her towers with his effulgent beams.

TEXT: Mary Anne Schimmelpenninck, *Biblical fragments* (London: Ogle, Duncan, and Co., 1821), xxxi–xxxii, 47–49, 233–36.

2   [Ed. Schimmelpenninck refers to typology, a method of biblical interpretation in which the interpreter locates types or symbols of New Testament (Christian) teachings in Old Testament writings.]

EDWARD IRVING
(1792–1834)
Living Word

Edward Irving, forerunner of the twentieth-century Pentecostal movement, was among the most dynamic and captivating preachers of the time. Born in Scotland, Irving entered Edinburgh University in 1805. After graduation, he found employment as a schoolmaster in Haddington (1810) and, later, at Kirkcaldy (1812), where he developed a friendship with Thomas Carlyle and commenced studies at Edinburgh for the ministry (part-time). By 1815 Irving was a licensed preacher in the Church of Scotland. From 1819 to 1822 he assisted Thomas Chalmers at the newly formed St. John's parish church in Glasgow and made regular household visits among members of the working class. In 1822 Irving accepted the opportunity to serve as minister of the Caledonian Chapel in London, where he transformed the small congregation through his lively preaching. Irving soon emerged as a celebrity in cosmopolitan London. He attracted large crowds by his prophetic sermons, formed friendships with illustrious figures such as S. T. Coleridge, wrote numerous books, and participated in leading controversies. After the publication of his *The Orthodox and Catholic doctrine of our Lord's human nature* (1830), Irving faced excommunication from the London presbytery for holding that Christ's human nature was capable of sin. Despite their condemnation of his teaching, Irving continued to preach with the blessing of the Church of Scotland. In association with the evangelist Henry Drummond (1786–1860), Irving founded a millennialist denomination known as the Catholic Apostolic Church. Increasingly, Irving's circle became associated with spiritual gifts reminiscent of the early Christians (including *glossolalia*), revivalist tendencies associated with premillennial expectations of the Second Coming of Christ, and the adoption of Anglo-Catholic practices (such as the use of clerical vestments). In 1833, having already faced expulsion for encouraging charismatic expressions of faith in his Regent Square church in London, Irving was formally discharged from ministry in the Church of Scotland. Nevertheless, so great was Irving's renown in Scotland that when he died of consumption at the age of forty-two, he was interred in the crypt of Glasgow Cathedral.

William Hazlitt's *The spirit of the age* (1825) portrays Irving as a force of nature in the pulpit, riveting audiences with a thundering voice that left them in a state of delight and astonishment. Irving's *For the oracles of God, four orations. For judgment to come, an argument* (1823) captures something of the powerful, authoritative presence that enraptured his London congregation. In the following selection, Irving exhorts readers to a deeper knowledge of God through a passionate appeal for the authority of the entire Bible. Scripture, Irving claims, has been reduced to dry statements of doctrine. In truth, he maintains, the Bible offers life and communion with God.

><del>~~</del>~><

SOURCES: *BDE*; Ralph Brown, "Victorian Anglican evangelicalism: the radical legacy of Edward Irving," *Journal of Ecclesiastical History* 58 (2007): 675–704; Stanley M. Burgess, ed., *Christian peoples of the Spirit: a documentary history of Pentecostal spirituality from the early church to the present* (New York: New York University Press, 2011); Tim Grass, *Edward Irving: the Lord's watchman* (Milton Keynes: Paternoster, 2011); William Hazlitt, *The spirit of the age; or, Contemporary portraits* (London: Henry Coburn, 1825); *ODCC*; *ODNB*.

EDWARD IRVING

For the oracles of God . . . For judgment to come
1823

If anyone who heareth me have the Word so believed, so treasured, so incorporated, the same is a perfect man and needeth only to preserve himself so. But as there is no one or hardly anyone so instated, I take the benefit of these arguments and illustrations to press home upon you the reading of the Word in another style than you are wont.

And, *first*, that which I have sketched of the soul's necessities needeth something more than to rake the Scriptures for a few opinions, which, by what authority I know not, they have exalted with the proud name of *the* doctrines—as if all Scripture were not profitable for doctrine [2 Tim 3:16]. Masterful men, or the masterful current of opinion, hath ploughed with the Word of God, and the fruit has been to inveigle the mind into the exclusive admiration of some few truths, which being planted in the belief and sacrificed to in all religious expositions and discourses, have become popular idols which frown heresy and excommunication upon all who dare stand for the unadulterated, uncurtailed testimony. . . . But, truly, there are higher fears than the fear even of the religious world, and greater loss than the loss of religious fame. Therefore, craving indulgence of you to hear us to an end, and asking the credit of good intention upon what you have already heard, we summon your whole unconstrained man to the engagement of reading the Word. Not to authenticate a meager outline of opinions elsewhere derived, but to prove and purify all the sentiments which bind the confederations of life; to prove and purify all the feelings which instigate the actions of life; many to annihilate; many to implant; all to regulate and reform; to bridle the tongue till its words come forth in unison with the Word of God and to people the whole soul with the population of new thoughts which that Word reveals of God and man—of the present and the future. These doctrines, truly, should be like the mighty rivers which fertilize our island, whose waters, before escaping to the sea, have found their way to the roots of each several flower and plant and stately tree, and covered the face of the land with beauty and with fertility—spreading plenty for the enjoyment of man and beast. So ought these great doctrines of the grace of God in Christ, and the help of God in the Spirit, and fallen man's need of both—to carry health and vitality to the whole soul and surface of Christian life. But it hath appeared to us that, most unlike such wide-spreading streams of fertility, they are often, as it were, confined within rocky channels of intolerance and disputation, where they hold noisy brawl with every impediment, draining off the natural juices of the soul; and, instead of fruits and graces, leaving all behind naked, barren, and unpeopled!—which makes us lament.

In the *second* place, that the catechetical[1] books of any church should have come to play such a conspicuous part in the foreground of the Christian stage, and have not kept their proper inferiority and served as handmaidens to the book of God. They are exhibitions not of the whole Bible, as is often thought, but of the abstract doctrines and formal commandments of the Bible; and this not upon any superhuman testimony, but after the judgment of fallible mortals like ourselves. We are not discontented with them on that account, but, on the other hand, we are proud to possess such as our church doth acknowledge. But we are very discontented that they should have stepped from their proper place of discerning heresy and preserving in the church a unity of faith; that from this useful office they should have come to usurp it as the great instrument of a religious education and the great storehouse of religious knowledge in our families, in our schools, and even in the ministry of our churches. Now they are not good instruments of education—being above the level of youth and the most of men, and addressing only the intellect, and that only with logical forms of truth, not with narrative, with example, with eloquence, or with feeling. And as to their being storehouses of religious knowledge, they want the most essential staples of our religion, for there is in them no authoritative voice of our God that we should fear them, no tender sympathetic voice of our Savior that we should tenderly affect them in return, no unction of the Holy One that we should depend upon them for healing power. . . . Moreover there is in them no feature of Christian imagery to catch the conception nor patterns of holy men, to awaken the imitation of excellence, and draw on the admiration of holiness; no joyful strains of hope and promised bliss to rouse nature's indolence, nor eager remonstrances against the world's ways, nor stern denouncements like the thunder of heaven upon the head of its transgressions, nor pathetic bursts of sympathy over nature's melancholy conditions and more melancholy prospects. . . . From the prevalence of this taste for doctrinal and catechetical statements, there hath sprung,

In the *third* place, this succession of practical evils over which we most bitterly lament. The Scriptures are not read for the higher ends of teaching the soul practical wisdom and overcoming the practical errors of all her faculties, of all her judgments, and of all her ways. Then the Word, which is diversified for men of all gifts, cometh to be prized chiefly as a treasure of intellectual truth, elements of religious dogmatism—often an armory of religious warfare. Then our spirits become intolerant of all who find in the Bible any tenets differing from our own, as if they had made an invasion upon the integrity of our faith and were plotting the downfall of religion itself. Then an accurate statement of opinion from the pulpit, from the lips of childhood, from the deathbed of age, becomes all in all; whereas it is nothing if not conjoined with the utterances of a Christian spirit and the evidences of a renewed life. Who can bear the logical and metaphysical aspect with which religion looks out from the temples of this land, playing about the head but starving the wellsprings of the heart and drying up the fertile streams of a holy and charitable life! . . .

---

[1] [Ed. Books of religious instruction, often in preparation for baptism or confirmation.]

O! Brethren, let me now drop this strain of censure which the honor of the Bible hath forced me to maintain against my better liking, and speak persuasively in your ear for a noble and more enlarged perception of the truth. Pour ye out your whole undivided heart before the command of God [Ps 62:8]. Give your enlarged spirit to the communion of his Word. Be free; be disentangled. Let it teach; let it reprove; let it correct; let it instruct in righteousness; let it elevate you with its wonderful delineations of the secrets of the divine nature and of the future destinies of the human race, higher than the loftiest poetry. And let it carry you deeper with its pictures of our present and future wretchedness than the most pathetic sentiment ever penned by the novelist. And let it take affection captive by its pictures of divine mercy and forgiveness, more than the sweetest eloquence. Let it transport you with indignation at that with which it is indignant, and take you with passion when it is impassioned; when it blames be ye blamed; when it exhorts be ye exhorted; when it condescends to argument by its arguments be ye convinced. Be free to take all its moods and to catch all its inspirations. Then shall you become instinct with all Christian feeling and pregnant with all holy fruits, "thoroughly furnished for every good word and work" [2 Tim 3:17].

Why, in modern times, do we not take from the Word that sublimity of design and gigantic strength of purpose which made all things bend before the saints, whose praise is in the Word and the church of God? Why have the written secrets of the Eternal become less moving than the fictions of fancy or the periodical works of the day; and their impressiveness died away into the imbecility of a tale that hath been often told? Not because man's spirit hath become more weak. Was there ever an age in which it was more patient of research or restless after improvement? Not because the Spirit of God hath become backward in his help or the Word divested of its truth, but because we treat it not as the all-accomplished wisdom of God. . . . We come to meditate it like armed men to consult of peace—our whole mind occupied with insurrectionary interests—we suffer no captivity of its truth. Faith, which should brood with expanded wings over the whole heavenly legend, imbibing its entire spirit—what hath it become? A name to conjure up theories and hypotheses upon. Duty likewise hath fallen into a few formalities of abstaining from amusements and keeping up severities, instead of denoting a soul girt with all its powers for its Maker's will. Religion also, a set of opinions and party distinctions separated from high endowments and herding with cheap popular accomplishments—a mere servingmaid of everyday life, instead of being the mistress of all earthly (and the preceptress of all heavenly) sentiments and the very queen of all high gifts and graces and perfections in every walk of life!

To be delivered from this dwarfish exhibition of that plant which our heavenly Father hath planted, take up this holy book. Let your devotions gather warmth from the various exhibitions of the nature and attributes of God. Let the displays of his power overawe you, and the goings forth of his majesty still you into reverend observance. Let his uplifted voice awake the slumber of your spirits and every faculty burn in adoration of that image of the invisible God which his Word reveals. If nature is reverend before him, how much more the spirit of man for whom he rideth forth in his state! Let his holiness, before which the pure seraph veils his face, and his justice, before which the heavens are rebuked, humble our frail spirits in the dust and awaken all their conscious guilt. Then let the richness of his mercy strike us dumb with amazement, and his offered grace revive our hopes anew;

and let his Son, coming forth with the embraces of his love, fill our spirits with rapture. Let us hold him fast in sweet communion, exchange with him affection's kindest tokens, and be satisfied with the sufficiency of his grace; and let the strength of his Spirit be our refuge, his all-sufficient strength our buckler and our trust!

Then, stirred up through all her powers, and awakened from the deep sleep of nature and oblivion of God (which among visible things she partaketh), our soul shall come forth from the communion of the Word full of divine energy and ardor, prepared to run upon this world's theatre the race of duty for the prize of life eternal. She shall erect herself beyond the measures and approbation of men into the measures and approbation of God. She shall become like the saints of old, who, strengthened by such repasts of faith, "subdued kingdoms, wrought righteousness, obtained promises, stopped the mouths of lions, quenched the violence of fire, escaped the edge of the sword, out of weakness were made strong, waxed valiant in fight, and turned to flight the armies of the aliens" [Heb 11:33-34].

TEXT: Edward Irving, *For the oracles of God, four orations. For judgment to come, an argument, in nine parts* (London: T. Hamilton, 1823), 37–42.

CONNOP THIRLWALL
(1797–1875)
Biblical Inspiration

Connop Thirlwall, bishop of St. David's, was a noted translator, historian, and liberal-minded theologian of the Church of England. Thirlwall was born in the parish of Mile End Old Town, London, where his father was a clergyman and author of several works. Thirlwall, considered a promising child from an early age, attended Charterhouse and became friends with the future broad churchman Julius Charles Hare. In 1814 Thirlwall matriculated at Trinity College, Cambridge, and by 1818 he was elected a fellow. After travels in Europe, Thirlwall studied law at Lincoln's Inn and practiced for two years. He was ordained deacon in 1827 and, one year later, priest. Thirlwall held a number of positions at Trinity, including junior dean and assistant tutor, before Christopher Wordsworth forced his resignation in 1834 on account of his support for the admission of dissenters to the universities. Thereafter Thirlwall took up the living of Kirby Underdale in Yorkshire, began publication of his *History of Greece* (8 vols., 1835–1844), and served in the senate of London University. In 1840 Lord Melbourne named Thirlwall bishop of St. David's, against the wishes of some Tractarians. Thirlwall applied the full force of his scholarly skills to the episcopacy. He learned Welsh within the year and personally inspected the schools and churches in order to invest in necessary improvements throughout the diocese. In subsequent decades, Thirlwall supported a number of highly contested positions, including Jewish political emancipation in 1848 and, two decades later, the disestablishment of the Church of Ireland. Surprisingly, given his introduction to and translation of F. D. E. Schleiermacher, Thirlwall supported the condemnation of *Essays and Reviews* (1860), the controversial work of biblical criticism in which several clergy openly advocated interpreting the Bible as literature.

Thirlwall's travels in the mid-1820s solidified his linguistic skills and brought him into contact with new theological movements. German philosophy and theology were widely distrusted in England during this period, and only a relative handful of scholars were capable of serious translation work. Thirlwall's anonymous translation and introduction to F. D. E. Schleiermacher's *A critical essay on the Gospel of St. Luke* (1825) marks an important moment in the history of English biblical criticism. While the work was not well received in England or North America, it remained one of few works by Schleiermacher to be translated into English during the nineteenth century. By the time Schleiermacher wrote his essay on the Gospel of Luke, he had already emerged as a pivotal figure in the rising Romantic movement in Germany. His critical approach to Luke deemphasized the possibility of reconstructing the life of Jesus and instead highlighted the theological and historical-contextual commitments of the Gospel writers. In England, Thirlwall's introduction to Schleiermacher's *Critical essay* was regarded as no less important than the translation itself. A significant portion of the introduction traces the state of research on the composition of the Gospels. In the following selection, Thirlwall defends a modified doctrine of biblical inspiration. He maintains that the Spirit's inspiring operation is not in "any temporary, physical, or even intellectual changes wrought in its subjects, but in the continual presence and action of what is most vital and essential in Christianity itself" (xix). In this way, Thirlwall rejects any theory of inspiration that reduced the biblical writers to passive automatons and yet asserts the Spirit's overarching work in the revelation of divine truth.

Sources: Nigel M. de S. Cameron, *Biblical higher criticism and the defense of infallibilism in 19th century Britain* (Lewiston: Edwin Mellen, 1987); *ODCC*; *ODNB*; John Connop Thirlwall, Jr., *Connop Thirlwall: historian and theologian* (London: SPCK, 1936); Terrence N. Tice, "Editor's introduction," in *Luke: a critical study*, by Friedrich Schleiermacher (Lewiston: Edwin Mellen, 1993); David A. Valone, "Theology, German historicism, and religious education at Cambridge: the controversies of Connop Thirlwall and Julius Hare, 1822–1834," *Anglican & Episcopal History* 78 (2009): 139–73.

CONNOP THIRLWALL
"Introduction by the translator"
1825

In the first place then, it must be admitted that all the hypotheses we have mentioned are equally and decidedly irreconcilable with that doctrine of inspiration once universally prevalent in the Christian church, according to which the sacred writers were merely passive organs or instruments of the Holy Spirit. This doctrine, however, has been so long abandoned that it would now be a waste of time to attack it. When I say it has been abandoned, I mean, of course, only by the learned, for undoubtedly it is still a generally received notion; and when those expressions which long usage has consecrated are used in public respecting the Scriptures, they will most frequently, unless particular care be taken to qualify and restrict them, be understood in this strictest sense. Among theologians, however, this doctrine of literal inspiration has been long softened into a milder and more flexible theory. Instead of an uniform, unremitting, indiscriminate operation, the agency of the Spirit was represented as accommodating itself to circumstances and assuming, as occasion required, two different forms. One of these was designated as the inspiration of suggestion, the other as the inspiration of superintendency; the object of the former was to reveal to the penmen of the Scriptures what was necessary to be revealed, that of the latter to secure them from any material error or mistake. This convenient division, which has been adopted by our most orthodox divines, enables the Church of England to comprehend within her bosom (as it is her wish to do on points of minor importance) very different and even opposite opinions on this subject. The inspiration of Scripture is a necessary and fundamental tenet on which she absolutely insists; but as to the nature and mode of that inspiration, she allows her members full liberty of private judgment. Those whose notion of revelation requires that every part of Scripture should have proceeded from a positive supernatural impulse will see in every passage the operation of the Holy Spirit. Those who consider such an agency of the Spirit as a continual miracle for which they can find no adequate occasion may still believe the sacred writers to have composed their works under his superintending control, which does not of necessity imply an active interposition. This seems a sufficient latitude of opinion, and it is difficult to conceive how any hypotheses respecting the origin of the Gospels can have required a larger license or have overstepped these very ample bounds. . . . The rational and orthodox medium (so far as it is possible to ascertain what has never been precisely defined) appears to be thought to consist in this: it recedes on the one hand from the ancient doctrine of verbal or, as it has been called, organic inspiration by rejecting all unnecessary exertions of supernatural influence, so that the evangelists may be believed to have written whatever fell within their own experience or was communicated to them by inspired witnesses without the aid of the Holy Spirit and only under his guardianship and protection; on the other hand, it shrinks from the boldness of the modern theories by maintaining that whatever was not known to the sacred historians by one or other of those ways was directly revealed to them from above. Those who insist upon this middle line seem to think that, although their view of the subject may leave some difficulties in our Gospels unexplained, it has at all events the advantage in point of piety and orthodoxy over the theories which suppose every part of our Gospels to have been derived by different processes from human sources. This superiority however, if we examine the foundation on which it rests, appears very questionable. For those who hold this opinion do not pretend to possess any peculiar information respecting the situation of the sacred writers and the opportunities and means of knowledge they enjoyed, so as to be able to determine where their ordinary sources failed them and the need of a divine interposition arose; still less do they profess to recognize by any marks the operation of the Spirit, and so to distinguish passages suggested and revealed from those derived from personal experience or testimony. The existence therefore of any passages of the former description is a merely arbitrary conjecture which rests entirely on a dogmatical ground. And even as opposed to the view of those who believe that the evangelists do not everywhere report either their own experience or the immediate testimony of eyewitnesses, but that they sometimes received their relations from second or third hand, the opinion we are examining possesses even in a dogmatical point of view no substantial advantage. For as the more rigid theory of inspiration was abandoned by the learned on account of the insuperable difficulties opposed to it by the discrepancies found in the Gospels, so these same discrepancies compel us to admit that the superintending control of the Spirit was not exerted to exempt the sacred writers altogether from errors and inadvertencies. And why need it be supposed that the variations which a narrative might undergo in passing through one or two hands must be more material than those produced by the difference in situation, character, memory, or other circumstances of the first witnesses? Yet unless we make this totally unfounded supposition, there appears to be no dogmatical necessity for denying that the evangelists drew from secondary sources or for maintaining that the use of these was superseded by the extraordinary suggestions of the Spirit. It would appear then that if there be any real difference between those who hold this, which passes for the more orthodox opinion, and the advocates of the modern hypotheses which they reprobate, it is one which does not affect the dogma of inspiration, which is or may be common to both, but only the mode of applying it—a wholly extraneous point, which can only be decided on historical or critical grounds.

But should we rest here, it might be imagined that the design of what has been hitherto said was not merely to defend from the charge of innovation the theories which have been proposed to explain the origin of the Gospels, but to attack the doctrine of inspiration itself; for the result of the argument seems to be that we can find no reason for believing the inspiration of suggestion was in any instance necessary to the composition of the Gospels and consequently that we cannot believe it was ever exerted. Now if this first kind of inspiration is totally excluded, it is evident that the second kind, that of superintendence, ceases to be anything positive and real, and exists only in possibility, or, at the utmost, it can only have operated in directing the Evangelists to the best sources; and it then becomes an ordinary dispensation of divine providence which might have been equally granted to a heathen historian of Christianity, so that we lose every idea of inspiration, in the proper sense of the word. Perhaps, however, this consequence, which is seemingly inevitable, does not flow from the nature of the doctrine itself, but from something erroneous or partial in the mode of considering it. And indeed, when we examine once more the common division of the subject, it seems in itself liable to considerable objections. In the first place, it implies an inequality in each Gospel, some passages being supposed to have been written under a more immediate influence of the Holy Spirit than others; of which nevertheless, as we have already observed, no one has hitherto professed to have discovered the slightest trace. In the next place, it assumes that the inspiration under which the historical parts of the New Testament were written was something essentially different from that experienced by the writers of the didactic parts; for in the latter no one certainly will contend that the positive agency of the Spirit could have been for a moment suspended or interrupted. The suspicion of any such break in the unity of those writings would, if well-founded, deprive them of all their value and authority; and there is no internal mark which in any degree justifies it. But perhaps it may be said that this difference naturally arises out of the different nature of the works; that in the composition of the historical parts the active influence of the Spirit was only occasionally needed to supply the defects of the writers or to prevent the consequences of their human infirmity. But surely this view of the subject exaggerates the importance of historical accuracy, which nevertheless it does not suppose to have been completely attained, while it underrates the magnitude and difficulties of the task which the evangelists have executed, and overlooks in their works what is most excellent and truly divine. For whoever considers the variety of delusions, prejudices, and errors which were rife in the pregnant age in which our Gospels were written and, dismissing for a time all critical analysis, contemplates each in the light in which it was intended to appear as a whole, and observes how pure and bright an image . . . it presents of the life and character which it describes—whoever takes all this into consideration will readily believe that the writers were filled with that Spirit which was to lead into all truth [John 16:13]. And we shall feel this still more strongly and shall subscribe still more willingly to the decision of the church, which consecrated these as the sole authentic Christian records, when we compare them with the fragments preserved to us even of the earlier apocryphal gospels. Perhaps then it may be desirable that the modern division (which seems indeed rather to have been devised as an expedient for getting rid of an apparent difficulty, than to have resulted from any independent view of the subject) should be discarded, and that we should return to the old opinion that the whole of Scripture proceeded from the constant and uniform operation of the Spirit; only we must clear that opinion of the exaggerations with which it has been loaded, and which were not implied in the judgment of the primitive church when it fixed the canon, and must seek the operation of the Spirit not in any temporary physical or even intellectual changes wrought in its subjects, but in the continual presence and action of what is most vital and essential in Christianity itself. With this view of our Gospels, we certainly need not be alarmed at the course which may be taken by any investigations instituted to explain their mutual relation or even scruple to prosecute them ourselves.

TEXT: Connop Thirlwall, "Introduction by the translator," in *A critical essay on the Gospel of St. Luke*, by [Friedrich] Schleiermacher (London: John Taylor, 1825), xi–xix.

IV

DOUBT

Christianity throughout the whole . . . exhibits proofs of its divine original, and its practical precepts are no less pure than its doctrines are sublime.

William Wilberforce, *A practical view* (1797)

GEORGE HORNE
(1730–1792)
Miracles

George Horne, bishop of Norwich, was born at the village of Otham (near Maid-stone), Kent. In 1746 Horne matriculated at University College, Oxford. There, Horne developed a close friendship with John Moore, the future archbishop of Canterbury, and William Jones of Nayland (see selection in Part I), Horne's future biographer. In subsequent years, Horne's gifts as a preacher and leader surfaced: he was elected fellow of Magdalen College, Oxford in 1750; selected as president of the College in 1768; vice chancellor of Oxford in 1776; dean of Canterbury in 1781, and finally bishop of Nor-wich in 1790. Although he ministered from high church principles, he remained open to the Methodists and, unlike some bishops, allowed John Wesley to preach within his diocese. Horne was a prolific controversialist. He opposed the mysticism of William Law's later writings, efforts to allow greater latitude in subscription to the Articles at Oxford, and the rise of Socinianism (early Unitarianism) in his diocese. His devotional and exegetical *Commentary on the Psalms* (1771) interprets the Old Testament in tradi-tional typological fashion.

Horne's *Letters on infidelity* (1784), a critique of David Hume and other skeptics, shows the interconnection between the debate over miracles and commitment to bib-lical authority in the late eighteenth century. Most English theologians considered the miracles of Christ and his fulfillment of the Old Testament prophecies to be irrefragable evidence for the veracity of the Bible and the divinity of Christ. Hume's "Of miracles," in his *Dialogues concerning natural religion* (1779), sought to dispel belief in the mirac-ulous by asserting the inadequacy of evidence for supposed departures from the laws of nature. In the following selection, Horne specifically targets a piece by one of Hume's fellow travelers: *The doubts of infidels, or queries relative to scriptural inconsistencies and contradictions* (1781), usually attributed to William Nicholson (1753–1815). Biblical skeptics, such as Nicholson, questioned the historicity of the miracles recorded in the Old and New Testaments, given that they "were all performed in those ages of which we have no credible history" and moreover "disappeared in proportion as men became enlightened and capable of discovering *imposture* and *priestcraft.*"[1] Horne contends that biblical miracles are attested by the highest possible historical verification, since eye-witnesses (including opponents of the Jews and Christians) affirmed the truth of the miracles in their own time as a testimony for later ages.

SOURCES: Nigel Aston, "Horne and heterodoxy: the defence of Anglican beliefs in the late Enlightenment," *English Historical Review* 108 (1993): 895–919; idem, "Infidelity ancient and modern: George Horne reads Edward Gibbon," *Albion* 27 (1995): 561–82; [William Nicholson,] *The doubts of infidels; or, Queries relative to scriptural inconsistencies and contradictions* (1781; London: Carlile, 1819); *ODCC*; *ODNB*; B.W. Young, *Religion and Enlightenment in eighteenth-century England: theological debate from Locke to Burke* (Oxford: Clarendon, 1998).

---

[1]   [William Nicholson], *The doubts of infidels; or, Queries relative to scriptural inconsistencies and contradictions* (1781; London: Carlile, 1819), 1–2.

GEORGE HORNE
Letters on infidelity
1784

The substance of this section [of Nicholson's essay], thrown into an argumentative form, stands thus: "Miracles are not wrought now; therefore they never were wrought at all."

One would wonder how the premises and the conclusion could be brought together. No man would in earnest assert the necessity of miracles being repeated for the confirmation of a revelation to every new generation and to each individual of which it is composed. Certainly not. If they were once wrought and duly entered on *record*, the record is *evidence* ever after. This reasoning holds good respecting them as well as other facts; and to reason otherwise would be to introduce universal confusion.

It is said, "They are things in their own nature far removed from common belief" [1].[1]

They are things which do not happen every day, to be sure. It were absurd from the very nature of them to expect that they should. But what reason can there be for concluding from thence that none ever were wrought? Why should it be thought a thing more incredible that the ruler of the world should interpose, upon proper occasions, to control the operations of nature than that he should direct them in ordinary? It is not *impossible* that a teacher should be sent from God. It may be *necessary* that one should be sent. If one be sent, he must bring *credentials* to show that he is so sent; and what can those credentials be but *miracles* or acts of almighty power such as God only can perform? In the case of Jesus, common sense spake by the mouth of the Jewish ruler, and all the sophistry in the world cannot invalidate or perplex the argument: "Master, thou art a teacher come from God; for no man can do the miracles which thou doest, except God be with him" [John 3:2].

"They (miracles) require something more than the usual testimony of history for their support" [1].

---

[1]   [Ed. All page numbers will appear in brackets in the main text for quotes from *The doubts of infidels; or, Queries relative to scriptural inconsistencies and contradictions* (1781; London: Carlile, 1819). Horne has made minor changes to each quote.]

Why so? If they *may* be wrought and good reasons are assigned for their *having been* wrought upon any particular occasion, "the usual testimony of history" is sufficient to evince that they *were* wrought. But the truth is that they *have* "something more than the usual testimony of history." They have *much* more. For no facts in the world ever were attested by such an accumulated weight of evidence as we can produce on behalf of the miracles recorded of Moses and Christ; insomuch that the mind of any person tolerably well informed concerning them, till steeled against conviction by the prejudices of infidelity, revolts at the very idea of their being accounted forgeries.

"When Livy speaks of shields sweating blood, of its raining hot stones, and the like, we justly reject and disbelieve the improbable assertions" [1].

Doubtless. But what comparison can be properly instituted between these hearsay stories concerning pagan prodigies and a series of miracles like those openly and publicly wrought for years together, in the face of the world, by Moses and by Christ? The historical facts related by Livy may be true, whatever becomes of his prodigies; but, in the other case, the miracles are interwoven with, and indeed constitute, the body of the history. No separation can possibly be made; the whole must be received or the whole must be rejected.

"Neither is any credit given to the wonderful account of curing diseases by the touch, said to be possessed by Mr. Greatrix,[2] though we find it in the *Philosophical transactions*" [1].

Mr. Greatrix's general method of curing diseases was not, as I remember,.simply and instantaneously by the *touch*, but by the operation of *stroking* the part affected, and that long continued or frequently repeated. Sometimes, it is said, this stroking succeeded and sometimes it failed. If (as we are informed in a note [1n.2]) Boyle, Wilkins, Cudworth, and other great men attested the fact that there were persons who found themselves relieved by this new device, undoubtedly there were such persons. But whether this relief were temporary; whether it were owing in any or what degree to the working of the imagination or to a real physical change effected by the application of a warm hand or any particular temperament in the constitution of the stroker—these are points which the reader may find discussed in Mr. Boyle's letter to Henry Stubbe written upon the occasion, in which he reproves Stubbe, as he well might, for supposing there was anything necessarily and properly miraculous in the affair.[3] Mr. Valentine Greatrix, by all accounts, was an honest, harmless, melancholy country gentleman of the kingdom of Ireland, who after having gained great reputation by *stroking* in England, returned to pass his latter days quietly and peaceably in his native country and was heard of no more. He had no new doctrine to promulgate, pretended to no divine mission, and, I daresay, never thought of his cures being employed to discredit those of his Savior. The wonders reported to have been wrought formerly by Apollonius Tyaneus, and more lately at the tomb of Abbé Paris, have been

[2]   [Ed. Valentine Greatrakes (1629–1683), nicknamed "the Stroker," was a public healer known for his alleged ability to cure various ailments by laying his hands on affected areas of the body. He came under official scrutiny for claiming to heal *scrofula* ("the king's evil"), a form of tuberculosis that was widely understood to be cured by monarchs alone.]

[3]   [Ed. Horne refers to Robert Boyle's response to *The miraculous conformist* (1666) by the physician Henry Stubbe (1632–1676).]

applied to the same purpose.[4] But their day is over and now all depends upon poor Mr. Valentine Greatrix!

"The miracles of the Old Testament were all performed in those ages of which we have no credible history" [1].

Pardon me. There cannot be a more credible history than that of Moses, since it is impossible that he could have written or the Israelites received his history had it not been true. Would he, think you, have called them together and told them to their faces—they had all heard and seen such and such wonders—when every man, woman, and child in the company knew they had never heard or seen anything of the kind? What? Not one honest soul to cry out *priest-craft* and *imposture!* [2]. Let these gentlemen try their hands in this way. They have often been requested to do it. Let one of them assemble the good people of London and Westminster, and tell them that on a certain day and hour he divided the Thames and led them on dry ground over to Southwark, appealing to them for the truth of what he says. I should like to see the event of such an appeal. There are many such appeals recorded of Moses to his nation, and the book in which these appeals are so recorded contains the municipal law by which that nation has been governed from the days of Moses to the dissolution of their polity. This is a fact without a parallel upon earth; and let any man produce an hypothesis to account for it, consistently with the idea of Moses being a deceiver, which will abide the test of common sense for five minutes. If the deists can reason us out of our faith, let them do so; but we are not weak enough, as yet, to be sneered or scoffed out of it.

"What reply can be made to those who affirm that miracles have always been confined to the early and fabulous ages?" [1].

The reply is easy: that miracles were performed by Christ and his apostles in the age of all others esteemed the most polite and learned, and that the adversaries of Christianity in those days never thought of denying the facts. It was a piece of assurance reserved for these latter times.

"That all nations have had them; but that they disappeared in proportion as men became enlightened and capable of discovering imposture" [1–2].

Many nations have had them—true or false; the false disappeared when discovered to be so, but the true will abide forever. The Jewish rulers had their senses about them as much as other people, and those senses sharpened to the utmost by envy and malice. Yet were they obliged to confess "This man doth many miracles" [John 11:47]. It may be added that had there been no genuine miracles, there would have been no counterfeits.

Upon the whole—in this section, on so leading an article—the infidels have made no considerable progress. Rather, they can hardly be said, in the nautical phrase, to have *got under way.*

Text: [George Horne,] *Letters on infidelity*, 2nd ed. (Oxford: Clarendon, 1786), 152–62.

[4]   [Ed. Apollonius of Tyana was a first-century Greek philosopher known for miraculous works. The grave of Abbé Paris, the Jansenist François de Pâris (1690–1727), attracted international attention due to reports of convulsions and miracles among those who visited his burial place. Hume's "Of miracles" singles out for scrutiny the extraordinary miracles associated with the Frenchman.]

WILLIAM WILBERFORCE
(1759–1833)
Unbelief

Unbelief, by some accounts, arose not from a careful examination of facts and evidence, but from prejudice and a depraved character. As the writings of Christian apologists in this period repeatedly assert, the unwillingness to be governed by any universal moral standard spawned infidelity. Few authors encouraged such a reading of the history of skepticism as effectively as the great abolitionist William Wilberforce.

Born at Hull, Wilberforce studied at the local grammar school until his father's death brought him to London, where he was influenced by George Whitefield. The impact of Whitefield's evangelical "enthusiasm" was, however, short lived. He matriculated at St. John's College, Cambridge in 1776, receiving a B.A. (1781) and M.A. (1788). In 1780, before graduating, Wilberforce won his first political appointment as MP for Hull. He was only twenty-one, but the election signaled a bright future. He won his second seat at only twenty-five, when Yorkshire, the largest county in England, elected him as representative. Under the influence of Isaac Milner, Wilberforce returned to evangelicalism in 1785. In time, Wilberforce's friendships read as a who's-who list of British evangelicals. His association with John Newton, Hannah More, and, from 1797, a group of evangelical Anglican clergy who came to be known as the "Clapham Sect" reflect the range of his connections in the religious sphere. Wilberforce helped to found or contributed to numerous charities, societies, and publications of note, including the Proclamation Society for the "Reformation of Manners" (1787), the Church Mission Society (1799), the *Christian Observer* (1801), and the British and Foreign Bible Society (1804). Still, no cause or interest occupied Wilberforce's attention more than abolitionism. From around 1787 Wilberforce championed abolition in Parliament. He lobbied bishops and laity, traveled tirelessly, and risked personal health and well-being in his efforts to end slavery. Wilberforce witnessed the end of the British slave trade in 1807 and the passage of the Emancipation Act in 1833.

Wilberforce's *A Practical view of the prevailing religious system of professed Christians* (1797) began as a tract published in 1793. When Wilberforce first proposed the work, his publisher doubted it would sell. The doubt proved unwarranted. Wilberforce's manifesto went through numerous editions and contributed to a broad revival in British evangelical Anglicanism. The work called for spiritual renewal, social activism, a reformation of morality, and clarity of doctrine—hallmarks of the new evangelical era. In the following selection, "Brief Observations Addressed to Skeptics and Unitarians," Wilberforce presents what he calls the "natural history" of skepticism, whereby an individual gradually succumbs first to confusion about matters of faith, then to prejudice against it, and eventually to immorality. He rejects any notion that unbelief emerges from thoughtful reflection: "Infidelity is, in general, a disease of the heart more than of the understanding."

><del>~~</del><

SOURCES: *BDE*; Bebbington; Jeffrey P. Greenman, "Anglican evangelicals on personal and social ethics," *Anglican Theological Review* 94 (2012): 179–205; William Hague, *William Wilberforce* (London: Harper Perennial, 2008); *OCEL*; *ODCC*; *ODNB*; *RCBEC*; Anne Stott, *Wilberforce: family and friends* (Oxford: Oxford University Press, 2012); Stephen Tompkins, *William Wilberforce: a biography* (Grand Rapids: Eerdmans, 2007).

WILLIAM WILBERFORCE
A practical view of the prevailing religious system of professed Christians
1797

There is another class of men—an increasing class, it is to be feared, in this country—that of absolute unbelievers, with which this little work has properly no concern. But may the writer, sincerely pitying their melancholy state, be permitted to ask them one plain question? If Christianity be not in their estimation true, yet is there not at least a presumption in its favor, sufficient to entitle it to a serious examination, from its having been embraced, and that not blindly and implicitly, but upon full inquiry and deep consideration by Bacon and Milton and Locke and Newton, and much the greater part of those, who—by the reach of their understandings or the extent of their knowledge, and by the freedom too of their minds, and their daring to combat existing prejudices—have called forth the respect and admiration of mankind? It might be deemed scarcely fair to insist on churchmen, though some of them are among the greatest names this country has ever known. Can the skeptic in general say with truth that he has either prosecuted an examination into the evidences of revelation at all, or at least with a seriousness and diligence in any degree proportioned to the importance of the subject? The fact is, and it is a fact which redounds to the honor of Christianity, that infidelity is not the result of sober inquiry and deliberate preference. It is rather the slow production of a careless and irreligious life, operating together with prejudices and erroneous conceptions concerning the nature of the leading doctrines and fundamental tenets of Christianity.

Take the case of young men of condition, bred up by what we have termed nominal Christians. When children, they are carried to church, and thence they become acquainted with such parts of Scripture as are contained in our public service. If their parents preserve still more of the customs of better times, they are taught their catechism and furnished with a little further religious knowledge. After a while, they go from under the eyes of their parents; they enter into the world and move forward in the path of life, whatever it may be, which has been assigned to them. They yield to the temptations which assail them and become, more or less, dissipated and licentious. At least they neglect to look into their Bible; they do not enlarge the sphere of their religious acquisitions; they do not even

140

endeavor by reflection and study to turn into what may deserve the name of knowledge and rational conviction, the opinions which, in their childhood, they had taken on trust.

They travel, perhaps, into foreign countries; a proceeding which naturally tends to weaken their nursery prejudice in favor of the religion in which they were bred, and, by removing them from all means of public worship, to relax their practical habits of religion. They return home and commonly are either hurried round in the vortex of dissipation or engage with the ardor of youthful minds in some public or professional pursuit. If they read or hear anything about Christianity, it is commonly only about those tenets which are subjects of controversy; and what reaches their ears of the Bible from their occasional attendance at church, though it may sometimes impress them with an idea of the purity of Christian morality, contains much which, coming thus detached, perplexes and offends them, and suggests various doubts and startling objections which a further acquaintance with the Scripture would remove. Thus growing more and more to know Christianity only by the difficulties it contains—sometimes tempted by the ambition of showing themselves superior to vulgar prejudice and always prompted by the natural pride of the human heart to cast off their subjection to dogmas imposed on them, disgusted perhaps by the immoral lives of some professed Christians, by the weaknesses and absurdities of others, and by what they observe to be the implicit belief of numbers whom they see and know to be equally ignorant with themselves—many doubts and suspicions of greater or less extent spring up within them. These doubts enter into the mind at first almost imperceptibly. They exist only as vague indistinct surmises and by no means take the precise shape or the substance of a formed opinion. At first, probably, they even offend and startle by their intrusion, but by degrees the unpleasant sensations which they once excited wear off. The mind grows more familiar with them. A confused sense (for such it is, rather than a formed idea) of its being desirable that their doubts should prove well founded, and of the comfort and enlargement which would be afforded by that proof, lends them much secret aid. The impression becomes deeper—not in consequence of being reinforced by fresh arguments, but merely by dint of having longer rested in the mind; and as they increase in force, they creep on and extend themselves. At length they diffuse themselves over the whole of religion and possess the mind in undisturbed occupancy.

It is by no means meant that this is universally the process. But, speaking generally, this might be termed, perhaps not unjustly, the *natural history* of skepticism. It approves itself to the experience of those who have with any care watched the progress of infidelity in persons around them; and it is confirmed by the written lives of some of the most eminent unbelievers. It is curious to read their own accounts of themselves . . . as they accord so exactly with the result of our own observation. We find that they once perhaps gave a sort of implicit hereditary assent to the truth of Christianity and were what, by a mischievous perversion of language, the world denominates *believers.* How were they then awakened from their sleep of ignorance? At what moment did the light of truth beam in upon them and dissipate the darkness in which they had been involved? The period of their infidelity is marked by no such determinate boundary. Reason and thought and inquiry had little or nothing to do with it. Having for many years lived careless and irreligious lives, and associated with companions equally careless and irreligious—not by force of study and reflection, but rather by the lapse of time—they at length attained to their infidel maturity. It is worthy of remark that where any are reclaimed from infidelity, it is generally by a process much more rational than that which has been here described. Something awakens them to reflection. They examine, they consider, and at length yield their assent to Christianity on what they deem sufficient grounds.

From the account here given, it appears plainly that infidelity is generally the offspring of prejudice and that its success is chiefly to be ascribed to the depravity of the moral character. This fact is confirmed by the undeniable truth that in *societies*, which consist of individuals, infidelity is the natural fruit not so much of a studious and disputatious as of a dissipated and vicious age. It diffuses itself in proportion as the general morals decline; and it is embraced with less apprehension when every infidel is kept in spirits by seeing many around him who are sharing fortunes with himself.

To any fair mind this consideration alone might be offered as suggesting a strong argument against infidelity and in favor of revelation. And the friends of Christianity might justly retort the charge, which their opponents often urge with no little affectation of superior wisdom, that we implicitly surrender ourselves to the influence of prejudice instead of examining dispassionately the ground of our faith and yielding our assent only according to the degree of evidence.

In our own days, when it is but too clear that infidelity increases, it is not in consequence of the reasonings of the infidel writers having been much studied, but from the progress of luxury and the decay of morals; and, so far as this increase may be traced at all to the works of skeptical writers, it has been produced not by argument and discussion but by sarcasms and points of wit which have operated on weak minds or on nominal Christians by bringing gradually into contempt opinions which, in their case, had only rested on the basis of blind respect and the prejudices of education. It may therefore be laid down as an axiom that *infidelity is, in general, a disease of the heart more than of the understanding.* If revelation were assailed only by reason and argument, it would have little to fear. The literary opposers of Christianity, from Herbert to Hume, have been seldom read. They made some stir in their day; during their span of existence, they were noisy and noxious; but like the locusts of the East, which for a while obscure the air and destroy the verdure, they were soon swept away and forgotten. Their very names would be scarcely found, if Leland had not preserved them from oblivion.[1]

TEXT: William Wilberforce, *A practical view of the prevailing religious system of professed Christians in the higher and middle classes in this country, contrasted with real Christianity*, 6th ed. (London: T. Cadell and W. Davies, 1798), 478–85.

[1]   [Ed. Wilberforce refers to the Presbyterian pastor and theologian John Leland, whose *A view of the principal deistical writers that have appeared in England in the last and present century* (1754), which appeared in several updated editions, identified contemporary opponents to Christian faith and practice.]

ROBERT HALL
(1764–1831)
Infidelity

Robert Hall was among the leading Baptist ministers and greatest orators of the early nineteenth century. Born at Arnesby, Leicestershire, Hall was a precocious child who was alleged to have composed hymns and read advanced theological works at an early age. In 1778 he was baptized at Arnesby. Hall entered the Baptist Academy at Bristol at the age of fourteen and began preparing for ministry. He attended Kings College, Aberdeen, on scholarship. After earning his M.A. degree in 1785, Hall began a preaching career that followed a circuit through Bristol (1785–1790), Cambridge (1791–1806), Leicester (1807–1825), and back to Bristol in the final years of his life (1826–1831). He was a Particular Baptist, reflecting the commitment to predestination found in much evangelicalism at this time, but theologically progressive on several contentious issues. He defended Joseph Priestley in *Christianity consistent with a love of freedom* (1791), argued for civil liberties in *Apology for the freedom of the press and for general liberty* (1793), and admonished those who denied communion to believers in infant baptism in *On terms of communion* (1815). Hall's willingness to diverge from strict Calvinism led some to question his Christian orthodoxy.

Hall's greatest work, *Modern infidelity* (1800), warns readers that the ideas of British skeptics such as David Hume lead to brazen immorality. Hall announces his work with the resonant words of Ephesians 2:12: "without God in the world," an indication that the violent revolution in France—including the execution of Louis XVI, the Reign of Terror, and the rise to power of Napoleon—continued to frighten English contemporaries as to the practical consequences of skepticism. Infidelity, he claims, rises from "the joint off-spring of an irreligious temper and unholy speculation" among critics more interested in "detecting the vices and imperfections of professing Christians" than "examining the evidences of Christianity" (12). In turn, Britain's "modern infidels" undermine morality as well as revelation in their effort to sever society from its Christian moorings. Hall matches a commitment to Christianity as the spiritual foundation for peace and good will with profound alarm over unbelief and the threat of political revolution.

ᔓᕽᐁᕽ

SOURCES: *BDE*; E. Paxton Hood, *Robert Hall* (London: Hodder and Stoughton, 1881); Graham W. Hughes, *Robert Hall* (London: Carey, 1943); *ODCC*; *ODNB*; Timothy Whelan, "'I am the greatest of the prophets': a new look at Robert Hall's mental breakdown, November 1804," *Baptist Quarterly* 42 (2007): 114–26.

ROBERT HALL
Modern infidelity
1800

As the Christian ministry is established for the instruction of men throughout every age in truth and holiness, it must adapt itself to the ever-shifting scenes of the moral world and stand ready to repel the attacks of impiety and error under whatever form they may appear. The church and the world form two societies so distinct and governed by such opposite principles and maxims that, as well from this contrariety as from the express warnings of Scripture, true Christians must look for a state of warfare—with this consoling assurance, that the church, like the burning bush beheld by Moses in the land of Midian, may be encompassed with flames, but will never be consumed [Exod 3].

When she was delivered from the persecuting power of Rome, she only experienced a change of trials. The oppression of external violence was followed by the more dangerous and insidious attacks of internal enemies. The freedom of inquiry claimed and asserted at the Reformation degenerated—in the hands of men who professed the principles without possessing the spirit of the Reformers—into a fondness for speculative refinements and consequently into a source of dispute, faction, and heresy. While Protestants attended more to the points on which they differed than to those in which they agreed, while more zeal was employed in settling ceremonies and defending subtleties than in enforcing plain revealed truths, the lovely fruits of peace and charity perished under the storms of controversy.

In this disjointed and disordered state of the Christian church, they who never looked into the interior of Christianity were apt to suspect that to a subject so fruitful in particular disputes must attach a general uncertainty, and that a religion founded on revelation could never have occasioned such discordance of principle and practice amongst its disciples. Thus infidelity is the joint offspring of an irreligious temper and unholy speculation employed not in examining the evidences of Christianity but in detecting the vices and imperfections of professing Christians. It has passed through various stages, each distinguished by higher gradations of impiety; for when men arrogantly abandon their guide and willfully shut their eyes on the light of heaven, it is wisely ordained that their errors

145

shall multiply at every step until their extravagance confutes itself and the mischief of their principles works its own antidote. That such has been the progress of infidelity will be obvious from a slight survey of its history.

Lord Herbert,[1] the first and purest of our English freethinkers, who flourished in the beginning of the reign of Charles the First, did not so much impugn the doctrine or the morality of the Scriptures, as attempt to supersede their necessity by endeavoring to show that the great principles of the unity of God, a moral government, and a future world are taught with sufficient clearness by the light of nature. Bolingbroke[2] and others of his successors advanced much further and attempted to invalidate the proofs of the moral character of the Deity, and consequently all expectations of rewards and punishments, leaving the supreme Being no other perfections than those which belong to a first cause or almighty contriver. After him, at a considerable distance, followed Hume,[3] the most subtle, if not the most philosophical of the Deists, who, by perplexing the relations of cause and effect, boldly aimed to introduce an universal skepticism and to pour a more-than-Egyptian darkness into the whole region of morals. Since his time, skeptical writers have sprung up in abundance and infidelity has allured multitudes to its standard; the young and superficial by its dexterous sophistry, the vain by the literary fame of its champions, and the profligate by the licentiousness of its principles. Atheism, the most undisguised, has at length begun to make its appearance.

Animated by numbers and emboldened by success, the infidels of the present day have given a new direction to their efforts and impressed a new character on the ever-growing mass of their impious speculations.

By uniting more closely with each other, by giving a sprinkling of irreligion to all their literary productions, they aim to engross the formation of the public mind and, amidst the warmest professions of attachment to virtue, to effect an entire disruption of morality from religion. Pretending to be the teachers of virtue and the guides of life, they propose to revolutionize the morals of mankind, to regenerate the world by a process entirely new, and to rear the temple of virtue—not merely without the aid of religion, but on the renunciation of its principles and the derision of its sanctions. Their party has derived a great accession of numbers and strength from events the most momentous and astonishing in the political world, which have divided the sentiments of Europe betwixt hope and terror, and, however they may issue, have, for the present, swelled the ranks of infidelity. So rapidly, indeed, has it advanced since this crisis that a great majority on the continent—and in England a considerable proportion—of those who pursue literature as a profession may justly be considered as the open or disguised abettors of atheism.

‡

[1]   [Ed. Edward Herbert (1582–1648), first Lord Herbert of Cherbury, was a forerunner of English Deism.]

[2]   [Ed. Henry St. John (1678–1751), first Viscount Bolingbroke, was a Deist and author of the noted *Reflections concerning innate moral principles* (1752).]

[3]   [Ed. David Hume (1711–1776), Scottish philosopher and prominent skeptic, received many of the most hostile reviews in the period.]

Settle it therefore in your minds as a maxim never to be effaced or forgotten that atheism is an inhuman, bloody, ferocious system, equally hostile to every useful restraint and to every virtuous affection; that—leaving nothing above us to excite awe, nor around us to awaken tenderness—it wages war with heaven and with earth. Its first object is to dethrone God, its next to destroy man.

‡

Religion being primarily intended to make men "wise unto salvation" [2 Tim 3:15], the support it ministers to social order, the stability it confers on government and laws, is a subordinate species of advantage which we should have continued to enjoy without reflecting on its cause but for the development of deistical principles and the experiment which has been made of their effects in a neighboring country.[4] It had been the constant boast of infidels that their system, more liberal and generous than Christianity, needed but to be tried to produce an immense accession to human happiness; and Christian nations, careless and supine, retaining little of religion but the profession, and disgusted with its restraints, lent a favorable ear to these pretensions. God permitted the trial to be made. In one country—and that the center of Christendom—revelation underwent a total eclipse; while atheism, performing on a darkened theater its strange and fearful tragedy, confounded the first elements of society, blended every age, rank, and sex in indiscriminate prescription and massacre, and convulsed all Europe to its center that the imperishable memorial of these events might teach the last generations of mankind to consider religion as the pillar of society, the safeguard of nations, the parent of social order, which alone has power to curb the fury of the passions and secure to everyone his rights: to the laborious, the reward of their industry; to the rich, the enjoyment of their wealth; to nobles, the preservation of their honors; and to princes, the stability of their thrones.

We might ask the patrons of infidelity, what fury impels them to attempt the subversion of Christianity? Is it that they have discovered a better system? To what virtues are their principles favorable, or is there one which Christians have not carried to a higher perfection than any of whom their party can boast? Have they discovered a more excellent rule of life or a better hope in death than that which the Scriptures suggest? Above all, what are the pretensions on which they rest their claims to be the guides of mankind; or which embolden them to expect we should trample upon the experience of ages and abandon a religion which has been attested by a train of miracles and prophecies, in which millions of our forefathers have found a refuge in every trouble and consolation in the hour of death; a religion which has been adorned with the highest sanctity of character and splendor of talents, which enrolls amongst its disciples the names of Bacon, Newton, and Locke—the glory of their species—and to which these illustrious men were proud to dedicate the last and best fruits of their immortal genius?[5]

If the question at issue is to be decided by argument, nothing can be added to the triumph of Christianity; if by an appeal to authority, what have our adversaries to oppose to these great names? Where are the infidels of such pure, uncontaminated morals, unshaken probity, and attended benevolence that we should be in danger of being seduced

---

4   [Ed. Hall refers to France and the notorious excesses of the French Revolution.]
5   [Ed. Francis Bacon (1561–1626), Sir Isaac Newton (1642–1727), and John Locke (1632–1704).]

into impiety by their example? Into what obscure recesses of misery, into what dungeons have their philanthropists penetrated to lighten the fetters and relieve the sorrows of the helpless captive? What barbarous tribes have their apostles visited, what distant climes have they explored, encompassed with cold, nakedness, and want to diffuse principles of virtue and the blessings of civilization? Or will they rather choose to waive their pretensions to this extraordinary, and in their eyes, eccentric species of benevolence (for infidels, we know, are sworn enemies to enthusiasm of every sort), and rest their character on their political exploits, on their efforts to reanimate the virtue of a sinking state, to restrain licentiousness, to calm the tumult of popular fury, and—by inculcating the spirit of justice, moderation, and pity for fallen greatness—to mitigate the inevitable horrors of revolution? Our adversaries will at least have the discretion, if not the modesty, to recede from this test.

More than all, their infatuated eagerness, their parricidal zeal to extinguish a sense of deity, must excite astonishment and horror. Is the idea of an almighty and perfect Ruler unfriendly to any passion which is confident with innocence or an obstruction to any design which it is not shameful to avow? Eternal God! On what are thine enemies intent? What are those enterprises of guilt and horror that, for the safety of their performers, require to be enveloped in a darkness which the eye of heaven must not pierce! Miserable men! Proud of being the offspring of chance; in love with universal disorder, whose happiness is involved in the belief of there being no witness to their designs, and who are at ease only because they suppose themselves inhabitants of a forsaken and fatherless world!

TEXT: Robert Hall, *Modern infidelity considered with respect to its influence on society, in a sermon preached at the Baptist meeting, Cambridge*, 3rd ed. (Cambridge: M. Watson, 1800), 11–15, 51, 72–76.

WILLIAM PALEY
(1743–1805)
Evil

For much of the nineteenth century, almost every student at Cambridge studied the writings of the Christian apologist and Utilitarian thinker William Paley. Born at Peterborough, in 1759 he matriculated at Christ's College, Cambridge, where he studied natural sciences, logic, and metaphysics, and in 1761 received the highest mathematical award at Cambridge: the Bunting scholarship. He was elected a fellow of Christ's College in 1766, ordained priest in 1767, and made archdeacon of Carlisle in 1782. His abilities as a lecturer attracted attention across Cambridge. Professors adopted Paley's first book, *The Principles of moral and political philosophy* (1785), almost immediately. Unlike Bentham, Paley incorporated traditional Christian beliefs about the afterlife into his Utilitarian ethics. Paley's defense of Christianity informed his *Horae Paulinae* (1790), which examined the historicity of the New Testament through a critical, comparative study of Paul's writings. His *A view of the evidences of Christianity* (1794), yet another response to Hume's critique, examined the standard arguments for the truth of Christianity. The work solidified Paley's reputation as a leading philosopher and theologian in England.

Paley's *Natural theology* (1802) developed a case for the existence of God based on evidences from nature. The work—which should be read, in part, as a response to David Hume's *Dialogues concerning natural religion* (1779)—begins with the famous analogy of the watch: "In crossing a heath, suppose I pitched my foot against a stone and were asked how the stone came to be there, I might possibly answer that, for anything I knew to the contrary, it had lain there forever . . . But suppose I had found a *watch* upon the ground, and it should be inquired how the watch happened to be in that place, I should hardly think of the answer which I have before given, that, for anything I knew, the watch might have always been there" (1–2). Paley's text quickly became a standard work of Christian apologetics and natural theology. Each chapter reviews different cases of apparent design in nature—from the plant and animal worlds to the intricate structures of the human body. In the following selection, Paley concludes *Natural theology* with a defense of divine benevolence. While Hume's *Dialogues* had alleged the incompatibility of the existence of evil and the goodness of God, Paley contends that many natural evils—such as apparent imperfections, finitude, and pain—are the result of intentional gradations in creation. The death of loved ones, for example, leads to suffering among the living, but the pain of grief is merely a consequence of the gift of rationality. Civil evils based on inequality, by contrast, result from class distinctions that *"must* be found" in every country (540); war, tyranny, and rebellion result from human rationality and free agency—and these by divine intent.

SOURCES: John T. Baldwin, "God and the world: William Paley's argument from perfection tradition—a continuing influence," *Harvard Theological Review* 85 (1992): 109–20; Cragg; D. L. LeMahieu, *The mind of William Paley: a philosopher and his age* (Lincoln: University of Nebraska Press, 1976); Nockles; *ODCC*; *ODNB*; *RCBEC*.

WILLIAM PALEY
Natural theology
1802

Of the *origin of evil* no universal solution has been discovered. I mean no solution which reaches to all cases of complaint. The most comprehensive is that which arises from the consideration of *general rules*. We may, I think, without much difficulty, be brought to admit the four following points. First, that important advantages may accrue to the universe from the order of nature proceeding according to general laws. Secondly, that general laws, however well set and constituted, often thwart and cross one another. Thirdly, that from these thwartings and crossings frequent particular inconveniences will arise. And, fourthly, that it agrees with our observation to suppose that some degree of these inconveniences takes place in the works of nature. These points may be allowed; and it may also be asserted that the general laws with which we are acquainted are directed to beneficial ends. On the other hand, with many of these laws we are not acquainted at all, or we are totally unable to trace them in their branches and in their operation; the effect of which ignorance is that they cannot be of importance to us as measures by which to regulate our conduct. . . . The consideration, therefore, of general laws, although it may concern the question of the origin of evil very nearly (which I think it does), rests in views disproportionate to our faculties and in a knowledge which we do not possess. It serves rather to account for the obscurity of the subject than to supply us with distinct answers to our difficulties. However, whilst we assent to the above-stated propositions as principles, whatever uncertainty we may find in the application, we lay a ground for believing that cases of apparent evil for which *we* can suggest no particular reason are governed by reasons which are more general, which lie deeper in the order of second causes, and on that account are removed to a greater distance from us.

‡

Of *bodily pain* the principal observation, no doubt, is that which we have already made and already dwelt upon, viz. "that it is seldom the object of contrivance;[1] that, when it is so, the contrivance rests ultimately in good."

To which, however, may be added that the annexing of pain to the means of destruction is a salutary provision, inasmuch as it teaches vigilance and caution, both gives notice of danger and excites those endeavors which may be necessary to preservation. The evil consequence which sometimes arises from the want of that timely intimation of danger which pain gives is known to the inhabitants of cold countries by the example of frostbitten limbs. I have conversed with patients who have lost toes and fingers by this cause. They have in general told me that they were totally unconscious of any local uneasiness at the time. Some I have heard declare that, whilst they were about their employment, neither their situation nor the state of the air was unpleasant. They felt no pain; they suspected no mischief, till, by the application of warmth, they discovered, too late, the fatal injury which some of their extremities had suffered. I say that this shows the use of pain and that we stand in need of such a monitor. I believe also that the use extends further than we suppose or can now trace; that to disagreeable sensations we and all animals owe or have owed many habits of action which are salutary, but which are become so familiar as not easily to be referred to their origin.

Pain also itself is not without its *alleviations.* It may be violent and frequent, but it is seldom both violent and long continued; and its pauses and intermissions become positive pleasures. It has the power of shedding a satisfaction over intervals of ease, which, I believe, few enjoyments exceed. A man resting from a fit of the stone or gout is, for the time, in possession of feelings which undisturbed health cannot impart. They may be dearly bought, but still they are to be set against the price. And, indeed, it depends upon the duration and urgency of the pain, whether they be dearly bought or not. I am far from being sure that a man is not a gainer by suffering a moderate interruption of bodily ease for a couple of hours out of the four-and-twenty. Two very common observations favor this opinion. One is that remissions of pain call forth from those who experience them stronger expressions of satisfaction and of gratitude towards both the author and the instruments of their relief than are excited by advantages of any other kind. The second is that the spirits of sick men do not sink in proportion to the acuteness of their sufferings, but rather appear to be roused and supported, not by pain, but by the high degree of comfort which they derive from its cessation—whenever that occurs—and which they taste with a relish that diffuses some portion of mental complacency over the whole of that mixed state of sensations in which disease has placed them.

In connection with bodily pain may be considered bodily *disease,* whether painful or not. Few diseases are fatal. I have before me the account of a dispensary in the neighborhood which states six years' experience as follows: "admitted 6,420—*cured* 5,476—dead 234." And this I suppose nearly to agree with what other similar institutions exhibit. Now, in all these cases, some disorder must have been felt or the patients would not have applied for a remedy; yet we see how large a proportion of the maladies which were brought forward have either yielded to proper treatment or, what is more probable, ceased of their own accord. . . .

---

[1] [Ed. A divine scheme or plot.]

Of *mortal* diseases the great use is to reconcile us to death. The horror of death proves the value of life. But it is in the power of disease to abate or even extinguish this horror, which it does in a wonderful manner, and, oftentimes, by a mild and imperceptible gradation. Every man who has been placed in a situation to observe it is surprised with the change which has been wrought in himself when he compares the view which he entertains of death upon a sickbed with the heart-sinking dismay with which he should some time ago have met it in health. There is no similitude between the sensations of a man led to execution and the calm expiring of a patient at the close of his disease. Death to him is only the last of a long train of changes in his progress through which it is possible that he may experience no shocks or sudden transitions.

Death itself, as a mode of removal and of succession, is so connected with the whole order of our animal world that almost everything in that world must be changed to be able to do without it. It may seem likewise impossible to separate the fear of death from the enjoyment of life or the perception of that fear from rational natures. Brutes are in a great measure delivered from all anxiety on this account by the inferiority of their faculties; or rather, they seem to be armed with the apprehension of death just sufficiently to put them upon the means of preservation and no further. But would a human being wish to purchase this immunity by the loss of those mental powers which enable him to look forward to the future?

Death implies *separation*, and the loss of those whom we love must necessarily be accompanied with pain. To the brute creation nature seems to have stepped in with some secret provision for their relief under the rupture of their attachments. In their instincts towards their offspring and of their offspring to them, I have often been surprised to observe how ardently they love and how soon they forget. The pertinacity of human sorrow (upon which time also, at length, lays its softening hand) is probably, therefore, in some manner connected with the qualities of our rational or moral nature. One thing, however, is clear, viz. that it is better that we should possess affections (the sources of so many virtues and so many joys), although they be exposed to the incidents of life as well as the interruptions of mortality, than by the want of them be reduced to a state of selfishness, apathy, and quietism.

‡

As we approach the summits of human greatness, the comparison of good and evil with respect to personal comfort becomes still more problematical—even allowing to ambition all its pleasures. The poet asks, "What is grandeur, what is power?"[2] The philosopher answers, "Constraint and plague; *et in maxima quaque fortuna minimum licere.*"[3] One very common error misleads the opinion of mankind upon this head, viz. that, universally, authority is pleasant, submission painful. In the general course of human affairs, the very reverse of this is nearer to the truth. Command is anxiety, obedience ease.

Artificial distinctions sometimes promote real equality. Whether they be hereditary or be the homage paid to office or the respect attached by public opinion to particular

---

[2]   [Ed. Thomas Gray, "Ode for music" (performed in the Senate House at Cambridge, 1769), 5.1.]
[3]   [Ed. The Latin (from Cicero) may be translated, "They that stand on the pinnacle of fortune are the least free."]

professions, they serve to *confront* that grand and unavoidable distinction which arises from property and which is most overbearing where there is no other. It is of the nature of property not only to be irregularly distributed but to run into large masses. Public laws should be so constructed as to favor its diffusion as much as they can. But all that can be done by laws, consistently with that degree of government over his property which ought to be left to the subject, will not be sufficient to counteract this tendency. There must always therefore be the difference between rich and poor; and this difference will be the more grinding when no pretension is allowed to be set up against it.

So that the evils, if evils they must be called, which spring either from the necessary subordinations of civil life or from the distinctions which have naturally, though not necessarily, grown up in most societies, so long as they are unaccompanied by privileges injurious or oppressive to the rest of the community, are such as may, even by the most depressed ranks, be endured with very little prejudice to their comfort.

The mischiefs of which mankind are the occasion to one another—by their private wickednesses and cruelties, by tyrannical exercises of power, by rebellions against just authority, by wars, by national jealousies and competitions operating to the destruction of third countries, or by other instances of misconduct either in individuals or societies—are all to be resolved into the character of man as a *free agent*. Free agency in its very essence contains liability to abuse. Yet, if you deprive man of his free agency, you subvert his nature. You may have order from him and regularity, as you may from the tides or the trade winds, but you put an end to his moral character, to virtue, to merit, to accountableness, to the use indeed of reason. To which must be added the observation that even the bad qualities of mankind have an origin in their good ones. . . . Human passions are either necessary to human welfare or capable of being made and, in a great majority of instances, in fact, made conducive to its happiness. These passions are strong and general; and, perhaps, would not answer their purpose unless they were so. But strength and generality . . . become, if left to themselves, excess and misdirection.

>︵⌣︵<

Text: William Paley, *Natural theology; or, Evidences of the existence and attributes of the Deity, collected from the appearances of nature*, 2nd ed. (London: R. Faulder, 1802), 527–29, 531–37, 545–47.

RICHARD WHATELY
(1787–1863)
Miracles and Testimony

Richard Whately, one of the so-called Noetics at Oxford, represents the rise of a group of like-minded, Church of England intellectuals writing in defense of Christianity against the tide of skepticism. Whately was born at Cavendish Square, London, into a family who had strong political and ecclesial connections. He matriculated at Oriel College, Oxford in 1805 and graduated with the B.A. (1808) and M.A. (1812). A fellow of Oriel from 1811 until his marriage in 1821, Whately returned to Oxford in 1825 after his mentor Edward Copleston assumed the chancellorship of the University and named Whately principal of St. Alban Hall. With the help of a young John Henry Newman, Whately improved the academic reputation of St. Alban. A prodigious writer, he emerged as a leading intellectual in the liberal-minded Noetic circle, publishing numerous works that established his theological reputation, including *Essays on some of the peculiarities of the Christian religion* (1825), *Essays on some of the difficulties of the writings of St. Paul* (1828), and *The errors of Romanism traced to their origin in human nature* (1830). In 1831 the prime minister appointed Whately archbishop of Dublin. He participated in church reform, challenged the leaders of the Oxford Movement, and contributed to the national conversation on religious education during an especially challenging period of ecclesial history.

Whately's first major publication, *Historic doubts relative to Napoleon Buonaparte* (1819), opposes David Hume's critique of religion and miracles. Whately's work began as an answer to a September 1814 essay in the *Edinburgh Review* that praised Hume's philosophical contribution. Whatley's book is a satirical attempt to deny the historicity of Napoleon—the accounts of his achievements being no more plausible than Hume found apostolic testimony regarded biblical miracles and the life of Christ. Whately made no secret of his intention: his style of argumentation closely follows Hume's works, and he includes numerous quotations from Hume's "Essay on Miracles" in the footnotes (most have been removed from the present edition). Whately's *Historic doubts* may be among the most creative responses to Hume's work in the decades following the philosopher's death.

SOURCES: Donald H. Akenson, *A Protestant in purgatory: Richard Whately, archbishop of Dublin* (Hamden, Conn.: Archon, 1981); Boyd Hilton, *The age of atonement: the influence of evangelicalism on social and economic thought, 1795–1865* (Oxford: Clarendon, 1988); *ODCC*; *ODNB*; *VC*.

RICHARD WHATELY

Historic doubts relative to Napoleon Buonaparte
1819

Long as the public attention has been occupied by the extraordinary personage from whose ambition we are supposed to have so narrowly escaped, the subject seems to have lost scarcely anything of its interest. We are still occupied in recounting the exploits, discussing the character, inquiring into the present situation, and even conjecturing as to the future prospects of Napoleon Bonaparte.

Nor is this at all to be wondered at, if we consider the very extraordinary nature of those exploits and of that character: their greatness and extensive importance, as well as the unexampled strangeness of the events, and also that strong additional stimulant, the mysterious uncertainty that hangs over the character of the man. If it be doubtful whether any history (exclusive of such as is avowedly fabulous) ever attributed to its hero such a series of wonderful achievements compressed into so small a space of time, it is certain that to no one were ever assigned so many dissimilar characters. . . . Neither the friends nor the enemies of Philip of Macedon or of Julius Caesar ever questioned their *courage* or their *military skill.*[1] With Bonaparte, however, it has been otherwise. This obscure Corsican adventurer—a man, according to some, of extraordinary talents and courage; according to others, of very moderate abilities and a rank coward—advanced rapidly in the French army, obtained a high command, gained a series of important victories, and, elated by success, embarked in an expedition against Egypt, which was planned and conducted, according to some, with the most consummate skill; according to others, with the utmost wildness and folly. He was unsuccessful, however, and leaving the army of Egypt in a very distressed situation, he returned to France and found the nation, or at least the army, so favorably disposed towards him that he was enabled with the utmost ease to overthrow the existing government and obtain for himself the supreme power: at first under the modest appellation of Consul, but afterwards with the more sounding[2] title of Emperor.

---

[1] [Ed. Philip II of Macedon (382–336 B.C.), father of Alexander the Great; Julius Caesar (100–44 B.C.).]

[2] [Ed. Sounding imposing but insubstantial.]

While in possession of this power, he overthrew the most powerful coalitions of the other European states against him, and though driven from the sea by the British fleets, overran nearly the whole continent triumphant; finishing a war, not infrequently in a single campaign, he entered the capitals of most of the hostile potentates, deposed and created kings at his pleasure, and appeared the virtual sovereign of the chief part of the continent, from the frontiers of Spain to those of Russia. Even those countries we find him invading with prodigious armies—defeating their forces, penetrating to their capitals, and threatening their total subjugation—but at Moscow his progress is stopped. A winter of unusual severity, cooperating with the efforts of the Russians, totally destroys his enormous host; and the German sovereigns throw off the yoke and combine to oppose him. He raises another vast army which is also ruined at Leipzig; and again another, with which, like a second Antaeus,[3] he for some time maintains himself in France, but is finally defeated, deposed, and banished to the island of Elba, of which the sovereignty is conferred on him. Thence he returns in about nine months at the head of 600 men to attempt the deposition of King Louis,[4] who had been peaceably recalled; the French nation declares in his favor, and he is reinstated without a struggle. He raises another great army to oppose the allied powers, which is totally defeated at Waterloo. He is a second time deposed, surrenders to the British, and is placed in confinement at the island of St. Helena. Such is the outline of the eventful history presented to us; in the detail of which, however, there is almost every conceivable variety of statement, while the motives and conduct of the chief actor are involved in still greater doubt, and the subject of still more eager controversy.

‡

Let those then who pretend to philosophical freedom of inquiry—who scorn to rest their opinions on popular belief and to shelter themselves under the example of the unthinking multitude—consider carefully, each one for himself, what is the evidence proposed to himself in particular for the existence of such a person as Napoleon Bonaparte (I do not mean whether there ever was a person bearing that *name*, for that is a question of no consequence, but whether any such person ever performed all the wonderful things attributed to him). Let him then weigh well the objections to that evidence (of which, I have given but a hasty and imperfect sketch) and if he then finds it amount to anything more than a probability, I have only to congratulate him on his easy faith.

But the same testimony which would have great weight in establishing a thing intrinsically probable will lose part of this weight in proportion as the matter attested is improbable and, if adduced in support of anything that is at variance with uniform experience, will be rejected at once by all sound reasoners. Let us then consider what sort of a story it is that is proposed to our acceptance. How grossly contradictory are the reports of the different authorities, I have already remarked. But consider by itself the story told by any one of them; it carries an air of fiction and romance on the very face of it; all the events

---

3   [Ed. In Greek mythology Antaeus wrestled opponents and slaughtered them upon defeat. Hercules defeated the giant, however, upon realizing that his powers of rejuvenation ceased when Antaeus was held in the air and separated from the earth.]

4   [Ed. King Louis XVIII (1755–1824) reigned in France between 1814 and 1824—with the exception of the Hundred Days of 1815, when Napoleon attempted to reestablish his empire.]

are great, and splendid, and marvelous;[5] great armies, great victories, great frosts, great reverses, "hairbreadth escapes," empires subverted in a few days; everything happening in defiance of political calculations and in opposition to the *experience* of past times; everything upon that grand scale, so common in epic poetry, so rare in real life; and thus calculated to strike the imagination of the vulgar and to remind the sober-thinking few of *The Arabian Nights*.[6] Every event too has that roundness and completeness which is so characteristic of fiction; nothing is done by halves; we have *complete* victories—*total* overthrows, *entire* subversion of empires, *perfect* reestablishments of them—crowded upon us in rapid succession. To enumerate the improbabilities of each of the several parts of this history would fill volumes; but they are so fresh in everyone's memory that there is no need of such a detail. Let any judicious man, not ignorant of history and of human nature, revolve them in his mind and consider how far they are conformable to experience,[7] our best and only sure guide. In vain will he seek in history for something similar to this wonderful Bonaparte: "naught but himself can be his parallel."[8]

Will the conquests of Alexander[9] be compared with his? They were effected over a rabble of effeminate undisciplined barbarians; else his progress would hardly have been so rapid. Witness his father Philip, who was much longer occupied in subduing the comparatively insignificant territory of the warlike and civilized Greeks, notwithstanding their being divided into numerous petty states, whose mutual jealousy enabled him to contend with them separately. But the Greeks had never made such progress in arts and arms as the great and powerful states of Europe, which Bonaparte is represented as so speedily overpowering. His empire has been compared to the Roman. Mark the contrast. He gains in a few years that dominion, or at least control, over Germany—wealthy, civilized, and powerful—which the Romans in the plenitude of their power could not obtain during a struggle of as many centuries against the ignorant half-savages who then possessed it!

Another peculiar circumstance in the history of this extraordinary personage is that when it is found convenient to represent him as defeated—though he is by no means defeated by halves, but involved in much more sudden and total ruin than the personages of real history usually meet with—yet, if it is thought fit he should be restored, it is done as quickly and completely as if Merlin's rod had been employed. . . . Does anyone believe all this and yet refuse to believe a miracle? Or, rather, what is this but a miracle? Is it not a violation of the laws of nature? For surely there are moral laws of nature as well as physical, which, though more liable to exceptions in this or that particular case, are no less true as general rules than the laws of matter and therefore cannot be violated and

---

[5]   "Suppose, for instance, that the fact which the testimony endeavors to establish partakes of the extraordinary and the marvelous; in that case, the evidence resulting from the testimony receives a diminution, greater or less, in proportion as the fact is more or less unusual" (Hume's *Essay on miracles*).

[6]   [Ed. For more on the history and disparate translations of *The Arabian Nights*, see Saree Makdisi and Felicity Nussbaum, eds., *The Arabian Nights in historical context: between East and West* (Oxford: Oxford University Press, 2008).]

[7]   "The ultimate standard by which we determine all disputes that may arise is always derived from experience and observation" (Hume's *Essay on miracles*).

[8]   [Ed. *Memoirs of the life and writings of Alexander Pope*, ed. William Ayre (London, 1745), 2:12.]

[9]   [Ed. Alexander III of Macedon (356–323 B.C.), commonly known as "Alexander the Great."]

contradicted beyond a certain point without a miracle.[10]. . . Wherever we turn to seek for circumstances that may help to account for the events of this incredible story, we only meet with such as aggravate its improbability. Had it been told of some distant country, at a remote period, we could not have told what peculiar circumstances there might have been to render probable what seems to us most strange; and yet in that case every philosophical skeptic, every freethinking speculator, would instantly have rejected such a history as utterly unworthy of credit. What, for instance, would the great Hume or any of the philosophers of his school have said if they had found in the antique records of any nation such a passage as this:

> There was a certain man of Corsica whose name was Napoleon, and he was one of the chief captains of the host of the French; and he gathered together an army, and went and fought against Egypt: but when the king of Britain heard thereof, he sent ships of war and valiant men to fight against the French in Egypt. So they warred against them, and prevailed, and strengthened the hands of the rulers of the land against the French, and drove away Napoleon from before the city of Acre. Then Napoleon left the captains and the army that were in Egypt, and fled, and returned back to France. So the French people took Napoleon and made him ruler over them, and he became exceeding great, insomuch that there was none like him of all that had ruled over France before.

What, I say, would Hume have thought of this, especially if he had been told that it was at this day generally credited? Would he not have confessed that he had been mistaken in supposing there was a peculiarly blind credulity and prejudice in favor of everything that is accounted sacred; for that, since even professed skeptics swallow implicitly such a story as this, it appears there must be a still blinder prejudice in favor of everything that is *not* accounted sacred.

‡

Now if a freethinking philosopher, one of those who advocate the cause of unbiased reason and despised pretended revelations, were to meet with such a tissue of absurdities as this in an old Jewish record, would he not reject it at once as too palpable an imposture to deserve even any inquiry into its evidence? Is that credible then of the civilized Europeans now, which could not, if reported of the semi-barbarous Jews 3,000 years ago, be established by any testimony? Will it be answered that "there is nothing *supernatural* in all this?"[11] Why is it then that you object to what is *supernatural*—that you reject every account of miracles—if not because they are improbable? Surely then a story equally or still more improbable is not to be implicitly received merely on the ground that it is not miraculous; though in fact, as I have already . . . shown from Hume's authority, it really is miraculous. The opposition to experience has been proved to be as complete in this case as in what are commonly called miracles; and the reasons assigned for that contrariety by the

---

[10]   This doctrine, though hardly needing confirmation from authority, is supported by that of Hume . . . Accordingly, in the tenth essay, his use of the term "miracle," after having called it "a transgression of a law of nature," plainly shows that he meant to include *human* nature . . .

[11]   [Ed. David Hume, *Essay on miracles*.]

defenders of them cannot be pleaded in the present instance. If then philosophers, who reject every wonderful story that is maintained by priests, are yet found ready to believe everything else, however improbable, they will surely lay themselves open to the accusation brought against them of being unduly prejudiced against whatever relates to religion.

‡

I call upon those therefore who profess themselves advocates of free inquiry—who disdain to be carried along with the stream of popular opinion, and who will listen to no testimony that runs counter to experience—to follow up their own principles fairly and consistently. Let the same mode of argument be adopted in all cases alike; and then it can no longer be attributed to hostile prejudice, but to enlarged and philosophical views. If they have already rejected some histories on the ground of their being strange and marvelous—of their relating facts, unprecedented, and at variance with the established course of nature—let them not give credit to another history which lies open to the very same objections—the extraordinary and romantic tale we have been just considering. If they have discredited the testimony of witnesses, who are said at least to have been disinterested, and to have braved persecutions and death in support of their assertions, can these philosophers consistently listen to and believe the testimony of those who avowedly get money by the tales they publish and who do not even pretend that they incur any serious risk in case of being detected in a falsehood? If in other cases they have refused to listen to an account which has passed through many intermediate hands before it reaches them and which is defended by those who have an interest in maintaining it, let them consider through how many, and what very suspicious hands, this story has arrived to them without the possibility (as I have shown) of tracing it back to any decidedly authentic source after all;[12] and likewise how strong an interest, in every way, those who have hitherto imposed on them have in keeping up the imposture. Let them, in short, show themselves as ready to detect the cheats and despise the fables of politicians as of priests. But if they are still wedded to the popular belief in this point, let them be consistent enough to admit the same evidence in other cases which they yield to in this. If, after all that has been said, they cannot bring themselves to doubt of the existence of Napoleon Bonaparte, they must at least acknowledge that they do not apply to that question the same plan of reasoning which they have made use of in others, and they are consequently bound in reason and in honesty to renounce it altogether.

TEXT: [Richard Whately,] *Historic doubts relative to Napoleon Buonaparte* (London: J. Hatchard, 1819), 1–5, 24–34, 38–39, 46–48.

---

[12]   For let it not be forgotten that these writers themselves refer to no better authority than that of an unnamed and unknown foreign correspondent.

JEREMY BENTHAM
(1748–1832)
Pain and the Afterlife

John Stuart Mill once claimed that everyone in England during the early nineteenth century was a follower of either Jeremy Bentham or Samuel Taylor Coleridge. The former, the father of Utilitarianism, was born in London. Bentham studied at Westminster, where he excelled in Greek and Latin, and matriculated at Queen's College, Oxford in 1760, receiving his B.A. in 1764 and M.A. in 1767. He then studied law at Lincoln's Inn, during which time he became increasingly radical in his political and economic opinions. Bentham's most celebrated work, *An introduction to the principles of morals and legislation* (1789), famously based morality on pleasure and pain. In later years, pursuing increasingly radical political proposals, he published *Plan of parliamentary reform* (1817), founded the *Westminster Review* (1823), and attempted to influence the codification of laws in numerous governments worldwide. Influenced in part by his friend Southwood Smith, who wrote on the need for cadavers for advanced medical training, Bentham's will instructed that his body be dissected in front of his friends, reconstructed with wires, and placed in effigy in a glass-front case (the auto-icon remains on display at University College, London).

Many of Bentham's close associates revised drafts of his works and prepared them for publication. George Grote (1794–1871), a historian and political philosopher in his own right, contributed to Bentham's *Analysis of the influence of natural religion on the temporal happiness of mankind* (1822)—the authorship of the work remains a matter of some dispute, but there is little doubt that Bentham's drafts provide its basis. In order to avoid prosecution for blasphemy, the two men published the volume under the pseudonym Philip Beauchamp. In the fashion of Utilitarianism, Bentham claims that religion (by which he means both natural and revealed) is pernicious, and religious hope for future rewards or punishments in the afterlife only leads to pain and misery in the present. Against both deistic and orthodox claims that evidence of design in the universe points to a benevolent Deity, Bentham maintains that believers live in a state of apprehension that disables true virtue in the present life. Self-denial, ascetic privations, and unwarranted beliefs harm both individuals and society by diminishing the value of experience in the formation of morality. In the following selection, Bentham argues that pain is the natural state of the human and postulates that religion's promise of a postmortem future leads to fear rather than hope.

Sources: M. L. Clarke, *George Grote: a biography* (London: Athlone, 1962); James E. Crimmins, *Secular utilitarianism: social science and the critique of religion in the thought of Jeremy Bentham* (Oxford: Clarendon, 1990); Boyd Hilton, *The age of atonement: the influence of evangelicalism on social and economic thought, 1795–1865* (Oxford: Clarendon, 1988); *ODNB*; *RCBEC*.

JEREMY BENTHAM

Analysis of the influence of natural religion on the temporal happiness
of mankind
1822

The pains and pleasures which are believed to await us in a posthumous existence may be anticipated either as conditional and dependent upon the present behavior of the believer, or as unconditional dispensations which no conduct on his part can either amend or aggravate. Though perhaps it is impossible to produce any case in which the belief has actually assumed this latter shape, yet it will be expedient to survey it in this most general and indeterminate form before we introduce the particular circumstances which have usually accompanied the reception of it. A few considerations will suffice to ascertain whether expectations of posthumous pains and pleasures, considered in themselves and without any reference to the direction which they may give to human conduct, are of a nature to occasion happiness or misery to the believer.

Nothing can be more undeniable than that a posthumous existence, if sincerely anticipated, is most likely to appear replete with impending pain and misery. The demonstration is brief and decisive.

A posthumous state of existence is necessarily unknown and impervious to human vision. We cannot see the ground which is before us. We possess not the slightest means of knowing whether it resembles that which we have already trodden. The scene before us is wrapped in impenetrable darkness. In this state of obscurity and ignorance, the imagination usurps the privilege of filling up the void, and what are the scenes which she portrays? They are similar to those with which the mind is overrun during a state of earthly darkness—the product of unmixed timidity and depression. Fear is the never-failing companion and offspring of ignorance, and the circumstances of human life infallibly give birth to such a communion. For the painful sensations are the most obtrusive and constant assailants which lie in ambush round our path. The first years of our life are spent in suffering under their sting, before we acquire the means of warding them off. The sole acquisition applicable to this purpose is knowledge—knowledge of the precise manner and occasion in which we are threatened, and of the antidote which may obviate it. Still however the painful sensations are continually on the watch to take advantage of every unguarded moment, nor is there a single hour of our life in which the lessons of experience are not indispensably necessary for our protection against them.

Since then it is only to knowledge that we owe our respite from perpetual suffering, wherever our knowledge fails us and we are reduced to a state of unprotected helplessness, all our sense of security, all anticipations of future ease, must vanish along with it. Ignorance must generate incessant alarm and uneasiness. The regular economy of the universe—by which nature is subjected to general laws, and the past becomes the interpreter of the future—is often adduced as a reason for extolling the beneficence of the Deity; and a reliance on the stability of *events*, as well as in the efficacy of the provision we have made against the future, is justly regarded as the most indispensable ingredient in human happiness. Had we no longer any confident expectation that tomorrow would resemble yesterday, were we altogether without any rule for predicting what would occur to us after this night, how shocking would be our alarm and depression? The unknown future which was about to succeed would be pregnant to our affrighted imaginations with calamity from which we knew not how to shelter ourselves. Infants are timorous to a proverb, and perhaps there is scarcely any man possessed of vision whom darkness does not impress with some degree of apprehension and uneasiness. Yet if a man fancies himself unsheltered when only the visible prognostics of impending evil are effaced, while all his other means of foresight and defense remain inviolate, how much keener will be the sense of his unprotected condition when all means of predicting or averting future calamity are removed beyond his reach? If, in the one case, his alarmed fancy peoples the darkness with unreal enemies, and that too in defiance of the opposing assurances of reason, what an array of suffering will it conjure up in the other, where the ignorance and helplessness upon which the alarm is founded is so infinitely magnified and where reason cannot oppose the smallest tittle of evidence?

I have thus endeavored to show that from the unintermitting peril to which human life is exposed, and the perpetual necessity of knowledge to protect ourselves against it, mankind must infallibly conceive an unknown future as fraught with misery and torment. But this is not the only reason which may be assigned for such a tendency. Pain is a far stronger, more pungent, and more distinct sensation than pleasure; it is more various in its shapes, more definite and impressive upon the memory, and lays hold of the imagination with greater mastery and permanence. Pain, therefore, is far more likely to obtrude itself upon the conceptions where there exists no positive evidence to circumscribe their range than pleasure. Throughout the catalogue of human suspicions, there exists not a case in which our ignorance is so profound as about the manner of a posthumous existence; and since no reason can be given for preferring one mode of conceiving it to another, the strongest sensations of the past will be perfectly sure to break in and to appropriate the empty canvas. Pain will dictate our anticipation, and a posthumous life will be apprehended as replete with the most terrible concomitants which such a counselor can suggest.

Besides, pain alone and want or uneasiness, which is a species of pain, are the standing provisions of nature. Even the mode of appeasing those wants is the discovery of human skill; what is called *pleasure* is a secondary formation, something superadded to the satisfaction of our wants by a further reach of artifice, and only enjoyable when that satisfaction is perfect for the present as well as prompt and certain for the future. Want and pain, therefore, are natural; satisfaction and pleasure, artificial and invented: and the former will on this ground also be more likely to present itself as the characteristic of an unknown state than the latter.

The preceding arguments seem to evince most satisfactorily that a posthumous existence, if really anticipated, is far more likely to be conceived as a state of suffering than of enjoyment. Such anticipation, therefore, considered in itself and without any reference to the direction which it gives to human conduct will assuredly occasion more misery than happiness to those who entertain it.

Though believers in a posthumous existence seldom in fact anticipate its joys or torments as unconditionally awaiting them and altogether independent of their present conduct, yet it is important to examine the effects and tendency of the belief when thus entertained. We frequently hear the hope of immortality magnified as one of the loftiest privileges and blessings of human nature, without which man would be left in a state of mournful and comfortless destitution. To all these vague declamations, by which it is attempted to interest the partiality of mankind in favor of the belief in question, the foregoing arguments furnish a reply: they demonstrate that such anticipations, so far from conferring happiness on mankind, are certain to fasten in preference upon prospects of torments and to occasion a large overplus of apprehension and uneasiness—at least until some revelation intervenes to settle and define them, and to terminate that ignorance which casts so terrific a character over the expected scenes.

He who imagines himself completely mortal suffers no apprehension or misery in this life from the prospect of death, except that which the pains attending it and the loss of present enjoyments unavoidably hold out. A posthumous existence, if anticipated as blissful, would doubtless greatly alleviate the disquietude which the prospect of death occasions. It cannot be denied that such a persuasion would prove the source of genuine happiness to the believer. But the fact is that a posthumous existence is not, by the majority of believers, anticipated as thus blissful, but as replete with terrors. The principles of human nature, to which reference has been made in the foregoing arguments, completely warrant this conclusion, supposing no revelation at hand to instill and guarantee more consoling hopes. It is obvious therefore that natural religion, alone and unassisted, will to the majority of its believers materially aggravate the disquietude occasioned by the prospect of death. Instead of soothing apprehensions which cannot be wholly dispelled, it would superadd fresh grounds of uneasiness wrapped up in an uncertainty which only renders them more painful and depressing.

TEXT: [Jeremy Bentham with George Grote,] *Analysis of the influence of natural religion on the temporal happiness of mankind* (London: R. Carlile, 1822), 4–9.

HUGH JAMES ROSE
(1795–1838)
Faith and Reason

Skepticism in France was notorious, but the decline of religion in Germany made many scholars wary of association with its theology, biblical criticism, and literature. Hugh James Rose, best known for his contributions to the Oxford Movement of the 1830s, fostered anxieties about the future of Christianity in England based on his firsthand knowledge of the deteriorating situation in Germany. Rose received his earliest education from his father at Uckfield School and later studied at Trinity College, Cambridge. He was ordained a priest in 1819 and subsequently ministered as vicar at Horsham, West Sussex (1821–1830), and at Hadleigh, Suffolk (1830–1833). He served as a select preacher at Cambridge during the latter half of the 1820s, where he promoted high church principles, the leadership of the clergy, and a rigorous defense of Christian doctrine. In subsequent years, Rose published numerous works of theology that brought him wide acclaim, including *Christianity always progressive* (1829), *An apology for the study of divinity* (1833), and *The study of church history recommended* (1834). In 1832 Rose founded the *British Magazine*, which published on high church doctrines and issues. Tractarians such as John Henry Newman found a congenial collaborator in Rose, and many date the founding of the Oxford Movement to a conference held at Rose's Hadleigh rectory in July 1833. The University of Durham named Rose the first regius professor of divinity in 1833, though he resigned the post after only a brief period due to illness. In 1836 he became principal of King's College, London, but died two years later at the age of only forty-three.

In the mid-1820s, Rose's intellectual development shifted in dynamic new directions. He spent a year in Germany to convalesce from a spate of medical troubles. During this time, the young apologist (who had already made a name for himself through various writings in defense of Christianity) encountered the latest forms of rationalism and theological liberalism in German theological scholarship. He published *The state of the Protestant religion in Germany* (1825) as a warning to England of the dangers simmering abroad. Throughout the work, Rose targets J. S. Semler (1725–1791), J. G. Eichhorn (1752–1827), F. W. J. Schelling (1775–1854), and (to some extent) F. D. E. Schleiermacher

(1768–1834). In the following selection, Rose confronts the modern tendency to vacillate between extremes. Reason nullifies biblical truths held faithfully by generations of Christians, while a capricious imagination renders the claims of reason ever uncertain and subject to whimsy.

SOURCES: Paul Avis, *Anglicanism and the Christian church: theological resources in historical perspective*, rev. ed. (London: T. and T. Clark, 2002); Hylson-Smith; Nockles; *ODCC*; *ODNB*; Michael Ramsey, *Durham essays and addresses* (London: S.P.C.K., 1956); *VC*.

HUGH JAMES ROSE
The state of the Protestant religion in Germany
1825

Thy wisdom and thy knowledge, it hath perverted thee.

Isaiah 47:10

A very remarkable characteristic of the age in which we live is its tendency to exalt and exaggerate the powers and capacities of the human mind. In former ages, the philosopher in his closet might speculate on a subject so flattering to human vanity and read in the success of his present enquiries the grateful assurance that in [the] future nothing would be denied to his penetration. But the reveries of the philosopher are the waking dreams of the million in our days, the object of their belief and the ground of their practice. This belief may be traced in the almost exclusive attention paid to subjects which favor and foster it, and the neglected state of those pursuits where the powers of the human understanding appear to be checked, where it is compelled to look beyond itself for light, and where docility, thought, and patience take the place of subtle inquiry and brilliant invention. But in no subject which presents itself to our view is this tendency and belief more clearly to be traced than in the speculations of the age on religious truth; on no subject is the boundless extent of the powers of the understanding more fully and entirely recognized. The preliminary condition indeed at present of any consideration of a religious subject is not only the *moral right* but the *full capacity* of each individual to judge of it. That indeed in what concerns individual salvation, the individual should be the sole judge, and that reason was given him especially that he might become so, are assertions which neither admit nor require any answer. The view on which they proceed and which represents the Deity as in a separate relation with each individual is itself false and partial; and although by his own progress in holiness made through God's grace each man will be judged at last, there want many links in the argument which thence infers that he can best judge how to gain the wisdom which is to make him wise unto salvation [2 Tim 3:15] and that he is to seek it in a blind confidence in his own powers. Without any reference to the direct arguments on the subject, every satisfactory and extended view

169

of human nature so constantly and universally represents man as a dependent being, dependent for life and light and knowledge at every portion and period of his existence, as to lead almost irresistibly to the conclusion that in this most important point where his infirmities must be the most strongly felt and productive of the greatest evil, it was never intended that he should be left to his own strength or his own weakness. . . . The advocates for the supremacy of the human understanding to whom I allude, not content with judging of the evidences offered in support of the truth of the Christian system, proceed much further and first establish reason as the sole and sufficient arbiter of the truth or falsehood of the various doctrines which that system contains, the umpire from whose judgment there is to be no appeal in matters of religious controversy. First, I say, for this is indeed only the preliminary step to that long career on which they are entering. Reason, which is to be the sole judge, must, if its office be rightly bestowed, at least be *capable* of deciding on everything offered to her examination; that is to say, in religion thus subjected to the decision of human reason, there must be nothing which it is beyond the power of human reason to *comprehend*, for without comprehension there can be no decision. Those things in religion which to others are obscure and difficult, to those who pursue this road must be as clear as the windows of the morning. They must explain them or explain them away. But when religion is thus placed at the mercy of reason, it is manifest that the first step will be to treat religious matters like any other science within the province of reason. . . . The same methods which the natural philosopher pursues in arriving at the knowledge which he presumes he possesses of chemistry or geology must be employed by the religious philosopher in arriving at Christian truth. Truth (according to the scientific plan of religion) as set before us in Scripture is the raw material which is to be worked up by human ingenuity, or rather the hieroglyphic system, the solution of which is to be achieved by human penetration. The doctrines which have commanded the assent, directed the faith, and warmed the hopes of the great, the wise, and the good in every age of Christianity may perhaps in every age of Christianity have been misunderstood or not understood at all. The theologian must *mine* for the long-hidden treasure of truth and, like the naturalist, must make new discoveries and modify his belief accordingly. When a sufficient number of facts is *discovered*, a system must be formed to which reason can form no objection: that is to say, a system which contains nothing transcending her powers. But as the name of *Christianity* is still to be written upon this system, it must at all events profess to rest, as we have said, on the basis of Scripture; and as the words and the facts of Scripture are occasionally somewhat more refractory than the imaginations of the human heart, new systems of interpretation must be devised, and the words and facts of Scripture must change their meaning at the omnipotent command of reason, and must be made to accord with the system which her wisdom has erected; or when this is impossible, portions (or rather masses) of Scripture must be wiped away from the canon and branded with spuriousness and imposture. Truth must no longer be recognized by external characters, but by its coincidence with the dictates of reason. And probabilities from external circumstances must afford us no matter for thought or conviction, but the system must itself be the measure and arbiter of probabilities.

But it must doubtless appear that I am detailing the mere fancies and caprices of madness or imbecility. Would it were so! On the contrary, although I speak of nothing which actually exists in this country, where the great body of dissenters has nothing which deserves the name of a system and where the rationalist party is below contempt, I am only giving a very feeble and imperfect sketch of the theory and practice which have for many years been entertained in one of the most enlightened and assuredly very far the most learned nation of Europe. It will be said, however, that such dreams must have been confined, as infidelity (at least in former days) was in this country, to the few who are misled by a fondness for speculation on subjects which surpass their powers, or to the superficial inquirer whose vanity is charmed at overcoming what he deems old and established prejudices, and whose ignorance prevents him from understanding their value and the worthlessness of his own principles. . . . But this is the very point at which I wish to arrive. So far are these hopes and suppositions from truth that a large portion of the Protestant churches of Germany hailed these principles with delight and spread with eagerness this purer system of Christianity. It was taught by her divines from the pulpit, by her professors from the chairs of theology. It was addressed to the old as the exhortation which was to free them from the weight and burden of ancient prejudices and observances, and to the young as that knowledge which alone could make them truly wise or send them into life with right or rational views. Nor could the result be different in a church which contains no power of control over the speculations of her ministers, when the principle which exalts reason to the exercise of full dominion is once admitted. But although this is the natural, it is not the *whole* result. There are in the mind of man two almost antagonist principles—the reason and the imagination—which ought to check and balance each other; and it never fails to happen that where one has exerted more than its due share of influence, the other resumes its rights with proportionate violence, and one extreme leads almost invariably to the indulgence in another. Thus in the German churches not only was the mischief such as we have adverted to, but the opposition which these evil principles produced was as mischievous as they were. For although these doctrines were undoubtedly opposed (in what Christian age or Christian country could they have been silently admitted?), yet what was the opposition offered and from what sources did it spring? It proceeded not from the dignity of a church possessing a clear and decided system of faith; not from those calm and lucid views of theology, which, while they reject all the traditions of men and their fond inventions and additions to Scripture, receive that Scripture in its plain and obvious sense; and while they seek not to deceive mankind with fresh tales of wonder are humbly thankful for that miraculous evidence with which God has been pleased to confirm the truth of Christianity, though such operations transcend their comprehension. The opposition, I say, proceeded not from such sources, but from a party which, shocked at the tendency of the rationalist doctrines, proceeded to the very opposite extreme. The one referring all to the judgment of reason was led to deny the truth of all that was above reason in religion; the other referred all to *sense* and contended that without *evidence* they had an immediate and intuitive perception of all the mysteries and all the most exalted truths within the sphere of Christianity.[1] The philosophical division of this party considered that everything in religion was to be referred for evidence to the imagination—that Christianity was poetry in its highest and most exalted sense—and that its doctrines were, in fact, merely symbolical presentations of certain eternal and

---

[1]   [Ed. Rose likely refers, at least in part, to the contrasting rationalism of philosophers such as J. S. Semler (1725–1791) and the theological liberalism of F. D. E. Schleiermacher (1768–1834).]

philosophical truths. Some in sounding these depths of mysticism were led to atheism, and some of the most lofty minds among them indulged in speculations to which no other name but that of pantheism can be applied. The less philosophical multitude of this party allowed the mind to lose itself in uncertain and indefinite sensations of religious feeling, in mystic meditation, and in vain aspirations after a union with God and an intuitive perception of his glorious attributes.

Such are the elements of which the Protestant world in Germany is, or was till a very recent period, composed. It need not be added that the Protestant church of that country is the mere shadow of a name. For this abdication of Christianity was not confined to either the Lutheran or Calvinistic profession, but extended its baneful and withering influence with equal force over each. It is equally unnecessary to add that its effects were becoming daily more conspicuous in a growing indifference to Christianity in all ranks and degrees of the nation. But it is rather to the *means* by which such dreadful results were effected that I am anxious to direct your attention. And those means were unquestionably the deficient constitutions of the Protestant German churches, the entire want of control in them over the opinions of their own ministers, and the consequent wild and licentious exercise of what was deemed not the base merely, but the essence of Protestantism—the right of private judgment—on every question however difficult or however momentous. These churches, in fact, are guilty of the extraordinary absurdity of first laying down their views of Scripture truth, and then allowing the very ministers who are ordained by their authority for the purpose of inculcating these views to reject them either in part or entirely at their own pleasure. And their ministers did not throw away the boon of liberty of opinion thus offered. They, and not the laity, are the sole authors of the fatal opinions which have taken from Christianity in Germany almost everything but its name, or at least have deprived it of almost all the marks and characteristics of a revelation. The evil, therefore, is to be imputed entirely to the absence of all control over religious speculation in the German churches.

‡

. . . If then it be an essential principle of a Protestant church that she possess a constant power of varying her belief, let us remember that we are assuredly no Protestant church. The dispute is not here whether we be right or wrong in our doctrines; but the principle on which we separated from the Roman church was—not that we had discovered any new views of Scripture doctrines, but that we desired to return to the primitive confession—the views held by the apostles and early Fathers of the church. And as the founders of our church firmly and hopefully believed that God had led them by his Spirit into these views of truth, so they as firmly and hopefully believed that he would continue and strengthen the church in them to the end. And with these feelings they have given us a declaration of faith (without subscription[2] to which, as thank God, no one can be a teacher in the church), so if he afterwards depart from it, he must depart also from communion with the church which holds it, and not disturb our peace by inculcating what his fancy dictates as a more excellent way. Here then is a marked difference between our own and

---

[2]   [Ed. Subscription to the Thirty-Nine Articles and adherence to the teachings of the Church of England.]

other Protestant churches. Our church receives only what was received in those ages when truth must have been known; the others profess that perhaps in no age has truth yet been recognized and that her genuine form may still remain to discover. . . . How can we fix on our minds today what tomorrow may teach us to reject? But even further, how can we teach others what we so doubtfully receive ourselves or offer to their notice anything but a cold system of moral truth resting on no higher ground than its expediency? Can we teach the repentant sinner to look for comfort to the cross of a dying Savior or to the mediation of that Savior glorified, when these doctrines of redemption and intercession may be mere speculative fancies? Can we teach him in his infirmities to rely for help on the ever-present Spirit, when we know not so much as whether there be any Holy Spirit; can we point the troubled look of suffering, of age, and of infirmity to the resurrection of Jesus as a certain token that they are themselves to be one day the inhabitants of a brighter and a better country when we doubt whether the very narration of the resurrection may not be a mere imposture and fabrication? If this be Protestantism, if it be Protestantism to doubt of every sacred truth or at least to receive none with confidence, may that gracious providence which has ever yet preserved the Church of England preserve her still from the curse of Protestantism; may it teach her that he who has given her Scripture as a guide has given her also the power of understanding the truths it contains; that she has not been in past times—that she is not now—left to wander in uncertainty and error but possesses a light which will guide her to truth and to peace.

TEXT: Hugh James Rose, *The state of the Protestant religion in Germany, in a series of discourses preached before the University of Cambridge* (Cambridge: J. Deighton and Sons, 1825), 1–11, 21–24.

V

ENTHUSIASM

Enthusiasm . . . denotes that self-sufficient spirit which, placing the conceits of human fancy on a level with real inspiration, has ever proved by its very fruit that it is not of God.

George Frederic Nott, *Religious enthusiasm* (1802)

WILLIAM LAW
(1686–1761)
Spiritual Life

The Nonjuror and devotional writer William Law was born in Northamptonshire and entered Emmanuel College, Cambridge in June 1705. His degrees at Cambridge were temporarily degraded and he was deprived of his fellowship after several inauspicious comments intimated Jacobite sympathies. In 1714, unwilling to take the Oath of Allegiance to George I, Law joined the Nonjurors. He served as a private tutor to Edward Gibbon, father of the historian, and wrote influential devotional works, including *A practical treatise upon Christian perfection* (1726) and *A serious call to a devout and holy life* (1728). Law reclaimed the idea of the imitation of Christ that had been central to the piety of the late Middle Ages; his beliefs, in turn, influenced many leading English writers in the following decades, including John and Charles Wesley, and Samuel Johnson. Later works by Law, such as *The spirit of prayer* (1749–1750), revealed the influence of the seventeenth-century German mystic Jakob Böhme, which dissatisfied many of his admirers (including John Wesley). In 1740 Law retired to his hometown of King's Cliffe. During these years, Law sought to live out his teachings through various practices of spiritual discipline, including regular prayer, acts of charity, establishing a lending-library of pious literature, and founding a school for poor girls.

In *An humble, earnest, and affectionate address to the clergy* (1761), completed shortly before his death, Law attacks William Warburton (1698–1779). While Warburton was well-known as an apologist for the Church of England, his scathing criticism of opponents (including Deists and evangelicals alike) frequently left him open to attack from all sides. Although Law typically avoided theological controversies, in *An humble, earnest, and affectionate address to the clergy*, Law counters Warburton's polemical sermons against mysticism and enthusiasm. The work displays Law's unique blend of keen intellect and devotional spirit. Reflecting his late emphasis on inner illumination by the indwelling Spirit, Law encourages readers to deny the desires of self, know the fire of divine love in the soul, and forego natural reason in favor of spiritual inspiration: "Show me a man whose heart has no desire or prayer in it but to love God with his whole soul and spirit, and his neighbor as himself, and then you have shown me the man who knows Christ" (140).

SOURCES: Donald S. Armentrout, "Law, William," *Biographical dictionary of Christian theologians*, ed. Patrick W. Carey and Joseph T. Lienhard (Peabody, Mass.: Hendrickson, 2002), 319–20; Paul Avis, *Anglicanism and the Christian Church: theological resources in historical perspective*, rev. ed. (London: T. and T. Clark, 2002); Cragg; Alan P. R. Gregory, *Quenching hell: the mystical theology of William Law* (New York: Seabury, 2008); *ODCC*; *ODNB*; *RCBEC*; Keith Walker, *William Law: his life and thought* (London: S.P.C.K., 1973).

WILLIAM LAW
An humble, earnest, and affectionate address to the clergy
1761

The reason of my humbly and affectionately addressing this discourse to the clergy is not because it treats of things not of common concern to all Christians, but chiefly to invite and induce them, as far as I can, to the serious perusal of it; and because whatever is essential to Christian salvation—if either neglected, overlooked, or mistaken by them—is of the saddest[1] consequence both to themselves and the churches in which they minister. I say essential to salvation, for I would not turn my own thoughts or call the attention of Christians to anything but the one thing needful, the one thing essential and alone available[2] to our rising out of our fallen state and becoming as we were at our creation: an holy offspring of God and real partakers of the divine nature.

If it be asked what this one thing is, it is the *Spirit of God* brought again to his *first power of life in us*. Nothing else is wanted by us, nothing else intended for us by the Law, the Prophets, and the gospel. Nothing else is or can be effectual to the making sinful man become again a godly creature.

Everything else, be it what it will, however glorious and divine in outward appearance, everything that angels, men, churches, or reformations can do for us, is dead and helpless, but so far as it is the immediate work of the Spirit of God breathing and living in it.

‡

The matter therefore plainly comes to this: nothing can do or be the good of religion to the intelligent creature but the power and presence of God really and essentially living and working in it. But if this be the unchangeable nature of that goodness and blessedness, which is to be had from our religion, then of all necessity the creature must have all its religious goodness as wholly and solely from God's immediate operation[3] as it had its first

---

1   [Ed. Serious or grave.]
2   [Ed. Able to be availed of.]
3   [Ed. Immediate here means "without intervention" and indicates that all goodness derives from the being of the divine.]

goodness at its creation. And it is the same impossibility for the creature to help itself to that which is good and blessed in religion by any contrivance, reasonings, or workings of its own natural powers, as to create itself. For the creature after its creation can no more take anything to itself that belongs to God than it could take it before it was created. And if truth forces us to hold that the natural powers of the creature could only come from the one power of God, the same truth should surely more force us to confess that that which comforts, that which enlightens, that which blesses, which gives peace, joy, goodness, and rest to its natural powers, can be had in no other way nor by any other thing but from God's immediate, holy operation found in it.

Now the reason why no work of religion but that which is begun, continued, and carried on by the living operation of God in the creature can have any truth, goodness, or divine blessing in it, is because nothing can in truth seek God but that which comes from God. Nothing can in truth find God, as its good, but that which has the nature of God living in it; like can only rejoice in like; and therefore no religious service of the creature can have any truth, goodness, or blessing in it but that which is done in the creature—in and through and by a principle and power of the divine nature begotten and breathing forth in it all holy tempers, affections, and adorations.

All true religion is or brings forth an essential union and communion of the spirit of the creature with the Spirit of the Creator: God in it and it in God; one life, one light, one love. The Spirit of God first gives or sows the seed of divine union in the soul of every man; and religion is that by which it is quickened, raised, and brought forth to a fullness and growth of a life in God. Take a similitude of this, as follows: the beginning or seed of animal breath must first be born in the creature from the spirit of this world,[4] and then respiration, so long as it lasts, keeps up an essential union of the animal life with the breath or spirit of this world. In like manner, divine faith, hope, love, and resignation to God are, in the religious life, its acts of respiration, which, so long as they are true, unite God and the creature in the same living and essential manner as animal respiration unites the breath of the animal with the breath of this world.

Now as no animal could begin to respire or unite with the breath of this world but because it has its beginning to breathe begotten in it from the air of this world; so it is equally certain that no creature, angel or man could begin to be religious or breathe forth the divine affections of faith, love, and desire towards God but because a living seed of these divine affections was by the Spirit of God first begotten in it. And as a tree or plant can only grow and fructify by the same power that first gave birth to the seed, so faith and hope and love towards God can only grow and fructify by the same power that begot the first seed of them in the soul. Therefore divine, immediate inspiration and divine religion are inseparable in the nature of the thing. . . .

A religious faith that is uninspired, a hope or love that proceeds not from the immediate working of the divine nature within us, can no more do any divine good to our souls or unite them with the goodness of God than a hunger after earthly food can feed us with the immortal bread of heaven. All that the natural or uninspired man does or can do in the church has no more of the truth or power of divine worship in it than that which he

---

4   [Ed. *Spiritus* means "breath" or "air" in Latin. Law may also imply semen, as in Shakespeare's "the expense of spirit in a waste of shame" (Sonnet 129), to build on the metaphor of the seed.]

does in the field or shop through a desire of riches. And the reason is because all the acts of the natural man, whether relating to matters of religion or the world, must be equally selfish, and there is no possibility of their being otherwise. For self-love, self-esteem, self-seeking, and living wholly to self are as strictly the whole of all that is or possibly can be in the natural man, as in the natural beast; the one can no more be better or act above this nature than the other. Neither can any creature be in a better or higher state than this till something supernatural is found in it; and this supernatural something, called in Scripture the *Word* or *Spirit* or *inspiration* of God is that alone from which man can have the first good thought about God or the least power of having more heavenly desires in his spirit than he has in his flesh. . . .

No man, therefore, can reach God with his love or have union with him by it, but he who is inspired with that one same Spirit of love with which God loved himself from all eternity and before there was any creature. Infinite hosts of new created heavenly beings can begin no new kind of love of God nor have the least power of beginning to love him at all but so far as his own Holy Spirit of love, wherewith he hath from all eternity loved himself, is brought to life in them. This love that was then in God alone can be the only love in creatures that can draw them to God; they can have no power of cleaving to him, of willing that which he wills, or adoring the divine nature, but by partaking of that eternal Spirit of love; and therefore the continual, immediate inspiration or operation of the Holy Spirit is the one only possible ground of our continually loving God. And of this inspired love, and no other, it is that St. John saith, "He that dwelleth in love, dwelleth in God" [1 John 4:16]. Suppose it to be any other love, brought forth by any other thing but the Spirit of God breathing his own love in us, and then it cannot be true that he who dwells in such love, dwelleth in God.

‡

Let then the writers against continual, immediate divine inspiration take this for a certain truth—that by so doing, they do all they can to draw man from that which is the very truth and perfection of the gospel state, and are and can be no better than pitiable advocates for a religion of self, more blamable and abominable now than that which was of old condemned by Christ. For whatever is pretended to be done in gospel religion by any other spirit or power but that of the Holy Ghost bringing it forth—whether it be praying, preaching, or practicing any duties—is all of it but the religion of self, and can be nothing else. For all that is born of the flesh is flesh, and nothing is spiritual but that which has its whole birth from the Spirit. But man, not ruled and governed by the Spirit, hath only the nature of corrupt flesh, is under the full power and guidance of fallen nature, and is that very natural man to whom the things of God are foolishness. But man, boldly rejecting and preaching against a continual, immediate divine inspiration is an anti-apostle; he lays another foundation than that which Christ hath laid [1 Cor 3:11]: he teacheth, that Christ needeth not, must not, be all in all in us, and is a preacher up of the folly of fearing to grieve, quench, and resist the Holy Spirit. For when, or where, or how could every one of us be in danger of grieving, quenching, or resisting the Spirit unless his holy breathings and inspirations were always within us? Or how could the sin against the Holy Ghost have a more dreadful nature than that against the Father and the Son but because the continual immediate guidance and operation of the Spirit is the last and highest manifestation of the Holy Trinity in the fallen soul of man?

TEXT: William Law, *An humble, earnest, and affectionate address to the clergy* (London: J. Richardson, 1761), 1–2, 6–12, 34–36.

WILLIAM WARBURTON
(1698–1779)
Divine Grace

William Warburton, bishop of Gloucester, was a theologian, editor, and controversialist. After practicing law until about age twenty-five, Warburton took orders in the Church of England. *The alliance between church and state* (1736), in which he defended this alliance as a matter of individual and national good, made him an author of note in England's so-called conservative Enlightenment. Warburton's subsequent *The divine legation of Moses* (1737–1741) defended the divine origin of the Mosaic law against deistic opponents by paradoxically claiming that only a work of divine inspiration could wholly neglect a doctrine of future blessings and punishments. *The divine legation* proved his most famous writing and continued to receive attention into the next century (most notably from Gladstone's critique in *The state in its relations with the church* [1838]). In 1766 Warburton, though a dedicated Whig, condemned slavery in a sermon before the Society for the Propagation of the Gospel in Foreign Parts, which had connections to plantations worked by slaves in the Caribbean. Despite a propensity for conflict and polarizing personality (Moorman calls him "a man of very strong feelings" [277]), he was friends with several leading writers of the times—including Alexander Pope, Samuel Richardson, Henry Fielding, Laurence Sterne, and Robert Lowth—and published editions of the works of both Shakespeare (1741) and Pope (1751). Warburton held several ecclesiastical offices, including dean of Bristol in 1757 and bishop of Gloucester from 1759.

In *The doctrine of grace* (1762), Warburton combines biblical research, rational argumentation, and close textual analysis in a stinging corrective to Methodism (and evangelicalism broadly). The bulk of Warburton's discourse on grace, enthusiasm, and the Spirit is directed at the writings of both Conyers Middleton (1683–1750) and, especially, John Wesley (to whom Warburton ironically sent the manuscript for correction). Middleton denied the Spirit's inspiration of the entire New Testament—a position that Warburton vehemently opposed. Wesley, Warburton alleges, claimed inspiration by the Spirit for himself and miraculous powers similar to the original apostles. In Warburton's view, Wesley, like other evangelical "enthusiasts" and mystics of the day, is a "fanatic" driven by self-interest, and the Methodist revival is a result of fraud, imprudence, partiality, and hypocrisy. In the following selection, Warburton argues that modern enthusiasts disavow the New Testament teaching that miraculous signs and spiritual gifts were intended for the age of the apostles alone.

Sources: Robert G. Ingram, "William Warburton, divine action, and enlightened Christianity," in *Religious identities in Britain, 1660–1832*, ed. William Gibson and Robert G. Ingram (Aldershot: Ashgate, 2005), 97–117; J. H. R. Moorman, *A history of the Church in England*, 3rd ed. (Harrisburg: Morehouse, 1980); *ODNB*; *RCBEC*; Robert M. Ryley, *William Warburton* (Boston: Twayne, 1984); David Sorkin, "William Warburton: the middle way of 'heroic moderation,'" *Dutch Review of Church History / Nederlands Archief voor Kerkgeschiedenis* 82 (2002): 262–300; John Selby Watson, *The life of William Warburton, D.D.* (London: Longman, 1863).

WILLIAM WARBURTON
The doctrine of grace
1762

Having now established the fact that miraculous gifts were to pass away with the first ages of the church, we may safely and reasonably inquire into the fitness of the thing.

There appear to have been two causes of the extraordinary operations of the Holy Spirit: the manifestation of his mission as it was predicted, and the comfort and instruction of a suffering church as it was promised.

To the first we have observed that in the early propagation of our holy faith it was fit [that] the Sanctifier as well as the Redeemer should support his presence by miracles. But the same considerations which show this fitness to be no more in the one case show it likewise in the other. For the divine original of our faith being once established, it supports itself ever after on the same credibility of human testimony which all other truths do that are founded on facts.

1. As to his extraordinary operations for the comfort and instruction of the church, we may observe that on his first descent upon the apostles, he found their minds rude and uninformed, strangers to all celestial knowledge, prejudiced in favor of a carnal law, and utterly averse to the genius[1] of the everlasting gospel. The minds of these he illuminated and, by degrees, led into all the truths necessary for the professors of the faith to know or for the propagators of it to teach. For a rule of faith not being yet composed, some extraordinary infusion of his virtue was still necessary both to regulate the faith of him who received it and to constitute the authority of him who was to communicate of what he had received to others. But when now the rule of faith was perfected in an authentic collection of the apostolic writings, part of this office was transferred upon the sacred canon; and his enlightening grace was not to be expected in so abundant an effusion as would make the recipients infallible guides to others, but only in a measure adequate to the direction of themselves.

---

[1]   [Ed. The distinctive character or tendency of.]

These reasons for the change of economy[2] in the dispensations of the Holy Spirit are sufficient to discredit the false confidence of modern fanatics who pretend to as high a degree of divine communications as if no such rule of faith was in being; or at least as if that rule was so obscure as to need the further assistance of the Holy Spirit to explain his own meaning; or so imperfect as to need a new inspiration to supply its wants. But these men read the history of the dispensations to the first propagators of our holy faith; they look with admiration on the privileges and powers conferred on those chosen instruments, their imagination grows heated, they forget the difference between the present and the past economy of things, they seem to feel the impressions they hear of, and they assume the airs and mimic the authority of prophets and apostles.

2. Again, the nature and genius of the gospel were so averse to all the religious institutions of the world that the whole strength of human prejudices was set in opposition to it. To overcome the obstinacy and violence of these prejudices, nothing less than the power of the Holy One was sufficient. He did the work of man's conversion and reconciled an unbelieving world to God. At present, whatever there may be remaining of the bias of prejudice (as such will mix itself even with our best conclusions), it draws the other way. So much then of his task was finished, and the faith from thenceforth had a favorable hearing. Indeed, were we to make our estimate of the present state of the religious world from the journals of modern fanatics, we should be tempted still to think ourselves in a land of pagans with all their prejudices full blown upon them. For the account they give us of their provincial missions always runs on in such strains as these: the name of Jesus is preached up in this city, the glad tidings of the gospel conveyed to that hamlet, a new light springs up in a land of darkness, and life and immortality is now first offered to those who sit in the shadow of death.

3. A further reason for the abatement of the influences of the supporting spirit of grace is the peace and security of the church. There was a time when the powers of this world were combined together for its destruction. At such a period, nothing but superior aid from above could support humanity in sustaining so great a conflict as that which the holy martyrs encountered with joy and rapture—the horrors of death in torment. But now the profession of the Christian faith is attended with ease and honor, and the conviction which the weight of human testimony and the conclusions of human reason afford us of its truth is abundantly sufficient to support us in our religious perseverance.

But the obstinate and continued claims of fanatics in all ages to this primitive abundance of the Spirit may make it expedient to examine their pretensions yet more minutely and exactly. And to this inquiry Scripture itself, which foresaw and foretold the evil, directs us to the remedy, where it exhorts us to try the spirits. "Beloved, believe not every spirit," says St. John, "but try the spirits whether they be of God; because many false prophets are gone out into the world" {1 John 4:6}. At the time this precept was given there was a more than ordinary attention requisite to guard against the delusions of false prophets. For the abundant effusion of the Holy Spirit on the rising religion gave encouragement to impostors to counterfeit and a handle to enthusiasts to mimic all that was equivocal in its operations.

---

[2]   [Ed. Warburton refers to a change in "the method of divine government of the world" (*OED*).]

‡

This the reader should have in mind when we bring him to apply these marks to the features of modern fanaticism, especially as they are seen in the famed leader of the Methodists, Mr. John Wesley; and not *seen* either, as Sancho Pancho saw his mistress,[3] by hearsay (which indeed has been too much the custom in the representations of this transcendent man), but as he appears in person in his own *Journals*. For by those indelible marks alone, there traced out and by his own pen, I purpose to try in him chiefly the spirits of all modern pretenders to supernatural powers.

TEXT: William Warburton, *The doctrine of grace; or, The office and operations of the Holy Spirit vindicated from the insults of infidelity and the abuses of fanaticism*, 3rd ed. (London: A. Millar and J. and R. Tonson, 1763), 81–84, 87.

---

[3]   [Ed. Sancho Pancho, a farmer, serves as Don Quixote's squire in Miguel de Cervantes' *Don Quixote de la Mancha* (1605).]

WILLIAM ROMAINE
(1714–1795)
Spirit and Conscience

The appeal to an interior work of the Spirit often coincides with an appeal to conscience. While British evangelicals exemplified the historic Protestant commitment to the Bible, they commonly also affirmed the Spirit's work in compelling, emboldening, and animating the conscience. The Bible remained the standard of faith and practice, but the enlightening work of the Spirit was no less indispensable for both an individual assent to the truths of the gospel and the pursuit of holiness.

William Romaine, an evangelical minister in the Church of England, was educated at Hart Hall and later Christ Church, Oxford. Romaine excelled in Hebrew studies, producing an important edition of the Hebrew concordance of Marius de Calasio in 1748. He was ordained deacon in 1736 and priest in 1738. After preaching several university sermons against William Warburton's *The divine legation of Moses*, the two engaged in extended public debate. Briefly attracted to the teachings of John Wesley, Romaine eventually took up George Whitefield's Calvinist evangelicalism. As with Whitefield and the Wesleys, Romaine's preaching, teaching, and writings became widely popular among the poor and working class. As with other evangelicals, numerous pulpits were closed to him and harassment was common, stemming in part from his popularity with the poor, who packed churches in order to hear him preach. After serving in various short-term posts, Romaine found security until the end of his life in an incumbency at St. Andrew by the Wardrobe with St. Ann Blackfriars in London. Romaine was the only evangelical to hold a benefice in London until John Newton in 1780.

In *The walk of faith*, which John Wesley thought tainted by antinomian disregard for moral responsibility (a common charge against Calvinists), Romaine offers a characteristic example of evangelical "heart religion." He traces the path of faith from reconciliation with God to final rest in a state of blessed triumph. Along the way, the believer carries the cross of Christ: outwardly suffering trials and temptations with patience, inwardly growing in virtue by a work of the Holy Spirit. In the following selection, Romaine offers a dark, Calvinist account of the fallen mind and explains how the believer walks with

God by a right conscience. He rejects the scholastic association of conscience with the "synderesis," according to which every person has an innate knowledge of good and evil, a knowledge that makes possible moral choice. Rather, the mind is ignorant, without innate principles, and utterly alienated from God. Romaine instead appeals to Scripture and the Spirit. The Bible alone provides "the only rule of right and wrong." In an act of grace, the Holy Spirit enlightens the mind to recognize sin and enter the promises of God. All that remains is self-examination: "O my soul, consider whether God has taught thee this knowledge of thyself."

SOURCES: Bebbington; William Bromley Cadogan, *The life of the Rev. William Romaine* (London: T. Bensley, 1796); *ODCC*; *ODNB*; Tim Shenton, *"An iron pillar": the life and times of William Romaine* (New York: Evangelical, 2004).

WILLIAM ROMAINE
The walk of faith
1771

"It is written in the prophets—they shall be all taught of God" [John 6:45]—every one of his children shall be brought to the knowledge of the truth, and what they have been taught in the understanding shall be made practical that it may have its proper effect upon the conscience. And this is answered[1] when it comes under the authority and power of the Word of God, and faithfully accuses or condemns according to that unerring rule.

Conscience supposes the knowledge of some rule, and it consists in comparing a man's state or actions with that rule, in order to discover whether they agree with it or not.

The rule is the Scripture, the whole revealed will of God, which is the unerring and the only standard of right and wrong: for all Scripture is given by the inspiration of God, and is profitable for doctrine, to teach the man of God what is truth, and to make him wise in it unto salvation [2 Tim 3:16]. Fallen man has no means of discovering the will of God, but as it is revealed to him. He has no innate knowledge. He has no implanted principles. He is born as ignorant of God and of the things of God, as a wild ass' colt. His understanding is darkened, being alienated from the life of God through the ignorance that is in him, because of the blindness of his heart. And he has no means in his own power of attaining any divine knowledge; for he cannot, by searching, find out God. The world by its wisdom never did find him out. The Hottentots[2] know as much of him as the Greeks and Romans did. Indeed the natural man, let him be ever so wise, knoweth not the things of the Spirit of God, neither can he know them, because they are spiritually discerned [1 Cor 2:14].

The Scripture, then, is the only rule of right and wrong. Conscience has no direction but this rule. Neither ethics nor metaphysics, no fancied light of dark nature, no lawless law of rebel nature, no human science (whether pretended to be implanted or by the use of reason to be acquired), have any right to guide the conscience. These are blind leaders of the blind [Matt 15:14]; they undertake what they are not only unfit but what they have

---

[1]   [Ed. Fulfilled.]
[2]   [Ed. *Hottentot* is a derogatory term for the Khoikhoi people of South Africa.]

no warrant for. A parcel of felons in jail may think what they will of their state. They may take it upon them to form a mock court and to try one another. They may acquit or condemn as they please; but the judge and the jury will pay no regard to their foolish proceedings. There is a word which is to try us at the last day, and by that we should try ourselves at present. It was revealed for this purpose. And when the revealed truth is clearly understood, then conscience is acting aright—if it finds a true verdict for God— either accusing or else excusing, according to the direction of his unerring Word.

And this is the work of the Holy Spirit. He enlightened the judgment with the knowledge of the truth in order to make it practical, which he effects by bringing the conscience to submit to the sovereignty of God in the law and to submit to the righteousness of God in the gospel. Herein he displays the omnipotent power of his grace, according to the promise. He carries with demonstration the conviction of guilt and the conviction of righteousness to the conscience. By the former, he gives the sinner a real heartfelt sense of his sin and misery and he acknowledges himself a convict of the law, justly deserving all its penalties in time and eternity. By the latter, he sets open a door of hope, showing him the perfect righteousness of the God-man, wrought out for such guilty creatures as he is. He enables him to plead it before the throne and to trust in it for his acceptance, by which means he finds relief in his conscience and comfort in his heart. Being justified by faith, he has peace with God through Jesus Christ our Lord [Rom 5:1].

What the Holy Spirit teaches has life as well as light in it. He accompanies his doctrine with the power of God. What he has revealed concerning the state of mankind under the Fall, he applies with divine evidence to the conscience. Under his influence, the sinner reads those Scriptures and feels the truth of them: "As by one man sin entered into the world, and death by sin, so death passed upon all men, for that all have sinned [Rom 5:12]; through the offense of one, judgment came upon all men to condemnation [Rom 5:18]; for it is written, 'There is none righteous, no, not one: there is none that understandeth, there is none that seeketh after God. They are all gone out of the way, they are together unprofitable; there is none that doeth good, no, not one.' Now we know that what things soever the law saith, it commands them who are under the law, that every mouth may be stopped, and all the world may become guilty before God" [Rom 3:10-12, 19]. His mouth is stopped. He has no plea to make. No excuse left. What the law saith, he subscribes to. The law brings him in guilty before God, and in his conscience he bears his testimony to the law. He acknowledges it to be holy, just, and good, even in its penalties, which he deserves to suffer. Formerly he tried in his own strength and took great pains to escape them, but now he gives over all those self-righteous attempts. He found that he labored in vain to atone for his sins or to make himself holy. He groans, being burdened under the ruins of the Fall. His ignorance, rebellion, apostasy, his corruption in every faculty of soul and body, render him unable to take one step in his return to God. He owns it and confesses that without Christ he can do nothing.

O my soul, consider whether God has taught thee this knowledge of thyself. It is absolutely necessary to reconcile thee to him and to his ways. Thou wilt never heartily agree to walk with him by faith so long as thou hast anything of thine own to trust in or to draw comfort from. Examine then: art thou sensible of thy fall and dost thou feel the sad effects of it? Dost thou know what it is to be alienated from the life of God? What! Dost thou find to this day the opposition of thy sinful nature to the holy law, the flesh lusting in thee against the Spirit [Gal 5:17]? Has God thus convinced thee of sin? If he has, then in thy conscience thou submittest to what the law says of thy state. Thy mouth is stopped, and thou art guilty before God [Rom 3:19]. Thou hast nothing of thine own to urge in arrest of judgment. This is an enlightened conscience, so far as it speaks for God and is guided by his unerring word. O pray to the Lord the Spirit and beg of him to guide thee into all truth, that he may bring thy conscience to submit to the righteousness of Jesus and to be a faithful witness for him.

TEXT: William Romaine, *Treatises on the life, walk, and triumph of faith*, 4th ed. (Glasgow: W. Collins, 1830), 178–82.

JOHN FOSTER
(1770–1843)
Evangelical Intellect

The Baptist author John Foster was the son of John Foster (d. 1814), a leading Baptist minister in Halifax, Yorkshire. The younger Foster worked on the family farm and studied under the Particular Baptist John Fawcett (1740–1817) at Brearley Hall. In 1791 he entered the Bristol Baptist Academy. Foster began preaching in dissenting meeting houses from May 1792, later serving various congregations and schools in Newcastle, Dublin, and Chester. In Dublin, his association with "violent Democrats" exposed him to "imminent danger."[1] After the success of his *Essays in a series of letters to a friend* (1805), Foster, who suffered from a throat condition, resigned his preaching post and became a regular contributor to the *Eclectic Review*: between 1806 and 1839 he wrote more than 180 articles, including *A discourse on missions* (1818) and *On the evils of popular ignorance* (1820). Foster's beliefs were contentious: he rejected eternal punishment, protested the Corn Laws (which enriched rural landowners at the expense of the urban poor), and favored wider public education, Catholic emancipation, and parliamentary reform. His friends included leading British Romantics: S. T. Coleridge, Robert Southey, and the publisher Joseph Cottle (1770–1853). A recent article by Timothy Whelan describes Foster's underappreciated contribution: "Foster . . . produced a body of critical literature between 1791 and 1843 that combined a marked Romantic ideology with a moderate Calvinistic theology, advocating a distinctly intellectual Dissenting tradition in literature, politics, and culture that established him as 'one of the most profound and eloquent' minds . . . ever produced in England."[2]

Foster's *Essays in a series of letters to a friend* went through thirty-five British and American editions between 1805 and 1920. The final essay, with a running title "On the aversion of men of taste to evangelical religion," challenges the widespread distrust of

[1]   Timothy Whelan, "William Hazlitt and radical West Country dissent," *Coleridge Bulletin* n.s. 38 (2011): 111–27 (122).

[2]   Timothy Whelan, "John Foster and Samuel Taylor Coleridge," *Christianity and Literature* 50 (2001): 631–56 (631).

evangelical religion through a twofold assessment. Foster acknowledges that many evangelicals lack philosophical sophistication, engage in strange or emotional practices, and rely on peculiar linguistic forms to express religious ideas. However, he also insists that his readers acknowledge that the cultivation of what is called "taste" often uproots the genuine truths of Christianity.

Sources: *ODNB*; Timothy Whelan, "John Foster and Samuel Taylor Coleridge," *Christianity and Literature* 50 (2001): 631–56; idem, "William Hazlitt and radical West Country dissent," *Coleridge Bulletin* n.s. 38 (2011): 111–27.

JOHN FOSTER
"On the aversion of men of taste to evangelical religion"
1805

It is true that many persons of taste have, without any precise disbelief of the Christian truth, so little concern about religion in any form that the unthinking dislike which they may occasionally feel to the evangelical principles hardly deserves to be described. These are to be assigned, whatever may be their faculties or improvements, to the numerous class of triflers, on whom we can pronounce only the general condemnation of irreligion, their feelings not being sufficiently marked for a more discriminative censure. But the feelings of aversion to the evangelical system in a mind which is too serious for the follies of the world and the neglect of all religion, and which is often compelled to reflect on the design of a revelation acknowledged by it to have the decisive evidence of truth, are of a more defined character. If a person of such a mind disclosed himself, he would tell you that the glowing admiration with which he contemplates other elevated objects is confounded, when this peculiar aspect of truth comes in his view, by a feeling of inexpressible strangeness and sinks mortified into the heart. It seems to require a total change of his mental habits to receive this as the noblest object of all, even while he is awed by the consciousness that it does, notwithstanding, advance the most solemn claims. The claims of religion in a general and refined sense he willingly admits, but the evangelical system appears to him an uncouth detail. He feels, at the sight of it, as though he saw an angel divested of his radiance and ethereal subtlety and confined in a human form. He clearly perceives that a direct manifestation was necessary to define and embody, as it were, that divine abstraction, which would else be too imperfectly known to have on mankind the influence of a reality; but he is tempted to ask, while yet scarcely daring to approve or utter the question, whether the Almighty could not have constructed for the form of this manifestation a somewhat different economy, discovering a less entire contempt of human speculations and less converting the grand generalities of religion (in a manner which seems to preclude our reverting to them as generalities any more) into the form of specific and often humiliating doctrines. The gospel appears to him like the image in Nebuchadnezzar's dream, refulgent indeed with a head of gold; the sublime truths which are independent of every dispensation, as being antecedent to all, are luminously exhibited; but the parts which are added, in order to modify the view of these great truths into a peculiar dispensation, appear less splendid and as if descending towards the qualities of iron and clay.[1] This portion of the system, presenting itself in an infallible revelation, is admitted by him, of necessity, as a part of the truth; but his feelings amount to the wish that a different theory *had been true*. It is therefore with a degree of shrinking reluctance that he sometimes adverts to the ideas peculiar to the gospel, which he has an habitual propensity to slide under a more ample, general theory of religion. Or at least, he is very unwilling to lose every wider speculation in that one specific scheme of doctrine by which God has circumscribed and concentrated into a practical dispensation all the religion which he wills to be known or to be useful to our world. He feels it difficult to keep his mind in obedience to the authority of even his own conviction that the gospel is so far from being merely one mode or even the best mode of religion; that it is, as to us, the comprehensive and exclusive mode; or rather that it is religion itself, insomuch that he who has not a religion concordant with the New Testament, has none, even though his ideas concerning the Deity and a future state were ever so sublime. He suffers himself to pass the year in a dissatisfied uncertainty and a most criminal neglect of deciding whether his cold reception of the specific view of Christianity will render useless his regard for many of the truths which it comprehends, or whether it will be safe to rest in a system composed of the general principles of wisdom and goodness taken indifferently from the evangelical ground and from the philosophical, harmonized by reason and embellished by taste. If it were safe, he would rather be the revered professor of a philosopher's religion than yield himself to be completely peculiarized into a submissive disciple of Jesus Christ. That religion would not only modify some of the less acceptable doctrines of the evangelical school, but would also tolerate some different maxims respecting what is the noblest model of human excellence.

‡

The injurious impressions have perhaps struck his mind in many ways. For instance, he has met with a great number of zealous Christians who not only were very slightly acquainted with the evidences of the truth and the illustrations of the reasonableness of their religion, but who actually felt no interest in the inquiry and some of whom perhaps even endeavored to deter him from pursuing it by representing it as a useless or a dangerous employment.

He may sometimes have heard the discourse of sincere Christians whose religion involved no intellectual exercise and, strictly speaking, no subject of intellect. Separately from their feelings, it had no definition, no topics, no distinct succession of views. And if he or any other person attempted to talk on some part of the religion itself, as a thing definable and important, independently of the feelings of any individual, and as consisting in a vast congeries of ideas in the various forms of doctrine, morals, prophecy, and so on, they seemed to have no concern with that religion and impatiently interrupted the subject with the observation—that is not experience.

[1]   [Ed. Foster refers to the account of Nebuchadnezzar's dream in Dan 2:31-35.]

Others he has heard continually recurring to three or four intellectual points, selected perhaps arbitrarily or perhaps in conformity to a system, as being the life and offense of Christianity; those points he has heard, though not argumentatively, yet zealously defended even when not attacked or questioned; perhaps too he has heard them abruptly applied in eager haste to any sentiment which he has happened to express concerning religion, as a test of its quality and a proof its corruptness.

‡

. . . He has perhaps even heard them make a kind of merit of their indifference to knowledge, as if it were the proof or the result of a higher value for religion. If a hint of wonder was insinuated at their reading so little and within so very confined a scope, it would be replied that they thought it enough to read the Bible (as if it were possible for a person whose mind fixes with inquisitive attention on what is before him, even to read through the Bible without at least ten thousand such questions being started in his mind as can be answered only from the sources of knowledge extraneous to the Bible). But he perceived that this reading the Bible was no work of inquisitive thought, and indeed he has commonly found that those who have no wish to obtain anything like extended information have no disposition for the real business of thinking even in religion and that their discourse on that subject is the disclosure of intellectual poverty. He has seen them live on from year to year content with the same confined views, the same meager list of topics, and the same uncouth religious language. . . .

He may not infrequently have heard pious but illiterate persons expressing their utmost admiration of sayings, sermons, or passages in books, which he could not help perceiving were but very imperfectly sense. While, on the other hand, when he has introduced a favorite passage or an admired book, they have, perhaps, discovered no perception of its beauty or expressed a doubt of its tendency from its not being in the language of commonplace. Or perhaps they have directly avowed that they could not understand it, in a manner that very plainly implied that *therefore* it was certainly of no value and that he was very foolish for finding in it anything to admire. Possibly even when he has expressed his high admiration of some of the aspects of the gospel, such for instance as struck the mind of Rousseau,[2] he has been mortified to find that what shone so resplendently in his view could not be rendered visible in theirs.

If he had generally found in those Christian professors whose intellectual powers and attainments were small, a candid humility instructing them, while expressing their animated and grateful delight for what acquaintance with religion they had been enabled to attain and for the immortal hopes springing from it, to feel that they had but a confined view of a subject which is of immense variety and magnitude, he would have been too much pleased by this amiable feeling to be much repelled by the defective character of their conceptions and expressions. But often, on the contrary, he has observed a complacent sense of sufficiency in the little sphere, as if it comprised everything which it is possible or which it is of consequence for any mind to see in the Christian religion. They

2   [Ed. In writings such as "The profession of faith of the Savoyard Vicar" (1762) and part of the novel *Emile*, Jean Jacques Rousseau (1712–1778) challenged traditional Christian assumptions about the Bible.]

are like persons who should be angry with a man who has a telescope for seeing, or rather as they think pretending to see, many more stars in the sky and a much stronger luster in those which are visible to the naked eye than they can perceive.

Many Christians may have appeared to him to attach an extremely disproportioned importance to the precise *modes* of religious observances, not only in the hour of controversy, when this is almost always the case, but in the habitual course of their religious references. These observances may be either those of a more general institution which distinguish a religious community or those which are the conception and the peculiarity of the individual or the family.

The religious habits of some Christians may have revolted him excessively. Everything, which could even distantly remind him of grimace,[3] would inevitably do this, as, for instance, a solemn lifting up of the eyes, artificial impulses of the breath, grotesque and regulated gestures and postures in religious exercises, an affected faltering of the voice, and, I might add, abrupt religious exclamations in common discourse, though they were even benedictions to the Almighty, which he has often heard so ill-timed as to have an irreverent and almost a ludicrous effect. In a mind such as I am supposing, even an increased veneration for religion will but increase the dislike to these habits. Nor will it be reconciled to them by a conviction, ever so perfect, of the sincere piety of the persons who practice them.

‡

After thus describing some of the more prominent circumstances of repellency—to which others might be added—it would be most unjust not to observe that some Christians of a subordinate intellectual order are distinguished by an unassuming simplicity, by so much refinement of conscience, and by a piety so fervent and even exalted, that it would imply a very perverted state of mind in a cultivated man if these examples did not operate, notwithstanding the confined scope of their ideas, to attract him toward the faith which renders them so happy and excellent, rather than to repel him from it. But I am *supposing* his mind to be in a perverted state and am infinitely far from the impiety of defending or excusing him. This however being supposed, I feel no surprise on surveying the majority of the persons composing evangelical communities that this man has acquired an accumulation of prejudices against some of the distinguishing features of the gospel. Permitting his mind to take all the circumstances which thus diminish or distort the evangelical views, as if they belonged to those views, he is inclined to regret that there should be any divine sanctions against his forming for himself, perhaps indeed on the foundation of those principles in Christianity which he cannot but admire, a more enlarged religion.

It was especially unfortunate if such a man's *education* was in the society and under the inspection and control of persons, whether parents or any other friends, whose religion was in a form so unattractive to taste. . . . They believed these articles through the habit of hearing them and maintained them by the habit of believing them. The recoil of his feelings therefore did not alarm his conscience with the conviction of its being absolutely the truth of God that, under this uninviting form, he was reluctant to embrace. Unaided by such a conviction, and unarmed with a force of argument sufficient to impress it, the

---

3   [Ed. Foster's use of *grimace* here means, quite literally, facial distortions.]

seriousness—perhaps, sometimes, rugged seriousness of his friends—incessantly asserting his mind to be in a fatal condition till he should think and feel exactly as they did was little likely to conciliate his repugnance. When sometimes their admonitions took the mild or pathetic tone, his respect for their piety and his gratitude for their affectionate solicitude had perhaps a momentary effect to make him earnestly wish he could abdicate every intellectual refinement and adopt the entire assemblage of their feelings and ideas. But as the contracted views, the rude figures, and the mixture of systematic and illiterate language recurred, his mind would again revolt and compel him to say, "This cannot, will not, be my mode of religion."

TEXT: John Foster, *Essays in a series of letters to a friend*, 2 vols. (London: Longman, Hurst, Rees, and Orme, 1805), 2:100–105, 118–19, 121–25, 128–32.

LEIGH HUNT
(1784–1859)
Dangers of Methodism

Two decades after the death of John Wesley, Methodism showed no signs of decline. Methodists continued to preach, gather members in societies, and publish widely of conversions to a new way of holy living. Yet, in the midst of numerous dissenting bodies in England, why was Methodism facing so many hostile attacks? At least part of the answer—setting aside the exponential growth of the movement—relates to double allegiance. In the early decades of the nineteenth century, Methodism could not yet be regarded as an exclusively dissenting religion. Many Methodists, as Knight explains, "may have regarded themselves primarily as Anglicans, and as only occasional 'hearers' at the chapel, and were perhaps perceived by the Methodists as among the uncommitted and unconverted."[1] In time, people began to attend church and chapel—or eventually only the chapel, which was often conveniently close to home—heightening the separation: "In many places almost everybody now had an alternative to the established Church within a convenient distance to their doorstep." Methodism, in short, threatened the unity and authority of the Church of England.

Not all critics of Methodism, however, defended the Establishment. Leigh Hunt was born at Southgate, Middlesex, to loyalists who fled America at the time of the Revolution. Hunt's father Isaac eventually received ordination, but his parents later became Unitarians and embraced political radicalism. Hunt's earliest years were spent in the King's Bench prison, where his parents were imprisoned for unpaid debts. This scarred Hunt and likely contributed to lifelong sicknesses (and a stammer that prohibited his acceptance to university). Hunt attended grammar school at Christ's Hospital, London, where S. T. Coleridge and Charles Lamb had recently completed their studies. He then turned to writing poetry, reviews, and political criticism. From 1808 Hunt edited *The Examiner* with his brother John. The weekly offered controversial political opinions on a wide range of issues. In 1812 Hunt's article "The prince on St. Patrick's day" led to libel charges

---

[1]   Frances Knight, *The nineteenth-century church and English society* (Cambridge: Cambridge University Press, 1995), 31.

against the brothers and imprisonment for two years due to their unflattering portrait of the prince regent (George IV). They nonetheless continued *The Examiner* from prison—where Hunt was accompanied by his family and visited by friends, including Jeremy Bentham, William Hazlitt, Maria Edgeworth, and Charles Lamb. In later years, Hunt wrote poetry, an autobiography, and literary criticism.

Hunt's "An attempt to show the folly and danger of Methodism" (1808), a series of six essays, appeared in *The Examiner*. Hunt begins by insisting on his commitment to political toleration and liberty; he opposes the Methodists not because they claim individual favor from God, but because they deny others the same divine approval. He highlights, in particular, the apparent contradiction between constant providential care (amounting, he thought, to superstition) and the immoral behaviors of many Methodists. Ignorant preachers depreciate reason in favor of mysticism, emotion, and delusional claims that reduce religious life to little more than thinly sublimated sensuality. Methodists, in such a view, are hypocritical bigots: their neighbors are damned for depravity, while they themselves profane God's name with amorous ramblings that offend against good taste and moral decency.

SOURCES: Jasper Cragwall, *Lake Methodism: polite literature and popular religion in England, 1780–1830* (Columbus: Ohio State University Press, 2013); Leigh Hunt, *The autobiography of Leigh Hunt*, ed. J E. Morpurgo (London: Cresset, 1949); Frances Knight, *The nineteenth-century church and English society* (Cambridge: Cambridge University Press, 1995); *ODNB*; Nicholas Roe, *John Keats and the culture of dissent* (Oxford: Clarendon, 1997); James R. Thompson, *Leigh Hunt* (Boston: Twayne, 1977).

LEIGH HUNT
"An attempt to show the folly and danger of Methodism"
1808

I do not oppose the Methodists from an intolerant spirit, but simply from a love of toleration. This is no solecism. My country, my reason, my veneration for the doctrines of Jesus Christ have all taught me the beauty and reason of a tolerant spirit; and it is merely because this spirit is threatened with annihilation by one of intolerance and gloom, by a phantom raised out of the vapors of spleen and the fumes of vanity, that I have ventured to encounter the supernaturals of Methodism. I do not attack, I merely defend. Not a day passes but the Methodists are endeavoring to overthrow the episcopal Church by a thousand weapons open and secret; by railing against the regular clergy, by the distribution of thousands of tracts, by their hosts of missions abroad and at home, by tampering with the consciences of the gloomy, and inflaming the fancies of the impassioned. . . .

The most striking difference between the Methodists and the other sects is their universal passion for preaching. In the churches of England, of France, and of Rome, the unlearned have been content to receive the mysteries of their faith from those men whose education has enabled them to search into the original languages of the Scriptures and the antiquities of the church, and who are, therefore, the only men competent to search into the truth of what they teach. But among the Methodists everybody teaches—men and boys, learned and unlearned. The great disproportion of the gentry to the vulgar in their persuasion produces a great overbalance of ignorant professors of divinity, and a melancholy barber has nothing to do but to receive the *new light*, and he instantly begins to "shine before men" [Matt 5:16]. The worst of it is that these preachers neglect the morality of the Scriptures, which is the only part they are likely to comprehend, and addict themselves to mysteries which have called forth all the learning and ingenuity of the Christians since the days of their origin. . . .

. . . But how are their ignorant preachers to know what to reject and what to retain? Not only is their want of education a satire upon almost every word they utter, but their superiors, who have really had an education, confirm them in all their ignorance by teaching them to despise scholastic learning, which they entitle "worldly wisdom," "carnal

201

knowledge," and "the learning of this world" [1 Cor 3:18-19; Jas 3:15]. As to reason, it is altogether useless and abominable: the world indeed has generally imagined that it was a most excellent gift of God and assisted us considerably in discerning truth from falsehood, but the Methodists will have nothing to do with it. If you dispute the subject, they tell you it is "carnal reason," "the blind guide," the "old Adam";[1] that faith has nothing to do with common sense; that you must not pretend to be wise before God; in short, that you must be excessively stupid and have a perfect comprehension of mysteries. Thus they utterly reject reason, and then proceed to give you the reason why. God has given us "ears to hear and eyes to see" [Matt 13:16], but these men stop their ears and pretend to judge of harmony; they shut their eyes and firmly believe that such a piece of cloth is of the color of blue without seeing it.

‡

All this arises from ignorance. If liberal and learned men differ upon the interpretation of Scripture, how is the question to be settled by prejudiced, uneducated men, who know nothing of the Scripture but a translation of it full of apparent contradictions, which they reconcile by *forcing* them to shake hands. If the Scriptures are to be explained by every vulgar man who shall persuade himself he has found grace in the eyes of heaven, he might as well teach Greek at once, for he must give us the essence of this language in his explanations of the Testament. . . . I shall be told that God can enlighten the darkest understanding and that "out of the mouths of babes and sucklings he has ordained praise" [Ps 8:2]. So he has, but he has not ordained preaching. The Methodists, who are always comparing themselves to Christ and his disciples, produce the example of the apostles to prove the innecessity of learning; but what is it they mean by these extravagant comparisons? If the literary deficiency of the Methodists is defensible on the same ground as that of the apostles, either the apostles were not divinely inspired, and are therefore like the Methodists, or the Methodists are divinely inspired, and are therefore like the apostles. A pious and modest conclusion!

‡

Jesus Christ showed his attachment to human virtue by placing his affection on the most amiable of his disciples, who always lay next [to] his master at table and was therefore said to lie in his bosom; but if you hear the Methodists talk, you would think that he had considerably altered his nature. The most vulgar and insolent of the inspired are continually boasting of their union with the dear Jesus and the sweet Jesus; they talk of lying in his bosom, and they grow absolutely the more fond in proportion as they consider themselves the more unworthy. This friendship is of too familiar a nature not to be used on the most common occasions, and therefore the enthusiasts leap at once over petty views and common providences and make God the immediate influence of their most indifferent actions. If a man is too lazy to work for a dinner, he puts his faith in God, goes walking into the fields or road, and is sure to pick up a shilling somewhere. If he wants to go out

---

[1]   [Ed. Hunt may refer to John Wesley, who frequently used such phrases and drew from New Testament passages such as 2 Cor 10:4; Matt 23:24; and Rom 6:6.]

of doors and the rain suddenly clears up, that is a miracle in his favor. If a preacher is going to a certain chapel and meets with a thunderstorm, that is a miracle to warn him against preaching. . . . In short, he cannot take a beefsteak or a walk, he cannot stumble upon a stone or a dinner, he cannot speak, look, or move without interesting the divine being most actively in his behalf; the whole order of nature is disturbed to indulge their little finger, and they talk as magnificently on every causal occurrence as the Spaniard who cried out, "I have torn my breeches as if heaven and earth were coming together!"[2]. . .

After all, however, the Methodists must acknowledge that it is somewhat unlucky for them to see their own miracles happening every day to almost everybody. Bad men as well as good, I am afraid, are continually picking up shillings and dinners, and it is plain that the Methodists have not yet managed to occupy the sunshine to themselves. But it is still more unlucky that other sects of at least equal veracity, not to mention the inspired Roman Catholics, claim these very same spiritual gifts and miracles, and we all know that two sects cannot be inspired with the same Spirit of truth, so that if the real Spirit moves the Quaker for instance, it must be one of very suspicious adulteration that inspires the multitude of Methodism.

‡

Fever and accidents make the great majority of Methodists. They are converted not by the sunshine but by the tempest: stomachaches, rheumatisms, and catarrhs, a constitution destroyed by debauchery and a mind debilitated by ignorance become precious helps to a communion with God; and the slave who would not be grateful for his master's kindness will drop on his knees under the whip and cry out with alarm, "How I love thee!"

In fact, their love of God—in its best state, in its warmest affection—can be founded upon nothing but his partiality to themselves; it has nothing to do with those qualities for which we love our fellow creatures, such as benevolence, good temper, and universal philanthropy; and since we can really love nothing but these qualities, it is evident that *they mistake the enjoyment of their own personal safety for spiritual attachment to their protector.* Their sweet experiences and divine assurances of safety will indeed sometimes render them as insane with joy as they are very often insane with horror. The Arminian Methodists cannot help being scandalized at their brethren the Calvinists, who in their exquisite humility are continually crying out, "Lord, why *me*? Why *me*?" But there appears nothing wonderful to me in the question. The Calvinists acknowledge, and indeed take a pride in saying, that they are the "vilest of vile sinners" [Ps 12:8], and if they really think as they talk, they may reasonably be surprised that God shows such a partiality to them, to the eternal prejudice of almost all mankind.

Thus the great prevailing feeling of the godly towards God is an extreme selfishness, which exhibits itself in the most abject fear, the most groveling flattery, and in a hard-hearted attempt to be perfectly comfortable while they look upon the great majority of their fellow creatures as eternally damned. They are continually, though perhaps unconsciously, attributing the worst of human passions to God, and therefore they are almost totally occupied in endeavoring to flatter the divine being by praises that would be

---

[2]   [Ed. Attributed to Sir John Chardin (1643–1713) in Jeremiah Whitaker Newman, *The lounger's common-place book*, 2 vols., new ed. (London, 1796), 1:98.]

contemptible from one man to another. If we examine their hymnbooks and sermons, we shall find the Deity praised more for his power than for any one virtue he possesses, and this sufficiently proves that the essence of their devotion is a fear and not a love of God. Patriots praise their monarch or their government for justice, for clemency, for an equal eye to all the nation, for the encouragement of wise and good men; but who but the vilest of slaves, or the vilest of sinners, would think of continually sounding the praise of mere power, or of professing to love a king because he chose the most undeserving of his subjects for favorites, and because he decreed that the great majority of the people should be racked every day by a malicious person, his sworn enemy, who had rebelled against him? The Africans worship the devil merely that he may do them no harm, and I am afraid that the Methodists worship the Deity upon no very different principle. . . .

‡

Superstitious people fly to sensual reveries for relief as the common hypochondriac flies to his bottle or to his mistress, and the effect is precisely the same: the animal spirits are exhausted, pleasure snaps with its own tension, and the changeful sufferer becomes doubly irritable and wretched. We may see directly what influence the body has upon this kind of devotion, if we examine the temperament of its professors. The female sex, for instance, are acknowledged to possess the greatest bodily sensibility, and it is the women who chiefly indulge in these lovesick visions of heaven; the men, after the usual system of the world, are more fond of the pride and ambition of favoritism. . . . The Methodist magazines abound in the dying raptures of the godly, and it is curious to observe what an infinite number of rapturous females there are in comparison with the men. It has been the same in all the Christian superstitions, from the perpetual virgin St. Teresa,[3] whom Christ espoused with a ring, down to Mrs. Rowe,[4] who wrote love letters to the divine being. The language of these women is so entirely earthly, that in general if you change the name of the object, you might think their devotion addressed to a mere lover. The Deity is personified and embodied in the grossest of images; the soul talks just as the body might be supposed to talk without a soul; and instead of the sense, God is adored with the senses. They tell us that they ascend to heaven in these raptures and leave earth behind them; but it appears to me that they are not quite so forgetful of their old acquaintance, or why should they adopt its language in a region so different? . . . I would not have the Methodists divest themselves of amatory feeling—it is one of the best of feelings in its proper state and towards its proper object—but I would admonish them to avoid the odious hypocrisy of pretending to get rid of all worldly feelings, when at the same time their very adoration of God convinces us they are full of them.

‡

This amorous spirit in the Methodists, and indeed in most other fanatical sects, has been strongly encouraged by the study of Solomon's Song,[5] a work which is a disgrace to the

---

    3   [Ed. The Spanish Carmelite mystic, St. Teresa of Ávila (1515–1582).]

    4   [Ed. Elizabeth Rowe (1674–1737), whose writings include *Devout exercises of the heart in meditation and soliloquy, prayer and praise* (1737).]

    5   [Ed. The Song of Solomon.]

sacred character of the Scriptures. If this indecent eclogue was really written by the Jewish king, as many excellent men have doubted, it is only an additional proof of his attachment to women. Some of it is elegant, more of it obscure, and much of it very obscene. I am not disposed to quarrel with the style of its metaphor and simile as too hyperbolical for the East, or to admire it as too delicate for vulgar comprehension. It is certainly not in the taste of the heathen poets. If the noses of Solomon's ladies were really like castle towers, their eyes like fish pools, and their bosoms like young roes [Song 4:4-5; 7:4], that was his concern: beauty is entirely a matter of taste; but what these similes can have to do with religion and the church is a matter that has puzzled men of much greater ingenuity than myself. . . .

The Methodists, to say the least of it, are very imprudent in admitting the amatory style of devotion into their meetings and societies. Granting that their old preachers and old women may really think more of heaven than of earth on those occasions, and not to mention that there is something ineffably disgusting in hearing old age murmuring and languishing in the phraseology of Solomon's Song, the young people, who have other duties to perform in this world besides praying, will not listen to them without effect. . . . and if you tell them they should not have excited the passions of youth by praying and singing so amorously, they shake their heads and pity your extreme want of purity.

⤙⤚

TEXT: Leigh Hunt, "An attempt to shew the folly and danger of Methodism. In a series of essays," *The Examiner* no. 19–22, 24, 28–29, 33, 35 (May–August 1808): 301–2, 334, 381–82, 445, 524–25, 555–56.

HANNAH MORE
(1745–1833)
Heart Religion

The Book of Common Prayer established uniformity throughout the nation, but new models of piety risked disrupting the stability of English Christendom. When the leader of such piety was a charismatic and illustrious woman, however, the potential for controversy rose dramatically, as the case of Hannah More amply demonstrates. More was born near Bristol and educated by her father. She began writing and teaching while at a school that she and her sisters helped found, leading to the publication of numerous works, including *The search after happiness* (1773), *Sacred dramas* (1782), and *Thoughts on the importance of the manners of the great to general society* (1788). She was engaged to one Edward Turner, but Turner's extraordinary shyness led to three postponed weddings and the eventual demise of their relationship (Turner settled an annuity of £200 on her, which secured her a stable income and freedom from marital attachments for the remainder of her life). Visits to London with her sisters placed Hannah within the literary bluestocking orbit of the times. Friendships shaped her life. The English playwright David Garrick and his wife Eva encouraged More to compose several dramatic works (some of which were staged). Her friendship with Ann Yearsley, an unlettered milk-woman, helped establish the latter's reputation, though their relationship ended badly due to More's paternalistic control of Yearsley's revenues. Wilberforce encouraged her to establish schools devoted to religious and professional training in and around Cheddar, as well as to take up political causes such as abolitionism. More published social, moral, and religious criticism, too. She opposed Thomas Paine's *Rights of man* in her *Village politics* (1792), penned a noted essay on aristocratic education in *Hints towards forming the character of a young princess* (1805), developed major Bible themes in *An essay on the character and practical writings of St. Paul* (1815), and published a highly successful novel (*Coelebs in search of a wife* [2 vols., 1809]). She was not a democrat: her *Cheap repository tracts* perpetuated class distinctions and paternalist attitudes, while the schools she established taught reading and religion but not writing (for fear that the skill would lead to discontent). This condescending attitude towards the lower classes, particularly when compared to leading contemporaries such as Mary Wollstonecraft, diminished her subsequent reputation.

The Blagdon controversy of 1800–1803 reveals a great deal about More's reputation as a religious leader in the English West Country. More found herself embroiled in a nasty row after the opening of her new school there in 1795. Although religious instruction under her influence led to remarkable increases in church attendance, the local curate denounced More's school for allegedly promoting Methodism. More was labeled a "she-bishop" by local clergymen—a sign of her growing public stature—and suffered the acerbic pen of the ecclesial polemicist Charles Daubeny. In fact, while More was friends with evangelicals such as Wilberforce and other members of the so-called Clapham Sect, she remained wary of the more emotive aspects of the evangelical revival throughout her life. The Blagdon controversy also provides some context for More's *Practical piety; or, The influence of the religion of the heart on the conduct of the life* (1811). More contends for a Christianity that is deeply pious and unabashedly practical. She advocates prayer as a yielding of the self to God and encourages the inculcation of devotion and love of God through virtue and self-denial. In the following selection from the opening chapter of *Practical piety*, More addresses the leading idea of the book, "Christianity an Internal Principle," in order to demonstrate the correspondence between the Spirit's work within the soul and the practice of piety in daily life.

Sources: *BDE*; Charles Howard Ford, *Hannah More: a critical biography* (New York: Peter Lang, 1996); *ODCC*; *ODNB*; Anne Stott, *Hannah More: the first Victorian* (Oxford: Oxford University Press, 2003).

HANNAH MORE
Practical piety
1811

Christianity bears all the marks of a divine original. It came down from heaven, and its gracious purpose is to carry us up thither. Its author is God. It was foretold from the beginning by prophecies which grew clearer and brighter as they approached the period of their accomplishment. It was confirmed by miracles which continued till the religion they illustrated was established. It was ratified by the blood of its author. Its doctrines are pure, sublime, consistent. Its precepts just and holy. Its worship is spiritual. Its service reasonable and rendered practicable by the offers of divine aid to human weakness. It is sanctioned by the promise of eternal happiness to the faithful and the threat of everlasting misery to the disobedient. It had no collusion with power, for power sought to crush it. It could not be in any league with the world, for it set out by declaring itself the enemy of the world. It reprobated its maxims, it showed the vanity of its glories, the danger of its riches, the emptiness of its pleasures.

Christianity, though the most perfect rule of life that ever was devised, is far from being barely a rule of life. A religion consisting of a mere code of laws might have sufficed for man in a state of innocence. But [a] man who has broken these laws cannot be saved by a rule which he has violated. What consolation could he find in the perusal of statutes, every one of which, bringing a fresh conviction of his guilt, brings a fresh assurance of his condemnation. The chief object of the gospel is not to furnish rules for the preservation of innocence, but to hold out the means of salvation to the guilty. It does not proceed upon a supposition, but a fact; not upon what might have suited man in a state of purity, but upon what is suitable to him in the exigencies of his fallen state.

This religion does not consist in an external conformity to practices which, though right in themselves, may be adopted from human motives and to answer secular purposes. It is not a religion of forms and modes and decencies. It is being transformed into the image of God. It is being like-minded with Christ.[1] It is considering him as our sanctifica-

---

[1]   [Ed. Biblical allusions permeate More's prose; these two sentences echo Rom 12:2: "And do not be conformed to this world, but be transformed by the renewing of your mind, so that you may prove what the will of God is, that which is good and acceptable and perfect."]

tion as well as our redemption. It is endeavoring to live to him here that we may live with him hereafter. It is desiring earnestly to surrender our will to his, our heart to the conduct of his Spirit, our life to the guidance of his Word. . . .

The sacred writings frequently point out the analogy between natural and spiritual things. The same Spirit which in the creation of the world moved upon the face of the waters, operates on the human character to produce a new heart and a new life.[2] By this operation the affections and faculties of the man receive a new impulse—his dark understanding is illuminated, his rebellious will is subdued, his irregular desires are rectified; his judgment is informed, his imagination is chastised, his inclinations are sanctified; his hopes and fears are directed to their true and adequate end. Heaven becomes the object of his hopes, an eternal separation from God the object of his fears. His love of the world is transmuted into the love of God. The lower faculties are pressed into the new service. The senses have a higher direction. The whole internal frame and constitution receive a nobler bent; the intents and purposes of the mind, a sublimer aim; his aspirations, a loftier flight; his vacillating desires find a fixed object; his vagrant purposes, a settled home; his disappointed heart, a certain refuge. That heart, no longer the worshipper of the world, is struggling to become its conqueror. Our blessed Redeemer, in overcoming the world, bequeathed us his command to overcome it also; but as he did not give the command without the example, so he did not give the example without the offer of a power to obey the command.

Genuine religion demands not merely an external profession of our allegiance to God, but an inward devotedness of ourselves to his service. It is not a recognition, but a dedication. It puts the Christian into a new state of things, a new condition of being. It raises him above the world while he lives in it. . . .

If Christianity does not always produce these happy effects to the extent here represented, it has always a tendency to produce them. If we do not see the progress to be such as the gospel annexes to the transforming power of true religion, it is not owing to any defect in the principle, but to the remains of sin in the heart—to the imperfectly subdued corruptions of the Christian. Those who are very sincere are still very imperfect. They evidence their sincerity by acknowledging the lowness of their attainments, by lamenting the remainder of their corruptions. Many an humble Christian whom the world reproaches with being extravagant in his zeal, whom it ridicules for being enthusiastic in his aims and rigid in his practice, is inwardly mourning on the very contrary ground. He would bear their censure more cheerfully, but that he feels his danger lies in the opposite direction. He is secretly abasing himself before his Maker for not carrying far enough that principle which he is accused of carrying too far. The fault which others find in him is excess. The fault he finds in himself is deficiency. He is, alas, too commonly right. His enemies speak of him as they hear. He judges of himself as he feels. But, though humbled to the dust by the deep sense of his own unworthiness, he is "strong in the Lord, and in the power of his might" [Eph 6:10]. "He has," says the venerable Hooker, "a Shepherd full of kindness,

---

2   [Ed. More alludes to Gen 1:2 ("And the earth was without form, and void; and darkness was upon the face of the deep. And the Spirit of God moved upon the face of the waters") and Ezek 36:26 ("A new heart also will I give you, and a new spirit will I put within you: and I will take away the stony heart out of your flesh, and I will give you an heart of flesh").]

full of care, and full of power."[3] His prayer is not for reward but pardon. His plea is not merit but mercy; but then it is mercy made sure to him by the promise of the Almighty to penitent believers.

‡

We must not, however, think falsely of our nature; we must humble but not degrade it. Our original brightness is obscured but not extinguished. If we consider ourselves in our natural state, our estimation cannot be too low; when we reflect at what a price we have been bought, we can hardly overrate ourselves in the view of immortality.

If, indeed, the Almighty had left us to the consequences of our natural state, we might, with more color of reason, have mutinied against his justice. But when we see how graciously he has turned our very lapse into an occasion of improving our condition— how from this evil he was pleased to advance us to a greater good than we had lost, how that life which was forfeited may be restored, how by grafting the redemption of man on the very circumstance of his fall, he has raised him to the capacity of a higher condition than that which he has forfeited, and to a happiness superior to that from which he fell— what an impression does this give us of the immeasurable wisdom and goodness of God, of the unsearchable riches of Christ.

The religion which it is the object of these pages to recommend, has been sometimes misunderstood and not seldom misrepresented. It has been described as an unproductive theory and ridiculed as a fanciful extravagance. For the sake of distinction it is here called *the religion of the heart.* There it subsists as the fountain of spiritual life; thence it sends forth, as from the central seat of its existence, supplies of life and warmth through the whole frame. There is the soul of virtue. There is the vital principle which animates the whole being of a Christian.

‡

The saints of old, so far from setting up on the stock of their own independent virtue, seem to have had no idea of any light but what was imparted, of any strength but what was communicated to them from above. Hear their importunate petitions! "O send forth thy light and thy truth!" [Ps 43:3]. Mark their grateful declarations! "The Lord is my strength and my salvation!" [Ps 62:2]. Observe their cordial acknowledgements! "Bless the Lord, O my soul, and all that is within me bless his holy name" [Ps 103:1].

Though we must be careful not to mistake for the divine agency those impulses which pretend to operate independently of external revelation—which have little reference to it, which set themselves above it—it is, however, that powerful agency which sanctifies all means, renders all external revelation effectual. Notwithstanding that all the truths of religion, all the doctrines of salvation are contained in the Holy Scriptures, these very Scriptures require the influence of that Spirit which dictated them to produce an influential faith. This Spirit, by enlightening the mind, converts the rational persuasion, brings the intellectual conviction of divine truth conveyed in the New Testament, into an operative

---

[3]   [Ed. Richard Hooker, "Sermon on Habakkuk 1:4," in *The works of that learned and judicious divine Mr. Richard Hooker*, ed. John Keble, 3 vols., 7th ed., rev. R. W. Church and F. Paget (Oxford: Clarendon, 1888), 3:481.]

principle. A man—from reading, examining, and inquiring—may attain to such a reasonable assurance of the truth of revelation as will remove all doubts from his own mind and even enable him to refute the objections of others; but this bare intellectual faith alone will not operate against his corrupt affections, will not cure his besetting sin, will not conquer his rebellious will, and may not therefore be an efficacious principle. A mere historical faith, the mere evidence of facts with the soundest reasonings and deductions from them, may not be that faith which will fill him with all joy and peace in believing.

An habitual reference to that Spirit which animates the real Christian is so far from excluding that it strengthens the truth of revelation, but never contradicts it. The Word of God is always in unison with his Spirit. His Spirit is never in opposition to his Word. . . . If then we refuse to yield to its [the Spirit's] guidance, if we reject its directions, if we submit not to its gentle persuasions (for such they are, and not arbitrary compulsions), we shall never attain to that peace and liberty which are the privilege, the promised reward of sincere Christians.

‡

On the whole then, the state which we have been describing is not the dream of the enthusiast; it is not the reverie of the visionary who renounces prescribed duties for fanciful speculations and embraces shadows for realities; but it is that sober earnest of heaven, that reasonable anticipation of eternal felicity, which God is graciously pleased to grant, not partially, nor arbitrarily, but to all who diligently seek his face, to all to whom his service is freedom, his will a law, his word a delight, his Spirit a guide; to all who love him unfeignedly, to all who devote themselves to him unreservedly, to all who with deep self-abasement, yet with filial confidence, prostrate themselves at the foot of his throne, saying, "Lord, lift thou up the light of thy countenance upon us" and we shall be safe [Ps 4:6, 8].

TEXT: Hannah More, *Practical piety; or, The influence of the religion of the heart on the conduct of the life*, 2 vols. (Boston: Munroe and Francis, 1811), 1:13–21, 26–29, 32–33.

JOANNA SOUTHCOTT
(1750–1814)
Prophecies

Some earned the label "enthusiast" for little more than encouraging individual spirituality. Others earned the label "enthusiast" through public claims of divine knowledge, political views that placed them at odds with king and country, or writings that related millenarian biblical themes to current events. The Baptist layman Richard Brothers (1757–1824), for example, was imprisoned for insanity in 1795 after declaring the French Revolution to be a sign of divine judgment and, later, for comparing London to Babylon. Enthusiasm, in Brothers' case, brought individual piety to the public square and, many believed, necessitated an equally public response in order to maintain social and political order.

Joanna Southcott similarly established herself as one of the most sensational religious figures in the Romantic period. Her writings, which fused visionary pretensions with savvy marketing, captured the attention of an eager reading public. While working as a household servant, this self-proclaimed prophetess developed a unique brand of spiritual biblical interpretation. Southcott joined the Methodists in 1791, but, unlike Whitefield and Wesley, she believed that her own words were divinely inspired. She soon began to claim prophetic, millenarian visions, sending her sealed prophecies to local clergy, so that, when the prophecies came true, the ministers' testimony would establish her reputation as an inspired prognosticator. Her predictions proved so compelling that the household in which Southcott worked (shrewdly, as it turns out) stockpiled food and prepared for the upheaval that would result from the war with France. Despite conflict with Anglican and dissenting ministers alike, around the turn of the century Southcott gained wide acclaim, particularly among the working classes, when she correctly predicted the death of a bishop and widespread food shortages.

Southcott began publishing her predictions with *The strange effects of faith* in 1801. The same year, Southcott's work attracted the attention of several clergymen who had previously supported Richard Brothers. Bolstered by their support, Southcott published several more parts of *The strange effects*. Not surprisingly, most clergy rejected Southcott's claims, suspecting a deception (if not mental illness). In London Southcott moved into the home of Jane Townley, who encouraged Southcott's work and provided her with the service of a permanent amanuensis (Ann Underwood). By this point, Southcott's prophecies amounted to a full-fledged movement. Her publications—which mixed biblical allusions with working-class themes and salacious details of local scandals—were widely distributed: "By one conservative estimate, a total of 108,000 copies of her various works were published and circulated from 1801 to 1816, making her one of the most popular writers of her time."[1] Southcott also mobilized her followers by developing special "seals" that affirmed devotees as members of the promised new Jerusalem.

Southcott's fame soared with her 1814 announcement that she would soon give birth to a child, the promised "Prince of Peace." Southcott portrayed herself as a new Mary sent to proclaim a message of good news for all who would follow her words. Publicity only increased when she claimed various signs of pregnancy (including intestinal pains and enlarged breasts) and reported that physicians had also confirmed signs of her divinely ordained pregnancy (this despite her advanced age and self-proclaimed virginity). The following selection from *Prophecies announcing the birth of the Prince of Peace* (1814) shows Southcott's unique rhetorical mix of hope for her followers, judgment towards those who reject her message, and confident apologetic regarding her own motivations.

Although Southcott claimed signs of laboring and even married a spiritual "Joseph" to legitimate the child before the law, her sudden death in late December 1814 terminated any further expansion of the movement. Some believed that keeping her body warm would allow for a resurrection, but four days after her death a group of physicians (joined by several of her followers) performed an autopsy. Her physician, Peter Mathias, reported on the results in *The case of Johanna Southcott* (1815). The autopsy revealed a considerable amount of abdominal fat, gall stones, enlarged breasts (due to a glandular disorder and large tumor), and severe intestinal flatus, but "neither the promised Shiloh nor any other fetus was found" within her womb.

SOURCES: Jasper Cragwall, *Lake Methodism: polite literature and popular religion in England, 1780–1830* (Columbus: Ohio State University Press, 2013); James K. Hopkins, *A woman to deliver her people: Joanna Southcott and English millenarianism in an era of revolution* (Austin: University of Texas Press, 1982); *ODCC*; *ODNB*.

---

[1] *ODNB.*

JOANNA SOUTHCOTT
Prophecies announcing the birth of the Prince of Peace
1814

Having brought together the principal prophecies concerning the Child that was to be born, but never understood till this revelation was given in what manner he should be born, I shall now bring forward some of the prophecies which were given to show how great the rage and fury would be in men when this was made known.

> The living waters are the living stream,
> That like a fountain will come from on high;
> But yet the sinners will it all defy;
> And as 'tis flowing, sin will sure abound;
> They'll froth with fury for to hear the sound.—
> So with the wicked it will certain be:
> They'll foam with fury, and the truth you'll see.[1]

How true I have found these words by experience! As I am now compelled to flee, not only from the face of my enemies, but from my friends likewise, to conceal myself in a place of safety, where I am not known by any person; and my name I am obliged to conceal, to preserve my life from malicious and inveterate enemies, who threatened to set the house on fire where I lived, and to take my life if they by any means could get me in their power. This my friends have heard them say, that their determination was to seek my life. As my enemies mock me, they mock the Scriptures likewise—then what can I expect from such men, if I fall into their hands? But this proves the truth of the following words:

> It is with Hell thou dost contend,
> For he in man doth speak;

[1] [Ed. Joanna Southcott, *The strange effects of faith, with remarkable prophecies, made in 1792, &c., of things which are to come*, in *Copies of letters sent to the clergy of Exeter from 1796 to 1800, with communications and prophecies put in the newspapers in 1813* (London: Marchant and Galabin, Ingram-Court, 1813), 162.]

And angels here do now appear,
For they do speak in man,
And tell thee for to persevere—
Like a good soldier stand.
So both are come the ranks to join,
And I'll join with my friends:
And Satan's come to join his own—
Mark well and see the end.[2]

Were not Satan to speak in men, such blasphemy would never be spoken, as I am now informed is spoken against my visitation, against the Scriptures, and against the gospel; for all are condemned together in the same manner. This showeth how infidelity is increasing, and how Satan is blinding the eyes of mankind. Concerning those men who said that they would not let me live to see whether the Child was born or not, I was answered in the following manner:

"Without the devil's speaking in men, to set them on with rage and fury, such expressions would not be made by men, as have been made concerning thee, so eagerly to seek thy life to destroy it. Because in men there is a curiosity wrought by nature; and from that curiosity they would wish to see thee live, to pass the time wherein it is said the Child will be born, so that they might have room to mock, without being put to shame and confusion, if no Child is born as mentioned by thee. But, on the other hand, so extraordinary an event to happen in the land, as never took place before, in any age of the world, the curiosity of men would make them long to see it, and what should follow such an extraordinary birth."

"Here I have shown thee what men are, as men, and what would be the language of their hearts, as men, wishing to preserve thy life, to see the effects of this extraordinary visitation that thou hast so published to the world. But how different from men dost thou now see thy enemies! No desire to come to the knowledge of the truth, but with rage and fury wishing to destroy the truth! And this is malice worked on by the devil; so that they may see the truth of the gospel before them: for as my enemies were worked on by the devil, when I became flesh and dwelt with men; perfectly so it is now I am come to visit in the Spirit, to bring in my kingdom that I died to redeem. . . . But let no man simply suppose, because it is said he rules the nations with a rod of iron, that it will be with a rod of cruelty unto any that love his appearing; but, as iron is strong, so will his strength be; and as iron will not break, so will he prove that my words cannot be broken; and that my mercies endure forever unto them that love my name. This is the rod of my strength, like a rod of iron, that will not be broken, but establish my kingdom in righteousness and peace. Happy are those that are longing for my coming and to see the Child born that I shall set upon my holy hill of Zion."

"And now let men view the different classes of people, how one part is filled with love, rejoicing in hope to see the glorious day approaching that the Child shall be born, which is spoken of throughout the Scriptures, to bring in the new heavens and new earth to man

---

[2] [Ed. Joanna Southcott, *The strange effects of faith: being a continuation of Joanna Southcott's prophecies of things which are to come* (London, 1802), 108.]

[Rev 21:1]. This is universally known, how men have shown their love and eager desire for the glory of God and the good of mankind, knowing how all is foretold and are now rejoicing that the fulfillment draweth near. This is publicly seen and known to be in man, while, on the other hand, all the rage and fury of the devil ye now see visibly in mankind; then what different answers and what different rods must these different men expect when I come in power to make a final end! The one will find the rod of my strength to deliver my friends from the hands of their enemies; the other will find the rod of my anger. And conscious guilt must condemn them all; as they have shown their anger and indignation at first, they must expect mine at the last. For now 'with the merciful man I will show mercy, and with the pitiful man I will show pity; but with the froward I shall show myself frowardly' [Ps 18:25-26]." . . .

Here I shall answer for myself, as I have brought forward the prophecy to show that it was foretold how the devil would speak in men the truth of these words of the Spirit, I can prove to be verified by the public newspapers, that have been for some time past daily filled with the most virulent and malicious abuse, and invented lies of various kind, which none but the devil himself could put into the heads or hearts of men, and cause them to utter them, which will bring an eternal disgrace on their characters, and prove that they themselves are the imposters, to impose on the minds of the vulgar and ignorant. For none but men void of understanding can for a moment give credit to such false and infamous reports. Every man of common sense must know that, if there was any truth in their assertions, those respectable gentlemen and ladies whom they allow have stood by me from the beginning, would have long ago deserted me, if there were any truth in the assertions that have been made in the newspapers.

With respect to those respectable friends, whom they acknowledge are enabled to make rich presents for the Prince of Peace in honor to the Lord; this, reason must tell every man, that it would not be done by respectable friends, if any of the assertions made against me were true: and therefore wisdom is justified of her children [Matt 11:19].

The rage of men against me showeth plainly to them, as well as to me, that such inveterate malice and envy must spring from the bottomless pit; as they have no grounds for the assertions they have made, calling me a mercenary impostor, that I sold the seals for a guinea and twelve shillings each.[3] Here the inventor discovers himself to be the impostor, to impose upon the public such falsehoods. For now I appeal to men of sense and reason, whether they judge any impostor that was wicked enough to sell the seals in that manner, would not have continued the sale, as thousands are now desirous of having them; and if they were purchased at only a shilling each, the gains would be great. This an impostor might do, but I never received anything for a seal in my life—neither would I for the world—and this is well known by all my friends, who cannot be imposed upon by such wicked inventions. . . .

---

[3] [Ed. Southcott's use of special "seals" invokes powerful biblical images, including Eph 4:30 ("And grieve not the Holy Spirit of God, whereby ye are sealed unto the day of redemption") and the seven seals of the scroll in Rev 5–8. Here, Southcott refers to the "seals" she created for members of her movement, which included a piece of paper, two signatures (her own and that of her follower), a few words of affirmation and acceptance, and a unique wax seal on the outside once the paper was folded. Some estimate that Southcott created twenty thousand of these seals (*ODNB*).]

They likewise have asserted that I announced that a miracle was to be performed by raising a corpse to life. This with my ascension to heaven, that was to take place in Bath, are their own inventions. The working of miracles I never pretended to; and were these men to be called to an account to answer for these assertions, how must they appear, when they cannot prove the truth of one word in a thousand that they have brought forward! But, as to myself, I can justify my conduct in all I have said and done, if I were called forward before all the bishops and clergy.

And now I shall come to their own words, "that all blasphemies against God are punishable." Out of their own mouths they condemn themselves, because I have heard my accusers make as great a mock of the Deity, and the Scriptures, as they have made of me, and condemned both at the same time; and had such men lived in the days of our Savior, they would have been as ready to have called him a blasphemer, and put him to death, as they are wishing to put me to death.[4]

Another of these reports I shall answer: they have said that I have presents to the amount of thirty thousand pounds, for the Child that is to be born, to establish the Jews in their own land; and that I was going to leave the country, taking these presents with me into France. This judgment they might draw from what they would do themselves, but I have acted a different way; for, as soon as I saw the friends, through faith, began to send in presents, I ordered a book to be made to enter every person's name, and what they sent, that if there was a possibility of my being deceived, all persons should have their presents returned to them again; and what I have received I have put out of my own possession; and others I have requested not to be sent till the Child is born.

Here I leave the world to judge whether I am a mercenary impostor or not; for I have enough of my own to support me the short time I shall live in this world (if it be possible for me to be deceived), without robbing my friends or injuring them.

Joanna Southcott

The above taken from Joanna Southcott's mouth, by me,

Ann Underwood
September 7, 1814

TEXT: Joanna Southcott, *Prophecies announcing the birth of the Prince of Peace* (London: W. Marchant [1814]), 34–40.

---

[4]   [Ed. Southcott's comparison of herself to Jesus Christ would undoubtedly have raised the ire of many readers—clergy and laity alike.]

JOSEPH JOHN GURNEY
(1788–1847)
Pure Christianity

The Quaker banker Joseph John Gurney was born in Norwich. His family was not strict in their practice: nearly half of his eleven siblings eventually joined the Church of England. As a youth, Gurney studied first in local boarding schools and then in Oxford with an Anglican tutor. He began attending a Church of England parish, finding the nearby Quaker meetinghouse unsatisfactory. Although as a dissenter he was unable to attend the university, he gained a strong knowledge of biblical and classical languages before returning to Norwich. He joined the family banking business and, after the death of his father, assumed responsibility for the family home, Earlham Hall. In 1812 Gurney committed to the conservative lifestyle of a plain or strict Friend. In 1818 Gurney's meetinghouse formally recognized him as a Quaker minister. He worried that his profession as a banker might conflict with the ministry but maintained both vocations until the end of his life. With his sister Elizabeth Fry (1780–1845), Gurney became an active voice in the prison-reform movement and the abolitionist cause. They visited numerous inmates and jails, and published their observations and proposals for improvements in *Notes on a visit made to some of the prisons in Scotland and the north of England* (1819). While Elizabeth continued to work towards social reform, Joseph John's attention increasingly turned to theological matters. Among several influential treatises are *Essays on the evidences, doctrines, and practical operations of Christianity* (1825) and *Biblical notes and dissertations, chiefly intended to confirm and illustrate the doctrine of the deity of Christ* (1830). He traveled to North America between 1837 and 1840; he preached, visited with numerous religious and political leaders, and observed the harmful effects of slavery. During the 1830s, Gurney increasingly maintained the consistency between evangelicalism and Quakerism. While he continued to believe in the universal light, his emphasis on biblical authority led to a major split among North American Friends: his evangelically inclined supporters became known as "Gurneyites," as opposed to followers of the American Quaker John Wilbur ("Wilberites"), who regarded the Bible as secondary to the authority of the universal inner light.

Gurney's *Sermons and prayers* (1832) includes three homilies delivered consecutively in May 1832 in the Friends' meetinghouse at Liverpool. The text exemplifies the controversial union that Gurney advocated between Quaker teaching and evangelical belief. Early Quaker doctrines of the divine light and obedience to the Holy Spirit merge with a fresh emphasis on the authority of the Bible and the centrality of Christ. To the dismay of many Quakers, Gurney appealed for a return to early Quaker teachings even as he promoted belief in salvation as an event (in opposition to the traditional Quaker understanding of justification as a gradual process over the course of an individual's life). In this way, Gurney fostered an evangelical vision of Quaker theology under the banner of primitive, "unadulterated" Christianity.

SOURCES: *BDE*; *ODCC*; *ODNB*; James A. Rawley, "Joseph John Gurney's mission to America, 1837–1840," *The Mississippi Valley Historical Review* 49 (1963): 653–74; David E. Swift, *Joseph John Gurney: banker, reformer, and Quaker* (Middletown, Conn.: Wesleyan University Press, 1962).

JOSEPH JOHN GURNEY
Sermons and prayers
1832

When our Lord Jesus Christ was drawing towards the close of his ministry, and when he was about to ascend into that glory from which he came, and wherein he was with the Father before the world was, he appeared to his disciples on the mountain . . . and he said to them when they were assembled together, "All power is given unto me in heaven and in earth" [Matt 28:18]. He therefore proclaimed his own supreme authority over all things visible and invisible under the Father, who gave him all authority as the glorious Mediator between God and man, in whom was the nature of the unchangeable God, and who had taken upon him the nature of man, but without sin. "All power is given unto me in heaven and in earth," and then followed his final commission, "Go ye, and teach all nations" (or make disciples of all nations), "baptizing them in the name" (or into the name, as the original words import), "baptizing them into the name of the Father and of the Son and of the Holy Ghost; teaching them to observe all things whatsoever I have commanded you; and behold I am with you always, even unto the end of the world" [Matt 28:19-20]. And blessed forever be the adorable name of the glorious Head of his own church [Col 1:18]; he is with his disciples always, even unto the end of the world; for it is their privilege to serve, worship, and obey an omnipotent and omnipresent Savior, who hath all power in heaven and in earth and who rules over the universe for the church's sake . . . And O my beloved friends, my soul is filled with an ardent desire that whatsoever may be our form of worship, whatsoever our name to religion, whatsoever the ceremonies which we practice or of which we avoid the practice, we may all be baptized under the power of the Lord Almighty into the name of the Father and of the Son and of the Holy Ghost; that ours may not be a barren, fruitless, speculative religion, but a religion which shall embrace the whole truth as it is in Jesus, and which shall be productive of that new creation wherein we may serve the Lord our God in the beauty of holiness [Ps 96:9] and be made meet for the final and full enjoyment of life everlasting: for "if any man be in Christ, it is a new creation; old things are passed away; behold all things are become new" [2 Cor 5:17]. And we may depend upon it, that we cannot live either by the practice of forms or by the absence of them, "for in Christ Jesus neither circumcision availeth anything, nor uncircumcision, but a new creation" [Gal 6:15]; and God grant, my beloved friends, that you may all experience this new creation by being baptized, under the influence of the Holy Spirit, into the name of the Father.

‡

My soul has been bowed in thankfulness in the remembrance at this time that the Lord condescends to guide us by the light of Scripture, my brethren; and I trust we increasingly feel the value, the inexpressible worth, of the light of an outward revelation, of which the divine origin is made abundantly clear by evidence which enlightened reason cannot resist. O friends, are we diligent in making a right use of this blessing? Do we endeavor to follow the guidance of the light of Scripture in all our ways, and in all our works? Are we satisfied with the superficial perusal of the book or do we endeavor to go down into the depth of it? Is it our daily study? Is it our daily delight? Are the Scriptures our evening friend and companion? O friends, how diligently did some of our forefathers in the early period of our Society study the holy Scriptures; how deeply were many of them imbued with their holiness; how many long hours did they spend in the perusal of them, of which we find a clear account written in many instances. They dared not lay the book on one side; they knew it from beginning to end; they studied deeply, many of them, of which you will find plain proofs and clear records in their history; and they were not afraid of applying to the sacred volume as the sure, safe test of their religious doctrine; and they invited their hearers on all occasions to follow the example of the Bereans, who "searched the Scriptures daily, that they might know whether these things are so."[1] And I long to encourage my young friends to make a more diligent, watchful, careful use of the light of Scripture, whereby the Shepherd of Israel condescends—as by one main, important means—to guide the children of God out of darkness into light; to bring their fellow men out of this blindness and ignorance to a knowledge of the truth, even into marvelous light; and I believe, friends, the more diligently, the more humbly, the more earnestly we devote our minds to the study of the sacred pages, the more we shall know of the fullness which is in Christ; the more we shall know, from our own experience, that he is a wonderful counsellor, an almighty friend; that in him are hid all the treasures of wisdom and knowledge [Col 2:3]. . . .

My dear friends, I trust we can, with one heart and one mind, set our seal to these truths; for they are plain, simple, and indubitable as the noonday light. . . . O friends, what a glorious privilege that there is an access open for us all to the Father, through the Son, by one Spirit [Eph 2:18]; and that God, in his matchless condescension, is pleased to make known his will to us by his Spirit, not in the disuse of the means appointed, but in the use of them. Friends, let us not deceive ourselves; let us be the children of prayer; let us wait upon God in true silence; let us devote some of our private hours to the patient perusal of Scripture with meditation and supplication; and then we shall know more of the guidance, even the immediate guidance of the Spirit of our God; and we shall realize our doctrine in our own experience.

---

[1]   [Ed. Gurney refers to Acts 17:10-15, where the people willingly received Paul and Silas, and compared their teaching to the Old Testament Scriptures.]

My beloved friends, there is but one foundation, and that is Christ crucified [1 Cor 1:23, 3:11] . . . And there is but one right superstructure, and that is the work of God's Spirit in the heart of man, producing a holy life and conversation worthy of our high vocation [Eph 4:1]. And those who come under this influence will be taught to worship God, who is a spirit, in spirit and in truth [John 4:24]; and the more they know of this influence, the less will they place their dependence on the wisdom and learning of man, even in the exercise of the Christian ministry; but they will find that the ministry of the gospel of Christ is as free as the air that we breathe; and the anointing in the universal church, under the immediate influence of the Lord's re-anointing, which, when it is poured forth, no man can stay rightly, and when it is withheld, no man can command. . . .

Let no man suppose that we would speak lightly of learning, knowledge, information. No! On the contrary, the servants of God and his children of every name are bound in conscience, are bound to provide themselves with knowledge of all things useful and honorable as far as lies in their power, that the instrument may be enlarged and improved for their Master's use.[2] For the exercise of their gifts in the ministry of the gospel, they must not depend on their own learning, but they must present their minds a living sacrifice unto their God [Rom 12:1], that, under the influence of his Holy Spirit, they may go forth in the work as good scribes, bringing forth from their treasury things new and old [Matt 13:52]. And then, friends, we shall know more of a native power—more of a spreading, diffusive influence in the Christianity of those who now profess it; and many will rally round the standard of Jesse's immortal Son; and the barren wilderness of this world shall blossom as the rose of Sharon [Isa 35:2].

O my beloved friends, would to God that all who name the name of Jesus would learn the lesson of silence; to be brought into true stillness before God; to know the creature, with all his imaginations and all his inventions, to be reduced as into nothing—that God may arise and perform his own work, and qualify his servants for the labors of love, that their offerings may be acceptable and pure.[3] And the Lord doth qualify his servants for their work by bringing them into secret suffering; they are brought into deep exercise of mind for the welfare of the cause; they fill up that which is behind of the afflictions of Christ for the body's sake, which is the church [Col 1:24]; and this appears to be described in the language of an ancient prophecy: "The Lord whom ye seek shall suddenly come to his temple; and who can stand when he appeareth? For he is like a refiner's fire and like fuller's soap, and he shall sit as a refiner and purifier of silver, and he shall purify the sons of Levi and purge them as gold and silver, that they may offer unto the Lord an offering in righteousness" [Mal 3:1-3]. . . . And I hope the day is coming when the Lord will pour forth of his Spirit on all flesh, and when our sons and our daughters shall prophesy, when on his servants and on his handmaids he will pour forth of his Spirit [Joel 2:28–29], and they shall proclaim the glad tidings of salvation under the immediate influence of that Spirit, making a diligent use of those materials which are contained in the holy Scriptures, which were put forth by God himself and are his glorious gift.

2   [Ed. Gurney may refer to Ps 4:1, where "enlarged" indicates freedom.]
3   [Ed. Gurney refers to the Quaker practice of stillness, or practice of silence in the worship meeting that reflects an interior state of spiritual awareness.]

Now, my beloved friends, may you all come more and more under the power of God; for the kingdom of God is not in word, but in power; and you must be saved not by word, but by power [1 Cor 1:18]. Come, I beseech you, as poor contrite sinners in the sight of God, and wash your garments from every stain in the blood of the Lamb which was shed for all men for the remission of sins [Rev 7:14]. And no longer depend on your own wisdom or on the wisdom of your fellow men in the things of religion, but come for yourselves, under the immediate influence of the Holy Ghost, that you may be baptized with the Holy Ghost; may be raised up by a power better than your own unto newness of life, and bring forth the fruits of the Spirit, which are joy, peace, long-suffering, faith, meekness, temperance [Gal 3:22-23]. . . .

There is nothing in the world—there is nothing under heaven, friends—so powerful and so pure as genuine, primitive, unmixed, unadulterated Christianity. And O that we might have it pure, friends; O that we might have it in its primitive, original force. O that we might divest it from the forms and systems and inventions of man, and become the living servants of that holy Lord, in whom dwelleth all virtue and all righteousness and all the beauty of holiness in its highest perfection. Do you understand it, friends? Let the great pattern be your standard, and "put ye on the Lord Jesus Christ, and fulfill not the desires of the flesh"; make not provision for the flesh, to fulfill the lusts thereof [Rom 13:14]; put ye on the Lord Jesus Christ: see that ye wear the robe of his righteousness [Isa 61:10]; for if ye go to the supper of the great king without the wedding garment, ye shall be "bound hand and foot, and cast into outer darkness; there shall be weeping and gnashing of teeth" [Matt 22:13]. . . .

TEXT: Joseph John Gurney, *Sermons and prayers, delivered by Joseph John Gurney, in the Friends' Meeting House, Liverpool, 1832*, 2nd ed. (Liverpool: Thomas Hodgson, 1832), 1–4, 25–29, 48–53.

VI

PSALMS

Songs and hymns in honor of their gods are found among all people who have either religion or verse.

James Montgomery, *The Christian psalmist* (1825)

CHARLES WESLEY
(1707–1788)
Family Hymns

The success of Methodism was due in no small part to the unparalleled achievement of Charles Wesley, one of the greatest hymn writers in the history of Christianity. The son of Samuel Wesley, rector of Epworth, and Susanna Annesley, daughter of a dissenting minister, Charles was born in Epworth, Lincolnshire, on December 18, 1707. He attended Westminster School from 1716 and matriculated at Christ Church, Oxford in 1726. Charles' brother, John, was a fellow of Lincoln College, Oxford, and the two began to study the writings of Thomas à Kempis, Jeremy Taylor, and William Law. They met regularly with a few friends including George Whitefield—the beginning of the so-called Holy Club. By 1732 the association was a formal society (the "Methodists") meeting regularly under John's leadership. After earning his B.A. in 1730 and taking a fellowship at Christ Church, Oxford in 1733, Charles was ordained a deacon and priest of the Church of England. He journeyed as a missionary clergyman to Georgia with his brother John, but left after only five months due to poor health and conflict with the colonists. Not long after his return, Charles experienced "a strange palpitation of heart" on Pentecost Sunday, May 21, 1738, preceding John's similar "heart-warming" experience at Aldersgate by three days. Subsequently, Charles continued to evangelize, first among prisoners and in open-air gatherings, and later, following his marriage to Sarah ("Sally") Gwynne (1726–1822) in 1749, through regular preaching in Bristol and London. Wesley penned some of the most beloved hymns in English history, including "Hark, the Herald Angels Sing" (1739), "Come, Thou Long Expected Jesus" (1745), and "Come, O Thou Traveler Unknown" (1742), with moving lines inspired by Jacob wrestling with the angel (Gen 32):

> Come, O thou Traveler unknown,
> Whom still I hold, but cannot see!
> My company before is gone,
> And I am left alone with thee;

With thee all night I mean to stay,
And wrestle till the break of day.

Charles Wesley remained faithful to the Church of England throughout his life, opposed John's unilateral ordination of ministers for the American colonies ("Wesley his hands on Coke hath laid, / but who laid hands on him?"), and left more than nine thousand poems and hymns in print or manuscript at the time of his death.

Methodist hymns fostered a sense of community and encouraged shared doctrine. Wesley's hymns were not used for large gatherings alone, as the title of the volume from which the following selections are drawn, *Hymns for the use of families* (1767), makes clear. These hymns, which include prayers for daily worship, expressions of pain and grief in times of trouble, and encouragement for various occasions of daily life, exhibit the practical theology of grace that characterizes the Methodist movement. Although Charles published the hymns for the assistance of Methodists generally, several hymns disclose personal anguish related to his wife's childbearing, and both struggles and tender affections associated with intimate family relations.

SOURCES: Jeffrey W. Barbeau, "Enthusiasts, rationalists, and Pentecost: The Holy Spirit in eighteenth-century Methodism," in *Spirit of God: Christian renewal in the community of faith* (Downers Grove, Ill.: IVP Academic, 2015); *BDE*; The Center for Studies in the Wesleyan Tradition, Duke Divinity School; *ECL*; Richard P. Heitzenrater, *Wesley and the people called Methodists* (Nashville: Abingdon, 1995); *ODNB*; *RCBEC*; John R. Tyson, *Assist me to proclaim: the life and hymns of Charles Wesley* (Grand Rapids: Eerdmans, 2007); idem, ed., *Charles Wesley: a reader* (Oxford: Oxford University Press, 1989).

CHARLES WESLEY
Hymns for the use of families
1767

For the evening

1.   O thou that hast our sorrows borne,
Help us to look on thee, and mourn,
    On thee whom we have slain,
Have pierced a thousand, thousand times,
And by reiterated crimes
    Renewed thy mortal pain.

2.   Vouchsafe us eyes of faith to see
The man transfixed on Calvary,
    To know thee, who thou art,
The one eternal God and true;
And let the sight affect, subdue,
    And break my stubborn heart.

3.   My heart all other means defies;
It dares against thy threat'nings rise,
    Thy righteous laws disdains;
More hardened than the fiends below,
With unconcern to hell I go,
    And laugh at hellish pains.

4.   Lover of souls, to rescue mine,
Reveal the charity divine
    That suffered in my stead,
That made thy soul a sacrifice,

And quenched in death those flaming eyes,
  And bowed that sacred head.

5. The unbelieving veil remove,
    And by thy manifested love
      And by thy sprinkled blood,
    Destroy the love of sin in me,
    And get thyself the victory,
      And bring me back to God.

6. Now by thy dying love constrain
    My heart to love its God again,
      Its God to glorify.
    And lo, I come thy cross to share,
    Echo thy sacrificial prayer,
      And with my Savior die.

‡

For a woman near the time of her travail

1. Righteous, O Lord, thy judgments are!
      Ordained by thy decree
    In sorrow to conceive and bear.
      I bow my soul to thee.
    Daughter of Eve, thy voice I hear
      Appointing my distress,
    And prostrate in the dust revere
      Thy awful[1] righteousness.

2. The misery of my fall I feel,
      And patiently sustain:
    But save me from th'extremest ill,
      The more than mortal pain:
    The utmost penalty decreed,
      The utmost wrath, forbear,
    And spare me, O thou woman's Seed,
      Thou Son of Mary, spare.

3. If once to swell the virgin's womb,
      Great God, thou didst not scorn,
    But man thyself for me become,
      Of thy own creature born;
    Partaker of our flesh and blood,

---

[1] [Ed. Worthy of reverence and respect.]

Our sorrows still partake,
And screen me from the curse of God
For thy own nature's sake.

4. O Son of man, assuage my woes,
My rising fears control,
And sanctify the mother's throes,
And save the mother's soul;
Thy blessed, sanctifying will
I know concerning me,
By faith assured I ne'er shall feel
That endless misery.

5. My Savior, from the wrath to come,
From present evil, save,
And further mitigate my doom,
Nor let me see the grave.
Still hold my soul in life, I pray,
A dying worm reprieve,
And let me all my lengthened day
Unto thy glory live.

6. Now, Lord, I have to thee made known
My troubled soul's request,
And sink in calm dependence down
Within thy arms to rest;
Secure in danger's blackest hour
Thy faithfulness to prove,[2]
Protected by almighty power,
And everlasting love.

‡

1. Father and friend of humankind,[3]
Supporter of this tottering clay,
I rest on thee my feeble mind,
On thee my shrinking flesh I stay,
And, called thy chastisement to bear,
Pour out a calmly pensive prayer.

---

[2]   [Ed. To show or demonstrate.]
[3]   [Ed. A manuscript in the hand of Charles Wesley's wife Sally indicates that she may have composed this poem. Note the difference in perspective between these verses and the previous selection: the first focuses on the condition of the mother, while the second appeals for the safe delivery of the infant.]

2. My life I know secured above,
      Hid in those gracious hands divine,
   But O, my heavier care remove,
      And claim my unborn child for thine;
   The burthen of my womb receive,
   Thine, only thine, to die or live.

3. If foreordained to see the light,
      It bursts into a world of woe,
   Seize the young sinner as thy right,
      Before it good or evil know,
   And cleanse in the baptismal flood,
   And wash my babe through Jesus' blood.

4. Ev'n from the sacred laver[4] take,
      And guard its favored infancy,
   Nor ever, Lord, thy charge forsake;
      Nor let thy charge depart from thee,
   But walk in all thy righteous ways,
   Till meet to see thy glorious face.

‡

Thanksgiving for her safe delivery

1. Blessing and praise and thanks and love
      Let God, the Savior-God, receive,
   Who sent the succors from above,
      And bade the dying sinner live!
   The bitterness of death is past,
      The mortal agony is o're[5]
   Brought through the fire, she lives at last
      To love and wonder and adore.

2. Long in the toils of hell she lay
      (While torture tore her tender frame),
   And meekly sighed her life away,
      A picture of the bleeding Lamb!
   Her eyes with looking upward failed,
      And sought the rest of endless night;
   But Christ her Advocate prevailed,
      And stopped the spirit in its flight.

4   [Ed. Wesley refers to the baptismal font.]
5   [Ed. That is, "over."]

3.　　When nature's strength and sense were gone,
　　　　And death's cold hand had grasped his prey,
　　God held her soul in life unknown,
　　　　And reinspired the breathless clay;
　　God heard his wrestling people plead,
　　　　Strong in the faith himself had given,
　　Mighty in prayer which wakes the dead,
　　　　In prayer which shuts and opens heaven.

4.　　Touched by the healing hand divine,
　　　　She lives, she lives to praise her Lord;
　　Jesus, the work and praise be thine,
　　　　Thy name be blest, revered, adored!
　　Thou hast thy gracious word fulfilled,
　　　　And saved her in her last distress;
　　The promise and the prayer is sealed,
　　　　Sealed on her heart in gospel-peace.

5.　　Wherefore with joyful lips and heart,
　　　　Thee, Jesus, Lord of life we own,
　　And sing how great and good thou art,
　　　　How near to help and save thine own!
　　To thee our grateful all we give,
　　　　Thine, wholly thine resolved to be,
　　And only for thy glory live,
　　　　And die a sacrifice to thee.

‡

At the baptism of a child

1.　　God of eternal truth and love,
　　　　Vouchsafe the promised grace we claim,
　　Thine own great ordinance approve,[6]
　　　　The child baptized into thy name
　　Partaker of thy nature make,
　　And give her all thine image back.

2.　　Born in the dregs of sin and time,
　　　　These darkest, last, apostate days,
　　Burthened with Adam's curse and crime
　　　　Thou in thy mercy's arms embrace,

---

[6]　[Ed. Wesley seeks God's faithfulness to impart grace through the sacrament of baptism.]

And wash out all her guilty load,
And quench the brand[7] in Jesus' blood.

3.   Father, if such thy sovereign will,
    If Jesus *did* the rite enjoin,
Annex thy hallowing Spirit's seal,
    And let the grace attend the sign;
The seed of endless life impart;
Seize for thy own our infant's heart.

4.   Answer on her thy wisdom's end
    In present and eternal good;
Whate'er thou didst for man intend,
    Whate'er thou hast on man bestowed,
Now to this favored babe be given:
Pardon and holiness and heaven.

5.   In presence of thy heavenly host
    Thyself we faithfully require;
Come Father, Son, and Holy Ghost,
    By blood, by water, and by fire,
And fill up all thy human shrine,
And seal our souls forever thine.

‡

For parents

1.   How fast the chains of nature bind
    Our poor degenerate race!
What darkness clouds the parent's mind
    If unrenewed by grace!
As sworn to take the tempter's part,
    They fatally employ
Their utmost power and utmost art
    Their offspring to destroy.

2.   By Satan's subtlety beguiled
    To Satan's school they send,
And each delights the favorite child
    To humor and commend:
The proud with ranker pride they fill,

[7]   [Ed. The phrase calls to mind John Wesley's spiritual self-assessment as "a brand plucked from the burning" (inspired by his need to be rescued from a burning home as a child).]

Heighten their worst disease,
And fondly soothe[8] the stubborn will
To tenfold stubbornness.

3.   With lust of pleasure, wealth, and fame
Their children they inspire,
And every vain desire inflame,
And every passion fire:
They wish them good, but rather great,
Religious, but genteel;
Pious, yet fond of pomp and state;
As heaven would mix with hell.

4.   Adorned in pearl and rich array
You see the murderer's prize!
As crowned with flowers, the victims gay
Are led to sacrifice;
Down a broad easy way they glide
To endless misery,
And curse their doting parents' pride
To all eternity.

5.   Others, an half-discerning few,
The fond excess condemn,
And rush with headlong zeal into
The merciless extreme;
They vent their passion's furious heat
In stern, tyrannic sway,
Their children as their beasts entreat,
And force the slaves t'obey.

6.   With notions fraught, the Stoics sour
Pursue their rigid plan,
In weakness look for perfect power;
In babes, the strength of man;
The wisdom ripe of hoary hairs
From children they require,
'Till time their schemes in pieces tears,
And all in smoke expire.

7.   Harassed by long domestic war
With scarce a truce between,
Their children's tender minds abhor
The Egyptian discipline;

[8]   [Ed. To encourage or cajole.]

They quite throw off the yoke severe,
  O're nature's wilds to rove,
And hate the objects of their fear
  Whom they could never love.

‡

For a sick child[9]

1. Father, God of pitying love,
    Let thy yearning bowels move,
    Let thine ear attend our cry,
    Help before our infant die.

2. Hear her help-imploring groan,
    Pained with sorrows not her own,
    Bruised, alas, for our offense
    Save her suffering innocence.

3. Whom but now thy mercy gave
    Keep her from the gaping grave,
    Whom thy love persists to give,
    Let her for thy glory live.

4. But if thou foreknow'st it best
    Not to grant our blind request,
    Snatch her from a length of pain,
    Take her to thine arms again.

5. Now her spotless soul remove
    To the innocents above,
    To her kindred in the skies,
    To an early paradise.

6. Only, while she hence departs,
    Let her carry up our hearts,
    Rend them, as she rends her clay,
    Tear them far from earth away.

7. Far above the world of pain
    Let our souls with hers remain,
    Far above its comforts soar,
    Stoop to earthly bliss no more.

[9]   [Ed. Charles wrote this hymn, and the following, in connection with the illness and death of his second child, Martha Maria Wesley (1755), who survived only one month after birth (see John R. Tyson, *Assist me to proclaim: the life and hymns of Charles Wesley* [Grand Rapids: Eerdmans, 2007], 170).]

On her death

1. Lovely-fair, but breathless clay,
       Whither is thy tenant gone?
    Would the soul no longer stay
       Prisoner in a world unknown?
    Surfeited with life and pain,
    Is she fled to heaven again?

2. Wherefore did she visit earth,
       Earth so suddenly to leave,
    Galled and burthened from the birth,
       Only born to cry and grieve?
    What was all her life below?
    One sad month of fruitless woe.

3. Count we now our mournful gains,
       We who called the child our own:
    Lo, she pays her mother's pains
       With her last expiring groan:
    Mocking all his fond desires,
    Lo, her father's hope expires!

4. Thus her parents' grief she cheers,
       Transient as a short-lived flower,
    Scarcely seen, she disappears,
       Blooms, and withers in an hour;
    Thus our former loss supplies,
    Thus our *promised* comfort dies!

5. But shall sinful man complain,
       Stripped by the divine decree?
    Dares our impious grief arraign
       Heaven's tremendous majesty?
    Rather let us meekly own
    All is right which God hath done.

6. God hath answered all our prayers,
       Mended after his own will;
    Numbered with salvation's heirs
       Her, whose happy change we *feel*;
    Her, whose bliss rebukes our sighs,
    Bids us follow to the skies.

7.   God, to enhance her joy above,
        Gave her a few painful days,
    Object of his richest love,
        Vessel of his choicest grace,
    Bade her suffer with his Son,
    Die to claim an earlier throne.

8.   Best for her so soon to die.
        Best for us, how can it be?
    Let our bleeding hearts reply,
        Torn from all, O Lord, but thee;
    To thy righteous will subdued,
    Panting for the sovereign good.

9.   Let them pant, and never rest
        'Till thy peace our sorrows heal;
    Troubled be our aching breast
        'Till the balm of love we feel,
    Love, which every want supplies,
    Love of One that never dies.

10.   Might we, Lord, thy love attain!
        Cure of every evil this;
    This would turn our loss to gain,
        Turn our misery into bliss:
    Love our Eden here would prove;
    Love would make our heaven above.

‡

A father's prayer for his son

1.   God of my thoughtless infancy
        My giddy youth and riper age,
    Pierced with thy love, I worship thee,
        My God, my guide through every stage;
    From countless sins, and griefs, and snares
        Preserved thy guardian hand I own,
    And borne and saved to hoary hairs,
        Ask the same mercy for my son.

2.   Not yet by the commandment slain,
        O may he uncorrupted live,
    His simple innocence retain,
        And dread an unknown God to grieve:

Restrained, prevented by thy love
   Give him, the evil to refuse,
And feel thy drawings from above,
   And good and life and virtue choose.

3.   When near the slippery paths of vice
      With heedless steps he runs secure,
   Preserve the favorite of the skies,
      And keep his life and conscience pure;
   Shorten his time for childish play,
      From youthful lusts and passions screen,
   Nor leave him in the wilds to stray
      Of pleasure, vanity, and sin.

4.   Soon may the all-inspiring Dove
      With brooding wings his soul o'respread;
   The hidden principle of love,
      The pure, incorruptible seed
   Hasten into his heart to sow;
      And when the word of power takes place,
   Let every blossom knit and grow,
      And ripen into perfect grace.

‡

Hymn for the head of an unconverted family

1.   Father of earth and heaven
      Permit me to complain
   Of those thy love to me hath given,
      Who bear thy name in vain;
      As yet I cannot see
      The marks of grace divine,
   Or one of all my family
      Adopted into thine.

2.   Strangers or foes to God,
      Dead, dead in sin they live,
   And thoughtless, with the worldly crowd,
      Their hearts to pleasure give;
      The paths of gospel-peace
      Alas, they have not known,
   But hate the power of godliness,
      And love themselves alone.

3. My life of faith and prayer
       As madness they condemn,
    My ways so strict they cannot bear,
       So contrary to them;
       My counsels they despise,
       When kindly I reprove,
    And stop their ears, and shut their eyes,
       And trample on my love.

4. Day after day I mourn,
       And wait their change to see:
    When wilt thou touch their hearts, and turn
       The wanderers back to thee?
       Mercy on them be showed
       In honor of thy Son;
    Nor let them perish in their blood
       For whom he poured his own.

5. Father, for Jesus' sake,
       Thy quick'ning Spirit breathe,
    And let their precious souls awake,
       Nor sleep in endless death;
       My household-foes convert,
       From Satan's power release,
    And then permit me to depart
       In everlasting peace.

‡

On the birthday of a friend[10]

1. Come away to the skies,
       My beloved arise,
    And rejoice on the day thou was born;
       On the festival day
       Come exulting away,
    To thy heavenly country return.

2. We have laid up our love
       And treasure above,
    Though our bodies continue below;

---

[10]   [Ed. Manuscript evidence indicates that Charles wrote these lines for his wife Sally.]

The redeemed of the Lord,
We remember his word,
And with singing to Zion we go.

3.   With singing we praise
The original grace
By our heavenly Father bestowed;
Our being receive
From his bounty, and live
To the honor and glory of God.

4.   For thy glory we are,
Created to share
Both the nature and kingdom divine;
Created again,
That our souls may remain
In time and eternity thine.

5.   With thanks we approve
The design of thy love
Which hath joined us, in Jesus his name,
So united in heart,
That we never can part,
Till we meet at the feast of the Lamb.

6.   There, there at his seat
We shall suddenly meet,
And be parted in body no more;
We shall sing to our lyres
With the heavenly choirs,
And our Savior in glory adore.

7.   Hallelujah we sing
To our Father and King,
And his rapturous praises repeat;
To the Lamb that was slain
Hallelujah again
Sing all heaven, and fall at his feet.

8.   In assurance of hope
We to Jesus look up,
Till his banner unfurled in the air

From our grave we doth see,
And cry out IT IS HE,
And fly up to acknowledge him there!

TEXT: Charles Wesley, *Hymns for the use of families, and on various occasions* (Bristol: William Pine, 1767), 20–21, 44–45, 55–56, 59–60, 63–67, 73–76, 118–19, 146–47, 174–76.

JOHN NEWTON (1725–1807)
WILLIAM COWPER (1731–1800)
Light Revealed

The hymns of John Newton and William Cowper (pronounced "Cooper") are among the most beloved in the English language. Newton's dramatic story from life as a slave trader to evangelical minister and author of "Amazing Grace" remains one of the most prominent conversion narratives in Christian history. Born in Wapping, London, Newton was raised in a dissenting home under the care of his mother. At her death, however, Newton's religious training ceased. After a brief stint at a boarding school, Newton traveled several times across the ocean with his father, a shipmaster who drowned at sea in 1750. The low point of Newton's life came during these years: he engaged in unsuccessful business opportunities, was forced into naval war service, deserted, and was imprisoned; then served on a merchant vessel engaged in the West African slave trade. During a severe storm on March 21, 1748, Newton turned to God in prayer. Despite this evangelical conversion, Newton subsequently served as master of three ships involved in the enslavement of Africans. In Liverpool, Newton was Tide Surveyor between 1755 and 1764 and, influenced by the evangelical preaching of George Whitefield's Calvinist Methodism, began to study ancient languages towards entrance into the ministry. Although he considered dissenting ministry for a time, the bishop of London ordained him in 1764, and he was placed in the curacy of Olney. The same year, he published a widely read account of his spiritual renewal in *An authentic narrative of some remarkable and interesting particulars in the life of —* (1764). From 1780 until his death, Newton served London's St. Mary Woolnoth, made significant contributions to the abolitionist movement, published sermons and reviews, and produced a valuable collection of letters.

At Olney, Newton developed a friendship and began collaborating with the poet William Cowper. Born at Great Berkhamstead, Cowper attended Westminster between 1741 and 1747. He studied for the bar at Middle Temple, worked unhappily in law, suffered from depression and mental instability, and required medical care throughout much of his adult life. After his father's death in 1756, Cowper was financially secure to pursue his love of literature. On July 26, 1764, a random reading from Romans 3:25 ("Whom God hath set forth to be a propitiation through faith in his blood, to declare his righteousness for the remission of sins that are past") led to a powerful experience of evangelical conversion. By 1773, however, continued mental illness and a disastrous amorous relationship led Cowper to renounce Christianity for the remainder of his life.

Olney hymns (1779), a powerful expression of Christian piety in verse, remains one of the great works of the English evangelical revival. Both men had known suffering through severe personal trials. Both regarded their adult conversions as life-changing examples of faith and saving grace. Cowper's literary skill was already apparent when the two men began their collaboration, and it was likely due to Newton's influence that Cowper published his own conversion account. Cowper's struggle with depression in the early 1770s nearly derailed the production of *Olney hymns*. Along with 66 hymns by Cowper, Newton published the collection of 348 pieces in 1779. The hymns, written individually by either Newton or Cowper, highlight the biblical orientation of evangelical religious experience, the centrality of divine grace, and intense spiritual brokenness.

SOURCES: Jonathan Aitkin, *John Newton: from disgrace to amazing grace* (Wheaton, Ill.: Crossway, 2007); Richard Arnold, *Trinity of discord: the hymnal and poetic innovations of Isaac Watts, Charles Wesley, and William Cowper* (New York: Peter Lang, 2012); *BDE*; D. B. Hindmarsh, "The Olney autobiographers: English conversion narrative in the mid-eighteenth century," *Journal of Ecclesiastical History* 49 (1998): 61–84; James King, *William Cowper: a biography* (Durham: Duke University Press, 1986); John Newton and D. Bruce Hindmarsh, *The life and spirituality of John Newton* (Vancouver, B.C.: Regent College, 1998); *ODCC*; *ODNB*; *RCBEC*.

JOHN NEWTON AND WILLIAM COWPER
Olney hymns
1779

Walking with God (Gen 5:24)

1. O for a closer walk with God,
       A calm and heavenly frame,
    A light to shine upon the road
       That leads me to the Lamb!

2. Where is the blessedness I knew,
       When first I saw the Lord?
    Where is the soul-refreshing view
       Of Jesus and his word?

3. What peaceful hours I once enjoyed,[1]
       How sweet their memory still!
    But they have left an aching void,
       The world can never fill.

4. Return, O holy Dove, return,
       Sweet messenger of rest;
    I hate the sins that made thee mourn,
       And drove thee from my breast.

5. The dearest idol I have known,
       Whatever that idol be,
    Help me to tear it from thy throne,
       And worship only thee.

[1] Ps 27:1, 2.

6.   So shall my walk be close with God,
      Calm and serene my frame;
    So purer light shall mark the road
      That leads me to the Lamb.[2]

‡

The Bitter Waters (Exod 15:23-25)

1.   Bitter, indeed, the waters are
      Which in this desert flow;
    Though to the eye they promise fair,
      They taste of sin and woe.

2.   Of pleasing draughts I once could dream;
      But now awake, I find,
    That sin has poisoned every stream,
      And left a curse behind.

3.   But there's a wonder-working wood,
      I've heard believers say,
    Can make these bitter waters good,
      And take the curse away.

4.   The virtues of this healing tree
      Are known and prized by few;
    Reveal the secret, Lord, to me,
      That I may prize it too.

5.   The cross on which the Savior died,
      And conquered for his saints;
    This is the tree, by faith applied,
      Which sweetens all complaints.

6.   Thousands have found the blessed effect,
      Nor longer mourn their lot;
    While on his sorrows they reflect,
      Their own are all forgot.

7.   When they by faith behold the cross,
      Though many griefs they meet;
    They draw a gain from every loss,
      And find the bitter sweet.[3]

---

[2]   [Ed. Book 1.3, Cowper.]
[3]   [Ed. Book 1.13, Newton.]

‡

Faith's Review and Expectation (1 Chron 17:16, 17)

1. Amazing grace! (how sweet the sound!)
    That saved a wretch like me!
    I once was lost, but now am found,
    Was blind, but now I see.

2. 'Twas grace that taught my heart to fear,
    And grace my fears relieved;
    How precious did that grace appear.
    The hour I first believed!

3. Through many dangers, toils, and snares,
    I have already come;
    'Tis grace has brought me safe thus far,
    And grace will lead me home.

4. The Lord has promised good to me,
    His word my hope secures;
    He will my shield and portion be,
    As long as life endures.

5. Yes, when this flesh and heart shall fail,
    And mortal life shall cease;
    I shall possess, within the veil,
    A life of joy and peace.

6. The earth shall soon dissolve like snow,
    The sun forbear to shine;
    But God, who called me here below.
    Will be forever mine.[4]

‡

The Future Peace and Glory of the Church (Isa 40:15-20)

1. Hear what God the Lord hath spoken:
    "O my people, faint and few;
    Comfortless, afflicted, broken,
    Fair abodes I build for you;
    Thorns of heartfelt tribulation
    Shall no more perplex your ways;

---

[4]   [Ed. Book 1.41, Newton.]

You shall name your walls, salvation,
And your gates shall all be praise.

2.   There, like streams that feed the garden,
Pleasures without end shall flow;
For the Lord, your faith rewarding,
All his bounty shall bestow;
Still in undisturbed possession,
Peace and righteousness shall reign;
Never shall you feel oppression,
Hear the voice of war again.

3.   Ye no more your suns descending,
Waning moons no more shall see;
But, your griefs forever ending,
Find eternal noon in me:
God shall rise, and shining o'er you,
Change today the gloom of night;
He, the Lord, shall be your glory,
God, your everlasting light."[5]

‡

Welcome to the Table

1.   This is the feast of heavenly wine,
    And God invites to sup;
The juices of the living vine
    Were pressed to fill the cup.

2.   Oh bless the Savior, ye that eat,
    With royal dainties fed;
Not heaven affords a costlier treat,
    For Jesus is the bread.

3.   The vile, the lost, he calls to them,
    Ye trembling souls, appear!
The righteous in their own esteem
    Have no acceptance here.

4.   Approach, ye poor, nor dare refuse
    The banquet spread for you.
Dear Savior, this is welcome news,
    Then I may venture too.

[5]   [Ed. Book 1.65, Cowper.]

5. If guilt and sin afford a plea,
      And may obtain a place,
    Surely the Lord will welcome me,
      And I shall see his face.[6]

‡

On the Commencement of Hostilities in America

1. The gathering clouds, with aspect dark,
      A rising storm presage;
    Oh! to be hid within the ark,
      And sheltered from its rage!

2. See the commissioned angel frown![7]
      That vial in his hand,
    Filled with fierce wrath, is pouring down
      Upon our guilty land!

3. Ye saints, unite in wrestling prayer,
      If yet there may be hope;
    Who knows but mercy yet may spare,
      And bid the angel stop?[8]

4. Already is the plague begun,[9]
      And fired with hostile rage,
    Brethren, by blood and interest one,
      With brethren now engage.

5. Peace spreads her wings, prepared for flight;
      And war, with flaming sword
    And hasty strides, draws nigh, to fight
      The battles of the Lord.

6. The first alarm, alas, how few,
      While distant, seem to hear!
    But they will hear, and tremble too,
      When God shall send it near.

[6] [Ed. Book 2.53, Cowper.]
[7] Rev 16:1.
[8] 1 Sam 24:16.
[9] Num 16:46.

7.   So thunder o'er the distant hills
      Gives but a murmuring sound;
   But as the tempest spreads, it fills
      And shakes the welkin[10] round.

8.   May we, at least, with one consent,
      Fall low before the throne;
   With tears the nation's sins lament,
      The church's and our own.

9.   The humble souls who mourn and pray,
      The Lord approves and knows;
   His mark secures them in the day
      When vengeance strikes his foes.[11]

‡

The Book of Creation

1.   The book of nature open lies,
      With much instruction stored;
   But till the Lord anoints our eyes,
      We cannot read a word.

2.   Philosophers have poured in vain,
      and guessed from age to age;
   For reason's eye could ne'er attain
      To understand a page.

3.   Though to each star they give a name,
      Its size and motion teach;
   The truths which all the stars proclaim,
      Their wisdom cannot reach.

4.   With skill to measure earth and sea,
      And weigh the subtle air;
   They cannot, Lord, discover thee,
      Though present everywhere.

5.   The knowledge of the saints excels
      The wisdom of the schools;
   To them his secrets God reveals,
      Though men account them fools.

---

[10]   Firmament or atmosphere.

[11]   [Ed. Book 2.64, Newton.]

6.   To them the sun and stars on high,
       The flowers that paint the field,[12]
   And all the artless birds that fly,
       Divine instructions yield.

7.   The creatures on their senses press,
       As witnesses to prove
   Their Savior's power and faithfulness,
       His providence and love.

8.   Thus may we study nature's book,
       To make us wise indeed!
   And pity those who only look
       At what they cannot read.[13]

‡

Joy and Peace in Believing

1.   Sometimes a light surprises
       The Christian while he sings;
   It is the Lord who rises
       With healing in his wings.[14]
   When comforts are declining,
       He grants the soul again
   A season of clear shining,
       To cheer it after rain.

2.   In holy contemplation,
       We sweetly then pursue
   The theme of God's salvation,
       And find it ever new.
   Set free from present sorrow,
       We cheerfully can say,
   E'en let th' unknown tomorrow[15]
       Bring with it what it may.

3.   It can bring with it nothing,
       But he will bear us through,
   Who gives the lilies clothing,
       Will clothe his people too.
   Beneath the spreading heavens

---

[12]   Matt 6:26–28.
[13]   Rom 1:20. [Book 2.81, Newton.—Ed.]
[14]   [Ed. Mal 4:2.]
[15]   Matt 6:34.

No creature but is fed,
And he who feeds the ravens
Will give his children bread.

4. The vine nor fig-tree neither[16]
Their wonted fruit shall bear;
Though all the field should wither,
Nor flocks nor herds be there.
Yet God the same abiding,
His praise shall tune my voice;
For while in him confiding,
I cannot but rejoice.[17]

TEXT: [John Newton and William Cowper,] *Olney hymns: in three books* (London: W. Oliver, 1779), 3–4, 14–15, 43, 66–67, 193–94, 202–03, 218–19, 284–85.

[16] Hab 3:17-18.
[17] [Ed. Book 3.48, Cowper.]

WILLIAM WORDSWORTH
(1770–1850)
English Church

Born at Cockermouth, Cumberland, in the English Lake District, William Wordsworth attended the Hawkshead Grammar School in Furness, Lancashire, before matriculating at St. John's College, Cambridge in 1787. He spent time in London and France in 1791 and 1792, during which time he began living with Annette Vallon (who later gave birth to their daughter Caroline). Wordsworth soon embraced radical political views. Late in 1792 he returned to England; he needed money to support Annette and his unborn child, and France was caught up in the turmoil of massacres and revolution. War between the nations made resumption of life in France impossible, so Wordsworth moved to the West Country of England, where he developed friendships with like-minded radicals such as S. T. Coleridge, John Thelwall, and Charles Lamb. In 1798 the *annus mirabilis* of English Romantic literature, Wordsworth and Coleridge published *Lyrical ballads*, which included poems such as "Lines written a few miles above Tintern Abbey" and "Lines written in early Spring." After traveling the continent with his sister Dorothy and friend Coleridge, Wordsworth returned to the Lake District, where he lived for the rest of his life with Dorothy, his wife Mary Hutchinson, and his children. In these years, Wordsworth wrote both poems and prose (including his *Guide to the lakes*, 1810), embraced the Church of England, and was honored as Poet Laureate in 1843. His later compositions, such as *The excursion* (1814), proved a significant influence on the religious verse of John Keble (anthologized later in this part) and other poets of the Oxford Movement. Wordsworth devoted much of his life to a spiritual autobiography, published posthumously as *The prelude* (1850).

If nature mediates divinity in the earliest poems, nature and the church work collaboratively as mediators of divine grace in Wordsworth's *Ecclesiastical sketches* (1822). His work, written during the contentious years of debate leading up to Roman Catholic emancipation, traces the history of Christianity in England from its earliest introduction until the early eighteenth century. The series of more than one hundred sonnets reveals "the Church as an evolving power in history, as a visible emblem of faith, and as a community of people, lay and ordained."[1]

SOURCES: M. H. Abrams, *Natural supernaturalism: tradition and revolution in Romantic literature* (New York: W. W. Norton, 1971); Jeffrey W. Barbeau, "Romantic religion, life writing, and conversion narratives," *The Wordsworth Circle* 47 (2016): 32–39; Lori Branch, *Rituals of spontaneity: sentiment and secularism from free prayer to Wordsworth* (Waco, Tex.: Baylor University Press, 2006); Stephen Gill, *William Wordsworth: a life* (Oxford: Oxford University Press, 1989); *ODCC*; *ODNB*; Stephen Prickett, *Romanticism and religion: the tradition of Coleridge and Wordsworth in the Victorian Church* (Cambridge: Cambridge University Press, 1976); Michael Wheeler, *The old enemies: Catholic and Protestant in nineteenth-century English culture* (Cambridge: Cambridge University Press, 2006); William Wordsworth, "Preface to *Lyrical ballads* (1802)," in *William Wordsworth: the major works*, ed. Stephen Gill (Oxford: Oxford University Press, 1984), 595–615.

[1] Stephen Gill, *William Wordsworth: a life* (Oxford: Oxford University Press, 1989), 344.

WILLIAM WORDSWORTH
Ecclesiastical sketches
1822

Corruptions of the Higher Clergy

"Woe to you, prelates! rioting in ease
And cumbrous wealth—the shame of your estate;
You on whose progress dazzling trains await
Of pompous horses; whom vain titles please,
Who will be served by others on their knees,
Yet will yourselves to God no service pay;
Pastors who neither take nor point the way
To heaven; for either lost in vanities
Ye have no skill to teach, or if ye know
And speak the word—" Alas! of fearful things
'Tis the most fearful when the people's eye
Abuse hath cleared from vain imaginings;
And taught the general voice to prophesy
Of Justice armed, and Pride to be laid low.

Abuse of Monastic Power

And what is Penance with her knotted thong,
Mortification with the shirt of hair,
Wan cheek, and knees indúrated with prayer,
Vigils, and fastings rigorous as long,
If cloistered Avarice scruple not to wrong
The pious, humble, useful secular,
And rob the people of his daily care,
Scorning that world whose blindness makes her strong?

Inversion strange! that unto One who lives
For self, and struggles with himself alone,
The amplest share of heavenly favor gives;
That to a monk allots, in the esteem
Of God and man, place higher than to him
Who on the good of others builds his own!

‡

Saints[1]

Ye, too, must fly before a chasing hand,
Angels and saints, in every hamlet mourned!
Ah! if the old idolatry be spurned,
Let not your radiant shapes desert the land:
Her adoration was not your demand,
The fond heart proffered it—the servile heart;
And therefore are ye summoned to depart,
Michael,[2] and thou St. George, whose flaming brand
The dragon quelled;[3] and valiant Margaret[4]
Whose rival sword a like opponent slew:
And rapt Cecilia, seraph-haunted Queen
Of harmony;[5] and weeping Magdalene,
Who in the penitential desert met
Gales sweet as those that over Eden blew![6]

The Virgin

Mother! whose virgin bosom was uncrost
With the least shade of thought to sin allied;
Woman, above all women glorified,
Our tainted nature's solitary boast;
Purer than foam on central ocean tost;
Brighter than eastern skies at daybreak strewn

[1]   [Ed. Wordsworth's recollection of great saints in this sonnet reminds readers of a long history in England of martyrdom, the rejection of idolatry, and faithful devotion to God.]

[2]   [Ed. The archangel Michael is frequently depicted as fighting a dragon with a sword.]

[3]   [Ed. St. George, patron saint of England, became a popular figure in English culture through the legendary account of his act of slaying the dragon in James of Voragine's *Golden legend* (ca. 1265).]

[4]   [Ed. St. Margaret of Antioch (sometimes called St. Marina) suffered martyrdom during the persecution of Christians under Diocletian; she is frequently depicted in combat with a dragon.]

[5]   [Ed. St. Cecilia, martyr of the second or third century, is known for having converted her husband and his brother (both subsequently martyred); she is the patroness of church music and often depicted playing the organ.]

[6]   [Ed. Wordsworth refers to the early English legend that Mary Magdalene spent her final days performing penance in a desert and, after her death, accomplished healing miracles.]

With fancied roses, than the unblemished moon
Before her wane begins on heaven's blue coast;
Thy image falls to earth. Yet some, I ween,
Not unforgiven, the suppliant knee might bend,
As to a visible Power, in which did blend
All that was mixed and reconciled in thee
Of mother's love with maiden purity,
Of high with low, celestial with terrene!

‡

Imaginative Regrets

Deep is the lamentation! Not alone
From sages justly honored by mankind,
But from the ghostly tenants of the wind,
Demons and spirits, many a dolorous groan
Issues for that dominion overthrown:
Proud Tiber grieves; and far-off Ganges, blind
As his own worshippers; and Nile, reclined
Upon his monstrous urn,[7] the farewell moan
Renews, through every forest, cave, and den,
Where frauds were hatched of old, hath sorrow past—
Hangs o'er the Arabian prophet's native waste
Where once his airy helpers schemed and planned,
'Mid phantom lakes bemocking thirsty men,
And stalking pillars built of fiery sand.

‡

Translation of the Bible

But, to outweigh all harm, the sacred Book,
In dusty sequestration wrapt too long,
Assumes the accents of our native tongue;
And he who guides the plough,[8] or wields the crook,
With understanding spirit now may look
Upon her records, listen to her song,[9]
And sift her laws—much wondering that the wrong,
Which faith has suffered, heaven could calmly brook.
Transcendent boon! noblest that earthly king

---

[7]   [Ed. Wordsworth imagines the rivers depicted on an urn.]

[8]   [Ed. William Tyndale (ca. 1494–1536) famously replied to criticism from Rome that, should he live long enough, he expected that the laboring child who drives the plow would soon learn more of the Scriptures than the pope.]

[9]   [Ed. The records and songs of the church.]

Ever bestowed to equalize and bless
Under the weight of mortal wretchedness!
But passions spread like plagues, and thousands wild
With bigotry shall tread the offering
Beneath their feet—detested and defiled.

The Point at Issue

For what contend the wise? for nothing less
Than that pure faith dissolve the bonds of sense;
The soul restored to God by evidence
Of things not seen—drawn forth from their recess,
Root there, and not in forms, her holiness;
That faith which to the patriarchs did dispense
Sure guidance, ere a ceremonial fence
Was needful round men thirsting to transgress;
That Faith, more perfect still, with which the Lord
Of all, himself a Spirit, in the youth
Of Christian aspiration, deigned to fill
The temples of their hearts—who, with his word
Informed, were resolute to do his will,
And worship him in spirit and in truth.

‡

Gunpowder Plot[10]

Fear hath a hundred eyes that all agree
To plague her beating heart; and there is one
(Nor idlest that!) which holds communion
With things that were not, yet were *meant* to be.
Aghast within its gloomy cavity
That eye (which sees as if fulfilled and done
Crimes that might stop the motion of the sun)
Beholds the horrible catastrophe
Of an assembled Senate unredeemed
From subterraneous treason's darkling power:
Merciless act of sorrow infinite!
Worse than the product of that dismal night,

---

10   [Ed. A group of Roman Catholics conspired to demolish the Houses of Parliament with gunpowder in 1605. Guy Fawkes (1570–1606) disclosed the plan under torture after being captured in the cellar while awaiting the time to fire the powder (*ODCC*).]

When gushing, copious as a thunder-shower,
The blood of Huguenots through Paris streamed.[11]

‡

Baptism

Blest be the Church, that, watching o'er the needs
Of infancy, provides a timely shower,
Whose virtue changes to a Christian flower
The sinful product of a bed of weeds!
Fitliest beneath the sacred roof proceeds
The ministration; while parental love
Looks on, and grace descendeth from above,
As the high service pledges now, now pleads.
There, should vain thoughts outspread their wings and fly
To meet the coming hours of festal mirth,
The tombs which hear and answer that brief cry,[12]
The infant's notice of his second birth,
Recall the wandering soul to sympathy
With what man hopes from heaven, yet fears from earth.

Catechizing

From little down to least—in due degree,
Around the pastor, each in new-wrought vest,
Each with a vernal posy at his breast,
We stood, a trembling, earnest company.
With low soft murmur, like a distant bee,
Some spake, by thought-perplexing fears betrayed;
And some a bold unerring answer made.
How fluttered then thy anxious heart for me,
Beloved mother! Thou whose happy hand
Had bound the flowers I wore, with faithful tie:
Sweet flowers! at whose inaudible command
Her countenance, phantom-like, doth re-appear.
O lost too early for the frequent tear,
And ill requited by this heart-felt sigh!

---

[11]   [Ed. Wordsworth refers to the St. Bartholomew's Day Massacre of 1572, when the French Catholics slaughtered between five thousand and ten thousand French Protestants.]

[12]   [Ed. As the child is brought forward for baptism, the tomb-lined walls echo in response to the cries of the infant.]

Confirmation

The young-ones gathered in from hill and dale,
With holiday delight on every brow—
'Tis passed away; far other thoughts prevail;
For they are taking the baptismal vow
Upon their conscious selves; their own lips speak
The solemn promise. Strongest sinews fail,
And many a blooming, many a lovely cheek
Under the holy fear of God turns pale,
While on each head his lawn-robed servant lays
An apostolic hand, and with prayer seals
The covenant. The Omnipotent will raise
Their feeble souls; and bear with *his* regrets,
Who, looking round the fair assemblage, feels
That ere the sun goes down their childhood sets.

Confirmation Continued

I saw a mother's eye intensely bent
Upon a maiden trembling as she knelt;
In and for whom the pious mother felt
Things that we judge of by a light too faint,
Tell, if ye may, some star-crowned muse, or saint!
Tell what rushed in, from what she was relieved—
Then, when her child the hallowing touch received,
And such vibration to the mother went
That tears burst forth amain. Did gleams appear,
Opened a vision of that blissful place
Where dwells a sister-child? And was power given
Part of her lost one's glory back to trace
Even to this rite? For thus *she* knelt, and, ere
The summer-leaf had faded, passed to heaven.

‡

Rural Ceremony[13]

Content with calmer scenes around us spread
And humbler objects, give we to a day
Of annual joy one tributary lay;
This day when, forth by rustic music led,

---

[13] This is still continued in many churches in Westmoreland. It takes place in the month of July, when the floor of the stalls is strewn with fresh rushes, and hence it is called the "rush-bearing."

The village children, while the sky is red
With evening lights, advance in long array
Through the still churchyard, each with garland gay,
That, carried sceptre-like, o'ertops the head
Of the proud bearer. To the wide church-door,
Charged[14] with these offerings which their fathers bore
For decoration in the papal time,
The innocent procession softly moves:—
The spirit of Laud is pleased in heaven's pure clime,
And Hooker's voice the spectacle approves![15]

Regrets

Would that our scrupulous sires had dared to leave
Less scanty measure of those graceful rites
And usages, whose due return invites
A stir of mind too natural to deceive;
Giving the memory help when she would weave
A crown for hope! I dread the boasted lights
That all too often are but fiery blights,
Killing the bud o'er which in vain we grieve.
Go, seek when Christmas snows discomfort bring
The counter spirit, found in some gay church
Green with fresh holly, every pew a perch
In which the linnet or the thrush might sing
Merry and loud, and safe from prying search,
Strains offered only to the genial Spring.

Mutability

From low to high doth dissolution climb,
And sinks from high to low, along a scale
Of awful notes, whose concord shall not fail;
A musical but melancholy chime,
Which they can hear who meddle not with crime
Nor avarice nor over-anxious care.
Truth fails not; but her outward forms that bear

---

14 [Ed. Filled.]
15 [Ed. In an earlier note, Wordsworth commented on the legacy of William Laud (1573–1645), archbishop of Canterbury, who was known for his emphasis on liturgical uniformity and anti-Puritanism before he was finally imprisoned and executed for "popery" during the Interregnum: "In this age a word cannot be said in praise of Laud, or even in compassion for his fate, without incurring a charge of bigotry; but, fearless of such imputation, I concur with Hume, 'that it is sufficient for his vindication to observe that his errors were the most excusable of all those which prevailed during that zealous period'" (452).]

The longest date do melt like frosty rime,[16]
That in the morning whitened hill and plain
And is no more; drop like the tower sublime
Of yesterday, which royally did wear
Its crown of weeds, but could not even sustain
Some casual shout that broke the silent air,
Or the unimaginable touch of time.

‡

New Churches

But liberty and triumphs on the main,
And laurelled armies—not to be withstood,
What serve they? if, on transitory good
Intent, and sedulous of abject gain,
The state (ah surely not preserved in vain!)
Forbear to shape due channels which the flood
Of sacred truth may enter—till it brood
O'er the wide realm, as o'er the Egyptian plain
The all-sustaining Nile. No more—the time
Is conscious of her want; through England's bounds,
In rival haste, the wished-for temples rise!
I hear their Sabbath bells' harmonious chime
Float on the breeze—the heavenliest of all sounds
That hill or vale prolongs or multiplies!

Church to be Erected

Be this the chosen site;—the virgin sod,
Moistened from age to age by dewy eve,
Shall disappear—and grateful earth receive
The corner-stone from hands that build to God.
Yon reverend hawthorns, hardened to the rod
Of winter storms, yet budding cheerfully;
Those forest oaks of Druid memory,
Shall long survive, to shelter the abode
Of genuine faith. Where, haply, 'mid this band
Of daisies, shepherds sate of yore and wove
May-garlands, let the holy altar stand
For kneeling adoration; while—above,

---

16   [Ed. "Hoar frost" or frozen mist that is "formed directly by water vapor turning to ice on contact with a cold object" (*OED*).]

Broods, visibly portrayed, the mystic Dove,
That shall protect from blasphemy the land.

Continued

Mine ear has rung, my spirit sunk subdued,
Sharing the strong emotion of the crowd,
When each pale brow to dread hosannas bowed
While clouds of incense mounting veiled the rood,
That glimmered like a pine tree dimly viewed
Through Alpine vapors. Such appalling rite[17]
Our Church prepares not, trusting to the might
Of simple truth with grace divine imbued;
Yet will we not conceal the precious cross,
Like men ashamed:[18] the Sun with his first smile
Shall greet that symbol crowning the low pile;
And the fresh air of "incense-breathing morn"[19]
Shall wooingly embrace it; and green moss
Creep round its arms through centuries unborn.

New Church-Yard

The encircling ground, in native turf arrayed,
Is now by solemn consecration given
To social interests and to favoring heaven;
And where the rugged colts their gambols played,
And wild deer bounded through the forest glade,
Unchecked as when by merry outlaw driven,
Shall hymns of praise resound at morn and even;
And soon, full soon, the lonely sexton's spade
Shall wound the tender sod.[20] Encincture small,[21]
But infinite its grasp of joy and woe!
Hopes, fears, in never-ending ebb and flow—
The spousal trembling—and the "dust to dust"—
The prayers, the contrite struggle, and the trust
That to the Almighty Father looks through all!

[17]   [Ed. The opening lines describe the Roman Catholic celebration of the Eucharist.]
[18]   The Lutherans have retained the cross within their churches; it is to be regretted that we have not done the same.
[19]   [Ed. Thomas Grey, "Elegy written in a country church-yard," line 17.]
[20]   [Ed. The sexton is responsible for the graveyard of a church.]
[21]   [Ed. A small enclosure.]

Cathedrals, etc.

Open your gates, ye everlasting piles![22]
Types of the spiritual church which God hath reared;
Not loth we quit the newly hallowed sward[23]
And humble altar, mid your sumptuous aisles
To kneel—or thrid your intricate defiles[24]—
Or down the nave to pace in motion slow;
Watching, with upward eye, the tall tower grow
And mount, at every step, with living wiles
Instinct—to rouse the heart and lead the will
By a bright ladder to the world above.
Open your gates, ye monuments of love
Divine! thou Lincoln, on thy sovereign hill!
Thou, stately York! and ye, whose splendors cheer
Isis and Cam,[25] to patient science dear!

‡

Ejaculation[26]

Glory to God! and to the Power who came
In filial duty, clothed with love divine;
That made his human tabernacle shine
Like ocean burning with purpureal flame,
Or like the alpine mount, that takes its name[27]
From roseate hues, far kenned at morn and even,
In hours of peace, or when the storm is driven
Along the nether region's rugged frame!
Earth prompts—heaven urges; let us seek the light,
Studious of that pure intercourse begun
When first our infant brows their luster won;
So, like the mountain, may we grow more bright
From unimpeded commerce with the sun,
At the approach of all-involving night.

---

22   [Ed. The opening line intimates the declaration of Ps 24:7: "Lift up your heads, O gates, and be lifted up, O ancient doors, that the King of glory may come in!"]

23   [Ed. That is, "not unwillingly do we leave the recently consecrated ground."]

24   [Ed. That is, "weave through narrow passages."]

25   [Ed. Isis and Cam refer, respectively, to the universities of Oxford and Cambridge, which stand along these rivers.]

26   [Ed. A short, emotional prayer.]

27   [Ed. Wordsworth comments: "Some say that Monte Rosa takes its name from a belt of rock at its summit—a very unpoetical and scarcely probable supposition" (455).]

Conclusion

Why sleeps the future, as a snake enrolled,
Coil within coil, at noon-tide? For the WORD
Yields, if with unpresumptuous faith explored,
Power at whose touch the sluggard shall unfold
His drowsy rings. Look forth! that stream behold,
THAT STREAM upon whose bosom we have passed
Floating at ease while nations have effaced
Nations, and Death has gathered to his fold
Long lines of mighty kings—look forth, my soul!
(Nor in this vision be thou slow to trust),
The living Waters, less and less by guilt
Stained and polluted, brighten as they roll,
Till they have reached the Eternal City—built
For the perfected spirits of the just!

TEXT: William Wordsworth, *Ecclesiastical sketches*, in *The poetical works of William Wordsworth*, 5 vols. (London: Longman, 1827), 3:377–78, 383–84, 386, 388–89, 401, 424–27, 429–31, 435–39, 443–44.

JAMES MONTGOMERY
(1771–1854)
Christian Hymnody

Many Christians in England and Scotland ranked James Montgomery with Isaac Watts and Charles Wesley during his lifetime. Montgomery was born in Irvine, Ayrshire, Scotland, to a Moravian family. Montgomery's father was a minister, and James was sent to a Moravian school in Leeds. His parents served in Barbados as missionaries and died when James was about twenty. He was briefly apprenticed to a baker before running away in search of better opportunities. In 1792 Montgomery took a position as clerk and book-keeper for the *Sheffield Register*. Soon, he was making regular contributions. The paper was briefly shut down, however, over allegations of treason. When the paper reopened, Montgomery worked as its editor, facing prosecution and a brief period of imprisonment for sedition. Upon release, Montgomery returned to the paper and developed a prosperous business as a publisher. In print and through several charitable endeavors, Montgomery advocated social and religious reform.

Montgomery's poetry and reviews are largely unknown today, but his hymns remain a lasting achievement. He not only contributed to the first authorized Anglican hymnal but also published *The Christian psalmist* (1825). In addition to selections by Watts, Wesley, and Toplady, Montgomery included his own original compositions on the ordinary life of families, women, children, and the poor. Verses from his hymn "A Visit to Bethlehem in Spirit" draw readers into an eyewitness account of the nativity in Luke 2:

> The scene around me disappears,
>   And borne to ancient regions;
> While Time recalls the flight of years,
>   I see angelic legions
> Descending in an orb of light,
> Amidst the dark and silent night;
>   I hear celestial voices.

"Tidings, glad tidings from above,
To every age and nation;
Tidings, glad tidings, God is love;
To man He sends salvation;
His Son beloved, his only Son,
The work of mercy hath begun;
Give to his name the glory."

Through David's city I am led;
Here all around are sleeping;
A light directs to yon poor shed,
There lonely watch is keeping:
I enter—ah! what glories shine!
Is this Immanuel's earthly shrine?
Messiah's infant temple?

It is, it is; and I adore
This Stranger meek and lowly,
As saints and seraphs bow before
The throne of God thrice holy;
Faith through the vale of flesh can see
The face of thy divinity,
My Lord, my God, my Savior![1]

Montgomery's introductory essay to *The Christian psalmist* demonstrates the close relationship between poetics and hymnody, and belongs alongside other, better-known and widely anthologized essays on Romantic verse. He contends that Christian hymns express the depths of human existence and the heart's strong longing for God. Against those who believed that poetry and Christian piety are antithetical pursuits, Montgomery illustrates how the great English hymn writers—among whom Cowper, Watts, and Charles Wesley rank highest—have used poetics to kindle devotion and "haunt the imagination."[2]

><~~<

SOURCES: Kenneth R. Johnston, *Unusual suspects: Pitt's reign of alarm and the lost generation of the 1790s* (Oxford: Oxford University Press, 2013); James Montgomery, *The poems of James Montgomery (1771–1854)*, ed. George Wiley (Sheffield: Hallamshire, 2000); *ODNB*.

[1]   James Montgomery, *The Christian psalmist; or, Hymns, selected and original*, 2nd ed. (Glasgow: Chalmers and Collins, 1825), 390–91.
[2]   Montgomery, *The Christian psalmist*, xv.

JAMES MONTGOMERY
The Christian psalmist
1825

Songs and hymns in honor of their gods are found among all people who have either religion or verse. There is scarcely any pagan poetry, ancient or modern, in which allusions to the national mythology are not so frequent as to constitute the most copious materials as well as the most brilliant embellishments. The poets of Persia and Arabia, in like manner, have adorned their gorgeous strains with the fables and morals of the Koran. The relics of Jewish song which we possess, with few exceptions, are consecrated immediately to the glory of God by whom, indeed, they were inspired. The first Christians were wont to edify themselves in psalms and hymns and spiritual songs [Eph 5:19]; and though we have no specimens of these left, except the occasional doxologies ascribed to the redeemed in the book of Revelation, it cannot be doubted that they used not only the Psalms of the Old Testament, literally or accommodated to the circumstances of a new and rising church, but that they had original lays of their own in which they celebrated the praises of Christ as the Savior of the world. In the Middle Ages, the Roman Catholic and Greek churches statedly adopted singing as an essential part of public worship; but this, like the reading of the Scriptures, was too frequently in an unknown tongue by an affectation of wisdom to excite the veneration of ignorance when the learned, in their craftiness, taught that "Ignorance is the mother of devotion";[1] and Ignorance was very willing to believe it. At the era of the Reformation, psalms and hymns in the vernacular tongue were revived in Germany, England, and elsewhere among the other means of grace of which Christendom had been for centuries defrauded.

‡

But turning more directly to the subject of these remarks . . . though our elder poets down even to the Revolution often chose to exercise their vein on religious topics, since that time there has been but one who bears a great name among them, who has condescended

---

[1]   [Ed. The common phrase is often attributed to Robert Burton, *The anatomy of melancholy* (1621), 3.4.1.2.]

to compose *hymns* in the commonly accepted sense of that word. Addison,[2] who has left several which may be noticed hereafter, though he ranks in the first class of prose writers, must take a place many degrees lower in verse. Cowper, therefore, stands alone among "the mighty masters" of the lyre as having contributed a considerable number of approved and popular hymns for the purposes of public or private devotion. Hymns, looking at the multitude and mass of them, appear to have been written by all kinds of persons except poets; and why the latter have not delighted in this department of their own art is obvious. Just in proportion as the religion of Christ is understood and taught in primitive purity, those who either believe not in its spirituality or have not proved its converting influence are careful to avoid meddling with it, so that if its sacred mysteries have been less frequently and ostentatiously honored by the homage of our poets within the last hundred and fifty years than formerly, they have been less disgraced and violated by absurd and impious associations.

‡

> The wretch, condemned with life to part,
>   Still, still on hope relies;
> And every pang that rends his heart
>   Bids expectation rise.
>
> Hope, like the glimmering taper's light,
>   Adorns and cheers the way;
> And still, as darker grows the night,
>   Emits a brighter ray.[3]

Is *this* poetry? Every reader feels that it is. Yet, if the same ideas were to be given in prose, they could not well be more humbly arrayed. Nothing can be more simple, nothing more exquisite; and hymns in the same pure and natural manner might be adapted to every subject in alliance with religion. But by whom? Not by one who had only the delicate ear, the choice expression, the melodious measures, and the fine conceptions of Goldsmith, but by him who, to all these, should add the piety of Watts, the ardor of Wesley, and the tenderness of Doddridge.[4] Had Goldsmith possessed these latter qualifications (and they were all within his reach), would he not have left hymns as captivating in their degree as any of those few but inestimable productions which have rendered him the most delightful of our poets to the greatest number of readers.

It may be superciliously answered that all this is mere speculation; and it may be reasonably demanded that some examples of hymns of merit should be adduced to establish beyond dispute the possible union of poetry with devotion. This shall be done in the sequel; at present, we will only offer a small extract from one of the best-known hymns

---

[2] [Ed. Joseph Addison (1672–1719) was an English essayist, poet, and politician best known for his play *Cato, a tragedy* (1712/1713).]

[3] [Ed. Oliver Goldsmith (1730–1774), playwright, "Song from the oratorio of the captivity."]

[4] [Ed. The English hymn writers Isaac Watts (1674–1748), Charles Wesley (1707–1788), and Philip Doddridge (1702–1751).]

of the only great poet of our country who has written such things; and we offer it as . . . showing that a heart filled with the peace of God has language suitable to its enjoyments and capable of communicating a sense of them to every other heart not dead to sympathy:

> The calm retreat, the silent shade,
>   With prayer and praise agree,
> And seem by thy sweet bounty made
>   For those that follow thee.
>
> There, if thy Spirit touch the soul,
>   And grace her mean abode,
> Oh, with what peace, and joy, and love,
>   She communes with her God!
>
> There, like the nightingale, she pours
>   Her solitary lays,
> Nor asks a witness to her song,
>   Nor sighs for human praise.[5]

Now if this be *not* poetry, the one-and-twenty enormous and unreadable volumes of Chalmers' English Poets[6] containing some four or five millions of lines must be burnt down to the size of *The Christian psalmist* before they will yield a *residuum* of finer standard. Yet will a profane world never be "smit with the love of *sacred song*."[7] The language of devotion, whether in prose or rhyme, cannot be relished because it is not understood by any but those who have experienced the power of the gospel as bringing salvation to them that believe [Rom 1:16]; for the same reason that the Bible itself is neither acceptable nor intelligible to those who are not taught by the Spirit of God. To such, though "I speak with the tongues of men and of angels" about divine things, "I am as sounding brass, or a tinkling cymbal" [1 Cor 13:1]. To those, on the other hand, who have "tasted the good word of God, and felt the powers of the world to come" [Heb 6:5], it will be easy to comprehend that poetry and piety may be as surely united on earth as they are in heaven before the throne, in the songs of angels and the spirits of just men made perfect [Heb 12:23].

A hymn ought to be as regular in its structure as any other poem; it should have a distinct subject and that subject should be simple, not complicated, so that whatever skill or labor might be required in the author to develop his plan there should be little or none required on the part of the reader to understand it. Consequently, a hymn must have a beginning, middle, and end. There should be a manifest gradation in the thoughts, and their mutual dependence should be so perceptible that they could not be transposed without injuring the unity of the piece; every line carrying forward the connection, and every

---

5   [Ed. William Cowper, "Far from the World, O Lord, I Flee," in *Olney hymns.*]
6   [Ed. Alexander Chalmers and Samuel Johnson, *The works of the English poets: from Chaucer to Cowper*, 21 vols. (1810).]
7   [Ed. John Milton, *Paradise Lost*, 3.29.]

verse adding a well-proportioned limb to a symmetrical body. The reader should know when the strain is complete and be satisfied, as at the close of an air in music; while defects and superfluities should be felt by him as annoyances in whatever part they might occur.

The practice of many good men in framing hymns has been quite the contrary. They have begun apparently with the only idea in their mind at the time; another, with little relationship to the former, has been forced upon them by a refractory rhyme; a third became necessary to eke out a verse; a fourth to begin one; and so on, till, having compiled a sufficient number of stanzas of so many lines, and lines of so many syllables, the operation has been suspended; whereas it might with equal consistency have been continued to any imaginable length and the tenth or ten-thousandth link might have been struck out or changed places with any other without the slightest infraction of the chain . . . Such rhapsodies may be sung from time to time and keep alive devotion already kindled, but they leave no trace in the memory, make no impression on the heart, and fall through the mind as sounds glide through the ear—pleasant it may be in their passage, but never returning to haunt the imagination in retirement or, in the multitude of the thoughts, to refresh the soul.

Of how contrary a character, how transcendently superior in value as well as in influence, are those hymns which, once heard, are remembered without effort, remembered involuntarily, yet remembered with renewed and increasing delight at every revival! It may be safely affirmed that the permanent favorites in every collection are those which, in the requisites before-mentioned or for some other peculiar excellence, are distinguished above the rest. This is so remarkably the case with the compositions of Watts, Wesley, and Newton—the most prolific writers of this class—that no further illustration is needful than a recurrence to their pages, when it will be found that the most neglected are generally inferior in literary merit to the most hackneyed ones which are in everybody's mouth and everybody's heart.

It may be added that authors who devote their talents to the glory of God and the salvation of men ought surely to take as much pains to polish and perfect their offerings of this kind as secular and profane poets bestow upon their works. Of these, the subjects are too often of the baser sort and the workmanship as frequently excels the material, while, on the other hand, the inestimable materials of hymns—the truths of the everlasting gospel, the very thoughts of God, the very sayings of Christ, the very inspirations of the Holy Ghost—are dishonored by the meanness of the workmanship employed upon them; wood, hay, straw, and stubble being built upon foundations which ought only to support gold, silver, and precious stones; work that will bear the fire and be purified by it [1 Cor 3:12-13]. The faults in ordinary hymns are vulgar phrases, low words, hard words, technical terms, inverted construction, broken syntax, barbarous abbreviations that make our beautiful English horrid even to the eye, bad rhymes (or no rhymes where rhymes are expected), but, above all, numbers without cadence. A line is no more meter because it contains a certain concatenation of syllables than so many crotchets and quavers pricked at random would constitute a bar of music. The syllables in every division ought to "ripple like a rivulet,"[8] one producing another as its natural effect, while the rhythm of each line, falling into the general stream at its proper place, should cause the verse to flow in

---

[8]   [Ed. Possibly a reference to Robert Southey's melodious "Inscription VII" in *Poems* (1797).]

271

progressive melody, deepening and expanding like a river to the close; or, to change the figure, each stanza should be a poetical tune played down to the last note. Such subservience of every part to the harmony of the whole is required in all other legitimate poetry, and why it should not be observed in that which is worthiest of all possible preeminence, it would be difficult to say; why it is so rarely found in hymns may be accounted for from the circumstance already stated—that few accomplished poets have enriched their mother tongue with strains of this description.

‡

Next to Dr. Watts[9] as a hymn writer undoubtedly stands the Rev. Charles Wesley. He was probably the author of a greater number of compositions of this kind, with less variety of matter or manner, than any other man of genius that can be named. . . . As the Poet of Methodism, he has sung the doctrines of the gospel as they are expounded among that people, dwelling especially on the personal appropriation of the words of eternal life to the sinner or the saint as the test of his actual state before God and admitting nothing less than the full assurance of faith as the privilege of believers:

> Faith, mighty faith, the promise sees,
>   Relies on that alone,
> Laughs at impossibilities,
>   And says—"It shall be done."[10]
>
> Faith lends her realizing light,
> The clouds disperse, the shadows fly,
> The Invisible appears in sight,
> And God is seen by mortal eye.[11]

These are glimpses of our author's manner—broad, indeed, and awful, but signally illustrative, like lightning out of darkness, revealing for a moment the whole hemisphere.

‡

In the composition of hymns, men of wealthier imaginations and happier utterance may furnish to others of susceptible hearts the means of bodying forth their own conceptions, which would otherwise be a burden to their minds or die in the birth without the joy of deliverance. The most illiterate person who understands his Bible will easily understand the most elegant or emphatic expression of all the feelings which are common to all; and, instead of being passive under them, when they are excited at particular seasons,

---

[9]   [Ed. Earlier, Montgomery praised Isaac Watts as nearly "the inventor of hymns in our language, for he so far departed from all precedent that few of his compositions resemble those of his forerunners, while he so far established a precedent to all his successors that none have departed from it otherwise than according to the peculiar turn of mind in the writer and the style of expressing Christian truths employed by the denomination to which he belonged" (xx).]

[10]   [Ed. From Charles Wesley's hymn, "Father of Jesus Christ, My Lord."]

[11]   [Ed. From Charles Wesley's hymn, "Author of Faith, eternal Word."]

he will avail himself of the songs put into his mouth and sing them with gladness and refreshment as if they were his own. Then, though like Milton's, his genius can ascend to the heaven of heavens or, like Shakespeare's, search out the secrets of nature through all her living combinations—blessed is the bard who employs his resources thus; who, from the fullness of his own bosom, pours his divinest thoughts, in his selectest words, into the bosoms of his readers and enables them to appropriate the rich communications to their personal exigencies without robbing him or hindering others from partaking of the same abundant fountain of human inspiration—a fountain flowing, like the oil at the command of the prophet, from one vessel into as many as could be borrowed without exhausting the first, though the whole were filled [2 Kgs 4:1-6]. If he who pens these sentiments knows his own heart . . . he would rather be the anonymous author of a few hymns which should thus become an imperishable inheritance to the people of God than bequeath another epic poem to the world which should rank his name with Homer, Virgil, and "our greater Milton."[12]

<hr>

TEXT: James Montgomery, "Introductory essay," in *The Christian psalmist; or, Hymns, selected and original*, 2nd ed. (Glasgow: Chalmers and Collins, 1825), v–vi, viii, xii–xvii, xxiii–xxiv, xxxii–xxxiii.

[12]   [Ed. Montgomery may be drawing on Anna Seward's memorable phrase in *Sonnet LXIV* of *The poetical works of Anna Seward* (1799).]

JOHN KEBLE
(1792–1866)

Nature's Praise

John Keble was a household name in nineteenth-century England. The son of a high church vicar at Coln St. Aldwyn, Keble was born at Fairford, Gloustershire, and gained distinction as a student at Corpus Christi College, Oxford. In 1811, having recently achieved a double first-class honors (a feat first accomplished only two years earlier by Robert Peel), Keble was elected a fellow of Oriel along with Richard Whately. In subsequent years, Keble was ordained deacon (1815) and priest (1816), and briefly served as a tutor at Oriel (1817–1823) before leaving for the Cotswolds where he assisted his father. During this period, Keble wrote one of the century's most successful books of poetry: *The Christian year* (1827). Keble was elected, without opposition, as professor of poetry at Oxford from 1831 to 1841. Keble's assize sermon at St. Mary the Virgin, Oxford (July 1833), has historically marked the formal commencement of the Oxford Movement. Keble was unflaggingly modest, avoiding popularity throughout his life, but the sermon was immediately published (*National apostasy*, 1833) and initiated high church renewal at Oxford and around England. With Newman and others, Keble wrote and published in the *Tracts for the times*, including contributions on apostolic succession, authority, and ministry (nos. 4, 52, 54, 57, 60), liturgy (no. 13), baptism (no. 40), and the mystical interpretation of the Bible (no. 89). His translation of Irenaeus for the *Library of the fathers* reflects his efforts to revive devotion to the early church within the Establishment. From 1836 until his death, Keble served as vicar of Hursley, near Winchester, publishing works of high church theology, such as his *On eucharistic adoration* (1857). Keble College, Oxford, was founded in his honor.

By many estimates, nearly every literate household in England owned a copy of *The Christian year* (1827). Keble's collection of "thoughts in verse" for Sundays and holy days was one of the most successful publications of the century. There were 16 editions by 1837, 95 by his death in 1866, and 158 editions by 1873. The devotional appealed to readers far outside Keble's own high church circle through biblical allusions, images from nature, and vivid compositions invoking mystery.

SOURCES: Hylson-Smith; Maria Poggi Johnson, "*The Christian year* and the typological imagination in John Keble's parochial sermons," *Pro Ecclesia* 9 (2000): 414–28; Joshua King, "John Keble's *The Christian year*: private reading and imagined national religious community," *Victorian Literature & Culture* 40 (2012): 397–420; Nockles; *ODCC*; *ODNB*; Stephen Prickett, *Romanticism and religion: the tradition of Coleridge and Wordsworth in the Victorian Church* (Cambridge: Cambridge University Press, 1976); Bernard M. G. Reardon, *Religious thought in the Victorian age: a survey from Coleridge to Gore*, 2nd ed. (London: Longman, 1995); *VC*.

JOHN KEBLE
The Christian year
1827

The Epiphany[1]

Behold, the star, which they saw in the east, went before them, till it came and stood over where the young child was; when they saw the star, they rejoiced with exceeding great joy.

Matt 2:9-10

Star of the East, how sweet art thou,
   Seen in life's early morning sky,
Ere yet a cloud has dimmed the brow,
   While yet we gaze with childish eye.

When father, mother, nursing friend,
   Most dearly loved and loving best,
First bid us from their arms ascend,
   Pointing to thee in thy sure rest.

Too soon the glare of earthly day
   Buries, to us, thy brightness keen,
And we are left to find our way
   By faith and hope in thee unseen.

What matter? If the waymarks sure
   On every side are round us set,
Soon overleaped, but not obscure?
   'Tis ours to mark them or forget.

[1]   [Ed. The last of the twelve days of Christmas, January 6 celebrates the manifestation of Christ to the Magi (and, thus, the Gentiles).]

What matter? If in calm old age
　　Our childhood's star again arise,
Crowning our lonely pilgrimage
　　With all that cheers a wanderer's eyes?

Ne'er may we lose it from our sight,
　　Till all our hopes and thoughts are led
To where it stays its lucid flight
　　Over our Savior's lowly bed.

There, swathed in humblest poverty,
　　On chastity's meek lap enshrined,
With breathless reverence waiting by,
　　When we our sovereign Master find.

Will not the long-forgotten glow
　　Of mingled joy and awe return,
When stars above or flowers below
　　First made our infant spirits burn?

Look on us, Lord, and take our parts
　　Even on thy throne of purity,
From these our proud yet groveling hearts
　　Hide not thy mild forgiving eye.

Did not the Gentile church find grace,
　　Our mother dear, this favored day?
With gold and myrrh she sought thy face,
　　Nor didst thou turn thy face away.

She too,[2] in earlier, purer days,
　　Had watched thee gleaming faint and far,
But wandering in self-chosen ways
　　She lost thee quite, thou lovely star.

---

[2]　The Patriarchal Church [of the Old Testament—Ed.].

Yet had her Father's finger turned
    To thee her first inquiring glance;
The deeper shame within her burned,
    When wakened from her willful trance.

Behold, her wisest throng thy gate,
    Their richest, sweetest, purest store
(Yet owned too worthless and too late)
    They lavish on thy cottage-floor.

They give their best—O tenfold shame
    On us their fallen progeny,
Who sacrifice the blind and lame,[3]
    Who will not wake or fast with thee!

First Sunday after Epiphany

They shall spring up as among the grass, as willows by the watercourses.

Isaiah 44:4

Lessons sweet of spring returning,
    Welcome to the thoughtful heart!
May I call ye sense or learning,
    Instinct pure, or heaven-taught art?
Be your title what it may,
Sweet the lengthening April day,
While with you the soul is free,
Ranging wild o'er hill and lea.

Soft as Memnon's harp at morning,[4]
    To the inward ear devout,
Touched by light, with heavenly warning
    Your transporting chords ring out.
Every leaf in every nook,
Every wave in every brook,
Chanting with a solemn voice,
Minds us of our better choice.

Needs no show of mountain hoary,
    Winding shore or deepening glen,

---

3   Mal 1:8.

4   [Ed. Cf. Byron's *The deformed transformed* (1824): "He shall be Memnon, from the Ethiop king / Whose statue turns a harper once a day" (1.531–532).]

Where the landscape in its glory
   Teaches truth to wandering men;
Give true hearts but earth and sky,
And some flowers to bloom and die,
Homely scenes and simple views
Lowly thoughts may best infuse.

See the soft green willow springing
   Where the waters gently pass,
Every way her free arms flinging
   O'er the moist and reedy grass.
Long ere winter blasts are fled,
See her tipped with vernal red,
And her kindly flower displayed
Ere her leaf can cast a shade.

Though the rudest hand assail her,
   Patiently she droops awhile,
But when showers and breezes hail her,
   Wears again her willing smile.
Thus I learn contentment's power
From the slighted willow bower,
Ready to give thanks and live
On the least that heaven may give.

If, the quiet brooklet leaving,
   Up the stony vale I wind,
Haply half in fancy grieving
   For the shades I leave behind,
By the dusty wayside drear,
Nightingales with joyous cheer
Sing, my sadness to reprove,
Gladlier than in cultured grove.

Where the thickest boughs are twining
   Of the greenest darkest tree,
There they plunge, the light declining,
   All may hear, but none may see.
Fearless of the passing hoof,
Hardly will they fleet aloof;
So they live in modest ways,
Trust entire, and ceaseless praise.

Second Sunday after Epiphany

Every man at the beginning doth set forth good wine, and when men have well drunk then that which is worse; but thou hast kept the good wine until now.

John 2:10

The heart of childhood is all mirth:
　　We frolic to and fro
As free and blithe, as if on earth
　　Were no such thing as woe.

But if indeed with reckless faith
　　We trust the flattering voice,
Which whispers, "Take thy fill ere death,
　　Indulge thee and rejoice";

Too surely, every setting day,
　　Some lost delight we mourn,
The flowers all die along our way,
　　Till we, too, die forlorn.

Such is the world's gay garish feast,
　　In her first charming bowl
Infusing all that fires the breast,
　　And cheats the unstable soul.

And still, as loud the revel swells,
　　The fevered pulse beats higher,
Till the seared taste from foulest wells
　　Is fain to slake its fire.

Unlike the feast of heavenly love
　　Spread at the Savior's word
For souls that hear his call, and prove
　　Meet for his bridal board.

Why should we fear youth's draught of joy,
　　If pure, would sparkle less?
Why should the cup the sooner cloy,
　　Which God hath deigned to bless?

For is it hope that thrills so keen
   Along each bounding vein,
Still whispering glorious things unseen?
   Faith makes the vision plain.

The world would kill her soon; but faith
   Her daring dreams will cherish,
Speeding her gaze o'er time and death
   To realms where naught can perish.

Or is it love, the dear delight
   Of hearts that know no guile,
That all around see all things bright
   With their own magic smile?

The silent joy, that sinks so deep,
   Of confidence and rest,
Lulled in a father's arms to sleep,
   Clasped to a mother's breast?

Who, but a Christian, through all life
   That blessing may prolong?
Who, through the world's sad day of strife,
   Still chant his morning song?

Fathers may hate us or forsake,
   God's foundlings then are we;
Mother on child no pity take,[5]
   But we shall still have thee.

We may look home, and seek in vain
   A fond fraternal heart,
But Christ hath given his promise plain
   To do a brother's part.

Nor shall dull age, as worldlings say,
   The heavenward flame annoy;
The Savior cannot pass away,
   And with him lives our joy.

Ever the richest tenderest glow
   Sets round the autumnal sun,

---

[5]   Can a woman forget her sucking child, that she should not have compassion on the son of her womb? Yea, they may forget, yet will I not forget thee (Isa 49:15).

But there sight fails, no heart may know
    The bliss when life is done.

Such is thy banquet, dearest Lord;
    O give us grace, to cast
Our lot with thine, to trust thy Word,
    And keep our best till last.

‡

Septuagesima Sunday[6]

*The invisible things of him from the creation of the world are clearly seen, being understood
by the things which are made.*

Romans 1:20

There is a book, who runs may read,[7]
    Which heavenly truth imparts,
And all the lore its scholars need:
    Pure eyes and Christian hearts.

The works of God above, below,
    Within us and around,
Are pages in that book, to show
    How God himself is found.

The glorious sky embracing all
    Is like the Maker's love,
Wherewith encompassed, great and small
    In peace and order move.

The moon above, the church below,
    A wondrous race they run,
But all their radiance, all their glow,
    Each borrows of its sun.

The Savior lends the light and heat
    That crowns his holy hill;
The saints, like stars, around his seat,
    Perform their courses still.[8]

6   [Ed. Septuagesima Sunday marks the third week before Ash Wednesday and the ninth Sunday before Easter.]

7   [Ed. For further consideration of this line, see "He may run that readeth," in *A dictionary of biblical tradition in English literature*, ed. David L. Jeffrey (Grand Rapids: Eerdmans, 1992), 335.]

8   Dan 12:3.

The saints above are stars in heaven—
    What are the saints on earth?
Like trees they stand whom God has given,[9]
    Our Eden's happy birth.

Faith is their fixed unswerving root,
    Hope their unfading flower,
Fair deeds of charity their fruit,
    The glory of their bower.

The dew of heaven is like thy grace,[10]
    It steals in silence down;
But where it lights, the favored place
    By richest fruits is known.

One name above all glorious names
    With its ten thousand tongues
The everlasting sea proclaims,
    Echoing angelic songs.

The raging fire,[11] the roaring wind,
    Thy boundless power display;
But in the gentler breeze we find
    Thy Spirit's viewless way.[12]

Two worlds are ours; 'tis only sin
    Forbids us to descry
The mystic heaven and earth within,
    Plain as the sea and sky.

Thou, who hast given me eyes to see
    And love this sight so fair,
Give me a heart to find out thee,
    And read thee everywhere.

‡

[9] Isa 9:21.
[10] Ps 68:9.
[11] Heb 12:29.
[12] John 3:8.

Whitsunday[13]

And suddenly there came a sound from heaven, as of a rushing mighty wind, and it filled all the house where they were sitting; and there appeared unto them cloven tongues, like as of fire, and it sat upon each of them, and they were all filled with the Holy Ghost.

Acts 2:2-3

When God of old came down from heaven,
    In power and wrath he came;
Before his feet the clouds were riven,
    Half darkness and half flame;

Around the trembling mountain's base
    The prostrate people lay,
Convinced of sin, but not of grace;
    It was a dreadful day.

But when he came the second time,
    He came in power and love,
Softer than gale at morning prime[14]
    Hovered his holy Dove.

The fires that rushed on Sinai down
    In sudden torrents dread,
Now gently light, a glorious crown,
    On every sainted head.

Like arrows went those lightnings forth
    Winged with the sinner's doom,
But these, like tongues, o'er all the earth
    Proclaiming life to come.

And as on Israel's awestruck ear
    The voice exceeding loud,
The trump, that angels quake to hear,
    Thrilled from the deep, dark cloud,

So, when the Spirit of our God
    Came down his flock to find,
A voice from heaven was heard abroad,
    A rushing, mighty wind.

[13]   [Ed. Also known as Pentecost, in remembrance of the outpouring of the Holy Spirit on the disciples in Acts 2.]

[14]   [Ed. That is, "softer than songs at morning prayer."]

Nor doth the outward ear alone
   At that high warning start;
Conscience gives back the appalling tone;
   'Tis echoed in the heart.

It fills the church of God; it fills
   The sinful world around;
Only in stubborn hearts and wills
   No place for it is found.

To other strains our souls are set;
   A giddy whirl of sin
Fills ear and brain, and will not let
   Heaven's harmonies come in.

Come, Lord; come, wisdom, love, and power,
   Open our ears to hear;
Let us not miss the accepted hour;
   Save, Lord, by love or fear.

TEXT: [John Keble,] *The Christian year: thoughts in verse for the Sundays and holy days throughout the year*, 2nd ed. (Oxford: W. Baxter, 1827), 45–54, 72–74, 163–65.

FELICIA HEMANS
(1793–1835)
Divine Mysteries

Felicia Dorothea Hemans (née Browne) was born in Liverpool. Her father, a merchant, followed her maternal grandfather as Tuscan and imperial consul in Liverpool. War unsettled the family, leading to their relocation in Wales between 1800 and 1809. Her father eventually emigrated to Canada, where he gradually lost contact with his family. In 1809 Felicia, with her mother and brothers, moved to St. Asaph in Flintshire, Wales. Felicia showed promise, even as a young girl, composing poetry and excelling as a student of languages (she learned French, Spanish, Portuguese, German, and Latin through a private tutor at home). Felicia published her first volume of poetry when she was only fourteen. In July 1812 she married Captain Alfred Hemans, a soldier. The two had five sons together, and she continued to publish, but the couple never made a good match. They separated in 1818. In long poems, theatrical works such as *The vespers of Palermo* (1823), and other miscellaneous pieces, Hemans combined historical, religious, and political details into a poetic vision that attracted admirers throughout Britain as well as abroad (American Unitarians applauded her works). Still, she wrote most often from necessity and without time for careful revisions, snatching moments between household duties to produce new lines for the presses. In 1826 the *Literary Chronicle* denominated her "the first poetess of the day."[1] *The forest sanctuary* (1825), *Songs of the affections* (1830), and *Scenes and hymns of life* (1834) reveal her increasing religiosity and, after a tour of Scotland and the Lake District in 1830, the heightened influence of William Wordsworth on her poetics. In autumn 1834 Hemans suffered from scarlet fever; her health quickly deteriorated, and she died at the age of forty-one in May 1835.

Hemans published hundreds of poems. Her most successful volume, *Records of woman, with other poems* (1828), contains a series of verse portraits of women who exemplify strength and tragic resilience in the face of overwhelming circumstances. Yet *Records of woman* includes other poems (including the following selections) that exhibit deep faith and spirituality within alternately patriotic, personal, or natural settings.

[1] Duncan Wu, *Romantic women poets: an anthology* (Oxford: Blackwell, 1997), 490.

SOURCES: Norma Clarke, *Ambitious heights: writing, friendship, love: the Jewsbury sisters, Felicia Hemans, and Jane Welsh Carlyle* (London: Routledge, 1990); Jerome J. McGann, *The poetics of sensibility: a revolution in literary style* (Oxford: Clarendon, 1996); Anne Nichols, "Glorification of the lowly in Felicia Hemans' 'Female characters of Scripture,'" *Victorian Poetry* 48 (2010): 559–75; *ODNB*; Nanora Sweet and Julie Melnyk, eds., *Felicia Hemans: reimagining poetry in the nineteenth century* (New York: Palgrave, 2001); Peter W. Trinder, *Mrs. Hemans* (Cardiff: University of Wales Press, 1984); Duncan Wu, *Romantic women poets: an anthology* (Oxford: Blackwell, 1997).

FELICIA HEMANS
Records of woman
1828

The Homes of England

Where's the coward that would not dare
To fight for such a land?

Marmion[1]

The stately homes of England,
   How beautiful they stand!
Amidst their tall ancestral trees,
   O'er all the pleasant land.
The deer across their greensward bound
   Through shade and sunny gleam,
And the swan glides past them with the sound
   Of some rejoicing stream.

The merry homes of England!
   Around their hearths by night,
What gladsome looks of household love
   Meet in the ruddy light!
There woman's voice flows forth in song,
   Or childhood's tale is told
Or lips move tunefully along
   Some glorious page of old.

---

[1]   [Ed. Walter Scott, *Marmion*, IV.30.34–35.]

The blessed homes of England!
 How softly on their bowers
Is laid the holy quietness
 That breathes from Sabbath hours!
Solemn, yet sweet, the church-bell's chime
 Floats through their woods at morn;
All other sounds, in that still time,
 Of breeze and leaf are born.

The cottage homes of England!
 By thousands on her plains,
They are smiling o'er the silvery brooks,
 And round the hamlet fanes.[2]
Through glowing orchards forth they peep,
 Each from its nook of leaves,
And fearless there the lowly sleep,
 As the bird beneath their eaves.

The free, fair homes of England!
 Long, long, in hut and hall,
May hearts of native proof be reared
 To guard each hallowed wall!
And green for ever be the groves,
 And bright the flowery sod,
Where first the child's glad spirit loves
 Its country and its God![3]

‡

Invocation

I called on dreams and visions, to disclose
That which is veiled from waking thought; conjured
Eternity, as men constrain a ghost
To appear and answer.

            Wordsworth[4]

Answer me, burning stars of night!
 Where is the spirit gone,
That past the reach of human sight,

---

 [2] [Ed. Parish churches.]
 [3] [Ed. Hemans only knew Britain at war with France from the time of her birth until 1815: "Heroism is not merely a patriotic pose well struck . . . Pride, defiance, courage in the face of inevitable defeat, even love: these are the virtues that pervade Felicia's poems" (Wu, *Romantic women poets*, 492).]
 [4] [Ed. William Wordsworth, "The excursion," 3.686–689.]

As a swift breeze hath flown?—
And the stars answered me—"We roll
 In light and power on high;
But, of the never-dying soul,
 Ask that which cannot die."

Oh! many-toned and chainless wind!
 Thou art a wanderer free.
Tell me if *thou* its place canst find,
 Far over mount and sea?—
And the wind murmured in reply,
 "The blue deep I have crossed,
And met its barks and billows high,
 But not what thou hast lost."

Ye clouds that gorgeously repose
 Around the setting sun,
Answer! have ye a home for those
 Whose earthly race is run?
The bright clouds answered—"We depart;
 We vanish from the sky.
Ask what is deathless in thy heart,
 For that which cannot die."

Speak then, thou voice of God within,
 Thou of the deep low tone!
Answer me, through life's restless din,
 Where is the spirit flown?—
And the voice answered—"Be thou still!
 Enough to know is given.
Clouds, winds, and stars *their* part fulfill;
 Thine is to trust in Heaven."

‡

The Spirit's Mysteries

And slight, withal, may be the things which bring
Back on the heart the weight which it would fling
 Aside forever;—it may be a sound—
A tone of music—summer's breath, or spring—
 A flower—a leaf—the ocean—which may wound—
Striking th' electric chain wherewith we are darkly bound.

Childe Harold[5]

---

[5] [Ed. George Gordon Byron, *Childe Harold*, 4.202–207.]

The power that dwelleth in sweet sounds to waken
    Vague yearnings, like the sailor's for the shore,
And dim remembrances, whose hue seems taken
    From some bright former state, our own no more;
Is not this all a mystery?—Who shall say
Whence are those thoughts, and whither tends their way?

The sudden images of vanished things,
    That o'er the spirit flash, we know not why;
Tones from some broken harp's deserted strings,
    Warm sunset hues of summers long gone by,
A rippling wave—the dashing of an oar—
A flower scent floating past our parents' door;

A word—scarce noted in its hour perchance,
    Yet back returning with a plaintive tone;
A smile—a sunny or a mournful glance,
    Full of sweet meanings now from this world flown;
Are not these mysteries when to life they start,
And press vain tears in gushes from the heart?

And the far wanderings of the soul in dreams,
    Calling up shrouded faces from the dead,
And with them bringing soft or solemn gleams,
    Familiar objects brightly to o'erspread;
And wakening buried love, or joy, or fear,—
These are night's mysteries—who shall make them clear?

And the strange inborn sense of coming ill,
    That ofttimes whispers to the haunted breast,
In a low tone which nought can drown or still,
    Midst feasts and melodies a secret guest;
Whence doth that murmur wake, that shadow fall?
Why shakes the spirit thus?—'tis mystery all!

Darkly we move—we press upon the brink
    Haply of viewless worlds, and know it not;
Yes! it may be, that nearer than we think,
    Are those whom death has parted from our lot!
Fearfully, wondrously, our souls are made—
Let us walk humbly on, but undismayed![6]

---

[6]   [Ed. These two lines allude to Ps 139:14 ("for I am fearfully, wonderfully made") and Mic 6:8 ("what doth the LORD require of thee, but to do justly, and to love mercy, and to walk humbly with thy God?").]

Humbly—for knowledge strives in vain to feel
    Her way amidst these marvels of the mind;
Yet undismayed—for do they not reveal
    Th' immortal being with our dust entwined?—
So let us deem! and e'en the tears they wake
Shall then be blest, for that high nature's sake.

‡

The Image in Lava[7]

Thou thing of years departed!
    What ages have gone by,
Since here the mournful seal was set
    By love and agony!

Temple and tower have moldered,
    Empires from earth have passed,—
And woman's heart hath left a trace
    Those glories to outlast!

And childhood's fragile image
    Thus fearfully enshrined,
Survives the proud memorials reared
    By conquerors of mankind.

Babe! Wert thou brightly slumbering
    Upon thy mother's breast,
When suddenly the fiery tomb
    Shut round each gentle guest?

A strange dark fate o'ertook you,
    Fair babe and loving heart!
One moment of a thousand pangs—
    Yet better then to part!

Haply of that fond bosom,
    On ashes here impressed,
Thou wert the only treasure, child!
    Whereon a hope might rest.

---

[7]   The impression of a woman's form, with an infant clasped to the bosom, found at the uncovering of Herculaneum [A town destroyed in 79 A.D. by the volcanic eruption of Mount Vesuvius.—Ed.].

Perchance all vainly lavished,
    Its other love had been,
And where it trusted, nought remained
    But thorns on which to lean.

Far better then to perish,
    Thy form within its clasp,
Than live and lose thee, precious one!
    From that impassioned grasp.

Oh! I could pass all relics
    Left by the pomps of old,
To gaze on this rude monument,
    Cast in affection's mold.

Love, human love! what art thou?
    Thy print upon the dust
Outlives the cities of renown
    Wherein the mighty trust!

Immortal, oh! immortal
    That art, whose earthly glow
Hath given these ashes holiness—
    It must, it *must* be so!

TEXT: Felicia Hemans, *Records of woman, with other poems* (Edinburgh: William Blackwood, 1828), 169–71, 242–44, 264–66, 307–10.

VII

MORALS

Pure religion and undefiled before God and the Father is this, To visit the fatherless and widows in their affliction, and to keep himself unspotted from the world.

James 1:27

HENRY VENN
(1725–1797)
Marriage

Henry Venn played a prominent role in the articulation of English evangelicalism. Venn was born at Barnes, Surrey, into a family that could trace the history of its ministers back for generations. He matriculated at St. John's College, Cambridge in 1742, and shortly after moved to Jesus College (B.A., 1745). Venn was ordained a deacon in 1747 and priest in 1749. Subsequently Venn worked as a minister in several small towns—to the surprise of many, he had considerable success in these staid communities. Perhaps for this reason, some local clergy regarded Venn as something of an enthusiast. In time, Venn began preaching extemporaneously, which no doubt contributed to rumors of Methodist influence. In 1754 Venn proceeded to the curacy of Clapham and frequently lectured in London. He soon formed friendships with leading evangelicals, including John Wesley, George Whitefield, and Selina Hastings, the countess of Huntingdon. As vicar of the vast parish of Huddersfield (from 1759), Venn was renowned for his extensive preaching (often, as with many Methodists, in the open air), teaching, and pastoral visitations. His personal life was darkened by severe illnesses that limited his ability to preach and the death of two wives (leaving him to care for several children on his own), yet his influence was far-reaching and extended to his own family: his son John Venn's leadership of the so-called Clapham Sect shaped English church and society long into the nineteenth century, a granddaughter wrote the beloved hymn "Just as I Am," and a grandson was honorary secretary of the Church Missionary Society for over three decades.

Venn's *The complete duty of man; or, A system of doctrinal & practical Christianity* (1763), written as an alternative to the popular high church guide *The whole duty of man* (ca. 1658), illustrates how eighteenth-century Christians connected the need for repentance with moral duty. In *The complete duty of man*, Venn explains the doctrinal basis for Christian practice: rejection of sin through repentance, justification by faith, and sanctification by the Holy Spirit to perform works of righteousness. The following section exemplifies the biblical and practical language that made evangelical Anglicanism so appealing for many in the period: he urges husbands and wives to form relationships based on mutuality, rejects the notion that a good marriage is only about material provision, and advises husbands and wives to support one another in serving God.

SOURCES: Bebbington; Michael Hennell, *John Venn and the Clapham sect* (London: Lutterworth, 1958); *ODCC*; *ODNB*; J. C. Ryle, *Five Christian leaders of the eighteenth century* (London: Banner of Truth Trust, 1960).

HENRY VENN
The complete duty of man
1763

As the ground of affection between Christian husbands and wives must be spiritual, so must the expressions and proofs of it. To be solicitous only in procuring a comfortable provision for your wife that she may not be left destitute or dependent, when your diligence or frugality might prevent it, is the affection every man must feel who is not sunk beneath a brute. On the other hand, the wife may express love to her husband by a most discreet management of the family, by cheerfully doing her utmost for its welfare, and by studying to make his life and home agreeable, yet be void of the least savor of Christian knowledge. Mutual and earnest endeavors to please each other are often found where the parties do a thousand things in open defiance of God's authority and, instead of meek remonstrance or disapproving silence on either side, they remain very well satisfied with each other's conduct. A perfidious sort of love this is, though everywhere prevalent. A confederacy against the truth and government of God, by which they strengthen one another in unbelief and profaneness, and are principal instruments of each other's endless misery.

In a manner quite the reverse will the affection of Christian husbands and wives for each other be discovered. Their spiritual good will be a chief and mutual concern. They will be tender-hearted inspectors of each other's conduct, meekly correcting errors which unnoticed would have struck root or pointing out faults before they are confirmed into habits.[1] They will converse together on the power, the glory, the mightiness of God's kingdom to increase their knowledge of his excellency and love of his name. They will prompt each other to holy vigilance and a diligent care and labor to please God, and encourage that sort of acquaintance and intimates whose principles, sentiments, and tempers are animating and exemplary. As the nuptial union gives the parties much influence to be either greatly serviceable or hurtful to each other's eternal interests, they must look upon themselves as bound in conscience to use all their weight against the corruptions of the heart: against pride, unbelief, and worldly lusts through which their salvation is most endangered.

[1]   [Ed. On this dubious advice, cf. Prov 11:12 and 17:9.]

Thus, with unspeakable advantage, Christian husbands and wives prove the spiritual nature of their conjugal affection—sure to find it equally constant in youth and age, sickness and health, indigence or plenty, lasting as their abode together, and redounding to their advancement in eternal glory after death.

True believers in Christ are the only persons capable of dwelling in the mutual exercise of such spiritual and permanent affection, since they only confess their innate depravity and, under an humbling sense of their vileness, use with success the means of grace.[2] They know how to persevere in importunate prayer for the remission of each other's sins, for daily supplies of strength against temptations, and help under various infirmities. These their devout sentiments and practices prove a fruitful source of mutual endearment; they forcibly impress upon them both the idea that they are connected by nobler ties than those of wedlock, that they are children of one heavenly Father, servants of one gracious Lord, members of his body, and heirs together of the grace of life.

A full persuasion of a common interest in such inestimable privileges is of powerful influence to unite even strangers to each other, at first view, in the bonds of friendship, and can instantly create delight in each other's company and welfare. Judge then the efficacy of this knowledge when increased and enlivened by daily prayer. It is a prevention of indifference to each other, and both persuades and inclines to love fervently.

We may observe also that satiety often proves the bane of conjugal affection. The parties grow insipid to each other upon more acquaintance; the husband becomes more reserved, or the wife loses her vivacity; in either case they are weary of each other. But the spiritual life of believers in Jesus prevents this satiety. An infinite grandeur in the objects of their common faith, the importance of their nuptial union with respect to them, joined to mutual desire of obtaining salvation, will not suffer that stagnation to take place in the married state which otherwise frequently follows.

Further, strife and contention often first cool, and then destroy, conjugal affection, but the devout exercises in which real Christians constantly engage effectually prevent this melancholy estrangement from each other. Should variance in any degree arise—they are checked, they are sharply upbraided in their own consciences, they have both offended and grieved their best friend. Before his throne of grace they are to appear, where they lament their failings and beg their trespasses may not be imputed but forgiven, as they forgive every offense against themselves. Hence they find it easy to make merciful allowances to each other: to divide the blame instead of placing it all to one side, as pride and self-will prompt men to do, thus inflaming the quarrel. With unfeigned self-abasement they will confess their depravity, from which they are so ready to kindle into rage, where Christian patience would scarcely be moved. By these concessions, contention ceases soon; and from mutual self-condemnation arises a desire of greater vigilance to guard against passion, and more earnest prayer to be kept for the future in harmony and love.

Though the vehement fondness, therefore, for each other, which usually precedes the nuptial union and flourishes for a time after it, may wear off, yet the married pair who,

---

[2]   [Ed. A hallmark teaching of John Wesley was that Christian faithfulness depends on the continual use of the "means of grace" or the "outward signs, words, or actions ordained of God . . . to be the *ordinary* channels whereby he might convey to men preventing, justifying, or sanctifying grace" ("The means of grace," §2.1).]

in the Scripture-phrase, are joined together in the Lord [Mark 10:9], may be sure a solid tender affection will ever remain; an affection true and refined, sufficient to produce substantial comfort, and ripening more and more as they improve themselves in every divine attainment.

Besides mutual fidelity and love, the common duty of both parties in the conjugal state, there are some offices peculiar to the husband, others to the wife; and the conscientious discharge of these respectively will be strictly regarded by the faithful in Christ Jesus.

The husband's peculiar province is to govern: "For the husband is the head of the wife, even as Christ is the head of the church" (Eph 5:23). When the husband, therefore, ceases to preside, giving up his authority to the wife, he transgresses no less than a military officer who should surrender the honor of his command to the impertinent intrusion of his inferior. But then as the head hath no interest distinct from the other parts of the body, nor any advantage over them (unless the care of direction and providing for them be one), so the husband has no interest separate from his wife. The authority entrusted in his hands by our God is designed for the direction and welfare of the wife; it never, therefore, can be exercised by a husband who fears God but to this excellent end. Never with arbitrary dominion, as tyrants rule slaves, but with such a benign influence, as the soul exerts over the body: for the command to the Christian church is, "So ought husbands to love their wives, even as their own bodies. He that loveth his wife, loveth himself, for no man ever yet hated his own flesh, but loveth it, and nourisheth it even as the Lord the church" [Eph 5:28-29]. So that the authority lodged with the husband, by being managed according to the appointed order, instead of proving burdensome or uneasy to the wife, shall become a source of greater peace and good to both.

Another peculiar branch of the husband's duty is to furnish his wife with things necessary and convenient according to his rank in life. He must express alacrity in letting her share the advantages he possesses and convince her he receives pleasure in seeing her use, within the limits of Christian moderation, his abundance.

The peculiar duty of the wife, which every real Christian from conscience towards God will observe, is to aid and comfort her husband in the midst of his business and labor. The good management of a family is a thing quite different from making provision for it. The former, in general, depends chiefly upon the wife; the latter is the husband's province. In this manner the labors of life are divided; and if either neglect their respective duty, much loss and confusion will follow, which marriage was designed to prevent.

A Christian wife, therefore, will not conform to corrupt custom and affect to be above the care of her family, as if she was made only to dress, visit, or, like a picture, be admired. She will look well to the ways of her household and not eat the bread of idleness [Prov 31:27]. She will give her husband a solid testimony of her affection for him by being careful to see his income, or the fruit of his labor, is not extravagantly consumed for want of female inspection at home.

A second instance of duty peculiar to the wife is obedience to her husband. When our common mother sinned through vain desire of being as the gods, she not only failed of the very end at which she aimed, but her proud desire of preeminence was made a reason of degrading her. "And thy desire shall be to thy husband, and he shall rule over thee" (Gen 3:16). Whenever, therefore, the wife affects to rule or refuses to submit to the authority of her husband, she resists the ordinance of God; she exalts herself in contempt of the divine decree published immediately after Eve's transgression and confirmed again by the Holy Ghost. "As the church is subject to Christ" (acknowledging and submitting to his authority, though contrary to natural inclination), "so let the wives be to their own husbands in everything" [Eph 5:22]. In every instance where the command of the husband does not contradict the command of God, the wife is obliged to comply and without a murmur give up her own will.

If it be urged that the wife has frequently more understanding and ability to govern than the husband, and on this account ought to be excused from living in subjection, the answer is obvious: she hath liberty to use her superior wisdom in giving counsel and producing such reasons as are proper to correct a mistaken judgment. But if her advice is not accepted, subjection is her duty. . . . An attempt, therefore, to gain the ascendency is an attempt to subvert the order which the sovereign Giver of all wisdom has appointed. Base return for his bounty! The Christian rule is positive against such an usurping spirit: the command is, "Let the wife see that she reverence her husband" [Eph 5:33]. In opposition to natural pride, let her carefully check the first desire to have her own will and see she be not wanting in submission, for this behavior is most becoming a woman professing godliness. Let her remember that God, the author of the marriage state, has appointed this subordination.

Such are the excellent tempers which husbands and wives must possess, and the extent of that duty which they must practice.

✂⌒⌒

Text: H[enry] Venn, *The complete duty of man; or, A system of doctrinal & practical Christianity* (New Brunswick: J. Simpson, 1811), 257–63.

SOAME JENYNS
(1704–1787)
Christian Virtue

In the latter half of the eighteenth century, English apologists (that is, defenders of religion) increasingly adopted moral arguments to demonstrate the supremacy of the Christian faith and life. Soame Jenyns composed one of the most compelling and controversial arguments in this mode. Born in London and raised on his family's estate in Cambridgeshire, he matriculated at St John's, Cambridge, in 1722 but soon left to pursue recreation and other distractions. During this time, Jenyns developed a reputation for an incisive wit and waggish personality—traits that made him especially popular at social gatherings in London and elsewhere. Jenyns married in 1740, but was abandoned by his wife after only two years (they had no children). A little more than a decade later, Jenyns married once again—this time, quite happily, to his cousin Elizabeth Gray. Stability in Jenyns' personal life was matched by an expanding degree of professional competence. For many decades, Jenyns represented conservative landowner interests in Parliament, first serving as a representative of Cambridgeshire (1741), then the rotten borough of Dunwich, and later the town of Cambridge. Although generally regarded as a poor public speaker, he nonetheless produced a steady stream of literary contributions, including poetry, a series of essays for *World* (1755), and other theoretical writings, such as one on theodicy in *A free inquiry into the nature and origin of evil* (1757). In *Miscellaneous pieces* (1761, 1770), bawdy verses on romantic affection are followed by aphorisms on political economy, virtue, and faith.

Perhaps the most significant (and controversial) work of Jenyns' professional life, however, was *A view of the internal evidence of the Christian religion* (1776). The title page, notably, contains an epigraph from Acts 26:28: "Almost thou persuadest me to be a Christian." In light of his reputation for satire, many readers were uncertain if Jenyns was himself a skeptic or some manner of Deist—though ostensibly the work was designed to confound precisely these views. For his "internal evidences," Jenyns appealed to morality and Christian virtue. The following selection was especially controversial and subject to scrutiny from all sides. Here, Jenyns compares biblical virtues such as humility and charity with "fictitious virtues" such as valor, patriotism, and friendship. Against the dominant mode of apologetics, Jenyns appeals not to miracles and prophecy as the foundation of Christian belief, but the moral character of the gospel. Critics worried that Jenyns only diminished Christian faith by undermining the force of classical virtues that Christians typically held in high regard. Undoubtedly, Jenyns' notoriety and unwillingness to defend his work contributed to the uncertainty of his readers. Still, despite this, the book was widely known and translated into French, Polish, and Greek.

SOURCES: *ODNB*; Ronald Rompkey, *Soame Jenyns* (Boston: Twayne, 1984).

SOAME JENYNS
A view of the internal evidence of the Christian religion
1776

... [F]rom this book called the New Testament may be collected a system of ethics in which every moral precept founded on reason is carried to a higher degree of purity and perfection than in any other of the ancient philosophers of preceding ages; every moral precept founded on false principles is entirely omitted, and many new precepts added, peculiarly[1] corresponding with the new object of this religion.

By moral precepts founded on reason, I mean all those which enforce the practice of such duties as reason informs us must improve our natures and conduce to the happiness of mankind: such are piety to God, benevolence to men, justice, charity, temperance, and sobriety, with all those which prohibit the commission of the contrary vices, all which debase our natures and, by mutual injuries, introduce universal disorder, and consequently universal misery. By precepts founded on false principles, I mean those which recommend fictitious virtues productive of none of these salutary effects and therefore, however celebrated and admired, are in fact no virtues at all: such are valor, patriotism, and friendship. . . .

Valor, for instance, or active courage, is for the most part constitutional and therefore can have no more claim to moral merit than wit, beauty, health, strength, or any other endowment of the mind or body; and so far is it from producing any salutary effects by introducing peace, order, or happiness into society, that it is the usual perpetrator of all the violences which from retaliated injuries distract the world with bloodshed and devastation. It is the engine by which the strong are enabled to plunder the weak, the proud to trample upon the humble, and the guilty to oppress the innocent; it is the chief instrument which ambition employs in her unjust pursuits of wealth and power and is therefore so much extolled by her votaries. . . . I object not to the praise and honors bestowed on the valiant—they are the least tribute which can be paid them by those who enjoy safety and affluence by the intervention of their dangers and sufferings. I assert only that active courage can never be a Christian virtue because a Christian can have nothing to do with

---

[1] [Ed. That is, "especially."]

it. Passive courage is indeed frequently and properly inculcated by this meek and suffering religion under the titles of patience and resignation. A real and substantial virtue this—and a direct contrast to the former—for passive courage arises from the noblest dispositions of the human mind, from a contempt of misfortunes, pain, and death, and a confidence in the protection of the Almighty; active from the meanest [dispositions]— from passion, vanity, and self-dependence; passive courage is derived from a zeal for truth and a perseverance in duty; active is the offspring of pride and revenge, and the parent of cruelty and injustice. In short, passive courage is the resolution of a philosopher, active the ferocity of a savage. . . .

Patriotism, also, that celebrated virtue so much practiced in ancient—and so much professed in modern—times; that virtue which so long preserved the liberties of Greece and exalted Rome to the empire of the world. This celebrated virtue, I say, must also be excluded because it not only falls short of, but directly counteracts the extensive benevolence of this religion. A Christian is of no country; he is a citizen of the world; and his neighbors and countrymen are the inhabitants of the remotest regions, whenever their distresses demand his friendly assistance. Christianity commands us to love all mankind; patriotism to oppress all other countries to advance the imaginary prosperity of our own. Christianity enjoins us to imitate the universal benevolence of our Creator, who pours forth his blessings on every nation upon earth; patriotism to copy the mean partiality of an English parish officer, who thinks injustice and cruelty meritorious whenever they promote the interests of his own inconsiderable village. This has ever been a favorite virtue with mankind because it conceals self-interest under the mask of public spirit—not only from others, but even from themselves—and gives a license to inflict wrongs and injuries not only with impunity, but with applause; but it is so diametrically opposite to the great characteristic of this institution that it never could have been admitted into the list of Christian virtues.

Friendship, likewise, although more congenial to the principles of Christianity, arising from more tender and amiable dispositions, could never gain admittance amongst her benevolent precepts for the same reason—because it is too narrow and confined, and appropriates that benevolence to a single object, which is here commanded to be extended over all. Where friendships arise from similarity of sentiments and disinterested affections, they are advantageous, agreeable, and innocent, but have little pretensions to merit; for it is justly observed, "If ye love them which love you, what thanks have ye? For sinners also love those that love them" {Luke 6:32}. But if they are formed from alliances in parties, factions, and interests, or from a participation of vices (the usual parents of what are called friendships among mankind), they are then both mischievous and criminal, and consequently forbidden, but in their utmost purity deserve no recommendation from this religion.

‡

Let us now examine what are those new precepts in this religion peculiarly corresponding with the new object of it, that is preparing us for the kingdom of heaven. Of these the chief are poorness of spirit, forgiveness of injuries, and charity to all men. . . .

"Blessed are the poor in spirit; for theirs is the kingdom of heaven" {Matt 5:3}. By which poorness of spirit is to be understood a disposition of mind, meek, humble, submissive to power, void of ambition, patient of injuries, and free from all resentment. This was so new, and so opposite to the ideas of all pagan moralists, that they thought this temper of mind a criminal and contemptible meanness which must induce men to sacrifice the glory of their country and their own honor to a shameful pusillanimity; and such it appears to almost all who are called Christians even at this day, who not only reject it in practice but disavow it in principle, notwithstanding this explicit declaration of their Master. We see them revenging the smallest affronts by premeditated murder: as individuals on principles of honor; and in their national capacities, destroying each other with fire and sword for the low considerations of commercial interests, the balance of rival powers, or the ambition of princes. We see them with their last breath animating each other to a savage revenge and, in the agonies of death, plunging with feeble arms their daggers into the hearts of their opponents. And, what is still worse, we hear all these barbarisms celebrated by historians, flattered by poets, applauded in theatres, approved in senates, and even sanctified in pulpits. But universal practice cannot alter the nature of things, nor universal error change the nature of truth. Pride was not made for man, but humility, meekness, and resignation; that is, poorness of spirit was made for man and properly belongs to his dependent and precarious situation, and is the only disposition of mind which can enable him to enjoy ease and quiet here, and happiness hereafter. . . .

Another precept, equally new and no less excellent, is forgiveness of injuries: "Ye have heard," says Christ to his disciples, "thou shalt love thy neighbor and hate thine enemy; but I say unto you, love your enemies, bless them that curse you, do good to them that hate you, and pray for them which despitefully use you and persecute you" {Matt 5:43-44}. This was a lesson so new and so utterly unknown, till taught by his doctrines and enforced by his example, that the wisest moralists of the wisest nations and ages represented the desire of revenge as a mark of a noble mind and the accomplishment of it as one of the chief felicities attendant on a fortunate man. But how much more magnanimous, how much more beneficial to mankind, is forgiveness! . . . . How much more exalted a character therefore is a Christian martyr, suffering with resignation and praying for the guilty, than that of a pagan hero, breathing revenge and destroying the innocent! . . . .

A third precept, first noticed and first enjoined by this institution, is charity to all men. What this is we may best learn from this admirable description, painted in the following words: "Charity suffereth long and is kind; charity envieth not; charity vaunteth not itself; is not puffed up; doth not behave itself unseemly; seeketh not her own; is not easily provoked; thinketh no evil; rejoiceth not in iniquity, but rejoiceth in truth; feareth all things; believeth all things; hopeth all things; endureth all things" {1 Cor 13:4-7}. Here we have an accurate delineation of this bright constellation of all virtues, which consists not (as many imagine) in the building of monasteries, endowment of hospitals, or the distribution of alms, but in such an amiable disposition of mind as exercises itself every hour in acts of kindness, patience, complacency, and benevolence to all around us, and which alone is able to promote happiness in the present life or render us capable of receiving it in another. . . . This benevolent disposition is made the great characteristic of a Christian, the test of his obedience, and the mark by which he is to be distinguished. This love for each other is that charity just now described and contains all those qualities which are there attributed to it—humility, patience, meekness, and beneficence—without which we must live in perpetual discord and consequently cannot pay obedience to this commandment by loving one another.

‡

I mean not by this to pass any censure on the principles of valor, patriotism, or honor. They may be useful, and perhaps necessary, in the commerce and business of the present turbulent and imperfect state; and those who are actuated by them may be virtuous, honest, and even religious men. All that I assert is that they cannot be Christians. A profligate may be a Christian, though a bad one, because he may be overpowered by passions and temptations, and his actions may contradict his principles; but a man whose ruling principle is honor, however virtuous he may be, cannot be a Christian, because he erects a standard of duty, and deliberately adheres to it, diametrically opposite to the whole tenor of that religion.

Text: Soame Jenyns, *A view of the internal evidence of the Christian religion*, 3rd ed. (London: J. Dodsley, 1776), 50–61, 63–74, 93–94.

THOMAS CLARKSON
(1760–1846)
Slavery

Some English Christians during the eighteenth and early nineteenth centuries considered slavery to be a moral, just, and even biblical practice. Gordon Turnbull, for example, defended the institution in his *Apology for Negro slavery* (1786), claiming that the treatment of enslaved Africans was far milder than typically depicted, even as he called for prohibiting kidnapping, murder, and inhumane working conditions. Others advocated for the religious education of the enslaved in order to foster submission to authority. Abolitionists, by contrast, believed that books and tracts defending the slave trade and ongoing practice of slavery not only distorted the concrete realities of the slave system but did so out of a repulsive commitment to economic self-interest.

Thomas Clarkson, one of the most significant English abolitionists of the eighteenth century, proved an especially trenchant activist. Born in Wisbech, Cambridgeshire, Clarkson attended the free grammar school where his father served as headmaster. Intending to follow his father's path, he took his B.A. at St. John's, Cambridge in 1783, but while preparing for ordination, Clarkson wrote a piece against slavery, which won first prize in Cambridge's 1785 Latin essay competition. Inspired by a religious conversion of sorts, Clarkson suspended his ministerial pursuits and recognized the campaign against slavery as his spiritual vocation. Through the support of several Quaker friends, an English translation of Clarkson's essay was published the following year as *An essay on the slavery and commerce of the human species* (1786). Clarkson soon found himself at the center of a lobbying group tasked with the responsibility for gathering information from port cities around England, establishing anti-slavery societies, and encouraging petitions to Parliament. His unceasing efforts cost him much of his health and small fortune. Clarkson was also influential in the establishment of a free Christian settlement in Sierra Leone. He published numerous tracts and other essays against slavery, including his *History of the rise, progress, and accomplishment of the abolition of the African slave-trade* (2 vols., 1808). Clarkson's advocacy in the towns, along with Wilberforce's efforts in Parliament, led to the abolition of the slave trade (1807) and the eventual emancipation of all slaves in the British Empire (1833).

Clarkson's *Essay* provides one of the most compelling arguments against the slave system during the period. In fact, the *Essay* spurred Wilberforce to enter the abolitionist cause. The work, which draws liberally from Anthony Benezet's influential *Some historical account of Guinea* (1772), includes three main sections. In the first part, Clarkson traces the history of slavery from the ancient world to his own day. Clarkson then turns to human rights. He refutes the main pro-slavery arguments by demonstrating how the slave system tramples on laws of commerce, maxims of equity, and the dictates of reason. Finally, in the third part, Clarkson confronts the claim that the slave system actually benefits African men and women. In the following selection, drawn from the book's conclusion, Clarkson addresses the so-called receivers, or advocates of the slave system, arguing that slavery undermines two fundamental principles of Christian morality: (1) the command to love one's neighbor and (2) divine judgment based on free moral choices.

SOURCES: Earl Leslie Griggs, *Thomas Clarkson: the friend of slaves* (London: Allen and Unwin, 1936); *ODCC*; *ODNB*; Ellen Gibson Wilson, *Thomas Clarkson: a biography* (New York: St. Martin's, 1990).

THOMAS CLARKSON

An essay on the slavery and commerce of the human species
1786

Neither does it escape our notice, when we are speaking of the fatal wound which every social duty must receive, how considerably Christianity suffers by the conduct of you receivers. For by prosecuting this impious commerce, you keep the Africans in a state of perpetual ferocity and barbarism; and by prosecuting it in such a manner as must represent your religion as a system of robbery and oppression, you not only oppose the propagation of the gospel as far as you are able yourselves, but throw the most certain impediments in the way of others who might attempt the glorious and important task.

Such also is the effect which the subsequent slavery in the colonies must produce. For by your inhuman treatment of the unfortunate Africans there, you create the same insuperable impediments to a conversion. For how must they detest the very name of Christians, when you Christians are deformed by so many and dreadful vices? How must they detest that system of religion which appears to resist the natural rights of men and to give a sanction to brutality and murder?

But, as we are now mentioning Christianity, we must pause for a little time to make a few remarks on the arguments which are usually deduced from thence by the receivers in defense of their system of oppression. For the reader may readily suppose that, if they did not hesitate to bring the Old Testament in support of their barbarities, they would hardly let the New escape them.

St. Paul, having converted Onesimus to the Christian faith, who was a fugitive slave of Philemon, sent him back to his master.[1] This circumstance has furnished the receivers with a plea that Christianity encourages slavery. But they have not only strained the passages which they produce in support of their assertions, but are ignorant of historical facts. The benevolent apostle, in the letter which he wrote to Philemon, the master of Onesimus, addresses him to the following effect: "I send him back to you, but not in his former capacity, not now as a servant, but above a servant, a brother beloved. In this

---

[1]   [Ed. The Epistle of Paul to Philemon contains instructions to treat the slave Onesimus as a brother in common service to Christ.]

manner I beseech you to receive him, for though I could enjoin you to do it, yet I had rather it should be a matter of your own will than of necessity."[2]

It appears that the same Onesimus, when he was sent back, was no longer a slave—that he was a minister of the gospel, that he was joined with Tychicus in an ecclesiastical commission to the church of the Colossians, and was afterwards bishop of Ephesus.[3] If language therefore has any meaning and if history has recorded a fact which may be believed, there is no case more opposite to the doctrine of the receivers than this which they produce in its support.

It is said again that Christianity, among the many important precepts which it contains, does not furnish us with one for the abolition of slavery. But the reason is obvious. Slavery at the time of the introduction of the gospel was universally prevalent, and if Christianity had abruptly declared that the millions of slaves should have been made free who were then in the world, it would have been universally rejected as containing doctrines that were dangerous, if not destructive, to society. In order therefore that it might be universally received, it never meddled by any positive precept with the civil institutions of the times. But though it does not expressly say that "you shall neither buy, nor sell, nor possess a slave," it is evident that in its general tenor it sufficiently militates against the custom.

The first doctrine which it inculcates is that of brotherly love. It commands good will towards men [Luke 2:14]. It enjoins us to love our neighbors as ourselves [Mark 12:31], and to do unto all men as we would that they should do unto us [Matt 7:12]. And how can any man fulfill this scheme of universal benevolence who reduces an unfortunate person against his will to the most insupportable of all human conditions—who considers him as his private property, and treats him not as a brother, nor as one of the same parentage with himself, but as an animal of the brute creation?

But the most important doctrine is that by which we are assured that mankind are to exist in a future state and to give an account of those actions which they have severally done in the flesh. This strikes at the very root of slavery. For how can any man be justly called to an account for his actions, whose actions are not at his own disposal? This is the case with the proper[4] slave. His liberty is absolutely bought and appropriated; and if the purchase is just and equitable, he is under the necessity of perpetrating any crime which the purchaser may order him to commit or, in other words, of ceasing to be accountable for his actions.

These doctrines, therefore, are sufficient to show that slavery is incompatible with the Christian system. The Europeans considered them as such when, at the close of the twelfth century, they resisted their hereditary prejudices and occasioned its abolition. Hence one among many other proofs that Christianity was the production of infinite wisdom: that though it did not take such express cognizance of the wicked national institutions of the times as should hinder its reception, it should yet contain such doctrines as, when it should be fully established, would be sufficient for the abolition of them all.

2   [Ed. Clarkson freely combines quotes and paraphrases from Phlm 8, 16, etc.]
3   [Ed. The name Onesimus appears again in Col 4:9 ("a faithful and beloved brother, who is one of you") and in the early Christian Epistle of Ignatius to the Ephesians, where Onesimus is named a bishop.]
4   [Ed. Clarkson refers to enslaved Africans here, rather than condemned criminals and others assigned to forced labor.]

Thus, then, is the argument of you receivers ineffectual, and your conduct impious. For, by the prosecution of this wicked slavery and commerce, you not only oppose the propagation of that gospel which was ordered to be preached unto every creature, and bring it into contempt, but you oppose its tenets also. First, because you violate that law of universal benevolence which was to take away those hateful distinctions of Jew and Gentile, Greek and barbarian, bond and free [Col 3:11], which prevailed when the gospel was introduced; and secondly, because, as every man is to give an account of his actions hereafter, it is necessary that he should be free.

TEXT: Thomas Clarkson, *An essay on the slavery and commerce of the human species, particularly the African . . .* (London: J. Phillips, 1786), 244–50.

JOHN WESLEY
(1703–1791)
Holy Living

The writings of John Wesley, one of the towering religious figures of eighteenth-century England, provide the theological basis of Methodist piety. In 1703 Wesley was born at Epworth, Lincolnshire, where his father was rector of the local parish. His mother, Susanna Wesley (née Annesley), educated John and his many siblings at home. He matriculated at Charterhouse in 1714 and entered Christ Church, Oxford in 1720. At Oxford, Wesley's study of Thomas à Kempis' *Imitation of Christ*, Jeremy Taylor's *Holy living* and *Holy dying*, and William Law's *Serious call to a devout and holy life* inspired deeper piety and commitment to the church. By the end of the decade, Wesley was a fellow of Lincoln College, Oxford, lecturer on the Greek New Testament, and ordained. Together with his brother Charles and George Whitefield, he formed the "holy club," whose members devoted themselves to charity work in prisons and orphanages, biblical study, and regular participation in the Eucharist. After unsuccessful missionary work in Georgia, John returned to England a broken man and uncertain of his salvation. On May 24, 1738, John famously experienced a "conversion" while reading Luther's "Preface" to Romans at Aldersgate Street: "I felt my heart strangely warmed. I felt that I did trust in Christ, Christ alone for salvation, and an assurance was given me that he had taken away *my* sins, even *mine*, and saved *me* from the law of sin and death." Subsequently, Wesley organized the Methodist movement in England and abroad: he took up open-air preaching, established Methodist meeting places in Bristol and London, and assigned numerous lay preachers to promote the renewal of the Church of England. Against his brother Charles' serious objections, Wesley implicitly separated the Methodists from the Church of England when he signed the Deed of Declaration in February 1784 and ordained Thomas Coke to serve with Francis Asbury as "Superintendents" (functionally bishops) of the American Methodists. Wesley was a prodigious author, editor, and publisher of numerous works. His sermons and other controversial writings (especially against Calvinists such as George Whitefield) continue to function as a leading source of Wesleyan theology today.

John Wesley's "The more excellent way" (1787) first appeared in two successive issues of *The Arminian Magazine*. The sermon reveals a shift in Wesley's thinking. Earlier in his ministry, Wesley had distinguished sharply between "altogether" and "almost" Christians. Such a rigid approach to holiness brought him into sharp conflict with fellow Anglicans. In this sermon based on 1 Cor 12:31 ("Covet earnestly the best gifts; And yet I show to you a more excellent way"), Wesley abandons the uncompromising spirit of his earlier sermons. He argues instead that all who are justified may be saved, regardless of the state of their sanctification. Wesley nonetheless admonishes his audience to pursue holiness in all aspects of life.

SOURCES: Frank Baker, *John Wesley and the Church of England*, new ed. (London: Epworth, 2000); *ELC*; Richard P. Heitzenrater, *Wesley and the people called Methodists* (Nashville: Abingdon, 1995); *ODCC*; *ODNB*; Albert C. Outler, *John Wesley* (New York: Oxford University Press, 1964); Albert C. Outler, *Sermons*, The Bicentennial Edition of the Works of John Wesley, vol. 3 (Nashville: Abingdon, 1986); Henry D. Rack, *Reasonable enthusiast: John Wesley and the rise of Methodism* (London: Epworth, 1992).

JOHN WESLEY
"The more excellent way"
1787

It is the observation of an ancient writer that there have been from the beginning two orders of Christians.[1] The one lived an innocent life, conforming in all things not sinful to the customs and fashions of the world, doing many good works, abstaining from gross evils, and attending the ordinances of God. They endeavored in general to have a conscience void of offense [Acts 24:16] in their outward behavior, but did not aim at any particular strictness, being in most things like their neighbors. The other sort of Christians not only abstained from all appearance of evil, were zealous of good works [Titus 2:14] in every kind, and attended all the ordinances of God, but likewise used all diligence to attain the whole mind that was in Christ [1 Cor 2:16] and labored to walk in every point as their beloved Master. In order to this, they walked in a constant course of universal self-denial, trampling on every pleasure which they were not divinely conscious prepared them for taking pleasure in God. They took up their cross daily [Luke 9:23]. They strove, they agonized without intermission, to enter in at the strait gate [Luke 13:24]. This one thing they did: they spared no pains to arrive at the summit of Christian holiness, "leaving the first principles of the doctrine of Christ, to go on to perfection" [Heb 6:1], to "know all that love of God which passeth knowledge, and to be filled with all the fullness of God" [Eph 3:19].

From long experience and observation, I am inclined to think that whoever finds redemption in the blood of Jesus, whoever is justified, has then the choice of walking in the higher or the lower path. I believe the Holy Spirit at that time sets before him the more excellent way and incites him to walk therein, to choose the narrowest path in the narrow way, to aspire after the heights and depths of holiness after the entire image of God. But if he does not accept this offer, he insensibly declines into the lower order of Christians.

[1]   [Ed. Several early Christian writings emphasize the difference between abandoning sinful behavior and seeking a higher knowledge of divine wisdom (see, for example, Clement of Alexendria, *Paedagogus*, 1.1–6).]

He still goes on in what may be called a good way, serving God in his degree, and finds mercy in the close of life through the blood of the covenant.

I would be far from quenching the smoking flax [Isa 42:3]—from discouraging those that serve God in a low degree. But I would not wish them to stop here. I would encourage them to come up higher, without thundering hell and damnation in their ears. Without condemning the way wherein they were, telling them it is the way that leads to destruction [Matt 7:13], I will endeavor to point out to them what is in every respect a more excellent way.

‡

I. To begin at the beginning of the day. It is the manner of the generality of Christians, if they are not obliged to work for their living, to rise, particularly in winter, at eight or nine in the morning after having lain in bed eight or nine if not more hours. I do not say now (as I should have been very apt to do fifty years ago) that all who indulge themselves in this manner are in the way to hell. But neither can I say they are in the way to heaven, denying themselves and taking up their cross daily. Sure I am, there is a more excellent way to promote health both of body and mind. From an observation of more than sixty years, I have learned that men in health require at an average from six to seven hours' sleep, and healthy women a little more, from seven to eight in four-and-twenty hours. I know this quantity of sleep to be most advantageous to the body as well as the soul. It is preferable to any medicine which I have known, both for preventing and removing nervous disorders. It is therefore undoubtedly the most excellent way, in defiance of fashion and custom, to take just so much sleep as experience proves our nature to require, seeing this is indisputably most conducive both to bodily and spiritual health.

‡

III. The generality of Christians, after using some prayer, usually apply themselves to the business of their calling. Every man that has any pretense to be a Christian will not fail to do this, seeing it is impossible that an idle man can be a good man—sloth being inconsistent with religion. But with what view? For what end do you undertake and follow your worldly business? "To provide things necessary for myself and my family." It is a good answer, as far as it goes, but it does not go far enough. For a Turk or a heathen goes so far—does his work for the very same ends. But a Christian may go abundantly further. His end in all his labor is to please God; to do not his own will, but the will of him that sent him into the world [John 6:38]—for this very purpose, to do the will of God on earth as angels do in heaven [Matt 6:10]. He works for eternity. He "labors not for the meat that perisheth" (this is the smallest part of his motive) "but for that which endureth to everlasting life" [John 6:27]. And is not this "a more excellent way"?

‡

V. The time of taking our food is usually a time of conversation also, as it is natural to refresh our minds while we refresh our bodies. Let us consider a little in what manner the generality of Christians usually converse together. What are the ordinary subjects of their conversation? If it is harmless (as one would hope it is), if there be nothing in it profane, nothing immodest, nothing untrue or unkind; if there be no tale-bearing, backbiting, or evil-speaking, they have reason to praise God for his restraining grace. But there is more than this implied in "ordering our conversation aright" [Ps 50:23]. In order to this it is needful, first, that "your communication," that is, discourse or conversation, "be good" [Eph 4:29]; that it be materially good, on good subjects, not fluttering about anything that occurs—for what have you to do with courts and kings? It is not your business to

Fight o'er the wars, reform the state,[2]

unless when some remarkable event calls for the acknowledgment of his justice or mercy. You must indeed sometimes talk of worldly things, otherwise we may as well go out of the world. But it should only be so far as is needful. Then we should return to a better subject. Secondly, let your conversation be "to the use of edifying" [Eph 4:29]; calculated to edify either the speaker or the hearers or both; to build them up, as each has particular need, either in faith, or love, or holiness. Thirdly, see that it not only gives entertainment, but in one kind or other "ministers grace to the hearers" [Eph 4:29].

‡

[VI.] Diversions are of various kinds. Some are almost peculiar to men, as the sports of the field—hunting, shooting, fishing—wherein not many women (I should say, ladies) are concerned. Others are indifferently used by persons of both sexes, some of which are of a more public nature, as races, masquerades, plays, assemblies, balls. Others are chiefly used in private houses, as cards, dancing, and music—to which we may add the reading of plays, novels, romances, newspapers, and fashionable poetry. . . .

But supposing these . . . to be quite innocent diversions, yet are there not more excellent ways of diverting themselves for those that love or fear God? Would men of fortune divert themselves in the open air? They may do it by cultivating and improving their lands, by planting their grounds, by laying out, carrying on, and perfecting their gardens and orchards. At other times they may visit and converse with the most serious and sensible of their neighbors, or they may visit the sick, the poor, the widows, and fatherless in their affliction [Jas 1:27]. Do they desire to divert themselves in the house? They may read useful history, pious and elegant poetry, or several branches of natural philosophy.[3] If you have time, you may divert yourself by music, and perhaps by philosophical experiments. But above all, when you have once learned the use of prayer, you will find that as

that which yields or fills
All space, the ambient air, wide interfused
Embraces round this florid earth;[4]

so will this, till through every space of life [prayer] be interfused with all your employments, and wherever you are, whatever you do, embrace you on every side.

---

2   [Ed. Matthew Prior (1664–1721), *The ladle* 1.96.]
3   [Ed. The natural sciences.]
4   [Ed. John Milton, *Paradise lost* 7.88–90.]

‡

[VII.] . . . I charge you in the name of God, do not increase your substance! As it comes daily or yearly, so let it go—otherwise you "lay up treasures upon earth" [Matt 6:19]. And this our Lord as flatly forbids as murder and adultery. By doing it therefore you would "treasure up to yourselves wrath against the day of wrath and revelation of the righteous judgment of God" [Rom 2:5].

But suppose it were not forbidden, how can you on principles of reason spend your money in a way which God may *possibly forgive*, instead of spending it in a manner which he will *certainly reward*? You will have no reward in heaven for what you *lay up*; you will for what you *lay out*. Every pound you put into the earthly bank is sunk: it brings no interest above. But every pound you give to the poor is put into the bank of heaven. And it will bring glorious interest, yea, and such as will be accumulating to all eternity.[5]

Who, then, is a wise man and endued with knowledge among you [Jas 3:13]? Let him resolve this day, this hour, this moment, the Lord assisting him, to choose in all the preceding particulars the more excellent way. And let him steadily keep it, both with regard to sleep, prayer, work, food, conversation, and diversions—and particularly with regard to the employment of that important talent, money. Let your heart answer to the call of God, "From this moment, God being my helper, I will lay up no more treasure upon earth; this one thing I will do, I will lay up treasure in heaven [Matt 6:19-20]. I will render unto God the things that are God's [Matt 22:21]. I will give him all my goods, and all my heart."

TEXT: John Wesley, Sermon XL ["The more excellent way"], *The Arminian Magazine* (July/August 1787): 343–45, 398–99; 400–403, 405–6.

---

[5]   [Ed. Wesley's rejection of the accumulation of wealth through banking interest weakens Max Weber's economic thesis of the "Protestant Ethic."]

MARY WOLLSTONECRAFT
(1759–1797)
Creation

Although best known today for her political radicalism, Mary Wollstonecraft (later, Godwin) wrote some of the most celebrated children's literature of the period. While some eighteenth-century educators believed that children ought to be protected from "the harsh and ugly realities of life" for as long as possible, others, including Wollstonecraft, thought observations of even severe incidents in the natural world provided the best guide for religious and moral formation. Born in London to a family of modest means, Wollstonecraft attained only a few years of formal education but eventually found employment as a governess and teacher. Her first book, *Thoughts on the education of daughters* (1787), provided a series of lessons on moral formation based on examples of love, benevolence, and ethical life. Wollstonecraft's stories—including a novel, *Mary: a fiction* (1788)—brought her into contact with rationalist dissenters such as Richard Price, Joseph Priestley, and the publisher Joseph Johnson, who encouraged her forays into radical political philosophy. Wollstonecraft published *A vindication of the rights of men* shortly after the appearance of Edmund Burke's *Reflections on the revolution in France* (1790). Two years later, Wollstonecraft followed up with a landmark defense of gender equality in *A vindication of the rights of woman* (1792). The latter work solidified Wollstonecraft's reputation as a leading intellectual. She married the political philosopher William Godwin in 1797 but died the same year, only days after delivering a daughter—Mary Wollstonecraft Godwin (later, Mary Shelley).

Wollstonecraft's *Original stories from real life, with conversations, calculated to regulate the affections, and form the mind to truth and goodness* (1788) exemplifies her commitment to female moral and social agency. *Original stories* is best understood as a supplement to her *Thoughts on the education of daughters*, which recommended beginning with "Stories of insects and animals" to "rouse the childish passions and exercise humanity, and then they will rise to man and from him to his Maker" (154). The central character in *Original stories* is Mrs. Mason, a surrogate mother to two adolescent girls charged to her care. Mason, as Mitzi Myers explains, "inculcates women's ways of coping with this hard world: rational reflection and religion, self-command and charity, 'strength of mind' and a humanitarian maternal ethic . . . She is a dream of strength and power" (42). In the following selection, Mason teaches the children through examples from nature. Mary and Caroline encounter small creatures—ants, snails, and birds—and learn a lesson on caring for all creatures even as the divine cares for all creation (cf. Matt 6:26). Joseph Johnson's 1791 edition included six etchings by William Blake.

SOURCES: Mitzi Myers, "Impeccable governesses, rational dames, and moral mothers: Mary Wollstonecraft and the female tradition in Georgian children's books," *Children's Literature* 14 (1986): 31–59; *ODNB*; Donelle Ruwe, *British children's poetry in the Romantic Era: verse, riddle, and rhyme* (New York: Palgrave Macmillan, 2014); Barbara Taylor, *Mary Wollstonecraft and the feminist imagination* (Cambridge: Cambridge University Press, 2003); Janet Todd, *Mary Wollstonecraft: a revolutionary life* (New York: Columbia University Press, 2000); Daniel E. White, *Early Romanticism and religious dissent* (Cambridge: Cambridge University Press, 2006).

William Blake, "Look what a fine morning it is" (in Mary Wollstonecraft,
Original stories from real life [1791]).

MARY WOLLSTONECRAFT
Original stories from real life
1788

One fine morning in spring, sometime after Mary and Caroline were settled in their new abode, Mrs. Mason proposed a walk before breakfast, a custom she wished to teach imperceptibly by rendering it amusing.

The sun had scarcely dispelled the dew that hung on every blade of grass and filled the half-shut flowers. Every prospect smiled, and the freshness of the air conveyed the most pleasing sensations to Mrs. Mason's mind. But the children were regardless[1] of the surrounding beauties, and ran eagerly after some insects to destroy them. Mrs. Mason silently observed their cruel sports without appearing to do it;[2] but stepping suddenly out of the footpath into the long grass, her buckle was caught in it, and, striving to disentangle herself, she wet her feet, which the children knew she wished to avoid, as she had been lately sick. This circumstance roused their attention, and they forgot their amusement to enquire *why* she had left the path; and Mary could hardly restrain a laugh when she was informed that it was to avoid treading on some snails that were creeping across the narrow footway. Surely, said Mary, you do not think there is any harm in killing a snail or any of those nasty creatures that crawl on the ground? I hate them and should scream if one was to find its way from my clothes to my neck! With great gravity, Mrs. Mason asked how she dared to kill anything unless it were to prevent its hurting her? Then, resuming a smiling face, she said: Your education has been neglected, my child. As we walk along attend to what I say, and make the best answers you can; and do you, Caroline, join in the conversation.

You have already heard that God created the world, and every inhabitant of it. He is then called the Father of all creatures, and all are made to be happy whom a good and wise God has created. He made those snails you despise, and caterpillars and spiders; and when he made them, did not leave them to perish, but placed them where the food that is most

1   [Ed. That is, "unaffected by."]
2   [Ed. An allusion to Shakespeare's *King Lear*: "As flies to wanton boys, are we to the gods. / They kill us for their sport" (4.1.36–37).]

proper to nourish them is easily found. They do not live long, but he who is their Father, as well as yours, directs them to deposit their eggs on the plants that are fit to support their young when they are not able to get food for themselves. And when such a great and wise Being has taken care to provide everything necessary for the meanest creature, would you dare to kill it merely because it appears to you ugly? Mary began to be attentive and quickly followed Mrs. Mason's example, who allowed a caterpillar and a spider to creep on her hand. You find them, she rejoined, very harmless; but a great number would destroy our vegetables and fruit; so birds are permitted to eat them, as we feed on animals, and in spring there are always more than at any other season of the year, to furnish food for the young broods. Half-convinced, Mary said: But worms are of little consequence in the world. Yet, replied Mrs. Mason, God cares for them and gives them everything that is necessary to render their existence comfortable. You are often troublesome—I am stronger than you—yet I do not kill you.

Observe those ants. They have a little habitation in yonder hillock. They carry food to it for their young and sleep very snug in it during the cold weather. The bees also have comfortable towns, and lay up a store of honey to support them when the flowers die and snow covers the ground—and this forecast is as much the gift of God as any quality you possess.

Do you know the meaning of the word "goodness"? I see you are unwilling to answer. I will tell you. It is, first, to avoid hurting anything; and, then, to contrive to give as much pleasure as you can. If some insects are to be destroyed to preserve my garden from desolation, I have it done in the quickest way. The domestic animals that I keep, I provide the best food for and never suffer them to be tormented; and this caution arises from two motives: I wish to make them happy; and, as I love my fellow-creatures still better than the brute creation, I would not allow those that I have any influence over to grow habitually thoughtless and cruel, till they were unable to relish the greatest pleasure life affords—that of resembling God, by doing good.

A lark now began to sing as it soared aloft. The children watched its motions, listening to the artless melody. They wondered what it was thinking of—of its young family, they soon concluded. For it flew over the hedge and, drawing near, they heard the young ones chirp. Very soon both the old birds took their flight together to look for food to satisfy the craving of the almost-fledged young. An idle boy, who had borrowed a gun, fired at them—they fell; and before he could take up the wounded pair, he perceived Mrs. Mason; and expecting a very severe reprimand, ran away. She and the little girls drew near, and found that one was not much hurt, but that the other, the cock, had one leg broken and both its wings shattered; and its little eyes seemed starting out of their sockets, it was in such exquisite pain. The children turned away their eyes. Look at it, said Mrs. Mason; do you not see that it suffers as much, and more, than you did when you had the smallpox, when you were so tenderly nursed. Take up the hen. I will bind her wing together. Perhaps it may heal. As to the cock, though I hate to kill anything, I must put him out of pain; to leave him in his present state would be cruel; and, avoiding an unpleasant sensation myself, I should allow the poor bird to die by inches and call this treatment tenderness when it would be selfishness or weakness. Saying so, she put her foot on the bird's head, turning her own another way.

They walked on, when Caroline remarked that the nestlings, deprived of their parents, would now perish—and the mother began to flutter in her hand as they drew near the hedge. Though the poor creature could not fly, yet she tried to do it. The girls, with one voice, begged Mrs. Mason to let them take the nest, and provide food in a cage, and see if the mother could not contrive to hop about to feed them. The nest and the old mother were instantly in Mary's handkerchief. A little opening was left to admit the air; and Caroline peeped into it every moment to see how they looked. I give you leave, said Mrs. Mason, to take those birds, because an accident has rendered them helpless; if that had not been the case, they should not have been confined.

They had scarcely reached the next field when they met another boy with a nest in his hand, and on a tree near him saw the mother, who, forgetting her natural timidity, followed the spoiler; and her intelligible tones of anguish reached the ears of the children, whose hearts now first felt the emotions of humanity. Caroline called him, and taking sixpence out of her little purse, offered to give it to him for the nest, if he would show her where he had taken it from. The boy consented, and away ran Caroline to replace it, crying all the way how delighted the old bird will be to find her brood again. The pleasure that the parent-bird would feel was talked of till they came to a large common and heard some young asses at the door of an hovel, making a most dreadful noise. Mrs. Mason had ordered the old ones to be confined, lest the young should suck before the necessary quantity had been saved for some sick people in her neighborhood. But after they had given the usual quantity of milk, the thoughtless boy had left them still in confinement, and the young in vain implored the food nature designed for their particular support. Open the hatch, said Mrs. Mason; the mothers have still enough left to satisfy their young. It was opened, and they saw them suck.

Now, said she, we will return to breakfast; give me your hands, my little girls, you have done good this morning; you have acted like rational creatures. Look what a fine morning it is. Insects, birds, and animals are all enjoying this sweet day. Thank God for permitting you to see it and for giving you an understanding which teaches you that you ought, by doing good, to imitate him. Other creatures only think of supporting themselves, but man is allowed to ennoble his nature by cultivating his mind and enlarging his heart. He feels disinterested love; every part of the creation affords an exercise for virtue, and virtue is ever the truest source of pleasure.

TEXT: Mary Wollstonecraft, *Original stories from real life, with conversations, calculated to regulate the affections, and form the mind to truth and goodness*, new ed. (London: J. Johnson, 1796), 1–9.

ADAM CLARKE
(1762–1832)
Tobacco

One of the most influential Methodists of the period was Adam Clarke, whom Thomas Langford calls "the epitome of all Wesley might have hoped for from his preachers: He combined biblical scholarship and practical concern in uncommon ways."[1] Clarke was born in Ireland, his mother a Presbyterian, his father an Anglican. Around sixteen years old, Clarke came under the influence of John Wesley and other Methodist preachers. Wesley set Clarke apart as one of his lay preachers in 1782, and Clarke was soon received into full connection (that is, with full rights and accountability to the Methodist conference). Clarke was largely self-educated, although Aberdeen University awarded him an honorary M.A. in 1807 and LLD in 1808. His lack of university education and Anglican ordination did not hinder him from becoming a trusted leader and scholar in the burgeoning Methodist movement. He worked tirelessly in far-flung regions of Methodist lay ministry, first preaching in the Bradford (Wiltshire) circuit and later ministering in Cornwall, the Channel Islands, Lancashire, and the Shetlands. In one year, Clarke preached more than 560 sermons, traveled hundreds of miles, and exhorted numerous Christians along the way. He resided from 1805 to 1815 in London and developed strong friendships with bishops and other prominent figures. These friendships left Clarke uniquely positioned to advocate for abolition and for relief of the poor in England and Ireland alike: "he built schools, planned a retirement home for Methodist preachers and their widows, led missionary efforts . . . organized drives to feed the hungry, and encouraged education for women in Northern Ireland."[2] This rare combination of strengths led him to the presidency of the Methodist conference in 1806, 1814, and 1822. Clarke's gifts as a biblical and linguistic scholar set him apart from many other Methodist preachers in his day. Clarke translated Christoph Christian Sturm's *Reflections on the works of God and his providence throughout all nature* (1804), Claude Fleury's *Manners of the ancient israelites*

---

[1]   Thomas A. Langford, *Practical divinity: theology in the Wesleyan tradition*, rev. ed., vol. 1 (Nashville: Abingdon, 1983), 47.

[2]   Langford, *Practical divinity*, 48.

(1805), and wrote an eight-volume *Commentary on the whole Bible* (1810–1824), one of the most significant commentaries of the time. After the appearance of Robert Southey's controversial *The life of Wesley, and the rise and progress of Methodism* (1820), Clarke was commissioned to produce a corrective study, published as *Memoirs of the Wesley family* (2 vols., 1822). Clarke devoted his final years to ministry and writing. He continued to produce tracts and sermons while serving congregations in England before succumbing to the cholera outbreak of 1831–1832.

Although Clarke's *Dissertation on the use and abuse of tobacco* (1797) may sound a bit stuffy to modern ears, the text actually demonstrates a thoughtful and pragmatic commitment to social reform. After reviewing recent medical literature on the dangers of tobacco (e.g., "it is known that a single drop of the chemical oil of tobacco, being put on the tongue of a cat, produced violent convulsions and killed her in the space of one minute" [231]), Clarke proceeds to explain the challenges that tobacco creates for Christian sanctification and, by implication, the salvation of individual users. In a remarkable description of late eighteenth-century social customs, Clarke complains that worshipers cannot even kneel for prayer in the churches without contacting the spittle of tobacco users. British Methodist opposition to tobacco use, so ably demonstrated by Clarke's essay, proved difficult to promote in the southern region of the United States, where American Methodism flourished through tacit acceptance of tobacco farming.

SOURCES: Maldwyn Edwards, *Adam Clarke* (London: Epworth, 1942); Thomas A. Langford, *Practical divinity: theology in the Wesleyan tradition*, rev. ed., vol. 1 (Nashville: Abingdon, 1983); *ODNB*; John Rogerson, *Old Testament criticism in the nineteenth century: England and Germany* (Philadelphia: Fortress, 1985).

ADAM CLARKE
A dissertation on the use and abuse of tobacco
1797

These facts, which are well authenticated, may suffice; and taken into connection with that word which says, "thou shalt do *no* murder" [Exod 20:13], should deter every person who wishes well to his body and his soul from the (at least immoderate) use of this herb.

That it is sinful to use it as most do, I have no doubt—if destroying the constitution and vilely squandering away the time and money which God has given for other purposes may be termed sinful.

Many persons I have known who were scarcely able to procure the necessaries of life, and yet, by sacrificing health and decency, have made a shift to procure the daily *quantum sufficit*[1] of tobacco. I have observed some whole families, and very poor ones too, who have used tobacco in all possible ways—and some of them for more than half a century. Now supposing the whole family—consisting of four, five, or six—to have used but 1*s*. 6*d*. worth in a week, then, in the mere article of tobacco, nearly 200*l*. sterling is totally irrecoverably lost in the course of fifty years![2] Were all the expenses attending this business enumerated, probably five times the sum in several cases would not be too large an estimate, especially if strong drink (its general concomitant), neglect of business, and appropriate utensils be taken into the account. Can any who profess to call themselves Christians vindicate their conduct in this respect?

A pious clergyman lately told me that he had a number of very poor families in his parish immoderately attached to the use of tobacco. He plainly saw that a large proportion of their daily earnings was destroyed in this way. He warned them in private and preached in public against it, but few of them had resolution enough to lay it aside.

The expense of one very poor family in snuff and tobacco he calculated, and found it to amount to nearly one third part of their yearly earnings!

---

[1] [Ed. That is, "as much as suffices."]
[2] To say nothing of the power of money to increase its value almost beyond credibility by compound interest, in which case the above weekly consumption would amount in 50 years to upwards of 800*l*. sterling, and in 54 years to upwards of 1000*l*.

But the loss of time in this shameful work is a serious evil. I have known some who (strange to tell!) have smoked three or four hours in the day, by their own confession, and others who have spent six hours in the same employment! How can such persons answer for this at the bar of God? "But it is prescribed to me by a physician." No man who values his character as a physician will ever prescribe it in this way. Whatever good effects may be attributed even to a moderate use of it can be produced by medicines of a more cleanly and less dangerous nature. . . .

I grant that a person who is brought under the dominion of the pipe or the snuffbox may feel great uneasiness in attempting to leave it off, and get some medical man, through a false pity or for money, to prescribe the continued use of it. But this does not vindicate it, and the person who prescribes thus is not to be trusted. He is either without principle or without skill.

> A mere licentiate without knowledge,
> The shame and scandal of the college.[3]

‡

The impiety manifested by several in the use of this herb merits the most cutting reproof. When many of the tobacco consumers get into trouble or under any cross or affliction, instead of looking to God for support, the pipe, the snuffbox, or the twist is applied to with quadruple earnestness—so that four times (I might say in some cases ten times) the usual quantity is consumed on such occasions. What a comfort is this weed in time of sorrow! What a support in time of trouble![4] In a word, what a god!

Again, the interruption occasioned in places of public worship by the use of the snuffbox is a matter of serious concern to all those who are not guilty. When the most solemn and important matters relative to God and man, eternal glory and eternal ruin, form the subject of a preacher's discourse, whose very soul is in his work, it is no unusual thing to see the snuffbox taken out and officiously handed about to half a dozen of persons on the same seat. Would there not be as much propriety in bringing forth and distributing some of the common necessaries of life? "But we do not go to the house of God to take our victuals." Neither should you to take physic.

Never did Pope Urban VIII act more like an apostolic man than when he made a bull to excommunicate all those who took tobacco in the churches.[5]

To the great scandal of religious people, the abominable customs of snuff-taking and chewing have made their way into many congregations and are likely to be productive of immense evil. Churches and chapels are most scandalously abused by the tobacco-chewers who frequent them, and kneeling before the Supreme Being, which is so becoming and necessary when sinners approach their Maker in prayer, is rendered in many

---

[3]   [Ed. William Meston, "Old Mother Grimm's tales: the cobbler," in *The poetical works of the ingenuous and learned William Meston*, 6th ed. (Edinburgh: Francis Robertson, 1767), 99.]

[4]   [Ed. Clarke contrasts dependence on tobacco with reliance on God: "God is our refuge and strength, a very present help in trouble" (Ps 46:1).]

[5]   [Ed. Clarke refers to a bull of Urban VIII (1568–1644) forbidding the use of tobacco during mass in 1624.]

seats impracticable because of the large quantity of tobacco saliva which is ejected in all directions.

‡

But are not many led into this practice of smoking by their pastors? I am sorry to have it to say that this idle, disgraceful custom prevails much at present among ministers of most denominations. Can such persons preach against needless self-indulgence, destruction of time, or waste of money? These men greatly injure their own usefulness. They smoke away their ministerial importance in the families where they occasionally visit, the very children and maidservants pass their jokes on the piping parson, and, should they unluckily succeed in bringing over the uninfected to their vile custom, the evil is doubled. I have known serious misunderstandings produced in certain families where the example of the idle parson has influenced a husband or wife, against the consent of the other, to adopt the use of the pipe or the snuffbox.

Should all other arguments fail to produce a reformation in the conduct of tobacco consumers, there is one which is addressed to good breeding and benevolence, which for the sake of politeness and humanity should prevail. Consider how disagreeable your custom is to those who do not follow it. An atmosphere of tobacco effluvia surrounds you whithersoever you go. Every article about you smells of it; your apartments, your clothes, and even your very breath. Nor is there a smell in nature more disagreeable than that of stale tobacco, arising in warm exhalations from the human body, rendered still more offensive by passing through the pores, and becoming strongly impregnated with that noxious matter which was before insensibly perspired.

Consider what pain your friends may be put to in standing near you in order to consult you on some important business or to be improved by your conversation. Will you oblige them to pay so heavy a tax for the benefit of your advice when it would have been more honorable to yourself, and comfortable to them, to have had that gratification in a less expensive way? I cannot help saying that I have often suffered a very painful nausea from the cause above assigned and on which I will dilate no further.

To those who are not yet incorporated with the fashionable company of tobacco-consumers, I would say, *never enter.* To those who are entered, I would say, *desist.* First, for the sake of your health, which must be materially injured, if not destroyed by it. Secondly, for the sake of your property, which, if you are a poor man, must be considerably impaired by it. But supposing you can afford this extra expense, consider how acceptable the pence (to go no further) which you spend in this idle, unnecessary employment would be to many who are often destitute of bread and to whom one penny would sometimes be as an angel of God. Thirdly, for the sake of your time—a large portion of which is irreparably lost, particularly in smoking. Have you any time to dispose of—to murder? Is there no need of prayer—reading—study? Fourthly, for the sake of your friends, who cannot fail to be pained in your company, for the reasons before assigned. Fifthly, for the sake of your voice, which continuance in snuff-taking will infallibly ruin, as the nasal passages are almost entirely obliterated by it. Sixthly, for the sake of your soul. Do you not think that God will visit you for your loss of time, waste of money, and needless self-indulgence? Have you not seen that the use of tobacco leads to drunkenness? Do you not know that habitual smokers have the drinking vessel often at hand, and frequently apply to it? Nor is it any wonder, for the great quantity of necessary moisture which is drawn off from the mouth, etc., by these means, must be supplied some other way. You tremble at the thought—well you may, for you are in great danger. May God look upon and save you before it be too late! It was this view of the subject that led Mr. Sylvester to imagine that the plant derived its name from Bacchus, the heathen god of the drunkards:

> Which of their weapons hath the conquest got,
> Over their wits: the pipe or else the pot? [. . .]
> For even the derivation of the name
> Seems to allude to, and include the same;
> Tobacco, as Τω Βαχχω, one would say;
> To cup-god *Bacchus* dedicated ay.[6]

It is with pain of heart that I am obliged to say, I have known several who through their immoderate attachment to the pipe have become mere sots. There are others who are walking unconcernedly in the same dangerous road—I tremble for them. Should this fall into their hands, may they receive it as a warning from God!

✂︎

TEXT: Adam Clarke, *A dissertation on the use and abuse of tobacco*, in *A discourse on the nature, design, and institution of the Holy Eucharist* . . . (New York: E. Sargeant and Griffin and Rudd, 1812), 231–34, 237–42.

---

6   [Ed. Joshuah Sylvester, "Tobacco Battered," in *Complete Works of Joshuah Sylvester*, ed. Alexander B. Grosart, 2 vols. (1880), 2:269 (lines 221–22, 225–28).]

ROBERT MALTHUS
(1766–1834)
Chastity

The sharp division between sacred and secular, so often taken for granted today, cannot be assumed for writers in England at the turn of the nineteenth century. Reflection on natural catastrophes, matters of pleasure and pain, and the perpetual conflicts that brought nations to war regularly implicated questions of divinity. Thus the economist Thomas Robert Malthus fuses analysis of the food supply with discussions of Christian virtue and divine benevolence.

Malthus was born to a family of independent means. Little is known of his early life and education except that his parents sent him to the dissenting academy at Warrington (the sole surviving evidence that the family belonged to a dissenting church). Malthus studied under the influential scholar Gilbert Wakefield, even after the school closed in 1783. Malthus matriculated at Jesus College, Cambridge in 1784, receiving the B.A. in 1788 and the M.A. in 1791. Malthus proceeded to ordination while a fellow at Jesus College, where he remained as a fellow until his marriage, at the age of thirty-eight, in 1804. The success of *An essay on the principle of population* (1798) helped to secure Malthus an appointment as professor of history and political economy at the East India College in Hertford. Malthus often preached with great success at the college, while continuing to write on political economy. He was awarded membership in the Royal Society (from 1818) and Royal Society of Literature (from 1825).

Malthus first published *An essay on the principle of population* anonymously in 1798. His argument pivots on the relationship between population and food supply. Food supply cannot keep pace with population, and historically the main ways the two have been brought back in balance are war, disease, and famine. In 1803 Malthus published a new edition of the work that expanded on several themes, including the possibility of controlling population by delaying marriage. The following selection, drawn from the edition of 1803, sets out the religious bases of Malthus' theory, according to which Christian sexual ethics turn out to be the key (in a world without reliable contraception) to preventing the mass starvation attendant upon overpopulation. Divine benevolence ordains chastity as a means of population control—one that increases human happiness, since children will be born into families with sufficient financial and emotional resources to care for them.

SOURCES: Alan Macfarlane, *Marriage and love in England: modes of reeproduction, 1300–1840* (Oxford: Blackwell, 1986); *ODNB*; William Petersen, *Malthus* (Cambridge, Mass.: Harvard University Press, 1979); Donald Winch, *Malthus* (Oxford: Oxford University Press, 1987).

ROBERT MALTHUS
An essay on the principle of population
1803

One of the principle reasons which has prevented an assent to the doctrine of the constant tendency of population to increase beyond the means of subsistence is a great unwillingness to believe that the Deity would, by the laws of nature, bring beings into existence which, by the laws of nature, could not be supported in that existence. But if, in addition to that general activity and direction of our industry put in motion by these laws, we further consider that the incidental evil arising from them are constantly directing our attention to the proper check to population—moral restraint—and if it appear that by a strict obedience to those duties which are pointed out to us by the light of nature and reason, and are confirmed and sanctioned by revelation, these evils may be avoided, the objection will, I trust, be removed and all apparent imputation of the goodness of the Deity be done away. . . .

If, for the sake of illustration, we might be permitted to draw a picture of society in which each individual endeavored to attain happiness by the strict fulfillment of those duties which the most enlightened of the ancient philosophers deduced from the laws of nature, and which have been directly taught and received such powerful sanctions in the moral code of Christianity, it would present a very different scene from that which we now contemplate. Every act which was prompted by the desire of immediate gratification, but which threatened an ultimate overbalance of pain, would be considered as a breach of duty; and, consequently, no man whose earnings were only sufficient to maintain two children would put himself in a situation in which he might have to maintain four or five, however he might be prompted to it by the passion of love. This prudential restraint, if it were generally adopted, by narrowing the supply of labor in the market, would, in the natural course of things, soon raise its price. The period of delayed gratification would be passed in saving the earnings which were above the wants of a single man and in acquiring habits of sobriety, industry, and economy, which would enable him, in a few years, to enter into the matrimonial contract without fear of its consequences. . . . As the wages of labor would thus be sufficient to maintain with decency a large family, and as every

333

married couple would set out with a sum for contingencies, all squalid poverty would be removed from society, or at least be confined to a very few who had fallen into misfortune against which no prudence or foresight could provide.

The interval between the age of puberty and the period at which each individual might venture on marriage must, according to the supposition, be passed in strict chastity, because the law of chastity cannot be violated without producing evil. The effect of anything like a promiscuous intercourse which prevents the birth of children is evidently to weaken the best affections of the heart and, in a very marked manner, to degrade the female character. And any other intercourse would, without improper arts, bring as many children into the society as marriage, with a much greater probability of their becoming a burden to it.

These considerations show that the virtue of chastity is not, as some have supposed, a forced produce[1] of artificial society, but that it has the most real and solid foundation in nature and reason, being apparently the only virtuous means of avoiding the vice and misery which result from the principle of population.

In such a society as we have been supposing, it might be necessary for both sexes to pass many of the early years of life in the single state; and if this were general, there would certainly be room for a much greater number to marry afterwards, so that fewer, upon the whole, would be condemned to pass their lives in celibacy. If the custom of not marrying early prevailed generally, and if violations of chastity were equally dishonorable in both sexes, a more familiar and friendly intercourse between them might take place without danger. Two young people might converse together intimately without its being immediately supposed that they either intended marriage or intrigue; and much better opportunity would thus be given to both sexes of finding out kindred dispositions and of forming those strong and lasting attachments without which the married state is generally more productive of misery than of happiness. The earlier years of life would not be spent without love, though without the full gratification of it. The passion, instead of being extinguished, as it now too frequently is by early sensuality, would only be repressed for a time, that it might afterwards burn with brighter, purer, and steadier flame; and the happiness of the married state, instead of an opportunity of immediate indulgence, would be looked forward to as the prize of industry and virtue, and the reward of a genuine and constant attachment.

The passion of love is a powerful stimulus in the formation of character, and often prompts to the most noble and generous exertions; but this is only when the affections are centered in one object and, generally, when full gratification is delayed by difficulties. The heart is perhaps never so much disposed to virtuous conduct, and certainly at no time is the virtue of chastity so little difficult to men, as when under the influence of such a passion. Late marriages, taking place in this way, would be very different from those of the same name at present, where the union is too frequently prompted by interested views and the parties meet, not unfrequently, with exhausted constitutions and generally with exhausted affection. The late marriages at present are indeed principally confined to the men; and there are few, however advanced in life they may be, who, if they determine to marry, do not fix their choice on the very young wife. A young woman, without fortune,

---

[1]   [Ed. That is, "a forced product."]

when she has passed her twenty-fifth year, begins to fear, and with reason, that she may lead a life of celibacy and, with a heart capable of forming a strong attachment, feels, as each year creeps on, her hopes of finding an object to rest her affections gradually diminishing, and the uneasiness of her situation aggravated by the silly and unjust prejudices of the world. If the general age of marriage among women were later, the period of youth and hope would be prolonged, and fewer would be ultimately disappointed.

That a change of this kind would be a most decided advantage to the more virtuous half of society, we cannot for a moment doubt. However impatiently the privation might be borne by the men, it would be supported by the women readily and cheerfully; and if they could look forward with just confidence to marriage at twenty-eight or thirty,[2] I fully believe, that if the matter were left to their free choice, they would clearly prefer waiting till this period to the being involved in all the cares of a large family at twenty-five. The most eligible age of marriage, however, could not be fixed, but must depend on circumstances and situation, and must be determined entirely by experience. There is no period of human life at which nature more strongly prompts to an union of the sexes than from seventeen or eighteen to twenty. In every society above that state of depression which almost excludes reason and foresight, these early tendencies must necessarily be restrained; and if, in the actual state of things, such restraint on the impulses of nature be found unavoidable, at what time we can be consistently released from it but at that period, whatever it may be, when in the existing circumstances of the society a fair prospect presents itself of maintaining a family.

The difficulty of moral restraint will perhaps be objected to this doctrine. To him who does not acknowledge the authority of the Christian religion, I have only to say that, after the most careful investigation, this virtue appears to be absolutely necessary in order to avoid certain evils which would otherwise result from the general laws of nature. According to his own principles, it is his duty to pursue the greatest good consistent with these laws and not to fail in this important end, and produce an overbalance of misery by a partial obedience to some of the dictates of nature while he neglects others. The path of virtue, though it be the only path which leads to permanent happiness, has always been represented by the heathen moralists as of difficult ascent.

To the Christian, I would say that the Scriptures most clearly and precisely point out to us as our duty to restrain our passion within the bounds of reason; and it is a palpable disobedience of this law to indulge our desires in such a manner as reason tells us will unavoidably end in misery. The Christian cannot consider the difficulty of moral restraint as any argument against its being his duty, since in almost every page of the sacred writings man is described as encompassed on all sides by temptations which it is extremely difficult to resist; and though no duties are enjoined which do not contribute to his happiness on earth as well as in a future state, yet an undeviating obedience is never represented as an easy task.

There is in general so strong a tendency to love in early youth that it is extremely difficult, at this period, to distinguish a genuine from a transient passion. If the earlier years of life were passed by both sexes in moral restraint, from the great facility that this would

---

[2]   [Ed. Not long after the publication of this expanded edition, Malthus married the twenty-eight-year-old Harriet Eckersall (1776–1864).]

give to the meeting of kindred dispositions, I might even admit of a doubt whether more happy marriages would not take place and, consequently, more pleasure from the passion of love than in a state such as that of America—the circumstances of which would allow of a very early union of the sexes. But if we compare the intercourse of the sexes in such a society as I have been supposing with that which now exists in Europe, taken under all its circumstances, it may safely be asserted that, independently of the load of misery which would be removed by the prevalence of moral restraint, the sum of pleasurable sensations from the passion of love would be increased in a very great degree.

⤛⤜

TEXT: T[homas] R. Malthus, *An essay on the principle of population; or, A view of its past and present effects on human happiness*, new ed. (London: J. Johnson, 1803), 494–500.

VIII

NATION

There are men who appear not insensible to the rules of morality as they respect individuals, and who unaccountably disclaim them with respect to nations.

Anna Letitia Barbauld, *Sins of government, sins of the nation* (1793)

SAMUEL PALMER
(1741–1813)
English Dissent

Samuel Palmer, dissenting minister, was born at Bedford and prepared for Christian ministry at the Daventry dissenting academy under the noted educator Caleb Ashworth, who also counted Joseph Priestley (see Part I) among his many students. In 1762 Palmer assisted William Hunt at the Independent congregation at Mare Street, Hackney. He was ordained the following year, and later succeeded Hunt, while also preaching at the Weigh-House chapel, Little Eastcheap. Palmer was a prolific author. In addition to regular essays in the *Protestant Dissenter's Magazine* and the *Monthly Repository*, Palmer penned apologies for Protestant dissent, among them *The nonconformist's memorial* (2 vols., 1775) and *The Calvinism of the Protestant dissenters asserted* (1786).

Palmer's best-known work, *The Protestant dissenter's catechism* (1772), provides a history of nonconformity and an apology for dissent from the Church of England. The following selection appeals to the authority of conscience in matters of religion, affirms religious freedom, and underscores the perseverance of faithful dissenters despite persecution. He defends the freedom of dissenters to gather as congregations, pray extemporaneously without liturgical forms, and preach directly from the Bible without fear of repercussion from the authorities. In the following selection, Palmer explains the differences between Christian denominations, defends the biblical grounds for dissent from the national church, and distinguishes between civil authority and individual conscience. The original text is heavily annotated with supporting biblical texts, but the heart of Palmer's work is found in the question-answer format of the catechism itself.

>━━◅

SOURCES: Bebbington; Mark Canuel, *Religion, toleration, and British writing, 1790–1830* (Cambridge: Cambridge University Press, 2002); Cragg; Frances Knight, *The nineteenth-century church and English society* (Cambridge: Cambridge University Press, 1995); *ODNB*; Daniel E. White, *Early Romanticism and religious dissent* (Cambridge: Cambridge University Press, 2006).

SAMUEL PALMER
The Protestant dissenter's catechism
1772

A Brief History of the Nonconformists

Q. 1. How many religions are there in the world?

A. Four: the Pagan (or Heathen), the Jewish, the Mahometan, and the Christian. Note, besides these, multitudes in all parts of Europe are Deists, who have not, as such, any form of religion or public worship. They profess to believe in God, and many of them in a future state, as the dictates of reason, but deny all revelation.

Q. 2. Who are generally comprehended under the name of Christians?

A. All who profess to receive the religion of Jesus Christ as divine.

Q. 3. What is the grand division which has taken place among Christians?

A. Christians (in this Western part of Europe) are divided into Papists[1] and Protestants.

Q. 4. Who are called Papists?

A. Those who are in communion with the Church of Rome, often called Roman Catholics, but more properly Papists, because of their subjection to the pope, whom the greater part of them receive and honor as Christ's vicar and universal bishop.

Q. 5. Who are meant by the term Protestants?

---

[1]   [Ed. *Papists* and *popery*, terms used throughout the period, are derogatory names associated with Roman Catholicism. In polemical arguments, the terms highlight Protestant rejection of the authority of the Roman curia.]

A. This name was given to those who first publicly protested against the errors of popery, viz., at Spire in Germany, 1529;[2] and from them it has been, to this day, applied to those Christians in general (in the West) who are not Papists.

Q. 6. Are the Protestants in England united in their faith and manner of worship?
A. No. They are divided into conformists and nonconformists or, as they are commonly called, churchmen and dissenters.

Q. 7. Who are called conformists or churchmen?
A. Those who conform to that mode of worship and form of church-government which are established and supported in England by the state.

Q. 8. Who are intended by the term dissenters?
A. The term properly signifies persons of a different opinion (in any matter) but now commonly denotes those in general who do not conform to the established Church, but meet for divine worship in places of their own; more especially those of the three following denominations: Presbyterians, Independents, and Baptists.

‡

The Reasons of the Protestant Dissent from the Established Church

Q. 1. What are the grand principles on which the Protestant dissenters ground their separation from the Church by law established?
A. The right of private judgment and liberty of conscience in opposition to all human authority in matters of religion, the acknowledgment of Christ alone as head of his church, and the sufficiency of the Holy Scriptures as the rule of faith and practice.

Q. 2. Doth not the Scripture require us {Rom 13:1-5; 1 Pet 2:13-14} to be subject to the civil magistrate as the minister of God for conscience sake?
A. Not in matters of religion, much less in things contrary to the law of God, for God cannot deny himself; so that all human laws which are inconsistent with the divine ought to be disobeyed.

Q. 3. But is every private man to judge for himself whether the laws of his country are agreeable to the laws of God?
A. Certainly in the affairs of religion every man ought to judge for himself, since every man must give an account of himself to God {Rom 14:12}, who has given us an infallible rule in his Word to guide us and reasonable faculties to understand it, which private persons are as capable of using to discover the way of truth and duty as magistrates and large bodies of men. Besides, religion is a

---

2   [Ed. The Diet of Speyer (1529), which gathered under the authority of Charles V, ended toleration of Lutherans throughout Europe. In response, five princes and fourteen cities formally protested the proceedings on the grounds of religious conscience, giving official rise to Protestant Christianity.]

personal thing, and no further deserves the name than as it is the effect of conviction and choice.

Q. 4. But are not priests our spiritual rulers and are we not expressly required {Heb 13:7-17} to obey them that rule over us?

A. They have no juster claim to implicit faith and unlimited obedience than civil magistrates, nor those supported by the state than others. The Word of God expressly forbids Christians giving up conscience to the direction of any men; and the apostles themselves disclaimed all dominion over it, and urged it upon their hearers to examine and judge for themselves.

Q. 5. Have we any instances in Scripture of wise and good men's refusing to conform to the national, established religion?

A. Yes. Daniel followed the dictates of his own conscience in praying to his God, as he had been used to do, when the king had issued out a decree against it {Dan 6:10}; as also did the three Hebrew youths in refusing to conform to the worship of the image which Nebuchadnezzar set up, though "the princes, the governors and captains, the judges, the treasurers, the counselors, the sheriffs, and all the rulers of the provinces, were gathered together at the dedication of it," nobly declaring when threatened with being cast for their nonconformity into the fiery furnace, "If it be so, our God whom we serve will deliver us out of thine hand, O King. But if not, be it known unto thee that we will not serve thy gods, nor worship the golden image which thou hast set up" {Dan 3:17, 18}.

In like manner the apostles of Christ disobeyed the Jewish priests and rulers in not conforming to the religion of their country, and when reproved by the high priest for violating their command, bravely answered, "We ought to obey God rather than men" {Acts 5:39}.

Q. 6. May a few men who are dissatisfied with the national religion publish their private sentiments and worship God according to them in places of their own?

A. If men have a right to think for themselves, they must have an equal right to act according to their judgment and conscience, and are in duty bound to do it. So that where persons think the established forms of religion unscriptural or defective, a regard to their own edification and the cause of pure religion requires them to dissent. On this principle the first Christians dissented from the Jewish church, the Gentile converts from pagan establishments, and the Church of England from the Church of Rome.

Q. 7. Ought we not to be very cautious of separating from any church of professed Christians and Protestants without very weighty reasons?

A. Doubtless it is not every trifling circumstance that will vindicate separations among Christians. But the dissenters apprehend that the grounds of their separation from the Church of England are so many and important as fully to justify them in it.

Q. 8. What are the principals of those things in the Church of England on which the dissent from it is founded?

A. 1. Its general frame and constitution as national and established.

2. The character and authority of certain officers appointed in it.

3. The imposition of a stated form of prayer called the Liturgy and many exceptionable things contained therein.

4. The pretended right of enjoining unscriptural ceremonies.

5. The terms on which ministers are admitted into it.

6. The want of liberty in the people to choose their own ministers. And

7. The corrupt state of its discipline.

Of the General Frame and Constitution of the Church of England

Q. 9. What do the dissenters think to be a true church of Christ?

A. A congregation or voluntary society of Christians who commonly meet together to attend gospel ordinances in the same place. And they think every such society has a right to transact its own affairs according to the judgment and conscience of the members thereof, independently of any other societies whatsoever, or without being accountable to any but Jesus Christ, or restrained by any laws but his.

Those who first maintained this opinion in England were called Congregationalists and also Independents. But in this respect the Presbyterians here are now agreed with them, as the Baptists always have been. This is the grand principle by which the Protestant dissenters are distinguished and in which they are all united. And this indeed is the only principle upon which their liberties can be maintained in their full extent; for if every Christian society have not the right above-mentioned, a door will be opened to human governors in affairs of religion; and it is no great matter whether they be the members of the legislature, of a convocation, or an assembly; the authority of either being equally void of foundation in Scripture and inconsistent with the natural rights of mankind.

Q. 10. Is this notion of a church of Christ supported by Scripture?

A. Yes. A number of Christians assembled for divine worship in a dwelling-house is there called a church {Rom 16:5}. A church is spoken of as coming together in one place {Acts 2:1, 46; 5:12, 14; 1 Cor 14:23}. And when affairs were to be determined relating to a church, all the members of it were called together to give their opinion {Acts 6:2, 5; 15:4, 22}. Nor do we find any human authority acknowledged or claimed in ecclesiastical affairs.

Q. 11. Wherein does the constitution of the Church of England differ from this account of a church in the New Testament?

A. The Church of England is not a voluntary society, the whole nation being considered as members of it, whether professedly so or not, and obliged by law (excepting those included in the Toleration Act)[3] at least thrice in the year to

---

3   [Ed. The Toleration Act (1688) granted freedom of worship to dissenters.]

communicate with it in the Lord's Supper. It is also incapable (as it is national) of being assembled in one place that the members of it may give their vote in ecclesiastical affairs; and the several congregations of which it consists are equally destitute of this liberty, being all obliged to an absolute uniformity in faith, worship, and discipline. . . .

Q. 13. In what respects does the Church of England appear to be a worldly constitution and therefore different from the church of Christ?

A. 1. Its origin is from the world, it being framed by human authority, and is properly a creature of the state; but the church of Christ is a "kingdom not of this world" {John 18:2}.

2. Its members are "men of the world" {Ps 17:14}, the whole nation being acknowledged as such; but those of Christ's church are holy and pious men, who "have their conversation in heaven" {John 17:16; 1 Pet 2:9; Phil 3:20}.

3. Its laws are of a worldly nature, being founded on acts of Parliament and enforced by mere worldly sanctions; but the laws of Christ's church are no other than the laws of God contained in the Scriptures and the sanctions of them are purely spiritual {Eph 2:20; 2 Cor 10:4}.

4. Its ground of support is the power and riches of the world; but that of Christ's church, the power and grace of God {2 Cor 4:7}.

5. Its supreme head is one of the princes of the world; but the supreme and only head of Christ's church is Jesus Christ himself {Eph 1:22}.

Q. 14. What power has the king in the Church of England, which constitutes him its supreme head and the church a worldly kingdom?

A. The king (or queen) "is vested with all power to exercise all manner of ecclesiastical jurisdiction; and archbishops, bishops, archdeacons, and other ecclesiastical persons have no manner of jurisdiction ecclesiastical but by and under the king's majesty, who hath full power and authority to hear and determine all manner of causes ecclesiastical, and to reform and correct all vice, sin, errors, heresies whatsoever."[4] The appointing of bishops also is his prerogative, and the power of ordination is derived from him and held during his pleasure.

Q. 15. What objection have dissenters to this authority of the king?

A. Though they think it their duty to honor and obey the king in civil matters, they apprehend such power as our present constitution gives him in affairs of religion to be not only foreign to the province of the civil magistrate, but highly derogatory to the honor of Christ, whom God hath appointed head over all things to the church, and a gross infringement on the liberty of Christians, who, in matters of faith and conscience, are forbid being the servants of men {1 Cor 7:23}.

Q. 16. May it not be of service to religion to have the authority of the chief magistrate engaged on its side?

4   [Ed. Henry VIII, Act of Supremacy, 1834 (Act 26, cap. 1).]

A. The religion of Jesus does not want the support of human power; his church is founded on a rock more stable than any earthly establishment, and the gates of hell shall never prevail against it {Matt 16:18}. The interference of the civil magistrate in matters of religion has often been more injurious than beneficial, and this authority in matters of faith is exceedingly dangerous; and indeed the claim is more absurd than that of the pope himself, who has the pretense of infallibility as the ground of it.

‡

Inferences from the Whole

Q. 125. What inferences may be drawn from the foregoing account of the Church of England?

A. 1. That it is very imperfectly reformed from popery and still bears too strong a resemblance to the Church of Rome.

2. That therefore it behooves those who have power in the church to exert themselves in order to carry on the Reformation, which the first Reformers never meant should be left so incomplete, and endeavor to perfect what they so nobly began (with greater difficulty and hazard than their successors have in the present day any reason to fear), that so the Church of England might be a true, consistent, Protestant church.

3. That while those on whom this work properly devolves are determined to take no steps towards a further reform in the church, but on the contrary endeavor to keep things as they are, it is the indispensable duty of those who are dissatisfied with them, and whose consciences would be uneasy with conformity, in a peaceable manner to dissent.

4. That the dissenters ought to be exceedingly thankful to God for, and diligent to the utmost to improve, the liberty they enjoy of separating from a national church which they think so corrupt, and of worshipping God in places of their own, in a manner agreeable to the dictates of their consciences, and, as they think, to the rules of God's holy Word; at the same time sympathizing with and praying for those of their Protestant brethren abroad who are deprived of this privilege.

5. That they should also be grateful to their civil governors, the king, and those in authority under him, through whose clemency they enjoy privileges (though no other than their natural right) far superior to what their ancestors enjoyed in former reigns; and to testify their gratitude by approving themselves good subjects, endeavoring to promote the prosperity of their country and preserve its peace in every instance that is consistent with a due regard to the liberty of the constitution.

6. That they ought to be zealous in maintaining those great principles on which their dissent from the Church is founded, and not only be steadfast in their adherence to the cause of nonconformity, but liberal and active to support and increase it by all such methods as are consistent with peace, liberty, and charity;

a proper regard to the cause of practical godliness and to the interest of Christ at large even in that Church from which they dissent.

They should love good men of every name and rejoice wheresoever "Christ is preached, and God is worshipped in Spirit" [John 4:24], though the mode be different from their own, making all proper allowances for the prejudices of education, which often have an amazing influence on the best of men. But a true catholic spirit does not require men to give up their own principles, or be indifferent to the support of them, or admit of conforming to those modes and forms, or submitting to those human impositions which we judge to be unscriptural, merely because they are received by those whom we believe to be eminent for piety, or because they hold the grand fundamental doctrines of the gospel.

TEXT: Samuel Palmer, *The Protestant dissenter's catechism*, 2nd ed. (London: J. Buckland, 1774), 1–3, 23–32, 79–81.

WILLIAM STEVENS
(1732–1807)
Spiritual Authority

Even as Christian dissenters advocated liberty of conscience and the right to private judgment, others thought dissent from the Church of England tantamount to opposition to the nation. Many Anglicans, both evangelical and high church, considered loyalty to the Church of England part of their Christian duty (consider Charles Wesley's stinging critique of his brother's decision to ordain superintendents for the American Methodists). Political conflict abroad—most notably in the conflict with the American colonies and again during the French Revolution—bolstered the belief that the spiritual and political wellbeing of the nation depended on loyalism, doctrinal orthodoxy, and anti-Jacobinism.

The high churchman William Stevens was born at Southwark to a tradesman's family. Stevens apprenticed under a hosier in 1746 and proved so successful in his work that he was named a partner in the business a year after the expiration of his apprenticeship in 1753. During his free time, Stevens studied theology, literature, and history. He became expert in classical and foreign languages alike. The writings of the early church and seventeenth-century divines such as Jeremy Taylor and Lancelot Andrews shaped his thought. In time, Stevens emerged as a leading figure, along with his cousin George Horne and William Jones, among the so-called Hutchinsonians, a group of high church Anglicans known for their emphasis on the sacramental and mystical elements of Christianity. Stevens published numerous writings defending high church theological and political views, including *A discourse on the English constitution* (1776), *Strictures on a sermon entitled "The principles of the revolution vindicated"* (1777), and *The revolution vindicated, and constitutional liberty asserted* (1777). His ecclesial service included strong support of episcopal clergy in Scotland, generous financial contributions to charitable societies, and dedicated collaboration with other clergy in various educational and political causes. Stevens' high church legacy extended from the "Club of Nobody's Friends," a group of noted churchmen who met regularly in his honor in early 1800s London, to the founders of the Oxford Movement.

Stevens' anonymous publication, *A treatise on the nature and constitution of the church* (1773), responds to the Feathers Tavern Petition of 1772, which sought to abolish ordinands' mandatory subscription to the Thirty-Nine Articles of the Church of England. Instead they advocated a simple declaration of belief in the Christian Bible. The measure was debated in the House of Commons in February 1772 and, owing to the influence of Edmund Burke, defeated by a vote of 217 to 71. Stevens' work—which echoes the standard arguments of Anglican ecclesiology from the Elizabethan era on—maintains that the true Christian church is not a voluntary congregation, but an *obligatory society* of Christians. The church is a *spiritual society*, insofar as it counters spiritual darkness, but it is also an *outward and visible society* that involves public rulers, public confession, and public actions. The following selection illustrates Stevens' commitment to the authority of the bishops to govern the Christian church as well as the necessity of obedience by those under their care.

SOURCES: Hylson-Smith; F. C. Mather, *High church prophet: Bishop Samuel Horsley (1733–1806) and the Caroline tradition in the later Georgian church* (Oxford: Clarendon, 1992); Nockles; *ODCC*; *ODNB*; E. A. Varley, *The last of the prince bishops: William Van Mildert and the high church movement of the early nineteenth century* (Cambridge: Cambridge University Press, 1992).

WILLIAM STEVENS

A treatise on the nature and constitution of the Christian church
1773

As the Holy Scriptures are the rule of our faith and practice, it is from them we are to learn the nature and constitution of the Christian church, the form of its government, the extent of its powers, and limits of our obedience.

I. From the account which the divine records have given us of the Christian church, it appears to be no confused multitude of men, independent one on another, but a well-formed and regular society. This is evident from the names and allusions by which it is described. It is called a family, whereof Christ is the master of "whom the whole family is named" {Eph 3:14, 15}. It is said to be the "city of the living God" {Heb 12:22}, whence Christian people are "fellow-citizens with the saints" {Eph 2:19}. And it is often mentioned as a kingdom, of which Christ is the king. Thus in our Lord's words, "Thou art Peter, and upon this rock I will build my church, and I will give unto thee the keys of the kingdom of heaven" {Matt 16:18, 19}, where the church and the kingdom of heaven mean the same thing. As a family, a city, and a kingdom are societies, and the Christian church is represented by them—that must likewise be a society.

‡

III. As no society can subsist without officers, so neither can it without power to do all things which are necessary to its own preservation and good government; and as it appears that the church is a society instituted by God and designed to last to the world's end, there can be no doubt but that he has invested it with all the powers which the nature of such a society requires.

First, as the church is a spiritual society, all the powers which belong to it are of the same nature and such as wholly relate to the next world; consequently, they are distinct from those of civil magistrates, which concern the affairs of this life and are designed for the present welfare of human societies. Our Lord himself wholly disclaimed all civil power and left the civil rights of mankind in the same state wherein he found them. And when the apostle exhorts the Hebrews to yield obedience to their pastors, he restrains it to the affairs of their souls, for which their pastors were accountable to God: "Obey them that have the rule over you, and submit yourselves, for they watch for your souls, as they that must give an account" {Heb 13:17}.

Secondly, as God has appointed officers to govern his church, the powers which he has committed to his church for its good government must ordinarily be executed by them. For every office implies power, and to say that the officers of the church have no power but what all private Christians may lawfully exercise is just the same as to say there are no such officers at all. And as there are distinct offices, so there must be distinct powers appropriated to every one of them; for as the notion of an office implies power, so distinct offices do necessarily imply distinct powers. And, therefore, though the Scriptures had been silent in this matter, it might safely have been concluded from the different kinds of officers whom Christ hath entrusted with the care and government of his church, not only that private Christians are excluded from the ordinary execution of any ecclesiastical power, but that some powers are appropriated in such a manner to the chief officers that they cannot lawfully be exercised by those of lower orders. The officers of the church are called God's stewards, who are entrusted with the care and government of his household—that is, his church—and whose business and duty it is to dispense their constant food, i.e., the Word and sacraments, to all the members of it; whence it is plain that private Christians have no power to dispense the ordinances of the gospel to others, but must themselves expect them from the hands of God's ministers. And the names of the apostles and angels, whereby the officers of the church were distinguished from other Christians in the apostolic age, manifestly imply that they acted by a commission from God to which the rest had no title. And however great the gifts and abilities of private Christians might be, none had power to exercise any function or office in the church who had not been first approved and commissioned by those whom God had invested with authority to that end. For through the whole New Testament the gifts or abilities of church officers are everywhere distinguished from their commission and described as previous qualifications to it.

‡

IV. As it appears that the church is a complete society, wherein some govern and others are governed, the next thing to be determined is what obedience is due from the private members of this society to their governors? That all lay Christians do owe some obedience to their spiritual rulers is evident from our Lord's command to "hear the church" {Matt 18:17} and the injunction of the apostle, "Obey them that have the rule over you, and submit yourselves, for they watch for your souls, as they that must give an account" {Heb 13:17}. The church which we are to hear is to be known from the foregoing description of it, and the rulers to whom we are to yield obedience and submit ourselves are they who derive their commission by an uninterrupted succession from Christ and his apostles. Wherein this obedience to our rulers consists and what are the limits of it, we may learn from the nature and extent of their power; for so far as they have a right to command, so far are we bound to obey. Now all things that are in the world may be divided into good, bad, and indifferent. The good oblige by their own nature and the command of God; in these things the authority of our governors is of no force. For whatever is enjoined by the positive command of God, we are bound to do, whether they require it or not. The evil are by the same forbidden, and we are obliged not to obey our governors if they should command them. So that it is the indifferent only whereto their authority reaches, and the things which are indifferent in themselves are all those which relate to the outward peace and order of the church—which are not enjoined by the express Word of God, but yet are in no respect contrary to it, in no wise forbidden by it. This authority was exercised by the governors of the church from the beginning (as hath been shown), and it undoubtedly belongs to them. For as they are evidently invested with some spiritual authority, and they can command in nothing at all if not in indifferent things, in all such things as are indifferent they certainly have a right to command. And as is their authority, such is to be our submission. So that the obedience we owe to our spiritual governors consists in observing all their injunctions that are contained within these bounds of their commission; in submitting to that discipline which they shall inflict either to recover us from a state of folly or to preserve us from falling into it; in attending their public administrations[1] at such times and places as they shall appoint, and upon such occasions as they shall judge proper to increase our piety and devotion; and in submitting to such regulations as they shall think conducive towards "the edifying or the body of Christ" [Eph 4:12]. This is our duty; for things which are indifferent in their nature, when commanded by lawful authority, are no longer indifferent to us, but become necessary in their use; and in disobeying them that have the rule over us, we disobey God, who has commanded us to be "subject for conscience sake" [Rom 13:5]; and therefore all this we are to do from a sense of that right which they have to command, entrusted to them by God our Savior, and of that great penalty to which we are liable by our contempt: "for he that despiseth them, despiseth him that sent them" [Luke 10:16].

TEXT: William Stevens, *A treatise on the nature and constitution of the Christian church, wherein are set forth the form of its government, the extent of its powers, and the limits of our obedience*, new ed. (London: F. and C. Rivington, 1799), 7–8, 21–24, 45–48.

---

[1]   [Ed. That is, "in exercising their sacramental and liturgical authority."]

GEORGE DYER
(1755–1841)
Religious Subscription

The University of Cambridge was a seedbed for political radicalism in the 1790s. One of the foremost radicals of the day was the poet, essayist, and political reformer George Dyer. Dyer was born in east London and studied classics at Christ's Hospital, where he moved in radical circles and within the orbit of the burgeoning Romantic movement. After graduation from Emmanuel College, Cambridge (B.A. 1778), Dyer found work as an usher at the Dedham grammar school and occasionally preached in dissenting circles. His platform for political reform in England centered on the plight of the poor. His *Complaints of the poor people of England* (1793) called for changes in taxation, prisons, and the education of children, but he also published histories of Cambridge and other volumes including *Poems, consisting of odes and elegies* (1792) and *Poems and critical essays* (1802).

Dyer's *An inquiry into the nature of subscription to the Thirty-Nine Articles* (1789) belongs to a national conversation on religious liberty. The title page promises an inquiry into the religious legitimacy of requiring subscription in light of four considerations: (1) the natural rights of humanity; (2) the powers of the human mind; (3) the principles of the British constitution; and (4) the doctrines and precepts of Christianity. The work shows the influence of William Frend, who had published on the same issue the previous year (*Thoughts on subscription to religious tests*, 1788). The first edition, from which the following selection is drawn, makes no reference to the French Revolution. In 1792 a second edition contained substantial revisions that reflect the mood of hope and expectancy that swept Europe in the first revolutionary years. Yet the earlier edition places readers squarely in the field of inquiry as it was *before* the social and political upheaval of the coming decade. Dyer questions why the universities were closed to men of academic merit on the sole basis of their refusing subscription to the Church of England's Thirty-Nine Articles. He advocates opening the English universities not only to Protestant dissenters, but also to Deists, Roman Catholics, and Jews, and, in consequence, the remaking of England into a fully *secular* nation.

Sources: M. Ray Adams, "George Dyer and English radicalism," *The Modern Language Review* 35 (1940): 447–69; *OCEL*; *ODNB*; Nicholas Roe, *The politics of nature: William Wordsworth and some contemporaries* (Basingstoke: Palgrave Macmillan, 2002).

GEORGE DYER

An inquiry into the nature of subscription to the Thirty-Nine Articles
1789

It is well known that places of public trust, extensive influence, and general utility are shut against many persons in England by a sacramental test.[1] Catholics, Protestant dissenters, Jews, and Deists are all affected by it; among whom will be found men who in point of virtue, honor, and political principle are of equal consideration with churchmen. But the doors by which they should enter to the enjoyment of their natural rights are, I say, shut against them by religious tests, improperly so-called: the *ne plus ultra*[2] to many a brave man. The Test Act was originally directed against Catholics, who at the time were said to be incapable of giving security to government, but was applied too successfully to men who most conscientiously could. The people to whom I allude were neither savages, idolaters, outlaws, nor aliens, but men whose origin is as respectable, whose complexion as fair, whose abilities as distinguished, whose religion as pure, whose pretensions in every respect as just as those of the reigning party. The Test laws affect all parties in England; and in the latter instance violate the rights of those who by the ties of nature, the bonds of society, and the engagements of religion are our brethren—in the most respectable sense, our equals. They are men, Christians, Britons, and Protestants. Now as every subscription is a test, so is every test a virtual subscription. A compliance with this requisition admits a man into those places of trust, influence, and advantage to which he had a previous title. The test, therefore, does but admit him to his just rank, while a noncompliance is a disqualification, and thrusts him down. And what does it argue whether I be a pupil of Spinoza[3] or a disciple of Jesus? Whether I embrace the creed of Arius or Athanasius or of

---

[1]   [Ed. The Test Act (1672) required a declaration against transubstantiation, reception of the sacrament according to the liturgy and usage of the Church of England, and oaths of supremacy and allegiance to the king by all government office holders.]

[2]   [Ed. That is, "the limit or boundary of their achievement."]

[3]   [Ed. Benedictus de Spinoza (1632–1677) was a Dutch Jewish philosopher and author of *Tractatus theologico-politicus* (1670). His philosophy is often associated with pantheism.]

Socinus?[4] *Homo sum et civis.*[5] A test which admits me to the enjoyment of a natural or civil right does in fact deprive me of them. Indeed, the law of exclusion not only injures those to whom it denies its protection, but those also whom it receives to its favor.

‡

And if the principles laid down be true, I am very far from thinking that Catholics, Protestant dissenters, Jews, and Deists are the only men injured by subscription. I must beg leave to ask another question: Does it not also injure those who call themselves the Church? We have already remarked that at Oxford no youth can be matriculated without subscribing to the Thirty-Nine Articles, and that, even at Cambridge, none are admitted to their first degree without a *bona fide* subscription. All our degrees in arts, law, physic, music, and divinity are guarded by subscription. If I have made a fair statement of natural rights, it will follow that such demands are impositions irreconcilable with the claims of general liberty and should be considered by the members of our learned seminaries a severe oppression. A literary qualification being supposed, should they not be admitted to their respective emoluments and employments without a religious test? For what does a religious test do for them? It gives them a power of entering on a possession where they had a right to enter before—making that a matter of reward which is a matter of justice.

‡

A relation of particulars will perhaps place this subject in a proper point of view. There are many Catholics—natural-born subjects of Britain. The voice of justice says that they are entitled to the privileges of citizens. But their religious profession exposes them to harsh penalties and excludes them from civil employments. From our universities, too, they are excluded by ecclesiastical restrictions. In vindication of these restraints, it has been said that they hold a disaffection to government which seeks its destruction—maintaining that no faith may be kept with heretics, that princes excommunicated by the sovereign pontiff may be dethroned, that dominion is founded in grace, and that they are in the interest of a foreign pretender. Some years ago, the fears to which such principles would give birth were not groundless. But in regard to the Catholics of modern times residing in Britain, they have it in their power to say,

Tempora mutantur, et nos mutamur in illis.[6]

They will tell you that in this whole system of fear there is something ideal; that the arguments which support it are derived from the maxims of more remote periods and from educational prejudices, not from modern facts and real life. It wants proof, they say, that modern Catholics believe that the pope has a right to supremacy in all Christian countries and that the church may dethrone monarchs. This power was indeed challenged by

---

4   [Ed. Dyer refers to a range of Christological positions: Arius (d. 336) maintained that Christ is a semi-divine creation responsible for the formation of the world; Athanasius (ca. 296–373) defended the Trinitarian teachings of the Council of Nicaea (325); Socinus refers to Fausto Paolo Sozzini (1539–1604), who provided the foundation for English Unitarianism by prioritizing the humanity of Christ.]

5   [Ed. That is, "I am both a human and a citizen."]

6   [Ed. That is, "times change, and we, too, change with them."]

several pontiffs, but by most liberal Catholics is considered as an obsolete claim. Those who reside in this nation have given many proofs of loyalty. . . . Catholics now make as good British subjects as Protestants. And, even if considerations of political necessity might operate to exclude them from offices of civil trust, the same would not apply to academical institutions.

To these we join "a philosophic sect"—I mean, the people whose principles will not allow them to bear arms, to take oaths, or to pay tithes.[7] Like the former, they are men, Britons, and Christians. But in regard to their political principles, the case is by no means parallel. The Quakers (as these people have been called) were never disaffected to the British government; they never professed allegiance to a foreign prince. Not allowing themselves to administer an oath, they are necessarily debarred some offices of magistracy. Equally averse to bearing arms, they are of course incapable of military distinctions. But this incapacity is of their own creating. Government need not exclude, but ought still to protect them, having found in their religious principles all that security which it can reasonably desire.

‡

The Baptists have been represented as the most violent and ungovernable of mankind; and many of our college statutes as well as our church canons guard expressly against them. The "anabaptistical errors," indeed, have been cried down all over Europe; and yet, by those who are best capable of speaking on this subject, it is affirmed to be no easy matter to ascertain what these "anabaptistical errors" have been—the Baptists, of all sects in Christendom, having professed the greatest diversity of political as well as of religious sentiments. . . . Upon an impartial inquiry it will be found that two of the grand "anabaptistical errors" in England have been those very sentiments which have rendered Milton, Sydney, Montesquieu, and Locke famous through Europe.[8]. . . Like the Quakers, the Baptists are men, Britons, Christians, and Protestants. But what does *alma mater* say of Baptists? No entrance for schismatics; and she turns the keys of the college gates on them.

Thus we treat schismatics. What shall we say to heretics? I mean to Arians and Socinians. We do not, they say, admit that Jesus Christ is the supreme God. We cannot grant that in the unity of the Godhead there be three persons of one substance. But we honor government. We are thankful for the gift of reason. We revere the sacred Scriptures. We hold the rights of all mankind sacred. Lardner and Leland, Emlyn and Taylor would not subscribe to the Thirty-Nine Articles.[9] They were heretics. What does *alma mater* say of Newton, Locke, and Whiston?[10] Yet deny it who will, they were all heretics. In the early

[7]   [Ed. Dyer refers to Voltaire's description of Quakers.]

[8]   [Ed. John Milton (1608–1674) Algernon Sydney (or Sidney) (1623–1683), Charles-Louis de Secondat, Baron de La Brède et de Montesquieu (1689–1755), and John Locke (1632–1704).]

[9]   [Ed. Nathaniel Lardner (1684–1768) was a nonconformist minister and New Testament scholar; John Leland (1691–1766) was a Presbyterian minister and author of *The advantage and necessity of the Christian revelation* (1764); Thomas Emlyn (1663–1741) was a dissenting minister and one of the first in England to take the name "Unitarian"; and, most likely, Henry Taylor (1711–1785), the controversial "Arian" theologian.]

[10]   [Ed. Dyer refers to three "natural philosophers" or scientists: Isaac Newton (1642–1727), John Locke (1632–1704), and William Whiston (1667–1752).]

part of life they subscribed to the Thirty-Nine Articles. But would they have done it at the close? They disbelieved our doctrinal Articles. Having reflected such honor on our universities, ought they to have been refused its privileges? What strange words would these have appeared when uttered by *alma mater* against these oracles of learning! *Bona fide*, ye are not of the church. Rebels and heretics, ye are disaffected to "King James's three darling articles."[11] . . .

It will, perhaps, appear an affected catholicism to place Jews and Deists on the same seat with orthodox Christians. Let it appear so. . . . The voice of justice speaks, "Hear, all ye inhabitants of the world! Ye disciples of Brumma,[12] of Mahomed, of Moses, and of Jesus. In whatever country ye are born, whatever ceremonies ye practice, into whatever doctrine ye are instructed, the law of nature is one, the rights of nature are invariable. The laws of baptism and of circumcision give no title and offer no bar to my impartial regard. Let me hold the scale, and remove rogues and fools, and all men weigh alike."

I affirm and feel indignation that the Jews have been cruelly treated by Christian states. Three hundred and four years they were banished from England but were at length recalled by Oliver Cromwell.[13] The forefathers of the present generation were consequently aliens and received into this country as foreigners. But ought not our modern Jews to be treated as the natural-born subjects of Britain? Are they not men? Are they not our brethren? And, living with us in a state of civil society, are they not entitled to the common privileges of citizens? They will be found, perhaps, equally qualified with the most devout Christians to preside in a corporation, to represent a borough, and to dispute in the schools. If the principles laid down be true, have they not as just a title?

Should Jews then be admitted to our universities? I see no reason for excluding them. Are these good arguments in support of our exclusive privilege? The sons of Israel killed Jesus. The justice of heaven is pursuing their children. They are banished from their beloved Canaan. They reject the Christian doctrine. Let all this be granted. What then? The Jews viewed Jesus as an imposter and nailed him to a cross, but the Jews are men. "That Christ should have been God before the world, and that he should submit to be made a man has appeared to their posterity not only impossible, but even absurd."[14] Yet the Jews are men. The Jews are circumcised. But the Jews are men, and equally capable as Christians of understanding this maxim, "What ye would, that men should do unto you, do ye even so to them" [Matt 7:12]. Some years ago two eminent Jews resided in a university town, and it is still reckoned no disgrace to read the Hebrew grammar of the father and the book of *Fluxions* of the son.[15] But, ye sons of the circumcised! Ye could not subscribe James' three darling articles.

---

[11] [Ed. Namely, acceptance of the Book of Common Prayer, the Thirty-Nine Articles, and the supremacy of the king in spiritual matters (see Michael A. Lawrence, *Radicals in their own time* [New York: Cambridge University Press, 2011], 21).]

[12] [Ed. Brumma or Brahma, one of three aspects of the supreme god of Hinduism.]

[13] [Ed. Oliver Cromwell (1599–1658) readmitted the Jews into England in 1656. They did not achieve formal political emancipation until 1858. On the Jews in England during this period, see Sheila A. Spector, ed., *The Jews and British Romanticism: politics, religion, culture* (New York: Palgrave Macmillan, 2005).]

[14] [Ed. Justin Martyr, *Dialogue with Trypho* 48.]

[15] [Ed. Dyer refers to the work of two prominent Jewish scholars from Cambridge: Israel Lyons, the elder (d. 1770), author of *A Hebrew grammar* (1763); and Israel Lyons, the younger (1739–1775), whose

And why should Deists, living among Christians, be treated like inhabitants of another world? The author of nature endues them with reason and presents them with revelation; and to him they are accountable for the use of both. A citizen of Geneva[16] loved the morality of Jesus, but held doubts concerning the Christian doctrines. Perhaps he did not understand them. . . . Why do we throw impediments in the way of Deists? Those impediments will but increase their power, and even give them a license to do mischief. Is a Deist a member of civil society, a man of humane sentiments, and a lover of the polite arts? Why then should we refuse him a place at our universities, though not choosing to attend our chapels or subscribe to our Articles?

✕⌒✕

TEXT: George Dyer, *An inquiry into the nature of subscription to the Thirty-Nine Articles* (Printed for the author, 1789), 11–12, 14–15, 17–25.

---

prodigious work on calculus, *A Treatise of Fluxions* (1758), was published before he had reached the age of twenty.]

   [16]   [Ed. Namely, Jean-Jacques Rousseau (1712–1778).]

EDMUND BURKE
(1729/30–1797)
Established Church

Edmund Burke served in the House of Commons for many years, where he proved an articulate spokesman for the Whigs. Born in Dublin, Burke was raised by a Roman Catholic mother and Protestant father. Burke adopted his father's Protestantism, but his sister grew up Roman Catholic. His early education included time at a Quaker school and attendance at Trinity College, Dublin, where he took a degree in 1748. In 1750 Burke left Ireland for London, where he attended the Middle Temple to prepare for a career in law. His first work, *A vindication of natural society* (1756), was an attack on Deism. In 1758 Burke cofounded the *Annual Register*, a periodical reviewing "History, Politics, and Literature." He wrote the bulk of the articles through the early 1760s and contributed until 1788. In time, the political dimension of Burke's career blossomed. He secured a seat in the House of Commons, in successive Parliaments representing Wendover (1766), Bristol (1774), and Malton (1781). He weighed in on the crisis in America, encouraged the impeachment of Warren Hastings (1788), and produced writings and speeches that shaped the national conversation. Burke's deeply conservative *Reflections on the revolution in France* (1790) attacked the French Revolution and its English supporters. He also devoted substantial energy to a range of emancipation causes: the abolition of slavery, freedom for the American colonies, political rights for Irish Catholics, and autonomy for India from the East India Company.

Reflections on the revolution in France (1790), the most famous and controversial of Burke's writings, is ostensibly a letter in reply to Charles DePont, a Frenchman who hoped to convince Burke of the merits of the revolutionary cause. In reality, Burke's *Reflections* challenges the radical reform politics of Richard Price (1723–1791), who hoped to generate in England the kind of change that revolutionaries in France had recently pursued. Burke regarded Price's ideas as a colossal assault on the English political traditions of monarchy, aristocracy, and church: "Burke set out his own statement of contrary values: of inherited manners that conferred honor and utility on institutions that might seem otherwise outmoded, of religious beliefs that were deeply ingrained in any civil society worthy of the name, of prescriptive customs and institutions, including property itself, that required protection against untried and arbitrary ideas of rationality" (*ODNB*). While most of the work addresses matters of state, several sections draw out his views on religion and the necessary interdependence of church and state. Burke asserts that civil society depends on religion, defends the wealth of the Church of England, and links his commitment to the national church with an assertion of free will and individual liberty. The text generated a substantial pamphlet war between Burke and writers including Thomas Paine, Mary Wollstonecraft, George Dyer, and James Mackintosh.

SOURCES: Cragg; Ian Crowe, *Patriotism and public spirit: Edmund Burke and the role of the critic in mid-eighteenth-century Britain* (Stanford: Stanford University Press, 2012); *OCEL*; *ODNB*; *RCBEC*.

EDMUND BURKE
Reflections on the revolution in France
1790

We know and, what is better, we feel inwardly, that religion is the basis of civil society, and the source of all good, and of all comfort. In England we are so convinced of this that there is no rust of superstition, with which the accumulated absurdity of the human mind might have crusted it over in the course of ages, that ninety-nine in a hundred of the people of England would not prefer to impiety. We shall never be such fools as to call in an enemy to the substance of any system to remove its corruptions, to supply its defects, or to perfect its construction. If our religious tenets should ever want a further elucidation, we shall not call on atheism to explain them. We shall not light up our temple from that unhallowed fire. It will be illuminated with other lights. It will be perfumed with other incense than the infectious stuff which is imported by the smugglers of adulterated metaphysics. If our ecclesiastical establishment should want a revision, it is not avarice or rapacity, public or private, that we shall employ for the audit or receipt or application of its consecrated revenue. Violently condemning neither the Greek nor the Armenian, nor, since heats are subsided, the Roman system of religion, we prefer the Protestant; not because we think it has less of the Christian religion in it, but because, in our judgment, it has more. We are Protestants, not from indifference but from zeal.

We know, and it is our pride to know, that man is by his constitution a religious animal; that atheism is against not only our reason but our instincts, and that it cannot prevail long. But if, in the moment of riot, and in a drunken delirium from the hot spirit drawn out of the alembic of hell, which in France is now so furiously boiling, we should uncover our nakedness by throwing off that Christian religion which has hitherto been our boast and comfort, and one great source of civilization amongst us, and among many other nations, we are apprehensive (being well aware that the mind will not endure a void) that some uncouth, pernicious, and degrading superstition might take place of it.

‡

361

It is on some such principles that the majority of the people of England, far from thinking a religious national establishment unlawful, hardly think it lawful to be without one. In France you are wholly mistaken if you do not believe us above all other things attached to it, and beyond all other nations; and when this people has acted unwisely and unjustifiably in its favor (as in some instances they have done most certainly), in their very errors you will at least discover their zeal.

This principle runs through the whole system of their polity. They do not consider their church establishment as convenient but as essential to their state; not as a thing heterogeneous and separable, something added for accommodation, what they may either keep up or lay aside, according to their temporary ideas of convenience. They consider it as the foundation of their whole constitution, with which, and with every part of which, it holds an indissoluble union. Church and state are ideas inseparable in their minds, and scarcely is the one ever mentioned without mentioning the other.

Our education is so formed as to confirm and fix this impression. Our education is in a manner wholly in the hands of ecclesiastics, and in all stages from infancy to manhood. Even when our youth, leaving schools and universities, enter that most important period of life which begins to link experience and study together, and when with that view they visit other countries, instead of old domestics whom we have seen as governors to principal men from other parts, three-fourths of those who go abroad with our young nobility and gentlemen are ecclesiastics: not as austere masters nor as mere followers, but as friends and companions of a graver character, and not seldom persons as well born as themselves. With them, as relations, they most commonly keep up a close connection through life. By this connection we conceive that we attach our gentlemen to the Church; and we liberalize the Church by an intercourse with the leading characters of the country.

So tenacious are we of the old ecclesiastical modes and fashions of institution that very little alteration has been made in them since the fourteenth or fifteenth century; adhering in this particular, as in all things else, to our old settled maxim, never entirely nor at once to depart from antiquity. We found these old institutions on the whole favorable to morality and discipline; and we thought they were susceptible of amendment, without altering the ground. We thought that they were capable of receiving and meliorating, and above all of preserving, the accessions of science and literature as the order of providence should successively produce them. And after all, with this gothic and monkish education (for such it is in the groundwork), we may put in our claim to as ample and as early a share in all the improvements in science, in arts, and in literature which have illuminated and adorned the modern world as any other nation in Europe; we think one main cause of this improvement was our not despising the patrimony of knowledge which was left us by our forefathers.

It is from our attachment to a church establishment that the English nation did not think it wise to entrust that great fundamental interest of the whole to what they trust no part of their civil or military public service: that is, to the unsteady and precarious contribution of individuals.[1] They go further. They certainly never have suffered and never will suffer the fixed estate of the Church to be converted into a pension, to depend on the

---

1   [Ed. Until the Tithe Commutation Act of 1836, which required monetary fees, tithes were paid to clergy of parish churches in produce, land, or money; for more on the state of the tithe during the Romantic

treasury, and to be delayed, withheld, or perhaps to be extinguished by fiscal difficulties; which difficulties may sometimes be pretended for political purposes and are, in fact, often brought on by the extravagance, negligence, and rapacity of politicians. The people of England think that they have constitutional motives, as well as religious, against any project of turning their independent clergy into ecclesiastical pensioners of state. They tremble for their liberty from the influence of a clergy dependent on the crown; they tremble for the public tranquility from the disorders of a factious clergy if it were made to depend upon any other than the crown. They therefore made their church, like their king and their nobility, independent. . . .

The men of England—the men, I mean, of light and leading in England—whose wisdom (if they have any) is open and direct, would be ashamed, as of a silly deceitful trick, to profess any religion in name which by their proceedings they appeared to condemn. If by their conduct (the only language that rarely lies) they seemed to regard the great ruling principle of the moral and the natural world as a mere invention to keep the vulgar in obedience, they apprehend that by such a conduct they would defeat the politic purpose they have in view. They would find it difficult to make others believe in a system to which they manifestly gave no credit themselves. The Christian statesmen of this land would indeed first provide for the *multitude* because it is the *multitude*, and is therefore, as such, the first object in the ecclesiastical institution and in all institutions. They have been taught that the circumstance of the gospel's being preached to the poor was one of the great tests of its true mission. They think, therefore, that those do not believe it, who do not take care it should be preached to the poor. But as they know that charity is not confined to any one description, but ought to apply itself to all men who have wants, they are not deprived of a due and anxious sensation of pity to the distresses of the miserable great. They are not repelled through a fastidious delicacy, at the stench of their arrogance and presumption, from a medicinal attention to their mental blotches and running sores. They are sensible that religious instruction is of more consequence to them than to any others; from the greatness of the temptation to which they are exposed; from the important consequences that attend their faults; from the contagion of their ill example; from the necessity of bowing down the stubborn neck of their pride and ambition to the yoke of moderation and virtue; from a consideration of the fat stupidity and gross ignorance concerning what imports men most to know, which prevails at courts, and at the head of armies, and in senates, as much as at the loom and in the field.

The English people are satisfied that to the great the consolations of religion are as necessary as its instructions. They too are among the unhappy. They feel personal pain and domestic sorrow. In these they have no privilege, but are subject to pay their full contingent to the contributions levied on mortality. They want this sovereign balm under their gnawing cares and anxieties, which being less conversant about the limited wants of animal life, range without limit, and are diversified by infinite combinations in the wild and unbounded regions of imagination. Some charitable dole is wanting to these, our often very unhappy brethren, to fill the gloomy void that reigns in minds which have nothing on earth to hope or fear; something to relieve in the killing languor and

---

period, see Eric J. Evans, *The contentious tithe: the tithe problem and English agriculture, 1750–1850* (London: Routledge, 1976).]

over-labored lassitude of those who have nothing to do; something to excite an appetite to existence in the palled satiety which attends on all pleasures which may be bought, where nature is not left to her own process, where even desire is anticipated, and therefore fruition defeated by meditated schemes and contrivances of delight; and no interval, no obstacle, is interposed between the wish and the accomplishment.

The people of England know how little influence the teachers of religion are likely to have with the wealthy and powerful of long standing, and how much less with the newly fortunate, if they appear in a manner no way assorted[2] to those with whom they must associate, and over whom they must even exercise, in some cases, something like an authority. What must they think of that body of teachers if they see it in no part above the establishment of their domestic servants? If the poverty were voluntary, there might be some difference. Strong instances of self-denial operate powerfully on our minds; and a man who has no wants has obtained great freedom and firmness, and even dignity. But as the mass of any description of men are but men, and their poverty cannot be voluntary, that disrespect which attends upon all lay poverty will not depart from the ecclesiastical. Our provident constitution has therefore taken care that those who are to instruct presumptuous ignorance, those who are to be censors over insolent vice, should neither incur their contempt nor live upon their alms; nor will it tempt the rich to a neglect of the true medicine of their minds. For these reasons, whilst we provide first for the poor, and with a parental solicitude, we have not relegated religion (like something we were ashamed to show) to obscure municipalities or rustic villages. No! We will have her to exalt her mitred front in courts and parliaments. We will have her mixed throughout the whole mass of life and blended with all the classes of society. The people of England will show to the haughty potentates of the world and to their talking sophisters, that a free, a generous, an informed nation honors the high magistrates of its church; that it will not suffer the insolence of wealth and titles, or any other species of proud pretension, to look down with scorn upon what they look up to with reverence; nor presume to trample on that acquired personal nobility, which they intend always to be, and which often is, the fruit, not the reward (for what can be the reward?) of learning, piety, and virtue. They can see, without pain or grudging, an archbishop precede a duke. They can see a bishop of Durham or a bishop of Winchester in possession of ten thousand pounds a year, and cannot conceive why it is in worse hands than estates to the like amount in the hands of this earl or that squire; although it may be true that so many dogs and horses are not kept by the former, and fed with the victuals which ought to nourish the children of the people. It is true, the whole Church revenue is not always employed, and to every shilling, in charity—nor perhaps ought it—but something is generally so employed. It is better to cherish virtue and humanity by leaving much to free will, even with some loss to the object, than to attempt to make men mere machines and instruments of a political benevolence. The world on the whole will gain by a liberty without which virtue cannot exist.

‡

We hear these new teachers continually boasting of their spirit of toleration. That those persons should tolerate all opinions, who think none to be of estimation, is a matter of

2   [Ed. That is, "matched."]

small merit. Equal neglect is not impartial kindness. The species of benevolence, which arises from contempt, is no true charity. There are in England abundance of men who tolerate in the true spirit of toleration. They think the dogmas of religion, though in different degrees, are all of moment; and that amongst them there is, as amongst all things of value, a just ground of preference. They favor, therefore, and they tolerate. They tolerate, not because they despise opinions, but because they respect justice. They would reverently and affectionately protect all religions because they love and venerate the great principle upon which they all agree, and the great object to which they are all directed. They begin more and more plainly to discern that we have all a common cause, as against a common enemy. They will not be so misled by the spirit of faction as not to distinguish what is done in favor of their subdivision, from those acts of hostility which, through some particular description, are aimed at the whole corps in which they themselves, under another denomination, are included. It is impossible for me to say what may be the character of every description of men amongst [us]. But I speak for the greater part; and for them, I must tell you, that sacrilege is no part of their doctrine of good works; that, so far from calling you into their fellowship on such title, if your professors are admitted to their communion, they must carefully conceal their doctrine of the lawfulness of the proscription of innocent men; and that they must make restitution of all stolen goods whatsoever. Till then they are none of ours.

TEXT: Edmund Burke, *Reflections on the revolution in France, and on the proceedings in certain societies in London relative to that event*, 2nd ed. (London: J. Dodsley, 1790), 134–35, 147–54, 221–22.

THOMAS PAINE
(1737–1809)
Toleration

Few authors can boast the celebrity and notoriety that the political reformer Thomas Paine achieved in Britain, France, and the United States during the eighteenth century. Born in Thetford, Norfolk, Paine was baptized and confirmed in the Church of England under his mother's influence, though his tenant farmer father was a Quaker. Paine's early years included difficult personal relationships and largely unsuccessful work as a sailor, stay-maker, excise officer, and teacher. Between 1774 and 1787, Paine lived in North America. He worked as an editor, promoted abolition and female emancipation, and won fame through his pamphlet in support of American independence: *Common sense* (1776). The work, which argued that the American cause was that of all humanity, proved a massive success. Upon returning to England, Paine stirred further controversy through his various political writings—none more important than *Rights of man*, which he published in two parts (1791, 1792). To avoid imprisonment for his rejection of monarchical and aristocratic power, Paine fled to France, where he continued to write, suffered scrutiny by the French government, and was briefly imprisoned in Paris. His deistic and highly critical assessment of Christianity, *Age of reason* (1794), led to numerous attacks on his character. In prison, he completed the second part of *Age of reason*, which he published the year after his release (1795). Paine lived most of the last decade of his life in the United States, though his antagonism towards Christianity left him unwelcome in many social circles he previously enjoyed.

Against Burke's *Reflections on the revolution in France* (1790) (see previous selection), Paine's first volume of *Rights of man* (1791) proposes that the French Revolution defeated the despotism of the monarchy and represents the freedom of each generation to govern itself. Paine's *Rights of man: part the second* (1792) turned to the American struggle for independence, rather than the increasingly ugly revolution unfolding in France. In the following selection from the first part, Paine supposes individual rights on the basis of a religious argument. All people, in such perspective, find their worth in having been made in the image of God. Whether man or woman, all alike belong to the unity of humanity.

Against Burke's assertion of institutional authority—whether civil or religious—Paine champions the rights of free individuals.

SOURCES: Craig Nelson, *Thomas Paine: Enlightenment, revolution, and the birth of modern nations* (New York: Penguin, 2006); *OCEL*; *ODCC*; *ODNB*; *RCBEC*.

THOMAS PAINE
Rights of man
1791

We are now got at the origin of man and at the origin of his rights. As to the manner in which the world has been governed from that day to this, it is no further any concern of ours than to make a proper use of the errors or the improvements which the history of it presents. Those who lived a hundred or a thousand years ago were then moderns, as we are now. They had *their* ancients, and those ancients had others, and we also shall be ancients in our turn. If the mere name of antiquity is to govern in the affairs of life, the people who are to live a hundred or a thousand years hence may as well take us for a precedent, as we make a precedent of those who lived a hundred or a thousand years ago. The fact is that portions of antiquity, by proving everything, establish nothing. It is authority against authority all the way, till we come to the divine origin of the rights of man at the creation. Here our inquiries find a resting place, and our reason finds a home. If a dispute about the rights of man had arose at the distance of a hundred years from the creation, it is to this source of authority they must have referred, and it is to the same source of authority that we must now refer.

Though I mean not to touch upon any sectarian principle of religion, yet it may be worth observing that the genealogy of Christ is traced to Adam. Why then not trace the rights of man to the creation of man? I will answer the question. Because there have been an upstart of governments thrusting themselves between and presumptuously working to *un-make* man.

If any generation of men ever possessed the right of dictating the mode by which the world should be governed forever, it was the first generation that existed; and if that generation did not do it, no succeeding generation can show any authority for doing it, nor set any up. The illuminating and divine principle of the equal rights of man (for it has its origin from the Maker of man) relates not only to the living individuals but to generations of men succeeding each other. Every generation is equal in rights to the generations which preceded it, by the same rule that every individual is born equal in rights with his contemporary.

Every history of the creation and every traditionary account, whether from the lettered or unlettered world, however they may vary in their opinion or belief of certain particulars, all agree in establishing one point—*the unity of man*—by which I mean that man is all of *one degree*, and consequently that all men are born equal, and with equal natural rights, in the same manner as if posterity had been continued by *creation* instead of *generation* (the latter being only the mode by which the former is carried forward); and consequently every child born into the world must be considered as deriving its existence from God. The world is as new to him as it was to the first man that existed, and his natural right in it is of the same kind.

The Mosaic account of the creation, whether taken as divine authority or merely historical, is fully up to this point, *the unity or equality of man*. The expressions admit of no controversy. "And God said, 'Let us make man in our own image.' In the image of God created he him; male and female created he them" [Gen 1:26-27]. The distinction of sexes is pointed out, but no other distinction is even implied. If this be not divine authority, it is at least historical authority and shows that the equality of man, so far from being a modern doctrine, is the oldest upon record.

It is also to be observed that all the religions known in the world are founded, so far as they relate to man, on the *unity of man*, as being all of one degree. Whether in heaven or in hell, or in whatever state man may be supposed to exist hereafter, the good and the bad are the only distinctions. Nay, even the laws of governments are obliged to slide into this principle by making degrees to consist in crimes and not in persons.

It is one of the greatest of all truths and of the highest advantage to cultivate. By considering man in this light and by instructing him to consider himself in this light, it places him in a close connection with all his duties, whether to his Creator or to the creation of which he is a part; and it is only when he forgets his origin, or, to use a more fashionable phrase, his *birth and family*, that he becomes dissolute. It is not among the least of the evils of the present existing governments in all parts of Europe that man, considered as man, is thrown back to a vast distance from his Maker, and the artificial chasm filled up by a succession of barriers or a sort of turnpike gates through which he has to pass. I will quote Mr. Burke's catalogue of barriers that he has set up between man and his Maker. Putting himself in the character of a herald, he says: "We fear God; we look with *awe* to kings; with affection to parliaments; with duty to magistrates; with reverence to priests; and with respect to nobility."[1] Mr. Burke has forgotten to put in "chivalry." He has also forgotten to put in Peter.[2]

The duty of man is not a wilderness of turnpike gates through which he is to pass by tickets from one to the other. It is plain and simple and consists but of two points. His duty to God, which every man must feel; and with respect to his neighbor, to do as he would be done by. If those to whom power is delegated do well, they will be respected; if not, they will be despised: and with regard to those to whom no power is delegated, but who assume it, the rational world can know nothing of them.

⁓⌒⌒⁓

TEXT: Thomas Paine, *Rights of man: being an answer to Mr. Burke's attack on the French Revolution* (London: J. S. Jordan, 1791), 44–48.

[1] [Ed. Edmund Burke, *Reflections on the revolution in France* (1790).]
[2] [Ed. A reference to the papacy.]

ANNA LETITIA BARBAULD
(1743–1825)
National Repentance

One of the leading English reformers of the revolutionary period, Anna Letitia Barbauld (née Aikin), was born to a prominent dissenting family at Kibworth Harcourt, Leicestershire. Barbauld's mother was responsible for Anna's earliest education, but her father, an influential Presbyterian schoolmaster and minister, taught her Latin and Greek and provided her with access to his library. In 1758 her father took a teaching position at Warrington, where he taught Latin literature and divinity—a move that shaped Barbauld's life. During that time, she began writing poetry on a wide range of topics (including politics, nature, and divinity). She also had extensive contact with Joseph Priestley (see Part I), her father's colleague at Warrington. Her first collection, *Poems* (1773), received positive reviews and sold well. In 1774 Anna married a graduate of Warrington, Rev. Rochemont Barbauld, and the two established a school for boys at Palgrave the same year. Barbauld's work at Palgrave led to the publication of two of her most influential books: *Lessons for children* (4 vols., 1778–1779) and *Hymns in prose for children* (1781). These works, devoted to literacy and religion, shaped pedagogy in England and abroad for several decades. Barbauld supported a number of dissenting social and philanthropic causes, wrote satirical pieces against slavery (*Epistle to William Wilberforce*, 1791), championed political freedom for nonconformists (*To Dr. Priestley*, 1792), and participated in a network of radical literati that included George Dyer (see earlier selection in this part), William Godwin, and others. In addition to writing prefaces for several literary collections, she edited the correspondence of Samuel Richardson (6 vols., 1804). Her husband, who became mentally ill, committed suicide in 1808. After his death, Barbauld worked tirelessly on various projects: she wrote more than three hundred contributions for the *Monthly Review*, compiled the fifty-volume *The British novelists* (1810), and published a darkly pessimistic verse account of British conflict with France in *Eighteen hundred and eleven* (1812).

Barbauld's biting sermon, *Sins of government, sins of the nation* (1793), challenged the entanglement of church and state in England implicit in their call for a national fast on April 9, 1793 in response to France's declaration of war on Britain. As was customary on national fast days, churches throughout Britain, both established and dissenting, were to use the official liturgy composed for the occasion, which included prayers of corporate repentance, collects for peace and grace, and blessings for the monarch. Barbauld, like other dissenters, used the fast day as an opportunity to challenge the national conscience and retrieve a tradition of Christian independence from the interests of the state. Barbauld begins with a subtle demonstration of support. Prayers of repentance have a primarily individual basis, but insofar as the nation is a composite of individuals, all are bound up in national sin. Barbauld then switches direction, excoriating the English for using their fast not to repent for their sins but to seek God's blessing on their exploitation of and aggression towards other nations. More than two centuries later, Barbauld's critique of church-state relations remains a prophetic warning against Christian political assimilation.

Sources: Felicity James and Ian Inkster, eds., *Religious dissent and the Aikin-Barbauld circle, 1740–1860* (Cambridge: Cambridge University Press, 2012); William McCarthy, *Anna Letitia Barbauld: voice of the Enlightenment* (Baltimore: Johns Hopkins University Press, 2008); *OCEL*; *ODNB*; *RCBEC*; Daniel E. White, *Early Romanticism and religious dissent* (Cambridge: Cambridge University Press, 2006).

ANNA LETITIA BARBAULD

Sins of government, sins of the nation

1793

Societies being composed of individuals, the faults of societies proceed from the same bad passions, the same pride, selfishness and thirst of gain, by which individuals are led to transgress the rules of duty; they require therefore the same curb to restrain them, and hence the necessity of a national religion. You will probably assert that most nations have one, but, by a national religion, I do not mean the burning a few wretches twice or thrice in a year in honor of God, nor yet the exacting subscription to some obscure tenets, believed by few and understood by none, nor yet the investing a certain order of men dressed in a particular habit with civil privileges and secular emolument. By national religion, I understand: the extending to those affairs in which we act in common and as a body; that regard to religion by which, when we act singly, we all profess to be guided. Nothing seems more obvious; and yet there are men who appear not insensible to the rules of morality as they respect individuals, and who unaccountably disclaim them with respect to nations. They will not cheat their opposite neighbor, but they will take a pride in overreaching a neighboring state; they would scorn to foment dissentions in the family of an acquaintance, but they will do so by a community without scruple; they would not join with a gang of housebreakers to plunder a private dwelling, but they have no principle which prevents them from joining with a confederacy of princes to plunder a province. As private individuals, they think it right to pass by little injuries, but as a people they think they cannot carry too high a principle of proud defiance and sanguinary revenge. This sufficiently shows that whatever rule they may acknowledge for their private conduct, they have nothing that can be properly called *national religion*; and, indeed, it is very much to be suspected that their religion in the former case is very much assisted by the contemplation of those pains and penalties which society has provided against the crimes of individuals. But the united will of a whole people cannot make wrong right, or sanction one act of rapacity, injustice, or breach of faith. The first principle, therefore, we must lay down is that we are to submit our public conduct to the same rules by which we are to regulate our private actions. A nation that does this is, as a nation, religious; a nation that does it not—though it should fast and pray and wear sackcloth and pay tithes and build churches—is, as a nation, profligate and unprincipled.

‡

There is a notion which has a direct tendency to make us unjust, because it tends to make us think God so; I mean the idea which most nations have entertained, that they are the peculiar favorites of heaven. We nourish our pride by fondly fancying that we are the only nation for whom the providence of God exerts itself; the only nation whose form of worship is agreeable to him; the only nation whom he has endowed with a competent share of wisdom to frame wise laws and rational governments. Each nation is to itself the fleece of Gideon and drinks exclusively the dew of science;[1] but as God is no respecter of persons [Acts 10:34], so neither is he of nations; he has not, like earthly monarchs, his favorites. There is a great deal even in our thanksgivings which is exceptionable on this account— "God, we thank thee, that we are not like other nations" [Luke 18:11]—yet we freely load ourselves with every degree of guilt; but then we like to consider ourselves as a child that is chidden, and others as outcasts.

When the workings of these bad passions are swelled to their height by mutual animosity and opposition, *war* ensues. War is a state in which all our feelings and our duties suffer a total and strange inversion; a state, in which,

> Life dies, death lives, and nature breeds
> Perverse, all monstrous, all prodigious things.[2]

A state in which it becomes our business to hurt and annoy our neighbor by every possible means; instead of cultivating, to destroy; instead of building, to pull down; instead of peopling, to depopulate; a state in which we drink the tears, and feed upon the misery of our fellow-creatures; such a state, therefore, requires the extremest necessity to justify it; it ought not to be the common and usual state of society. As both parties cannot be in the right, there is always an equal chance, at least, to either of them of being in the wrong; but as both parties may be to blame, and most commonly are, the chance is very great indeed against its being entered into from any adequate cause; yet war may be said to be, with regard to nations, the sin which most easily besets them. We, my friends, in common with other nations, have much guilt to repent of from this cause, and it ought to make a large part of our humiliations on this day. When we carry our eyes back through the long records of our history, we see wars of plunder, wars of conquest, wars of religion, wars of pride, wars of succession, wars of idle speculation, wars of unjust interference, and hardly among them one war of necessary self-defense in any of our essential or very important interests. Of late years, indeed, we have known none of the calamities of war in our own country but the wasteful expense of it; and sitting aloof from those circumstances of personal provocation, which in some measure might excuse its fury, we have calmly voted slaughter and merchandized destruction—so much blood and tears for so many rupees or

---

[1]   [Ed. Barbauld's references to Gideon's fleece (Jdg 6:36-40) and "the dew of science" imply that nations claim their own standards of morality and knowledge.]

[2]   [Ed. John Milton, *Paradise lost*, 2.624-625.]

dollars or ingots. Our wars have been wars of cool calculating interest, as free from hatred as from love of mankind; the passions which stir the blood have had no share in them. We devote a certain number of men to perish on land and sea, and the rest of us sleep sound, and, protected in our usual occupations, talk of the events of war as what diversifies the flat uniformity of life.

We should, therefore, do well to *translate* this word war into language more intelligible to us. When we pay our army and our navy estimates, let us set down—so much for killing, so much for maiming, so much for making widows and orphans, so much for bringing famine upon a district, so much for corrupting citizens and subjects into spies and traitors, so much for ruining industrious tradesmen and making bankrupts (of that species of distress at least, we *can* form an idea), so much for letting loose the demons of fury, rapine, and lust within the fold of cultivated society, and giving to the brutal ferocity of the most ferocious its full scope and range of invention. We shall by this means know what we have paid our money for, whether we have made a good bargain, and whether the account is likely to pass elsewhere. We must take in, too, all those concomitant circumstances which make war, considered as battle, the least part of itself, *pars minima sui*. We must fix our eyes not on the hero returning with conquest, nor yet on the gallant officer dying in the bed of honor, the subject of picture and of song, but on the private soldier, forced into the service, exhausted by camp sickness and fatigue; pale, emaciated, crawling to an hospital with the prospect of life, perhaps a long life, blasted, useless, and suffering. We must think of the uncounted tears of her who weeps alone because the only being who shared her sentiments is taken from her; no martial music sounds in unison with her feelings; the long day passes, and he returns not. She does not shed her sorrows over his grave, for she has never learnt whether he ever had one. If he had returned, his exertions would not have been remembered individually, for he only made a small imperceptible part of a human machine, called a regiment. We must take in the long sickness which no glory soothes, occasioned by distress of mind, anxiety, and ruined fortunes. These are not fancy pictures; and if you please to heighten them, you can every one of you do it for yourselves. We must take in the consequences, felt perhaps for ages, before a country which has been completely desolated lifts its head again; like a torrent of lava, its worst mischief is not the first overwhelming ruin of towns and palaces, but the long sterility to which it condemns the track it has covered with its stream. Add the danger to regular governments which are changed by war, sometimes to anarchy, and sometimes to despotism. Add all these, and then let us think when a general performing these exploits is saluted with "well done good and faithful servant" [Matt 25:23], whether the plaudit is likely to be echoed in another place.

In this guilty business there is a circumstance which greatly aggravates its guilt, and that is the impiety of calling upon the divine Being to assist us in it. Almost all nations have been in the habit of mixing with their bad passions a show of religion, and of prefacing these their murders with prayers and the solemnities of worship. When they send out their armies to desolate a country and destroy the fair face of nature, they have the presumption to hope that the sovereign of the universe will condescend to be their auxiliary, and to enter into their petty and despicable contests. Their prayer, if put into plain language, would run thus: "God of love, Father of all the families of the earth, we are going to tear in pieces our brethren of mankind, but our strength is not equal to our fury; we beseech thee to assist us in the work of slaughter. Go out, we pray thee, with our fleets and armies; we call them Christian, and we have interwoven in our banners and the decorations of our arms the symbols of a suffering religion that we may fight under the cross upon which our Savior died. Whatever mischief we do, we shall do it in thy name; we hope, therefore, thou wilt protect us in it. Thou, who hast made of one blood all the dwellers upon the earth [Acts 17:26], we trust thou wilt view us alone with partial favor, and enable us to bring misery upon every other quarter of the globe." Now if we really expect such prayers to [be] answered, we are the weakest, if not, we are the most hypocritical of beings.

Formerly, this business was managed better and had in it more show of reason and probability. When mankind conceived of their gods as partaking of like passions with themselves, they made a fair bargain with them on these occasions. Their chieftains, they knew, were influenced by such motives, and they thought their gods might well be so, too. Go out with us, and you shall have a share of the spoil. Your altars shall stream with the blood of so many noble captives, or you shall have a hecatomb of fat oxen, or a golden tripod. Have we anything of this kind to propose? Can we make anything like a handsome offer to the Almighty, to tempt him to enlist himself on our side? Such things have been done before now in the Christian world. Churches have been promised, and church lands, aye, and honestly paid too; at other times silver shrines, incense, vestments, tapers, according to the occasion. Oh how justly may the awful text be here applied! "He that sitteth in the heavens shall laugh, the Lord shall have them in derision" [Ps 2:4]. Christians! I shudder, lest in the earnestness of my heart I may have sinned, in suffering such impious propositions to escape my lips. In short, while we must be perfectly conscious in our own minds that the generality of our wars are the offspring of mere worldly ambition and interest, let us, if we must have wars, carry them on as other such things are carried on, and not think of making a prayer to be used before murder, any more than of composing prayers to be used before we enter a gambling house, or a place of licentious entertainment. Bad actions are made worse by hypocrisy; an unjust war is in itself so bad a thing that there is only one way of making it worse, and that is by mixing religion with it.

TEXT: [Anna Letitia Barbauld,] *Sins of government, sins of the nation; or, A discourse for the fast, appointed on April 19, 1793* (London: J. Johnson, 1793), 7–9, 24–33.

SAMUEL TAYLOR COLERIDGE
(1772–1834)
The Christian Church

Although the events surrounding the French Revolution gave rise to some of the period's most noteworthy writings on the church and state, ongoing interest in social and political reform inspired further reflection on their relation. The insights of Samuel Taylor Coleridge deserve special consideration. Coleridge was not only one of the great poets of English Romanticism, but also a philosopher, theologian, biblical scholar, and literary critic. Born at Ottery St. Mary, Devonshire, on October 21, 1772, Coleridge attended Christ's Hospital School, Hertford, and then from 1791 to 1794, Jesus College, Cambridge, where he soon embraced radicalism and Unitarianism. The watershed moment of his life came in 1798, when Coleridge published *Lyrical ballads* with his friend William Wordsworth. This early poetic promise was disrupted, though never wholly extinguished, by numerous personal crises. His marriage collapsed. He abandoned his wife and children to the care of Robert Southey. He was addicted to opium. The positive influence of Kantian philosophy coupled with a study of the English Trinitarian controversies, however, led him finally to declare in 1805: "No Trinity, no God." Coleridge's renewed belief naturally did not end his personal problems, but from this point his philosophical theology takes up a distinctly trinitarian outlook. Supported by his longsuffering friends, Coleridge continued to write: *Kubla Khan* and *Christabel* came out in 1816, *Biographia literaria*—one of the monuments of British Romantic literary criticism—the following year. In later years, Coleridge's books and personal correspondence often center explicitly on theological topics including biblical authority and inspiration, sin, redemption, and the church. Coleridge's *Aids to reflection* (1825), one of the most influential theological books in England and the United States during the 1820s and 1830s, encouraged the formation of critical reflection through attention to language and dependence on divine Ideas: "Christianity is not a theory, or a speculation; but a *life*. Not a *philosophy* of life, but a life and a living process."

By the time Coleridge published *On the constitution of the church and state* (1830), the political reality of Catholic emancipation had already been decided. The original title,

On the constitution of the church and state, according to the idea of each (the first edition further stated *"with aids toward a right judgment on the late Catholic bill"*), exemplifies Coleridge's application of theological and philosophical distinctions to the possibilities for a national church in a pluralistic age. In the following selection, Coleridge explains the *idea* of the church by distinguishing the Christian church from national churches such as the Church of England. Coleridge maintains that the Christian church is marked by characteristics such as universality and the absence of a visible head. By contrast, a national church promotes the well-being of the nation through the establishment of the *clerisy*—"the learned of all denominations," including experts in law, medicine, the arts, and theology. Protestantism, in such perspective, encourages the formation of democratic societies. Coleridge thereby articulated a modern Anglican ecclesiology while reconceptualizing the status of the national church in the nation.

SOURCES: Rosemary Ashton, *The life of Samuel Taylor Coleridge* (Oxford; Blackwell, 1996); Aimee E. Barbeau, "The 'hedge-girdle of the state': Coleridge and the social contract," *Coleridge Bulletin* n.s. 40 (2012): 15–24; Jeffrey W. Barbeau, *Coleridge, the Bible, and religion*, Nineteenth-Century Major Lives and Letters (New York: Palgrave Macmillan, 2008); idem, *Sara Coleridge: her life and thought* (New York: Palgrave Macmillan, 2014); David P. Calleo, *Coleridge and the idea of the modern state* (New Haven: Yale University Press, 1966); Graham Davidson, *Coleridge's career* (Basingstoke: Macmillan, 1990); *ECL*; John Stuart Mill, *Dissertations and discussions: political, philosophical, and historical*, 2 vols. (London: John W. Parker and Son, 1859); *OCEL*; *ODCC*; *ODNB*.

SAMUEL TAYLOR COLERIDGE
On the constitution of the church and state
1830

. . . Of the Christian *church* only, and of this no further than is necessary for the distinct understanding of the national church, it is my purpose now to speak: and for this purpose it will be sufficient to enumerate the essential characters by which the Christian church is distinguished.

FIRST CHARACTER. The Christian church is not a kingdom, realm (*royaume*), or state (*sensu latiori*)[1] of the world, that is, of the aggregate or total number of the kingdoms, states, realms, or bodies politic (these words being, as far as our present argument is concerned, perfectly synonymous) into which civilized man is distributed and which, collectively taken, constitute the civilized world. The Christian church, I say, is no state, kingdom, or realm of this world; nor is it an estate of any such realm, kingdom, or state; but it is the appointed opposite to them all, *collectively*—the sustaining, correcting, befriending opposite of the world! The compensating counterforce to the inherent[2] and inevitable evils and defects of the state, as a state, and without reference to its better or worse construction as a particular state; while whatever is beneficent and humanizing in the aims, tendencies, and proper objects of the state, it collects in itself as in a focus, to radiate them back in a higher quality; or, to change the metaphor, it completes and strengthens the edifice of the state, without interference or commixture, in the mere act of laying and securing its own foundations. And for these services the church of Christ asks of the state neither wages nor dignities. She asks only protection and *to be let alone.* These indeed she demands, but even these only on the ground that there is nothing in her constitution, nor in her discipline, inconsistent with the interests of the state, nothing resistant or impedimental to the state in the exercise of its rightful powers, in the fulfillment of its appropriate duties, or in the

[1]   [Ed. That is, "in a wider sense." I have been aided throughout by John Colmer's excellent critical edition, *On the constitution of the church and state*, Collected Works of Samuel Taylor Coleridge, 10 (Princeton: Princeton University Press, 1976); hereafter, *C&S.*]

[2]   [Ed. At this point Coleridge includes a lengthy footnote recommending his readers to pursue further evidence of his claims in the writings of G. E. Lessing—a helpful reminder of Coleridge's role as a mediator of German ideas to the English (and North American) reading public.]

effectuation of its legitimate objects. It is a fundamental principle of all legislation that the state shall leave the largest portion of personal free agency to each of its citizens that is compatible with the free agency of all and not subversive of the ends of its own existence as a state. And though a negative, it is a most important distinctive character of the church of Christ that she asks nothing [from the state] for her members as Christians which they are not already entitled to demand as citizens and subjects.

SECOND CHARACTER. The Christian church is not a secret community. In the once current (and well worthy to be reissued) terminology of our elder divines, it is objective in its nature and purpose, not mystic or subjective, i.e., not like reason or the court of conscience, existing only in and for the individual. Consequently the church here spoken of is not "the kingdom of God which is *within* and which cometh not with observation (Luke 17:20-21), but most observable" (Luke 21:28-31). A city built on a hill, and not to be hid [Matt 5:14]—an institution consisting of visible and public communities. In one sentence, it is the church visible and militant under Christ. And this visibility, this *publicity*, is its second distinctive character.

The THIRD CHARACTER reconciles the two preceding and gives the condition under which their coexistence in the same subject becomes possible. Antagonist forces are necessarily of the same kind. It is an old rule of logic that only concerning two subjects of the same kind can it be properly said that they are opposites. *Inter res heterogeneas non datur oppositio*, i.e., contraries cannot be opposites. Alike in the primary and the metaphorical use of the word, rivals (*rivales*) are those only who inhabit the opposite banks of *the same stream.*

Now, in conformity to character the first, the Christian church dare not be considered as a counter-pole to any particular state—the word state here taken in the largest sense. Still less can it, like the national clerisy, be opposed to the state in the narrower sense. The *Christian* church, as such, has no *nationalty* entrusted to its charge. It forms no counter-balance to the collective *heritage* of the realm. The phrase, church and state, has a sense and a propriety in reference to the *national* Church alone. The church of Christ cannot be placed in this conjunction and antithesis without forfeiting the very name of Christian. The true and only contra-position of the Christian church is to the world. Her paramount aim and object, indeed, is *another* world, not a world *to come* exclusively, but likewise *another world that now is* . . . and to the concerns of which alone the epithet spiritual can, without a mischievous abuse of the word, be applied. But as the necessary consequence and accompaniments of the means by which she seeks to attain this especial end, and as a collateral object, it is her office to counteract the evils that result by a common necessity from all bodies politic, the system or aggregate of which is the world. And, observe that the nisus, or counter-agency, of the Christian church is against the evil *results* only, and not (directly, at least, or by primary intention) against the defective institutions that may have caused or aggravated them.

But on the other hand, by virtue of the second character, the Christian church is to exist in every kingdom and state of the world in the form of public communities—is to exist as a real and ostensible power. The consistency of the first and second depends on, and is fully effected by, the THIRD CHARACTER of the church of Christ: namely, the absence of any visible head or sovereign—by the nonexistence, nay the utter preclusion, of any local or personal center of unity, of any single source of universal power. This fact may be thus illustrated. Kepler and Newton,[3] substituting the idea of the infinite for the conception of a finite and determined world (assumed in the Ptolemaic astronomy), superseded and drove out the notion of a one central point or body of the universe; and, finding a center in every point of matter and an absolute circumference nowhere, explained at once the unity and the distinction that coexist throughout the creation by focal instead of central bodies, the attractive and restraining power of the sun or focal orb in each particular system, supposing and resulting from an actual power, present in all and over all, throughout an indeterminable multitude of systems—and this, demonstrated as it has been by science and verified by observation, we rightly name the true system of the heavens. And even such is the scheme and true idea of the Christian church. In the primitive times, and as long as the churches retained the form given them by the apostles and apostolic men, every community, or in the words of a Father of the second century . . . every altar had its own bishop, every flock its own pastor, who derived his authority immediately from Christ, the universal Shepherd, and acknowledged no other superior than the same Christ, speaking by his spirit in the unanimous decision of any number of bishops or elders, according to his promise, "Where two or three are gathered together in my name, there am I in the midst of them" [Matt. 18:20].

Hence the unitive relation of the churches to each other, and of each to all, being equally *actual* indeed, but likewise equally ideal—i.e., mystic and supersensual, as the relation of the whole church to its one invisible Head, the church with and under Christ, as a one kingdom or state—is hidden.

‡

The FOURTH CHARACTER of the Christian Church, and a necessary consequence of the first and third, is its catholicity, i.e., universality. It is neither Anglican, Gallican, nor Roman—neither Latin nor Greek. Even the catholic and apostolic Church *of* England is a less safe expression than the Churches of Christ in England: though the Catholic church *in* England, or (what would be still better) the Catholic church under Christ throughout Great Britain and Ireland, is justifiable and appropriate. For through the presence of its only head and sovereign, entire in each and one in all, the church universal is spiritually perfect in every true church and of course in any number of such churches, which from circumstance of place, or the community of country or of language, we have occasion to speak of collectively. (I have already, here and elsewhere, observed, and scarcely a day passes without some occasion to repeat the observation, that an equivocal term, or a word with two or more different meanings, is never quite harmless. Thus, it is at least an inconvenience in our language that the term church—instead of being confined to its proper sense, Kirk, Aedes Kyriacae,[4] or the Lord's House—should likewise be . . . our term for the clerical establishment . . .) The true Church *of* England is the national Church or

---

[3]   [Ed. Coleridge's invocation of Johannes Kepler (1571–1630) and Isaac Newton (1643–1727) further demonstrates his conception of the centrality of Christ, the Logos, in the order and harmony of all created things.]

[4]   [Ed. In Coleridge's usage, "the Lord's House."]

clerisy. There exists (God be thanked!) a catholic and apostolic church *in* England—and I thank God also for the constitutional and ancestral Church *of* England.[5]

These are the four distinctions, or peculiar and essential marks, by which the church with Christ as its head is distinguished from the national Church, and *separated* from every possible counterfeit that has, or shall have, usurped its name.

TEXT: S. T. Coleridge, *On the constitution of the church and state, according to the idea of each, with aids toward a right judgment on the late Catholic bill* (London: Hurst, Chance and Co., 1830), 132–42, 146–47.

[5]   [Ed. Earlier in this work, Coleridge calls the existence of the true Christian church in England "a blessed accident, a providential boon, a grace of God" that supports and invigorates the national Church of England (59–60; cf. *C&S*, 55).]

IX
PAPACY

Here then our Protestant countrymen are called upon to place themselves in our situation . . .

Charles Butler, *An address to the Protestants of Great Britain and Ireland* (1813)

CHARLES BUTLER
(1750–1832)
Catholic Relief

The accession of Elizabeth I in 1558 led many English Catholics to flee to the Continent. Those who remained faced significant social, cultural, and political challenges. A series of Restoration-era Test Acts, requiring oaths of allegiance to the monarchy and denunciations of transubstantiation, were established to keep the reins of power out of Roman Catholic hands. The two English universities—Oxford and Cambridge—were closed to Catholics, although some pursued studies in France at the English College at Douai before returning home to a nation at odds with their faith.

In 1766 Charles Butler, the son of a linen draper and a mother who knew Greek and Latin, returned from studies at Douai and began working as a conveyancer (the only area of law open to Roman Catholics at the time). A decade later, he set up his own practice and entered Lincoln's Inn, though he was unable to take the necessary oaths for procession to the bar. He began writing on political topics in the 1770s, seeking support for the Catholic Relief Act (1778), whose provisions would allow Roman Catholics, after taking a loyalty oath, to hold and inherit real property. Having been made secretary to the Catholic Committee in 1782, Butler was asked to draft a new bill designed to improve the status of Catholics in England in 1788. His work included an oath that defined Roman Catholics as "Protesting Catholic Dissenters." Though his work had the support of William Pitt ("the younger") and several clerical and lay members of the committee, others—such as the eventual vicar apostolic, John Milner (see selection in this part)—thought Butler's work risked schism with the Roman Church for appearing to equate Rome with Protestant dissent. Milner distrusted a layman like Butler meddling in ecclesiastical policy, feared that Butler would promote factions among English Roman Catholics, and eventually censured him as "a rebel to ecclesiastical authority and a public sinner" (*ODNB*). In the end, insufficient support for Butler's attempt to enfold Catholic interests with Protestant dissenters led to the removal of his original language. When the rephrased bill finally passed in 1791, Butler became the first Roman Catholic to be called to the bar in over a hundred years. Subsequently, Butler championed the cause of

Catholic emancipation through numerous publications and political efforts. He founded the Cisalpine Club, whose mission it was "to resist any ecclesiastical interference which may militate against the freedom of English Catholics" (*ODNB*). Between 1819 and 1821, he also wrote a four-volume history of Catholics in Britain. In *The book of the Catholic Church* (1825), Butler provided a counter-narrative to Robert Southey's anti-Catholic *The book of the church* (1824). Despite Milner's fierce antagonism, Butler's lifelong efforts were rewarded with the passage of the Roman Catholic Relief Act of 1829 and an appointment to the king's council.

Butler worked tirelessly for Catholic emancipation throughout his life. His *An address to the Protestants of Great Britain and Ireland* (1813) urges a renewal of national conscience, asking that Protestants imagine themselves in the role of the religious minority. Likewise, he appeals to national self-interest, arguing that Catholic emancipation would free Catholics to contribute to the larger good and thereby benefit the nation as a whole.

SOURCES: Stuart Andrews, *Robert Southey: history, politics, religion* (New York: Palgrave Macmillan, 2011); *NCE*; *ODNB*.

CHARLES BUTLER

An address to the Protestants of Great Britain and Ireland
1813

In the last sessions of Parliament, the House of Commons came to a resolution that "the House would early in the next session take into its most serious consideration the laws affecting his Majesty's Roman Catholic subjects in Great Britain and Ireland, with a view to such final, conciliatory adjustment as might be conducive to the peace of the United Kingdom, stability of the Protestant establishment, and the general satisfaction and concord of all classes of his Majesty's subjects."[1]

Encouraged by this resolution, the Roman Catholics of England and Ireland intend presenting immediately separate petitions to each House of Parliament, "for a repeal of the penal and disabling statutes which still remain in force against them."

In the meantime they observe with great concern and surprise that attempts are made to prejudice the legislature against their application. Many erroneous, artful, and inflammatory publications of this tendency have been actively and extensively circulated. The charges brought in them against the Roman Catholics are of the most serious nature. The object of this address to you is to answer these charges and to state to you, succinctly, the grounds of the intended application of the English Roman Catholics to the legislature for relief. The greatest part of what is intended to be said in the address will apply, in great measure, as much to the situation of the Irish and Scottish, as to the situation of the English Roman Catholics; but as the penal codes of Ireland, Scotland, and England in respect to Roman Catholics are very different, it has been thought advisable to confine the present address to the case of the English Roman Catholics only.

I.

It is generally represented in the publications of which we complain that the English Roman Catholics labor under no real grievances; and that, if all the remaining penal laws

---

[1]   [Ed. *The parliamentary debates from the year 1803 to the present time*, vols. 24–25 (London: T. C. Hansard, 1913), 875.]

against them were repealed, the number of those who would be really benefited by the repeal would be too insignificant to make their relief an object of legislative concern.

But this representation is altogether erroneous—the English Catholics labor under many severe penalties and disabilities: their whole body is affected by them, and would be essentially benefited by their removal.

‡

II.

Such, fellow subjects, is the particular operation of the principal laws still remaining in force against your English Catholic brethren. The general effect of them is to depress every member of the body below his legitimate level in society.

Even in the very lowest order of the community, some actuations[2] conferring comfort, emolument, or distinction are open to the individuals of that class; and in proportion as the several classes of society rise into importance, these situations are multiplied. From all of them the law excludes the English Catholic. This effectually places him below his Protestant brethren of the same class and makes the whole body in the estimation of the community a depressed and insulated cast.

This the Roman Catholics severely feel, but it is not by its substantial effects alone that they feel their depression. Some avenues of wealth are still open to them—none to honors or distinctions. Thus, thousands of those possibilities, the prospect and hope of which constitute a large proportion of the general stock of human happiness, are peremptorily denied to the Roman Catholics. No hope of provision, of preferment, of honors, or dignity cheers their souls or excites their exertions. A Roman Catholic scarce steps into life when he is made to feel that nothing which confers them is open to him; and however successful his career may have been, it seldom happens that his success has not been, on more than one occasion, either lessened or retarded by the circumstance of his having been a Roman Catholic.

Here then our Protestant countrymen are called upon to place themselves in our situation and to reflect what their own feelings would be if, from a conscientious adherence to their religious principles, they belonged to a class thus legally degraded. How often would they substantially feel the effects of this degradation? How many of their hopes would it destroy? How many of their projects would it ruin? Surely a petition to the Legislature from any portion of his Majesty's subjects, for the removal of such a woe, is entitled to the sympathy and aid of every other portion of the community.

III.

We are sometimes told that however the repeal of the laws complained of by the Roman Catholics would benefit them, it would confer no real benefit on the state; and that, as no alteration of law should take place, unless it promotes the general welfare of the state, the laws complained of should remain in force.

But we beg leave to submit to the consideration of our countrymen that the whole kingdom would be essentially served by the repeal of the penal laws remaining in force

---

[2]   [Ed. Actions.]

against his Majesty's Roman Catholic subjects. On this head the writer of these pages requests your particular attention.

Two-thirds of the population of Ireland, and no inconsiderable proportion of the population of England, is composed of Roman Catholics. It is obvious that the feelings of this large proportion of the community are wounded, in the highest degree, by the penal and disabling laws to which they are subject, and that they consider themselves highly injured, insulted, and degraded by them. Now, must it not be beneficial to the state that this extensive feeling of insult, injury, and degradation should be healed? Do not wisdom and sound policy make it the interest of the state that every circumstance which leads this injured, insulted, and degraded but numerous portion of the community to think that any new order of things must end their injury, insult, and degradation and is, therefore, desirable, should be removed as soon as possible? Surely the removal of it must be as advantageous to the state, as it will be advantageous and gratifying to the persons individually benefited by it.

But this is not the only circumstance which would make the repeal of the penal laws a general benefit to the state. Again we request you to consider the immense number of his Majesty's Roman Catholic subjects and the great proportion which it bears to the rest of the community. What a proportion of genius, of talent, of energy, of everything else by which individuals are enabled to distinguish themselves and benefit and elevate their country must fall to their share! But all this, for the present, is lost to you in consequence of the penal codes. Is the subtraction of this prodigious mass of probable genius, talent, and wisdom from the general stock no detriment to the state? Surely it is a national loss. Thus while the penal code harasses the individual object of its infliction, it contracts and paralyzes, to an amazing degree, the strength, powers, and energies of the whole community.

⤜⤚

TEXT: Charles Butler, *An address to the Protestants of Great Britain and Ireland*, 2nd ed. (London: Booker, 1813), 2–3, 5–7.

JOHN MILNER
(1752–1826)
Papal Authority

While Charles Butler and his allies worked to gain political freedoms for Roman Catholics, others warned that any compromise with Protestantism risked diluting the purity of Catholic truth. The latter position is exemplified in one of the most unyielding Romanists of the period: John Milner. Born to Lancastrian Catholic parents, Milner matriculated at the English College at Douai in 1766. He returned to England, already ordained, more than a decade later. Initially, Milner worked around London, ministering to French prisoners of war, but was later sent to serve at the mission in Winchester. Here, Milner began a vocal campaign against the alleged liberalism of Butler and other likeminded Catholics. He opposed any move to compromise or secularize church teaching in exchange for political liberty. In the negotiations leading to the passage of the Catholic Relief Bill (1791), which abolished penal laws and legalized the celebration of the mass, Milner successfully appealed to high church bishops to eliminate language that referred to Roman Catholics as "Protesting Catholic Dissenters"—language designed to provide wider political freedoms for Catholics, but which Milner regarded as a dangerous conflation of Roman Catholic teaching with Protestant dissent. The papacy rewarded Milner with an appointment as the titular bishop of Castabala and in 1803 as the English vicar apostolic of the Midland district (functionally, a bishop responsible for the pastoral care of a missionary region). During the next decades, Milner worked to defend Catholic teaching in England, bolster the education of English Catholic clergy (particularly after the suppression of the English College at Douai during the French Revolution), and diminish the influence of the Catholic landed gentry over their clergy. After assuming control of the seminary at Oscott, Milner enforced a demanding rule of moral austerity that held priests to the highest standards of church obedience and separated them from the laity. Through these actions, Milner gained a reputation for his unwillingness to compromise with potential allies for the sake of emancipation.

Milner's most influential work was an apologetic volume written in the form of a catechism, *The end of religious controversy* (1818). Although he first wrote the work in

1801, he delayed its publication for nearly two decades at the request of Bishop Horsley, who hoped to advance the cause of Catholics through diplomacy. The following selection illustrates Milner's skill as a polemicist. He distances English Catholicism (and Catholicism broadly) from the abiding Protestant anxiety that the Roman pontiff sought political authority over temporal rulers. Rather, Milner maintains, when in prior ages the pope has enjoyed such authority, the power always was derived from the unity of the empire and the willing subordination of kings and princes to their chief spiritual pastor. In recent pluralistic times, however, the pope has relinquished this authority. Milner challenges Protestant readers by appealing to the Bible in favor of the Catholic position that Peter's authority (now manifest in the papacy) derives from the command of Jesus Christ.

SOURCES: Stuart Andrews, *Robert Southey: history, politics, religion* (New York: Palgrave Macmillan, 2011); *NCE*; *ODCC*; *ODNB*.

JOHN MILNER
The end of religious controversy
1818

I now appeal to you, dear sir, and to the respectable friends who are accustomed to deliberate with you on religious subjects, whether these observations and arguments of the ancient Fathers are not as strikingly true in this nineteenth century as they were during the six first centuries in which they wrote? Is there not, among the rival churches, one exclusively known and distinguished by the name and title of *the Catholic Church*, as well in England, Holland, and other countries which protest against this church as in those which adhere to it? Does not this effulgent mark of the true religion so incontestably belong to us—in spite of every effort to obscure it by the nicknames of papists, Romanists, etc.—that the rule of St. Cyril and St. Augustine is as good and certain now as it was in their times? What I mean is this: if any stranger in London, Edinburgh, or Amsterdam were to ask his way to the Catholic chapel, I would risk my life for it that no sober Protestant inhabitant would direct him to any other place of worship than to ours. On the other hand, it is notorious that the different sects of Protestants, like the heretics and schismatics of old, are denominated either from their founders (as the Lutherans, the Calvinists, the Socinians, etc.), or from the countries in which they prevail (as the Church of England, the Kirk of Scotland, the Moravians, etc.), or from some novelty in their belief or practice (as the Anabaptists, the Independents, the Quakers, etc.). The first father of Protestants was so sensible that he and they were destitute of every claim to the title of Catholic that in translating the Apostles' Creed into Dutch he substituted the word *Christian* for that of *Catholic*. The first Lutherans did the same thing in their catechism, for which they are reproached by the famous Fulke, who, to his own confusion, proves that the true church of Christ must be Catholic in name, as well as in substance.[1]

‡

---

[1]   [Ed. Milner refers to the Puritan theologian William Fulke (1537–1589).]

392

It is not, then, the faith of this church that the pope has any civil or temporal supremacy by virtue of which he can depose princes or give or take away the property of other persons out of his own domain. For even the incarnate Son of God, from whom he derives the supremacy he possesses, did not claim here upon earth any right of the above-mentioned kind. On the contrary, he positively declared that his "kingdom is not of this world" [John 18:36]! Hence, the Catholics of both our islands have, without impeachment even from Rome, denied, upon oath, that the pope "has any civil jurisdiction, power, superiority, or preeminence, directly or indirectly, within this realm."[2] But as it is undeniable that different popes in former ages have pronounced sentence of deposition against certain contemporary princes, and as great numbers of theologians have held (though not as a matter of faith) that they had a right to do so, it seems proper, by way of mitigating the odium which Dr. Porteus[3] and other Protestants raise against them on this head, to state the grounds on which the pontiffs acted and the divines reasoned in this business. Heretofore the kingdoms, principalities, and states composing the Latin church, when they were all of the same religion, formed, as it were, one Christian republic of which the pope was the accredited head. Now, as mankind have been sensible at all times that the duty of civil allegiance and submission cannot extend beyond a certain point, and that they ought not to surrender their property, lives, and morality to be sported with by a Nero or a Heliogabalus,[4] instead of deciding the nice point for themselves when resistance becomes lawful, they thought it right to be guided by their chief pastor. The kings and princes themselves acknowledged this right in the pope and frequently applied to him to make use of his indirect, temporal power on their behalf, as appears in numberless instances. In latter ages, however, since Christendom has been disturbed by a variety of religions, this power of the pontiff has been generally withdrawn. Princes make war upon each other at their pleasure and subjects rebel against their princes as their passions dictate,[5] to the great detriment of both parties, as may be gathered from what Sir Edward Sandys, an early and zealous Protestant writer, wrote: "The pope was the common father, adviser, and conductor of Christians to reconcile their enmities and decide their differences."[6] I have to observe, secondly, that the question here is not about the personal qualities or conduct of any particular pope, or of the popes in general; at the same time it is proper to state that in a list of 253 popes who have successively filled the chair of Saint Peter, only a small comparative number of them have disgraced it, while a great proportion of them have done honor to it by their virtues and conduct. On this head, I must again quote Addison, who says, "the pope is generally a man of learning and virtue, mature in years and experience,

---

[2] [Ed. From the Oath of Supremacy of the 1791 Catholic Relief Bill (31 George III, c. 32).]

[3] [Ed. Beilby Porteus (1731–1809) was bishop of London and an opponent of Catholic emancipation.]

[4] [Ed. The erratic and gluttonous Roman emperor Heliogabalus or Elagabalus (203–222) reigned from 218 until his assassination in 222.]

[5] [Ed. Here Milner produces a long note alleging "the total or partial deposition of the lawful sovereign" in every country where Protestantism spread, including England, France, and the United States, as well as other nations influenced by the teachings Luther, Müntzer, and Zwingli.]

[6] [Ed. Milner may refer to Sir Edwin Sandys' *A relation of the state of religion* (1605), which surveyed the state of Catholicism on the continent.]

who has seldom any vanity or pleasure to gratify at his people's expense, and is neither encumbered with wife and children, or mistresses."[7]

In the third place I must remind you and my other friends that I have nothing here to do with the doctrine of the pope's individual infallibility (when, pronouncing *ex cathedra*, as the term is, he addresses the whole church and delivers the faith of it upon some contested article), nor would you, in case you were to become a Catholic, be required to believe in any doctrines except such as are held by the whole Catholic church with the pope at its head. But, without entering into this or any other scholastic question, I shall content myself with observing that it is impossible for any man of candor and learning not to concur with a celebrated Protestant author, Causabon, who writes thus, "No one who is the least versed in ecclesiastical history can doubt that God made use of the Holy See during many ages to preserve the doctrines of faith!"[8]

At length we arrive at the question itself, which is, whether the bishop of Rome, who by preeminence is called *papa* ("pope" or "father of the faithful"), is or is not entitled to a superior rank and jurisdiction above other bishops of the Christian church, so as to be its spiritual head upon earth and his see the center of catholic unity? All Catholics necessarily hold the affirmative of these questions . . . Let us begin with consulting the New Testament in order to see whether or no the first pope or bishop of Rome, Saint Peter, was any way superior to the other apostles. St. Matthew, in numbering up the apostles, expressly says of him, *"the first*, Simon, who is called Peter" (Matt 10:2). In like manner, the other evangelists, while they class the rest of the apostles differently, still give the first place to Peter {Mark 3:16; Luke 6:14; Acts 1:13}. In fact, as Bossuet observes,[9] "St. Peter was the first to confess his faith in Christ {Matt 16:16}, the first to whom Christ appeared after his resurrection {Luke 24:34}; the first to preach the belief of this to the people {Acts 2:14}; the first to convert the Jews {Acts 2:37}; and the first to receive the Gentiles" {Acts 10:47}. Again I would ask, is there no distinction implied in Saint Peter's being called upon by Christ to declare three several times that he loved him and, in the end, that he loved him more than his fellow apostles, as likewise in his being each time charged to feed Christ's lambs and, at length, to feed his sheep also {John 21:17}. What else is here signified but that this apostle was to act the part of a shepherd not only with respect to the flock in general but also with respect to the pastors themselves? The same is plainly signified by our Lord's prayer for the faith of this apostle in particular, and the charge which he subsequently gave him: "Simon, Simon, behold Satan has desired to have you, that he may sift you, as wheat: but I have prayed for thee, that thy faith fail not; and thou, being once converted, confirm thy brethren" (Luke 22:31-32). Is there no mysterious meaning in the circumstance, marked by the evangelist, of Christ's "entering into Simon's ship" in preference to that of James and John, in order to "teach the people out of it," and in the subsequent miraculous "draught of fishes," together with our Lord's prophetic declaration to Simon: "Fear not, from henceforth thou shall catch men?" (Luke 5:3, 10). But the strongest proof of St. Peter's superior dignity and jurisdiction consists in the explicit and

---

7   [Ed. Milner draws this inexact quote—which substitutes "pope" for "prince"—from Joseph Addison's *Remarks on Italy*, 2nd ed. (London, 1718), 137.]

8   [Ed. The French polymath, Isaac Casaubon (1559–1614).]

9   [Ed. Jacques-Bénigne Bossuet (1627–1704) was a French bishop, orator, and leading theologian whose writings on papal restraint are often regarded as a high point in French Gallicanism.]

energetical declaration of our Savior to him, in the quarters of Caesarea Philippi, upon his making that glorious confession of our Lord's divinity: "Thou art Christ, the Son of the living God" [Matt 16:16]. Our Lord had mysteriously changed his name at his first interview with him, when Jesus, looking upon him, said, "Thou art Simon, the son of Jona: thou shall be called Cephas, which is interpreted, Peter" (John 1:42); and on the present occasion he explains the mystery, where he says, "Blessed art thou, Simon Bar Jona, because flesh and blood hath not revealed it to thee, but my Father, who is in heaven. And I say to thee, that thou art Peter (a rock), and *upon this rock I will build my church*, and the gates of hell shall not prevail against it; and I will give to thee the keys of the kingdom of heaven, and whatsoever thou shall bind on earth shall be bound in heaven; and whatsoever thou shalt loose on earth, shall be loosed also in heaven" (Matt 16:17-19). Where now, I ask, is the sincere Christian, and especially the Christian who professes to make Scripture the sole rule of his faith, who, with these passages of the inspired text before his eyes, will venture, at the risk of his soul, to deny that any special dignity or charge was conferred upon St. Peter in preference to the other apostles? I trust no such Christian is to be found in your society. Now, as it is a point agreed upon, at least in your church and mine, that bishops, in general, succeed to the rank and functions of the apostles; so, by the same rule, the successor of Saint Peter in the See of Rome succeeds to his primacy and jurisdiction. This cannot be questioned by any serious Christian who reflects that when our Savior gave his orders about "feeding his flock," and made his declaration about building his church, he was not establishing an order of things to last during the few years that St. Peter had to live, but one that was to last as long as he should have a flock and a church on earth—that is, to the end of time—conformably with his promise to the apostles and their successors in the concluding words of St. Matthew: "Behold I am with you always, even to the end of the world" (Matt 28:20).

TEXT: John Milner, *The end of religious controversy, in a friendly correspondence between a religious society of Protestants and a Roman Catholic divine* (Derby: Richardson and Son, 1842), 266–67, 434–40.

JOSEPH BLANCO WHITE
(1775–1841)
Catholic Tyranny

Tales of Roman Catholic atrocities, plots, and perversions, the vast majority of which proved fabricated, had been a staple of Protestant polemic since the beginning of the Reformation. When Joseph Blanco White, a former Spanish priest, published on the dangers of Catholicism, however, the warning was suddenly less implausible. Unlike old tales of Catholic conspiracies, White's writings commanded the attention of a nation facing the very real possibility of Catholic emancipation.

White was born José María Blanco y Crespo in Seville, Spain. His grandfather emigrated from Waterford, Ireland, in the early 1700s to form an import-export company in Seville. White's father gave his son a Spanish name, though he had him work among Irish clerks in the family business as a young man. White's fondness for literature and a desire to please his mother, María Gertrudis Crespo y Neve (niece of the founder of Los Angeles), led him to pursue the priesthood. He studied at the Dominican college of Santo Thomás from 1789 and matriculated at the University of Seville in 1790. By the turn of the century, White was an ordained priest and part of a community devoted to poetry, rhetoric, and Christian humanism. Soon, however, White faced unsettling doubts about his faith and the leadership of the church he served. He moved to Madrid in 1805, abandoned the priesthood, and fell in love with Magdalena Ezquaya, who eventually bore him a son. Meanwhile, political turmoil in the nation led White down an increasingly radical path. In 1810 he escaped to England. For the first several years, White worked as editor of a political journal he founded: *El español* (1810–1814). White's revolutionary articles left many of his former associates bewildered, but the journal was highly successful and widely reprinted in Spanish America. The influence of evangelical friends encouraged White to join the Church of England in 1812. Two years later, the bishop of London revalidated his orders, and he proceeded to Oxford for service as an Anglican minister. His writings in the 1820s—highly political and tied to controversies abroad—linked corruption and the practice of slavery overseas to the moral turpitude of the Catholic priesthood. In addition to ongoing work as editor of a Spanish-language magazine (*Variedades*) and author of books related to Spain, White wrote articles for the *New Monthly Magazine* and J. S. Mill's *London Review*. White's anti-Catholic writings earned him an M.A. at Oxford and honorary membership at Oriel College, where he associated with leading churchmen, including Thomas Arnold (see selection in this part), Richard Whately (see selection in Part IV), and John Henry Newman. In subsequent years, White moved briefly to Dublin with Whately, now bishop of Dublin, and continued to publish works including *Second travels of an Irish gentleman in search of a religion* (1833). In time, White's inquiring spirit led him to break with the Church of England. He continued to publish (for example, *Observations on heresy and orthodoxy* in 1835), but in the final years of his life he moved to Liverpool and embraced Unitarianism.

White believed that his experiences in Spain could shape the national conversation and forewarn of impending dangers in England. To this end—and with the encouragement of Robert Southey—White first published *Practical and internal evidences against Catholicism* (1825), followed by a simplified version, *The poor man's preservative against popery* (1825). In the following selection from the latter, White repeats many of the commonplace charges against Roman Catholics. What distinguishes his work, however, is that White writes as one familiar with Catholicism as it existed in a Catholic nation.

SOURCES: Martin Murphy, *Blanco White: self-banished Spaniard* (New Haven: Yale University Press, 1989); *OCEL*; *ODCC*; *ODNB*.

JOSEPH BLANCO WHITE
The poor man's preservative against popery
1825

A[uthor]. What would you think of a power, or authority, that would force you to act like a hypocrite?

R[eader]. I should think that it was no better than the government of the Turks, which, as I hear, treats men like beasts.

A. Well, now you will be able to understand what I meant by *religious tyranny*. The popes of Rome believe that they have a right to oblige all men who have been baptized, but more especially those who have been baptized by their priests, to continue Roman Catholics to their lives' end. Whenever anyone living under their authority has ventured to deny any of the doctrines which the Church of Rome believes, they have shut them up in prisons, tormented them upon the rack, and, if they would not recant and unsay what they had given out as their real persuasion, the poor wretches have been burnt as heretics. The kings of Spain, being Catholics upon these matters, acted according to the will of the pope; and, in order to prevent every Spaniard from being anything, at least in appearance, but a Papist, had established a court called the *Inquisition*, where a certain number of priests tried, in secret, such people as were accused of having openly denied any of the articles of the Roman Catholic faith. Whenever, moved by fear of the consequences, the prisoner chose to eat up his own words and declare that he was wrong, the priests sent him to do penance for a certain time or laid a heavy fine upon him; but, if the accused had courage to persist in his own opinion, then the priests declared that he was a heretic and gave him up to the public executioner to be burnt alive.[1]

R. Good heaven! You quite astonish me. Have you ever seen such doings, sir?

A. I well remember the last that was burnt for being a heretic in my own town, which is called Seville. It was a poor blind woman. I was then about eight years

---

[1] [Ed. The Spanish Inquisition, which was not abolished until 1834, conducted its last execution in 1826.]

old, and saw the pile of wood, upon barrels of pitch and tar, where she was reduced to ashes.

R. But are there many who venture their lives for the sake of what they believe to be the true gospel?

A. Alas! There was a time when many hundreds of men and women sacrificed themselves for the love of the Protestant religion which is professed in England. But the horrible cruelties which were practiced upon them disheartened all those who were disposed to throw off the yoke of the pope, and now people disguise their religious opinions in order to avoid the most horrible persecution.

R. And you, sir, of course, were obliged to disguise your own persuasion, in order not to lose your liberty and your life.

A. Just so. I lived ten years in the most wretched and distressed state of mind. Nothing was wanting to my being happy but the liberty of declaring my opinions; but that is impossible for a Roman Catholic who lives under the laws which the popes have induced most of the Roman Catholic princes to establish in their kingdoms. I could not say, as a Roman Catholic may under the government of Great Britain and Ireland, "I will no longer be a spiritual subject of the pope; I will worship God as my conscience tells me I should, and according to what I find in the Bible." No. Had I said so, or even much less— had any words escaped me in conversation, from which it might be suspected that I did not believe exactly what the pope commands—I should have been taken out of my bed in the middle of the night and carried to one of the prisons of the Inquisition. Often, indeed, very often have I passed a restless night under the apprehension that, in consequence of some unguarded words, my house would be assailed by the ministers of the Inquisition and I hurried away in the black carriage which they used for carrying dissenters to their dungeons. Happy indeed are the people of these kingdoms, where every man's house is his castle; and where, provided he has not committed some real crime, he may sleep under the protection of a mere latch to his door, as if he dwelt in a walled and moated fortress! No such feeling of safety can be enjoyed where the tyranny of popery prevails. A Roman Catholic *who is not protected by Protestant laws* is all over the world a slave, who cannot utter a word against the opinions of his church but at his peril. "The very walls have ears" is a common saying in my country. A man is indeed beset with spies; for the Church of Rome has contrived to employ everyone as such against his nearest and dearest relations. Every year there is publicly read at church, a proclamation, or (as they call it) a *bull* from the pope, commanding parents to accuse their children, children their parents, husbands their wives, and wives their husbands, of any words or actions against the Roman Catholic religion. They are told that whoever disobeys this command not only incurs damnation for his own soul, but is the cause of the same to those whom he wishes to spare. So that many have had for their accusers their fathers and mothers, without knowing to whom they owed their sufferings under the Inquisitors; for the name of the informer is kept a most profound secret, and the accused is tried without ever seeing the witnesses against him.

R. I am perfectly astonished at the things you say, sir; and did I not perceive by your manners that you are a gentleman, I should certainly suspect that you were trying to trepan[2] us poor unlearned people.

A. I neither wonder nor am offended at your suspicion. All I can say to remove it is that I am well known in London, that for the truth of everything you have already heard and will hear from me I am ready to be examined *upon oath*, and that there are many hundreds of Spaniards at this moment in England who will attest every word of mine about the Inquisition of the pope in Spain. I say the Inquisition of the pope because that horrible *court of injustice* was established, kept up, and managed by and under the pope's authority. And now I must add one word as to the effects of the pope's contrivance to make spies of the nearest relations, against those who might not believe every tittle of the Roman Catholic religion. I have told you that my parents were good and kind. My mother was a lady whom all the poor of the neighborhood loved for her goodness and charity; and indeed I often saw her denying herself even the common comforts of life that she might have the more to give away. I was her favorite child, being the eldest; and it is impossible for a mother to love with more ardent affection than that she showed towards me. Well, as I could not entirely conceal my own mind in regard to popery, she began to suspect that I was not a true Roman Catholic in my heart. Now, she knew that the pope had made it her duty to turn informer even against her own child in such cases; and dreading that the day might come when some words should drop from me against the Roman Catholic religion, which it would be her duty to carry to the judges, she used to avoid my company and shut herself up to weep for me. I could not, at first, make out why my dear mother shunned my company, and was cut to the heart by her apparent unkindness. I might to this day have believed that I had lost her affection, but that an intimate friend of hers put me in possession of the whole thing.

R. Upon my word, sir, you give me such horror of Roman Catholics that I shall in [the] future look with suspicion on some neighbors of mine of that persuasion.

A. God forbid that such should be the consequence of my communication with you. The Roman Catholic religion in itself, and such as the pope would make it all over the world if there were no Protestant laws to resist it, is the most horrible system of tyranny that ever opposed the welfare of man. But most of the Roman Catholics in these kingdoms are not aware of the evils which their religion is likely to produce. They have grown up under the influence of a constitution which owes its full freedom to Protestantism; and many of them are Protestants in feelings, whom their priests, I am sure, must lead with a very light rein-hand for fear of their running away. There is, indeed, no reason for either fear or suspicions with regard to the Roman Catholics of these kingdoms, as long as both the government and Parliament remain purely Protestant; but I would not answer for the consequences if the pope, through his priests, could obtain an underhand influence in either.

---

2   [Ed. That is, "entrap."]

R. But, sir, I want to know the rest of your own story, and how, though obliged to appear outwardly a Roman Catholic, you settled within yourself what you were to believe.

A. I will not delay to satisfy your curiosity, though that part of my story is the most painful to me. At all events you will be sure, when you hear it, that I am telling the truth, the whole truth, and nothing but the truth, since I do not spare myself. You must know, then, that from the moment I believed that the Roman Catholic religion was false, I had no religion at all and lived without God in the world [Eph 2:12].

‡

[A.] I will proceed with the account of myself. When I had in my own mind thrown off all allegiance to the Christian religion, though I tried to enjoy myself and indulge my desires, I could find neither happiness nor comfort. My mind was naturally averse to deceit, and I could not brook the necessity of acting publicly as the minister of a religion which I believed to be false. But what could I do? . . . Ten years of my life did I pass in this hot and cold fever, this ague of the heart, without a hope, without a drop of that cordial which cheers the very soul of those who sacrifice their desires to their duty under the blessed influence of religion. At last it pleased God to afford me a means of escaping from the tyranny of the pope and make me willingly and joyfully submit to the easy yoke of his blessed son Jesus Christ. The ways of providence for my change appear so wonderful to me that I feel almost overcome when I earnestly think upon them. In the first place, it was certain that I could not leave Spain for a Protestant country without giving a deathblow to my parents. Could any human being have foreseen in the year 1807 that in 1810 my own father and mother would urge me to leave my country for England? And yet, so it came to pass. You have heard how Bonaparte entered Spain with the design of placing his brother Joseph upon the throne of that country; how for a time he seemed to have obtained his wishes, when his armies advanced till they came within view of Cadiz, and threatened to extinguish the last hope of the Spaniards. I was at that time at Seville, my native town; and as the French troops approached it, all those who would not submit to their government, and had the means of removing to another place, tried to be beforehand with them by taking their flight to Cadiz. My parents could not abandon their home; but as they abhorred the French troops and hated the injustice of their invasion, they were anxious that I should quit the town. Here I saw the most favorable opening for executing my long delayed plan for escaping the religious tyranny under which I groaned, and pretending that I did not feel secure at Cadiz, prepared in four days to leave my country for England. I knew it was forever; and my heart bleeds at the recollection of the last view I took of my father and mother. A few weeks after I found myself on these shores.

‡

[A.] I found England as hospitable and generous as it had always been described to me. But one thing I found in it which I never expected—that was true and sincere religion. I have told you that in popish countries people are made to believe that whoever is not a Roman Catholic is only a Christian in name. I therefore supposed that in this Protestant country, though men appeared externally to have a religion, few or none would care anything about it. Now observe the merciful dispensations of providence with regard to me. Had I upon my first arrival fallen in with some of your infidels, I should have been confirmed in all my errors. But it pleased God so to direct events as to make me very soon acquainted with one of the most excellent and religious families in London. I had, in my former blindness and ignorance, believed that since in Spain, which is the most thoroughly Roman Catholic country in the world, the morals in general are very loose, a nation of Christians only in name (for such was my mistaken opinion of you) would be infinitely more addicted to vicious courses. But, when I began to look about me and observed the modesty of the ladies, the quiet and orderly lives of the greatest part of the gentry, and compared their decent conversation with the profane talk which is tolerated in my country, I perceived at once that my head was full of absurd notions and prepared myself to root out from it whatever I should find to be wrong. In this state of mind I went one Sunday to church, out of mere curiosity, for my thoughts were at that time very far from God and his worship. The unmeaning ceremonies of the Roman Catholics had made me sick of churches and church service. But when, in the course of the prayers, I perceived the beautiful simplicity and the warm heartiness, if I may say so, of your Prayer Book, my heart, which for ten years had appeared quite dead to all religious feelings, could not but show a disposition to revive, like the leafless trees when breathed upon by the first soft breezes of Spring. God had prevented its becoming a dead trunk: it gave indeed no signs of life, but the sap was stirring up from the root. This was easily perceived in the effect which the singing of a hymn had upon me that morning. It begins,

> When all thy mercies, O my God,
>   My rising soul surveys,
> Transported with the view I'm lost
>   In wonder, love, and praise.[3]

The sentiments expressed in this beautiful hymn penetrated my soul like the first rain which falls upon a thirsty land. My long impious disregard of God, the Father and supporter of my life and being, made me blush and feel ashamed of myself, and a strong sense of the irrational ungratefulness in which I had so long lived forced a profusion of tears from my eyes. I left the church a very different man from what I was when I entered it; but still, very far from being a true believer in Christ. Yet, from that day I began to put up a very short prayer every morning, asking for light and protection from my Creator, and thanking him

---

[3]   [Ed. Joseph Addison, "When all thy mercies, O my God" (1712).]

for his goodness. It happened about that time that some books concerning the truth of religion—a kind of works in which this country excels all others—fell in my way. I thought it fair to examine the matter again, though I imagined that no man could ever answer the arguments against it, which had become quite familiar to my mind. As I grew less and less prejudiced against the truth of divine revelation, I prayed more earnestly for assistance in the important examination in which I was engaged. I then began a careful perusal of the Scriptures, and it pleased God, at the end of two years, to remove my blindness, so far as to enable me with humble sincerity to receive the sacrament[4] according to the manner of the Church of England; which appeared to me in the course of my enquiries to be, of all human establishments, the most suited in her discipline to promote the ends of the gospel, and in her doctrines, as pure and orthodox as those which were founded by the apostles themselves. It is to me a matter of great comfort that I have now lived a much longer period in the acknowledgment of the truth of Christianity, than I spent in my former unbelief.

TEXT: Joseph Blanco White, *The poor man's preservative against popery: addressed to the lower classes of Great Britain and Ireland* (London: C. and J. Rivington, 1825), 4–9, 11–16.

---

4   [Ed. The Eucharist or the Lord's Supper.]

WILLIAM POYNTER
(1762–1827)
Christian Obedience

Those struggling for Roman Catholic emancipation in Britain can be divided into two ideological categories. Many lay Catholics, represented by writers such as Charles Butler, hoped to achieve greater freedom through small political compromises that linked the Catholic cause to that of Protestant dissenters. Many ordained Catholics, such as John Milner, vicar apostolic (ecclesiastic responsible for the pastoral care of a missionary region) of the Midlands, vigorously pursued emancipation without allowing for even a hint of conciliation to Protestantism. William Poynter, vicar apostolic of the London district, held the two in fragile unity. Poynter was born at Petersfield, Hampshire and studied at the English College at Douai (1775). He developed a love of scholastic theology, knowledge of several languages, and interpersonal skills that would prove essential to his work in England. Shortly after his ordination in 1786, Poynter was named prefect of the English College. When this was suppressed during the French Revolution, Poynter and others were initially confined to prison but allowed to return to England in 1795. There Poynter steadily ascended the ranks of the English Catholic hierarchy. He served as vice president (1795–1801) and president (1801–1813) of St. Edmund's College in Hertfordshire—the first Roman Catholic seminary in England—founded to replace the Douai. In 1803 Poynter was named coadjutor to the vicar apostolic of the London district, John Douglass, whom he succeeded in 1812. As bishop, Poynter's diplomacy and leadership were evident: he countered Milner's aggressive attacks on other Catholic leaders, gave numerous addresses to the English laity, and wrote a preface to a Catholic Bible Society edition of the New Testament (Milner opposed the publication).

Poynter was the guiding spirit behind one of the most important Roman Catholic documents in the nineteenth century: *Declaration of the Catholic bishops, the vicars apostolic and their coadjutors in Great Britain* (1826). Although the work represented all the vicars apostolic—ten bishops signed the *Declaration* in all—Poynter's leadership is evident. The document takes up the major areas of division between Catholics and Protestants in England, including the authority of the Bible (section three), the veneration of saints (section four), and the power to grant indulgences (section six), in order to defend Roman Catholics before the English people: "by publishing at the present time a plain and correct declaration of our real tenets on those points which are still so much misrepresented or misconceived—a better understanding may be established among his Majesty's subjects" (5). The following selections, which draw particular attention to matters of temporal and spiritual authority, reveals Poynter's firm and charitable approach to easing tensions in England.

SOURCES: *NCE*; *ODNB*; Bernard N. Ward, *The eve of Catholic emancipation, being the history of the English Catholics during the first thirty years of the nineteenth century* (London: Longmans, Green, and Co., 1911–1912).

WILLIAM POYNTER
Declaration of the Catholic bishops
1826

Preamble

When we consider the misrepresentations of the Catholic religion which are so industriously and widely propagated in this country, we are filled with astonishment. But our astonishment subsides when we call to mind that the character of Christ himself was misrepresented—he was charged with blasphemy, with breaking the Sabbath, and with forbidding tribute to be paid to Caesar {Matt 26:65; Mark 3:22; John 9:16; Luke 23:2}—that the apostles and disciples of Christ were misrepresented—they were charged with speaking blasphemous words against Moses and against God, with exciting sedition, and with many other grievous offenses entirely devoid of proof {Acts 6:11; 24:5; 25:7}—and that misrepresentation was the general lot of Christians in the first ages of the church. The primitive Christians were first calumniated and held up to public contempt, and then persecuted and deprived, not only of their civil rights and privileges, but of their property, and even of their very lives. They were charged with idolatry, with horrid cruelties and other flagitious crimes, even in their religious worship. In a word, their whole religion was described as a system of folly and superstition, grounded on no one rational principle. . . .

The Catholics of Great Britain have to lament and to complain that the doctrines and religious rites which, as Catholics, they are taught by their church to believe and observe, have been long grossly misconceived and misrepresented in this country, to the great injury of their religious character and temporal interests.

They are persuaded that many who are opposed to them on account of their religion suppose, without inquiry, that the Catholic Church really teaches all that she is reported by her adversaries to teach; and imagine that she is responsible for every absurd opinion entertained, and for every act of superstition performed, by every individual who bears the name of Catholic.

We hope that all who are animated with a love of truth and with sentiments of Christian charity will be disposed willingly to listen to the sincere declarations of their Catholic fellow countrymen, and will never impute to their religion principles or practices which,

406

as Catholics, they do not hold or observe and which their church condemns as errors or abuses.

In this hope and persuasion, the British Catholics have made repeated declarations of their religious doctrines and have shown, they trust to the satisfaction of all who have paid attention to them, that they hold no religious principles, and entertain no opinions flowing from those principles, that are not perfectly consistent with the sacred duties which, as Christians, they owe to Almighty God; with all the civil duties which, as subjects, they owe to their sovereign and the constituted civil government of their country; and with all the social duties which, as citizens, they owe to their fellow subjects, whatever may be their religious creed.

They had flattered themselves that the numerous and uniform expositions of their religious doctrines, given in public professions of the Catholic faith, in Catholic catechisms, in various authentic documents, and in declarations confirmed by their solemn oaths, would have abundantly sufficed to correct all misrepresentations of their real tenets.

But they have to regret that some grievous misconceptions regarding certain points of Catholic doctrine are, unhappily, still found to exist in the minds of many whose good opinion they value and whose good will they wish to conciliate. To their grief they hear that, notwithstanding all their declarations to the contrary, they are still exhibited to the public as men holding the most erroneous, unscriptural, and unreasonable doctrines: grounding their faith on human authority and not on the Word of God; as enemies to the circulation and to the reading of the Holy Scriptures; as guilty of idolatry in the sacrifice of the mass, in the adoration (as it is called) of the Virgin Mary, and in the worship of the saints, and of the images of Christ and of the saints; and as guilty of superstition in invoking the saints and in praying for the souls in purgatory; as usurping a divine power of forgiving sins, and imposing the yoke of confession on the people; as giving leave to commit sin by indulgences; as despising the obligation of an oath; as dividing their allegiance between their king and the pope; as claiming the property of the church establishment; as holding the uncharitable doctrine of exclusive salvation; and as maintaining that faith is not to be kept with heretics.

We are at a loss to conceive why the holding of certain religious doctrines—which have no connection with civil or social duties (whether those doctrines are taken in the sense in which they are misconstrued by others, or in the sense in which they are uniformly understood by Catholics)—should be made a subject of crimination against British Catholics by those who assume to themselves liberty of thinking what they please in matters of religious belief. It is difficult to understand why doctrines purely religious, in no wise affecting the duties which Catholics owe to their sovereign or to civil society, should be brought forward at all, when the question relates only to the civil rights and privileges which they claim as British subjects. It is much to be wished that those who declaim against what they call the errors and superstitions of popery would first learn from Catholics themselves, by inquiry, what their real doctrines are on the points above alluded to and in what sense Catholics understand the terms by which their doctrines are expressed. They would perhaps find that they have been hitherto contending not against the Catholic faith, but against the fictions of their own imaginations or against their own misconstructions of the language of the Catholic Church.

Section VII
On the obligation of an oath

Catholics are charged with holding that they are not bound by any oath and that the pope can dispense them from all the oaths they may have taken.

We cannot sufficiently express our astonishment at such a charge. We hold that the obligation of an oath is most sacred: for by an oath, man calls the almighty searcher of hearts to witness the sincerity of his conviction of the truth of what he asserts and his fidelity in performing the engagement he makes. Hence, whosoever swears falsely or violates the lawful engagement he has confirmed by an oath, not only offends against truth or justice, but against religion. He is guilty of the enormous crime of perjury.

No power in any pope or council, or in any individual or body of men invested with authority in the Catholic Church, can make it lawful for a Catholic to confirm any falsehood by an oath or dispense with any oath by which a Catholic has confirmed his duty of allegiance to his sovereign, or any obligation of duty or justice to a third person. He who takes an oath is bound to observe it in the obvious meaning of the words or in the known meaning of the person to whom it is sworn.

Section VIII
On allegiance to our sovereign and obedience to the pope

Catholics are charged with dividing their allegiance between their temporal sovereign and the pope.

Allegiance relates not to spiritual but to civil duties; to those temporal tributes and obligations which the subject owes to the person of his sovereign and to the authority of the state.

By the term *spiritual*, we here mean that which in its nature tends directly to a supernatural end or is ordained to produce a supernatural effect. Thus the office of teaching the doctrines of faith, the administration of the sacraments, the conferring and exercising of jurisdiction purely ecclesiastical are spiritual matters.

By the term *temporal*, we mean that which in its nature tends directly to the end of civil society. Thus the right of making laws for the civil government of the state, the administration of civil justice, the appointment of civil magistrates and military officers are temporal matters.

The allegiance which Catholics hold to be due and are bound to pay to their sovereign, and to the civil authority of the state, is perfect and undivided. They do not divide their allegiance between their sovereign and any other power on earth, whether temporal or ecclesiastical. They acknowledge in the sovereign and, in the constituted government of these realms, a supreme civil and temporal authority which is entirely distinct from, and totally independent of, the spiritual and ecclesiastical authority of the pope and of the Catholic Church. They declare that neither the pope nor any other prelate or ecclesiastical person of the Roman Catholic Church has, in virtue of his spiritual or ecclesiastical character, any right, directly or indirectly, to any civil or temporal jurisdiction, power, superiority, preeminence, or authority within this realm; nor has any right to interfere, directly or indirectly, in the civil government of the United Kingdom, or any part thereof; nor to oppose, in any manner, the performance of the civil duties which are due to his Majesty, his heirs and successors, from all or any of his Majesty's subjects; nor to enforce the performance of any spiritual or ecclesiastical duty, by any civil or temporal means. They hold themselves bound in conscience to obey the civil government of this realm in all things of a temporal and civil nature, notwithstanding any dispensation or order to the contrary had, or to be had, from the pope or any authority of the Church of Rome.

Hence we declare that by rendering obedience in *spiritual* matters to the pope, Catholics do not withhold any portion of their allegiance to their king and that their allegiance is entire and undivided; the *civil* power of the state and the *spiritual* authority of the Catholic Church being absolutely distinct and being never intended by their divine Author to interfere or clash with each other.

"Render unto Caesar the things that are Caesar's, and to God the things that are God's" [Matt 22:21].

‡

Section X
On the doctrine of exclusive salvation

Catholics are charged with uncharitableness in holding the doctrine of exclusive salvation.

Catholics are taught by their church to love all men without exception: to wish that all may be saved, and to pray that all may be saved and may come to the knowledge of the truth by which they may be saved.

If the Almighty himself has assigned certain conditions, without the observance of which man cannot be saved, it would seem to be an act of impiety to attempt to annul those divinely established conditions; and an act of great uncharitableness towards a fellow man to tell him that he may be saved without complying with the conditions prescribed by the Almighty.

The doctrinal principle of exclusive salvation belongs to the law of Christ.

Has not Christ, who commands the belief of his revealed doctrines, pronounced that he that "believeth not shall be condemned" (Mark 16:16)? Has not Christ, who instituted baptism for the remission of sins, declared that "except a man be born again of water and of the Holy Ghost, he *cannot* enter into the kingdom of God" (John 3:5)? Has not St. Paul enumerated a list of crimes, such as adultery, idolatry, hatred, seditions, heresies, murders, drunkenness, etc., of which he declares that "they who do such things shall not obtain the kingdom of God" (Gal 5:21)? Are not these exclusive conditions?

Whoever professes the law of Christ must profess the *principle* and doctrine of exclusive salvation. It is not the Catholic—it is God himself who will exclude from heaven those who are not duly qualified for it by faith and good works.

But the Catholic, whilst he is bound to admit and with firm faith to believe this doctrinal *principle*, is bound also by the divine commandment not to judge. He is not allowed therefore to pronounce sentence of condemnation on individuals who may live and die out of the external communion of the Catholic Church, nor to pronounce sentence of condemnation against those who may die in an apparent state of sin. All those he leaves to the righteous judgment of the great searcher of hearts, who at the last day will render to every man according to his works.

But surely charity as well as truth must forbid one Christian to deceive another in a matter of such infinite importance as the eternal salvation of his soul. He who should persuade his neighbor that no condition for salvation is required on the part of man would deceive him. He who admits that any one such condition is required by the Almighty admits the *principle* of exclusive salvation.

‡

Conclusion

Having, in the foregoing declaration, endeavored to state in the simplicity of truth such doctrines of our church as are most frequently misrepresented or misunderstood in this country, and to explain the meaning in which Catholics understand the terms by which these doctrines are expressed in the language of their church, we confidently trust that this declaration and explanation will be received by all our fellow subjects in a spirit of candor and charity, and that those who have been hitherto ignorant of or but imperfectly acquainted with our doctrines of faith will do us the justice to acknowledge that, as Catholics, we hold no religious principles, and entertain no opinions flowing from those principles, which are not perfectly consistent with our duties as Christians and as British subjects.

TEXT: *Declaration of the Catholic bishops, the vicars apostolic and their coadjutors in Great Britain* (London: Keating and Brown, 1826), 3–5, 13–16.

THOMAS HARTWELL HORNE
(1780–1862)
Rome

The long and strained history of Protestant-Catholic relations in Britain made the years leading up to Roman Catholic emancipation especially difficult. Few knew that contentious history as well as Charles Butler (see the previous selection in this part), English barrister and Roman Catholic historian, whose four-volume *Historical memoirs respecting the English, Irish, and Scottish Catholics from the Reformation to the present time* (1819–1821) provided the standard compendium of the period. One of Butler's research assistants, a devout Protestant named Thomas Hartwell Horne, used his knowledge of that same troubled history to dissuade public acceptance of Catholicism.

Horne was born in London and educated at Christ's Hospital as a classmate of S. T. Coleridge. The death of both parents left Horne unable to afford university, so he worked as a barrister's clerk, taking up literary projects to earn extra money on the side. Horne began working on his first book, *A brief view of the necessity and truth of the Christian revelation* (1800), when still a teenager. Not long after its publication, Horne joined the Wesleyan Methodists. A superb researcher and bibliographer, Horne assisted a wide array of writers on their projects. He also wrote an *Introduction to the study of bibliography* (2 vols., 1814) and began cataloguing the Harleian manuscripts in the British Library. During the same years, Horne was preparing to write a complete study of the Bible. This proved to be his lasting achievement. He completed bibliographical research between 1801 and 1812; for five more years, Horne devoted himself to writing. The final work, *An introduction to the critical study and knowledge of the Holy Scriptures* (3 vols., 1818; vol. 4, 1821), which showed awareness of German criticism yet upheld traditional Christian teaching, went through numerous editions and remained standard reading in English universities for several decades. Horne received an honorary M.A. from King's College. Having joined the Church of England, Horne was ordained by the bishop of London and named curate of Christ Church Greyfriars in 1819. He went on to serve as a rector and became a prebendary to St. Paul's in 1831. In his final years, he worked in the British Museum as senior assistant librarian in the department of printed books.

Like many theologians of the day, Horne engaged in controversy. He wrote against skepticism in *Deism refuted* (1819) and commended Nicene orthodoxy in *The Scripture doctrine of the Trinity briefly stated and defended* (1820). In *Romanism contradictory to the Bible* (1827), a work that first appeared in the *Christian Remembrancer*, Horne challenged the legitimacy of Catholic doctrine and practice. His command of the Bible and Christian history combined with a biting rhetoric to articulate deep-rooted Protestant objections to Roman Catholicism. His ominous recommendation in the final sentence of the following selection ("from such withdraw thyself") is a stark reminder of the lasting social and political consequences of the Reformation.

>⌒⌒<

Sources: *ODCC*; *ODNB*.

THOMAS HARTWELL HORNE
Romanism contradictory to the Bible
1827

Jesus Christ prohibited all disputes concerning rank and preeminency in his kingdom. "Ye know," he said, "that the princes of the Gentiles exercise dominion over them; and they that are great exercise authority upon them. But *it shall not* be so among you. But, whosoever will be great among you, let him be your minister; and whosoever will be chief among you, let him be your servant; even as the Son of Man came not to be ministered unto but to minister and to give his life a ransom for many" (Matt 20:25-28). St. Paul, addressing the Ephesians, says, "Ye are built upon the foundation of the *apostles and prophets*, Jesus Christ himself being the chief cornerstone" (Eph 2:20). It will be observed that the apostles and prophets are here put in the same rank, and are *all* equally called foundations. To Jesus Christ alone belongs the preeminence.

But the Church of Rome claims to be the supreme mistress of all churches and arrogates to the popes a primacy of dominion. "I acknowledge the Holy Catholic Apostolic Roman Church to be the mother and mistress of all churches; and I promise to swear true obedience to the pope of Rome, who is the successor of St. Peter, the prince of the apostles, and vicar of Jesus Christ."[1]

The Romish church is *not* the mother and mistress of all churches. *The* mother church was the church at Jerusalem, which was formed immediately after the ascension of Christ; next was formed the church at Samaria (Acts 8; A.D. 34); and, then, the churches in Cyprus and Phoenice and at Antioch by those Christians who were dispersed in consequence of the persecution that arose about Stephen (Acts 11:19-21). There is no evidence whatever that the church at Rome was founded by Peter, as the Romanists affirm, or by the joint labors of Peter and Paul. In the first council held at Nicaea, all other Christian churches were on an equality with that at Rome.[2] And in the fourth general council

---

[1]   [Ed. Horne cites the Creed of Pius IV, art. 23, but later readers would associate such authoritative language with the declarations of papal infallibility at Vatican Council I (1869–1870).]

[2]   [Ed. Horne rejects the controversial claim that the First Council of Nicaea (325) gave precedence to Rome above all other sees.]

(that convened at Chalcedon), it was declared that the church at Constantinople should have equal honors with that at Rome because the seat of imperial government was there.[3] Catholic, that is, universal, the Romish church *never was, nor is*; for ecclesiastical history attests that both the Asiatic and African churches formerly rejected her authority, and also that the Eastern churches to this day despise her pride and affectation of supremacy; and a simple inspection of the map of the globe will prove that the Romish Church is by no means universal. Over the united Church of England and Ireland, Rome can have no authority, for the churches of England and of Ireland were *more ancient* than the pope's supremacy. They were free churches from the first planting of Christianity among the ancient Britons and Irish; and whatever oppressions those churches suffered from papal intrusions, fraud, and violence, their natural freedom remained unaltered, and that freedom is justly maintained. The fiction of papal supremacy is unsupported by Scripture and is a novelty of the seventh century.

‡

Such are the dogmas of the Church of Rome, and such has been her practice for many centuries. Individuals of high character belonging to her communion (the sincerity of whose protestations cannot be doubted) have disclaimed them, but they remain unrescinded by the united church and court of modern Rome. These doctrines (the contrariety of which to Scripture, reason, and, in many instances, to morality cannot but have powerfully struck the reader's mind) have been promulgated by popes, councils, and canonists. They must be rescinded by the same authorities before Protestants can consent to give up those securities upon which their civil and religious liberties depend. Have we any concern for pure and undefiled religion, for the liberties of our country, and for the welfare of our children and posterity? Let us then "stand fast in the liberty wherewith Christ has made us free" [Gal. 5:1]; and "let the word of Christ" (and not human traditions) "dwell in us richly in all wisdom" (Col 3:16); "for other foundation can no man lay than that is laid, which is Jesus Christ" (1 Cor 3:11). We "have renounced the hidden things of dishonesty, not walking in craftiness, nor handling the Word of God deceitfully, but by manifestation of the truth, commending ourselves to every man's conscience in the sight of God."[4] "If any man teach otherwise and consent not to wholesome words, even the words of our Lord Jesus Christ and to the doctrine which is according to godliness, *from such withdraw thyself*" (1 Tim 6:3, 5).

TEXT: Thomas Hartwell Horne, *Romanism contradictory to the Bible; or, The peculiar tenets of the Church of Rome, as exhibited in her accredited formularies, contrasted with the Holy Scriptures*, new ed. (London: T. Cadell, 1827), 17–18, 45.

[3]   [Ed. By the time of the fourth ecumenical Council of Chalcedon (451), Constantinople had wide support in the East as a central seat of both political and ecclesial authority.]

[4]   [Ed. The original text incorrectly cites Col 1:28 rather than 2 Cor 4:2.]

THOMAS ARNOLD
(1795–1842)
Irish Catholicism

The events of the French Revolution and widespread fears that Roman Catholics owed their deepest allegiance to the papacy (a foreign power) left English Catholics in a position of political vulnerability. As a result, any proposals for emancipation required corresponding pledges and safeguards, namely, promises not to undermine either the Church of England or the government. Much of the struggle focused on those living in Ireland, where the emancipation of the Roman Catholic majority would inevitably lead to significant political gains and the formation of a strong Irish Catholic party in Parliament. Some responded to these contentious political issues in a new spirit of tolerance, laying the intellectual foundation for what W. J. Conybeare would later call the English broad church movement.

Thomas Arnold, a leading voice in the burgeoning movement, shaped key religious and political conversations in the 1820s and 1830s. Born on the Isle of Wight, where Arnold's father was postmaster, Arnold was sent to Warminster School in Wiltshire, where his performance won him a scholarship to Corpus Christi, Oxford in 1811. Having completed his B.A. in 1814, Arnold was elected a fellow of Oriel College (1815–1819) at a time during which the college enjoyed unparalleled fame and intellectual distinction. Arnold was made deacon in 1818, but unresolved religious doubts about some articles of the Athanasian Creed and Thirty-Nine Articles kept him from continuing on to the priesthood. Eventually he settled on teaching and helped to establish a private school at Laleham. In 1828 Arnold accepted a position as headmaster at Rugby, and, in order to facilitate his work there, was ordained priest, having received permission from the bishop of London to accept the Articles as "only articles of peace" (*ODNB*). The trustees of Rugby believed that Arnold could renew educational standards in England—and their hopes were fulfilled. His pupils, among them his son Matthew Arnold, Arthur Hugh Clough, and A. P. Stanley, achieved great success. Arnold shaped Rugby as a distinctly Christian institution, contributed to the national conversation on public education, and advocated for the union of sacred and secular spheres of life. Nonetheless, in the spirit of toleration, he publicly supported Catholic emancipation, the Reform Bill, and—against the Tractarians—R. D. Hampden's appointment as regius professor of divinity. Shortly before his death, Arnold received the honor of being named regius professor of modern history.

In *The Christian duty of granting the claims of the Roman Catholics* (1829), Arnold charges England's Protestants with responsibility for Irish hostility and Irish Catholicism alike. In the following selection, Arnold maintains that English Protestants brought Irish Catholics into a state of political subjection, treating the people as inferiors by nature rather than equals before God. In consequence, Catholicism thrived where it would have been cast off, and the religion of Protestants became associated with the politics of conquest. The solution to the present state of political unrest is therefore the establishment of truth, the righting of inequalities, and the restoration of human dignity.

SOURCES: Tod E. Jones, *The broad church: a biography of a movement* (Lanham, Md.: Lexington, 2003); Michael McCrum, *Thomas Arnold, headmaster: a reassessment* (Oxford: Oxford University Press, 1989); Nockles; *OCEL*; *ODCC*; *ODNB*; *VC*.

THOMAS ARNOLD
The Christian duty of granting the claims of the Roman Catholics
1829

And now I would ask of those who shrink from what they call "liberal opinions," as if they were connected with a disregard for Christianity, in what do the opinions which have been here expressed differ from the spirit of the gospel? Is it unchristian to labor to effect the destruction of injustice; to promote the growth of equal rights; to advance the physical and moral condition of mankind by applying to the constitution of society those notions of perfect goodness and wisdom which the gospel, and the gospel alone, has taught us? Or will it be said that all worldly objects are too insignificant to engage the attention of an heir of immortality? Yet it is only by the pursuit of some worldly object that we can perform our worldly duty, and so train ourselves up for immortality; it is by improving the various faculties that are given to us that we can fit ourselves for our everlasting habitations. Or can the relief of the ordinary physical wants of individuals be so high and essential a virtue, and yet the remedying those political evils—which affect both the physical and moral condition of millions—be no fit object of our exertions? And since in the present state of society we can scarcely avoid being called upon to act or to express an opinion, directly or indirectly, upon public matters which may influence the conduct of others, is it well to remain in such ignorance of the principles and facts of political science that our practice is but a leap in the dark and our advice and influence can do nothing but mislead?

‡

The origin of the present form of civil society in Ireland was conquest; and, what was more unfavorable to the establishment of just institutions, it was a conquest obtained over a barbarous people by another scarcely less barbarous, and of a race and language at once distinct and dissimilar. Now in that order of God's providence, by which even our wickedness is sometimes made to promote his purposes of good, it cannot be denied that the ultimate consequences of conquests have been in many instances highly beneficial to the conquered themselves: a better national character has been produced by the intermixture

417

of different races; and laws, commerce, and general civilization have been communicated by the conquerors to their subjects. To talk in this case of a continued right in the conquered people to regain by force that which they had lost by force is palpably foolish, for in a few generations there are neither conquerors nor conquered remaining, but one united people sprung from the intermixture of both; and professing in its improved moral and physical condition, reasons for remembering only with thankfulness the cause which first brought its two elements into contact. But where the wounds inflicted by the first conquest have never been suffered to heal; where the conquerors have continued to form a distinct people, and the conquered have been regarded as an inferior race; where conquest, in short, has never been softened into union, but retains all the harshness of its original features, aggravated by successive centuries of irritation—such a state of things is a perpetual crime, and the original guilt of the conquerors must forever extend to their posterity, so long as by neglecting to remedy or palliate its evil consequences they make themselves a party to it. It is too late then to talk of the inconveniences of extending the rights of citizens to those whose peculiar opinions disqualify them for an union with their conquerors. We brought them forcibly into our national society, and we must not shrink from the just consequences of our own act. And the plea of conscience—when urged as an excuse for not offering atonement for our crime, while we continue to profit by its fruits—is no better than self-deceit and hypocrisy. If Protestants urge that they cannot allow Catholics to have any voice in the government, why did they bring a Catholic people into political connection with themselves? If they so dread the infection of Catholic opinions, why do they oblige Catholics to live and breathe in the same society with themselves? But this they have chosen to do; and if their health be endangered, they have only themselves to thank for it.

In saying this, it will not be supposed that I am gravely arguing in favor of a total separation between this country and Ireland. When I urge that those who refuse to do Ireland justice (and make conscience their plea for the refusal) are bound not to be conscientious only where it suits their own interests, but to make restitution in full if they scruple at coming to a fair compromise, I mean to show the futility of their plea and to insist that it is only a deceived or self-deceiving conscience which advances it. In fact, it is a plea which would dissolve the whole fabric of society throughout Europe and would make it impossible for men of different religions to live together as fellow citizens, if they mutually insisted upon their own exclusive supremacy. The connection between this country and Ireland is not now to be torn asunder; the injustice which we have done cannot now in that manner be rendered undone; but it is our bounden duty to remedy its actual evil effects. What ought to have been done long since should at least no longer be delayed; we should hasten to remove all those marks of our original violence which leave us still guilty till they are wiped away. We should make it as impossible even to dream of a separation with Ireland as to break up England itself into the original elements of its heptarchy.[1]

‡

---

[1]   [Ed. The seven Anglo-Saxon kingdoms of England in late antiquity, including East Anglia, Essex, Kent, Mercia, Northumbria, Sussex, and Wessex.]

It may be urged, as a last plea for still calling upon Parliament to persevere in the iniquities of our ancestors, that exclusion from the full rights of citizenship is not directed against the Irish Catholics as Irishmen, but as Catholics; and that the Catholics of England are in some respects subjected to still greater disqualifications. This also is one of those arguments which men are liable to advance while they want the knowledge or the ability to connect the present state of things with the causes that produced it. That the majority of the Irish people are Catholics at this hour is almost demonstrably owing to the English conquest, combined with the neglect of those measures which repair the evil of conquest. Had Ireland been left to herself, she would have experienced in all human probability the same course of events with the other countries of the North of Europe. Her kings would have become impatient of the papal pretensions; her aristocracy would have been jealous of the wealth and consequence of the Church; her commons would have been alienated by the unworthy lives of the clergy; and with these predisposing causes to aid them, the doctrines of the Reformers would have taken root as effectually as they did in Scotland and in England. . . . But now Ireland is Catholic because Protestantism was associated in her eyes with subjugation and oppression; she clung the more fondly to her superstitions because they were renounced and persecuted by her enemy. And who can doubt but that the dread and hatred of popery which prevailed in England during the seventeenth century were at least greatly aggravated by causes arising out of her political relations with Ireland. If there was one thing more than another which made popery detestable, it was the Irish rebellion and massacre of 1642[2] or, at a later period, the support which Ireland gave to James the Second, and the Acts of James' Irish Parliament in 1689.[3] Now, although religious animosity had a great share in the violence of both these periods, yet it was so mixed up with feelings of national and political hatred that they ought not to be regarded as the mere effects of Catholic bigotry, but as the atrocious vengeance of a barbarous people upon those who had conquered and held them in subjection. In all these cases, to remember only the wickedness of the retaliation, and to pass over the injustice which provoked it, is at once morally and politically blamable. Let us abhor as much as we will the individual actors in scenes of cruelty, but let us not think that their guilt can cancel ours—or that because evil has been overthrown by worse evil, that therefore we are justified in restoring and upholding it.

‡

As a last resource, we are opposed by the argument "that men have no right to govern themselves, but only to be kindly and justly treated by their governors. That therefore the Irish Catholics may indeed claim exemption from persecution and tyranny, but that they have no right to a voice in the legislature, or to exercise the highest functions of free

---

[2] [Ed. The Irish Rebellion of 1641, including months of violence continuing into 1642, was an attempted coup led by Irish Catholics against the English government. The Rebellion stemmed, in part, from the failed assimilation of the Irish and dispossession of hereditary lands following English conquest during the sixteenth century. The Rebellion, which led to a Irish Catholic Confederation, furthered the polarization and distrust between Protestants and Catholics in subsequent years.]

[3] [Ed. In an attempt to further the independence of Ireland from English claims, James II called a single session of the Irish Parliament in 1689. They not only supported James' right to the crown but also affirmed the liberty of religious conscience.]

citizens: the administration of the whole state." Now if men—that is, if societies of men, for we are not speaking of individuals—have not a right to govern themselves, who has the right to govern them? Government is either a matter of agreement, as when the proprietors in a joint stock company depute some of their body to manage the concerns of the whole; or it arises out of a natural superiority, either temporary, as that of men over boys and children, or perpetual, as that of men over beasts. Now it is very true that beasts have no right to govern themselves, but only to be kindly and justly governed; for men have a natural superiority over them, which is perpetual and unalterable; and God has accordingly declared his will that to men they should be subject. It is true also that boys and children have no right to govern themselves while they remain boys and children, for there also is a natural superiority in their parents and elders over them; and God has accordingly in this case also sanctioned this authority by his express law. But as soon as boys arrive at manhood, the superiority of nature on the part of the parent expires. Then therefore the child has a right to govern himself, and this the law of Christian countries, justly (as I conceive) interpreting the divine law, has agreed to acknowledge. A child then has no right to govern himself while he is a child, but he has a right so to be governed as shall qualify him for governing himself hereafter; and what should we say of the guilt of that parent who should willfully neglect his son's education in order to protract the period of his own authority?

‡

The Christian Scriptures indeed enjoin conscientious submission to government on the part of individuals, resting this duty on the divine authority vested in it as the representative on earth of our supreme moral Governor. They strongly condemn the doctrines of the Fifth Monarchy men[4] and of the ancient Jews who held that the saints were not subject to any earthly society (especially when it consisted of heathens) because they had one only King in heaven. They discourage the notion, so common amongst religious bigots, that there is something profane in political institutions, with which the servants of God should not intermeddle. On the contrary, the apostles teach that these political institutions are God's appointed means of governing the world and that he so highly regards them as to invest them with one of his own attributes—the dispensation of good to the well-disposed and of punishment to the evildoer. If they are perverted from fulfilling these purposes, they are faulty and require amendment, and every servant of God should use his best endeavors to restore them to their designed purity. But that they who had so perverted them should be allowed to profit by their own wrong . . . affords altogether a melancholy instance of the art with which the great enemy of all goodness employs the pretext of respect for the gospel when he would most effectually prevent the gospel from bringing forth its proper fruits.

And now I would briefly recapitulate the proofs of my original position—that it is a direct Christian duty to grant the claims of the Roman Catholics, and a direct sin, however ignorantly committed, to endeavor to procure the rejection of them. We conquered Ireland unjustly and have perpetuated the evils (and consequently the guilt) of our first

---

4   [Ed. A seventeenth-century millenarian sect of political agitators who hoped to bring about the promised "fifth monarchy" of Dan 2:44.]

conquest. We refuse to admit the Irish nation into the pale of our civil society, whilst, by admitting into it those Protestant military colonies by which we have from time to time garrisoned Ireland, we keep up a broad line of distinction between union and conquest, between the small minority whom we make our fellow citizens and the majority whom we treat as subjects. We plead the inconveniences to ourselves of a connection with Ireland on equal and just terms, while we effected in the first instance, and still insist on maintaining, a connection on unequal and unjust terms. We talk of the sin of uniting ourselves with papists, yet we force papists to belong to us; and we plead the idolatry of the Catholics as a reason for not doing them justice, when our own injustice has been the cause of this idolatry still existing—and had it not been for us, Ireland would in all human probability have been at this moment Protestant. We confound an entire national society with particular orders or professions of society, and sacrifice the rights of one nation to the interests of another, because the interests of a part of a nation may lawfully be sacrificed to the paramount rights of the whole. We attempt sometimes to justify our conduct by an argument, which, if acted upon in private life, would cause a man to be banished from all honest society: namely, that we are not bound to repair an injustice done by others, even though we continue to reap the profits of it. . . . And we individually—that is, the clergy, gentry, farmers, and shopkeepers of this country—make ourselves each separately guilty of the injustice which we have committed as a nation, by calling upon our rulers to persevere in this wickedness, when they appear inclined to relieve us and our posterity from the curse which it must entail upon us, and to return at last to the path of duty.

‡

And for the application of all this to the great question which now engrosses the whole mind of England, I wish to impress upon the Christian opponents of concession that while I maintain the positive duty of granting the Catholic claims as an act of simple justice, it is also with the most deliberate conviction that thus, and thus only, can the spiritual improvement of our Catholic countrymen ever be effected. If Protestants will not endure to hear the language of impartiality and charity towards the Catholics, if they will only look upon them as men without truth and without humanity, as ferocious bigots and blasphemous idolaters, do they think that the Catholics can be more favorably disposed to them, when over and above their religious prejudices they must entertain against them the galling sense of national and civil injustice? What Protestant missionary, however holy and eloquent, can have any chance of influencing men who are not only daily reviled by Protestants, but actually degraded and oppressed by them—are treated as aliens in their own land, as unfit and unworthy to become citizens of their own country? They who are most zealous in their endeavors to convert the slaves in the West Indies to Christianity are also most eager to effect their temporal deliverance. They are regarded therefore as friends, and the gospel is doubly loved for the sake of those who offer the knowledge of it. Would the Negroes listen to a mission of tyrannical overseers who spoke to them with the whip in one hand and the Bible in the other, or to a set of plantation proprietors who had most steadily refused to adopt every measure recommended by the government of Britain for the improvement of their temporal condition? We have a great, a solemn duty to perform towards our Irish brethren; we have connected them with ourselves, and therefore we are bound first to do them justice, and then to do them kindness; to labor at this eleventh hour to atone for the long day during which we have not only neglected to do them good, but have heaped upon them evil, alike physical and moral.

TEXT: Thomas Arnold, *The Christian duty of granting the claims of the Roman Catholics* (Oxford: W. Baxter, 1829), 12–13, 22–26, 29–31, 38–39, 43–47, 99–101.

X

OUTSIDERS

Can we whose souls are lighted
With wisdom from on high,
Can we to men benighted
The lamp of life deny?
Salvation! Oh, salvation!
The joyful sound proclaim
Till each remotest nation
Has learn'd Messiah's name.

Reginald Heber, "From Greenland's Icy Mountains" (1819)

JOSEPH WHITE
(ca. 1746–1814)
Christianity and Islam

Arabic-Islamic sources permeate the writings of the Romantic era. Blake, Coleridge, and Byron, among many others, alluded to the Qur'an, Islamic history, and well-known tales such as the *Arabian nights*. Still, while the use of such sources became increasingly common in the Romantic period, hostility towards Muslims and Islam was widespread, as the Bampton Lectures of Joseph White make clear. Born in Ruscombe, Gloucestershire, White was raised by a broadloom weaver and his wife. A charity school in the area provided Joseph's earliest education. In 1765, with the financial support of wealthy neighbors, White matriculated at Wadham College, Oxford. He excelled in languages—including Hebrew, Arabic, and Syriac—and attained the D.D. degree in 1787. From 1774 White held the Laudian chair of Arabic. Four years later, White published an edition of the Syriac Gospels in the Philoxenian version (2 vols., 1778). Other publications appealed for a new translation of the Bible based on the latest manuscripts (1779), a harmony of the Gospels (1800), a study of Egyptian antiquities (1804), and a new edition of the Greek New Testament (1808). White, who received a prebend at Gloucester Cathedral from 1788, was named the regius professor of Hebrew at Oxford in 1804.

The Bampton Lectures, established by the will of John Bampton (1689–1751), canon of Salisbury, were annual lectures in defense of the Christian faith. White's contribution, *A comparison of Mahometism and Christianity, in their history, their evidence, and their effects* (1784), offers an historical and theological comparison of the two religions, with an assessment of the respective evidences and effects of each. While some Muslims migrated to England in the eighteenth century, arriving predominantly from India, there is no evidence that White had any contact with the Islamic community. The following selection, drawn from the ninth lecture, stems from the biblical warning in Matthew 7:16: "Ye shall know them by their fruits." White's caustic discourse contended that Christianity encourages political liberty and benevolence, while Islam fosters ignorance and violence. The lectures show little of the self-critical perspective that later comparativists would bring to bear on world religions but underscore the then commonplace English belief that Christianity (unique among the religions) promotes both individual freedom and national benevolence.

〜〜〜

SOURCES: Samar Attar, *Borrowed imagination: the British Romantic poets and their Arabic-Islamic sources* (Lanham, Md.: Lexington, 2014); Jeffrey Einboden, *Islam and Romanticism: Muslim currents from Goethe to Emerson* (London: Oneworld, 2014); Albert Hourani, *Islam in European thought* (Cambridge: Cambridge University Press, 1991); P. J. Marshall, "Oriental studies," in *The history of the University of Oxford*, vol. 5, *The eighteenth century*, ed. L. S. Sutherland and L. G. Mitchell (Oxford: Clarendon, 1986), 551–63; *ODCC*; *ODNB*; Joseph White, *A statement of Dr. White's literary obligations to the late Reverend Mr. Samuel Badcock* (Oxford: D. Prince and J. Cooke, 1790).

JOSEPH WHITE
A comparison of Mahometism and Christianity
1784

The characters of the religions which Christ and Mahomet have respectively founded are not more different than those of the nations which have embraced them. From the period of their primary establishment to the present hour, a different aspect seems to have belonged to them. Wherever they have spread themselves, they have communicated their distinguishing properties to the understandings and affections of the people whom they have converted; and, in opposition to former experience, the influences of climate, of government, and of manners have yielded to the effects of religious persuasion. The appearances they now give to those great divisions of mankind among which they are planted form a most striking part of the modern history of the world, and the investigation of the causes which produce those appearances would constitute one of the most splendid subjects of political speculation, even though it were not at the same time one of the most important to the interests of Christianity.

The view of mankind, as arranged under this distinction of religious opinion, presents to us very singular and permanent oppositions of national character.

The faith of Mahomet, wherever it is established, is united with despotic power. On the banks of the Ganges, and on the shores of the Caspian, under the influence of climates the most unlike and manners the most opposite, it is still found accompanied with servitude and subjection; every free and every gallant people whom it has involved in the progress of its power have abandoned their rights when they enlisted themselves under the banner of the prophet, and have forgotten in the title of the faithful the pride of independence and the security of freedom.

The religion of Christ, on the contrary, is found to exist and to flourish under every variety of political power. In the different periods of its history, it has been united with every form of government; and of the nations among whom it is now professed, the most general and perhaps the most discriminating[1] feature is that equal and courteous system of manners which has operated in so striking a manner to limit the progress of tyranny;

---

[1]   [Ed. Distinguishing.]

and which, even in the few countries where despotism is established, has served to soften the austerity of its administration.

The nations who have embraced Mahometism are distinguished by a spirit of hostility and hatred to the rest of mankind. Wherever it has established itself, the relations of situation, of language, and of national policy have been controlled by the influence of religious enmity. The regulations which it prescribes for the conduct of private life have a tendency to separate the Mussulman from all communion with other men, and all participation of the offices of humanity; and in every period of its history the pride, or the jealousy, which it has inspired seems to have represented the rest of mankind as enemies with whom, while they opposed the prophet's power, it were impious to converse and whom it was even meritorious to destroy.

The character of Christian nations is, on the contrary, marked by a spirit of benevolence and humanity, as new in the history of mankind as it is conducive to their welfare. The violence of national animosity, of old so fruitful a source of dissension, has given way in a great measure to the dictates of more enlarged humanity. Where the religion of Christ has not always directed the conduct of men, it has at least secretly influenced their opinions; and the union of European nations in the faith of the gospel has produced a general disposition to courtesy and humanity, which—in opposition to every distinction of language, of manners, and of national interests—has united the various people of whom it is composed in one firm and sacred bond of brotherhood and affection.

‡

It requires no uncommon effort of sagacity to discover the wide difference that subsists between the religions of Mahomet and Christ in their influence on the conceptions of the imagination and the direction of the appetites. The doctrines which the prophet of Arabia has taught concerning the divine perfections too frequently accord with the lowest ideas of the human mind; and though they are at times illuminated by sublime or magnificent images, yet many of the supposed beauties of the Koran consist rather in the brilliancy of the language than in the majesty of the thought. How much Mahomet was indebted to the writings of the Prophets and of the Evangelists for the greater part of what is sublime or beautiful in his theology, his compositions declare; but with this sacred and hallowed imagery, he blended the impure superstitions and gross conceptions of his countrymen. For the wild profusion and incongruous mixture of absurdity and sense which pervade his writings, it is scarcely possible to account on any other supposition than the natural incapacity even of the wisest man to form upon every subject, and to preserve upon every occasion, just and consistent notions of the divine perfections.

In what glowing colors is the greatness of the Deity displayed almost in the commencement of the Koran! And with what zeal does the imagination go along with descriptions which seem so suited to the supreme dignity of his nature and the glorious excellence of his works! Yet hardly is this enthusiasm excited before all the ardors of the mind are repressed, when we find this sublime Being descend to the meanest and most contemptible employments, prescribing laws which minister more to the appetites than to the interests of men, and regulating with the same care at one moment the order of secret and impure enjoyment, and, in the next, the discipline in which men are to be trained for eternity.

In the composition of the fanatical impostor, credulity is often intermixed with craft. The fervors, which are at first assumed voluntarily and insidiously, return by a kind of mechanical force; in process of time the glow of his fancy and the tumult of his passions are no longer artificial but real; and in this last stage of depravity combined with folly, the enthusiast is inseparably blended with the hypocrite in the whole mass of character; and in the same action we may discover the wiliness of the one and the weakness of the other. Hence the inconsistencies of Mahomet are to be ascribed partly to cunning, in accommodating his doctrines to the prejudices of other men, and partly to fanaticism, which prevented him from controlling the impetuous but uncertain sallies of his own mind.

Hence the God of Abraham and of Moses, the incomprehensible Being, who, in the language of Isaiah, "liveth from eternity to eternity" [Isa 43:13], is associated with the gross and limited attributes of Eastern idolatry; and the altar which is erected to the Father of universal nature is commanded to be approached with the slavish rites of a timorous and abject superstition.

Of that eternity, the representation of which forms so great a part of every religion, the ideas which Mahomet has given are not more pure or more consistent. Of such a system of opinions, so perplexed by inconsistency and so debased by impurity, the effect upon the mind is obvious. Though all men probably can feel the sublimity of those descriptions which sometimes occur, yet the impression is momentary; but the apprehensions which are entertained of the Deity from his agency, and the conceptions which are formed of futurity from its employments, are permanent. The beauties of the Koran may captivate the fancy, but its errors at once delude the judgment, degrade the spirit, and pollute the affections. How can the follower of Mahomet, therefore, feel any enlargement given to his understanding from representations of a deity who, though sometimes eloquently or magnificently described, is yet familiarized to his apprehension in the character of an impure or capricious being? How can he be excited to the exercise or improvement of the higher powers of his nature by the views which his religion affords him of a futurity in which these powers seem to be unemployed, in which the enjoyments of animal pleasure form a great part of the reward assigned to virtue, and to the relish of which no other preparation seems necessary than to assimilate the mind to an ambition as limited and to desires as impure?

⤛⤜

TEXT: Joseph White, *A comparison of Mahometism and Christianity, in their history, their evidence, and their effects*, new ed. (London: F. C. and J. Rivington, 1811), 295–98, 316–20.

WILLIAM KNOX
(1732–1810)
Native Americans

In 1537 Pope Paul III issued *Sublimus Deus*, a papal bull that forbade the enslavement of Native Americans, declared that indigenous people bear the image of God, and defended their inherent right to freedom and property. This proclamation, however, was often ignored in practice and had no authority for Protestants, whose missionary efforts to convert Native Americans more than 250 years later continued to be frustrated by misunderstanding, distrust, and ignorance. Not unlike the treatment of enslaved Africans, Native Americans were sometimes regarded as inferior and in need of civilization. Consistent with this long history, missionary organizations in the eighteenth and early nineteenth centuries struggled to develop effective policies that promoted Christianity among people from vastly different cultural backgrounds.

William Knox, one of the leading political figures of his day, was born in Monaghan, Ireland, and educated in Church of Ireland schools. His family claimed kinship with the Scottish theologian John Knox. He attended Trinity College, Dublin, and received instruction in Irish politics. In 1756 Knox was named provost marshal in the American colony of Georgia, where he amassed considerable wealth, including 8,400 acres and 122 slaves (this despite his evangelical doctrine). He distrusted colonial misgivings for imperial rule. In 1762 he moved to London, where as Georgia's colonial agent in London he endorsed increasingly hardline policies favoring British interests in the colonies. Between 1770 and 1782, he served as Senior Undersecretary in the Colonial Office. After the American War of Independence, Knox lost his plantation properties and spent years seeking compensation.

Knox's *Three tracts respecting the conversion and instruction of the free Indians and Negro slaves in the colonies* (1768; new ed. 1789) assesses British efforts to convert Native Americans and enslaved Africans based on his firsthand knowledge of life in the colonies. The tracts are addressed to members the Society for the Propagation of the Gospel in Foreign Parts (S.P.G.), which owned a Caribbean plantation worked by slaves. Knox's tracts defended slaveholding, yet, as he regarded both Native Americans and Africans as bearers of the divine image, he thought Christians had an obligation to provide for slaves' spiritual education. Similarly, in the following selection from a tract titled "Of the Indians in the colonies," Knox explains that Native Americans are fully capable of receiving the gospel, but he names numerous cultural impediments to the spread of Christianity. Knox criticizes Protestants, who had little success converting Native Americans, since their missionaries required the outright renunciation of all cultural practices. Roman Catholics, by comparison, willingly embraced the language, dress, and tribal practices of the people but replaced one form of superstition with another in the process. Knox instead advocates conversion through a preliminary civilizing process involving the introduction of private property, English farming techniques, and new educational and medical resources. Despite Knox's insistence that *"nothing is to be pressed upon them,"* such methods frequently led to a disturbing loss of cultural memory and self-determination.

SOURCES: Leland J. Bellot, "Evangelicals and the defense of slavery in Britain's old colonial empire," *Journal of Southern History* 37 (1971): 19–40; idem, "William Knox asks what is fit to be done with America?" in *Sources of American Independence*, ed. Howard H. Peckham (Chicago: University of Chicago Press, 1978); idem, *William Knox: the life and thought of an eighteenth-century imperialist* (Austin: University of Texas Press, 1977); *ODNB*.

WILLIAM KNOX
"Of the Indians in the colonies"
1789

The varieties of sects to be found amongst the European inhabitants of the colonies, though a thing to be lamented by a lover of unity among Christians and frequently urged as a proof of the little success attending the society's missions, is in truth the clearest evidence of the great service done to religion by the venerable Society for Propagating the Gospel, and the great benefits the people of America have derived from its establishment. . . .

But although one great purpose of the Society has been answered, and the descendants of the European settlers have been kept back from degenerating into the barbarism and ignorance of the natives, it is much to be lamented that so little has been done towards instructing the free Indians or Negro slaves in the colonies. The obstacles to the conversion of the Indians are indeed many and formidable. Were they only ignorant of our religion, their natural good sense would give hopes of their imbibing its doctrines, so soon as they were properly explained and set before them; but the misfortune is that they are not only ignorant of it, but what they do know and are taught is diametrically opposite to the doctrines of Christianity. While they are infants, they are taught to repeat the warlike achievements of their ancestors and the tortures they suffered or inflicted upon their enemies, and they are required to prove the sincerity of their professions to imitate such examples by patiently bearing hunger for several days, suffering their limbs to be lacerated by fishes' teeth, or standing resolutely under a plate of iron with burning coals upon their heads until the scalp is parched to a cinder. No wonder then that their wars are hereditary and that Indian resentments are so implacable. As the object of their wars is always the utter extirpation of their enemies, they are instructed to destroy an enemy in the manner the most safe for themselves . . . Hence their subtlety and their cruelty to the innocent and helpless inhabitants. No Indian can be considerable in his nation until he is dubbed a warrior, and that he can never be without producing a scalp, and hence the frequency of wars with each other. Of all our methods of making war, none appeared to them so ridiculous and absurd as our sparing prisoners, and many of their parties withdrew from us on that account. What, say they, after you have got your enemy in your power, will you let him go that he may kill you or your friends again? Vagrant in their manner of life, without social intercourse even among each other, jealous in the highest degree of their liberty and independency, and attached to their customs and nation with more than Spartan pride and tenacity—such we found them. They had, however, some notions of honesty in their little dealings, but those we have eradicated. Our traders and they now mutually deceive each other. Our traders cut short their measure, and they sow lead bullets in the ears and tails of their skins. Both expect to be cheated, and under that expectation each makes his bargain, and fraud is become so customary that it would be very difficult, if not impracticable, to establish an honest tariff between them. The Indians never complain of a trader cheating them unless he is remarkably dexterous and exorbitant, and then they only charge them with cheating them *too much.*

Very unpromising principles and dispositions these, on which to graft the meek, forbearing, equitable, and benevolent tenets of Christianity!

The cause is not, however, to be forsaken as altogether hopeless. Their conversion may, through God's blessing, still be effected, though a much greater compass must be taken than has hitherto been thought necessary to attain it.

The Protestant missionaries, in order to do themselves credit, make it their first object to get the Indians to submit to be baptized, and preparatory thereto they opened to them the most mysterious doctrines of Christianity, shocking their pride by displaying their original corruptions and blindness and exciting their jealousy by the change they are told is to be wrought in them. They inform them of the spiritual worship which is to be paid to the Deity, ridicule their talismans, and at once exhort them to cease to be Indians, lay aside all their own customs, quit their country and independency, and become a poor contemptible people among us. The Roman Catholic missionaries take a different method and have therefore been more successful. They first conciliate the good will of the Indians by following their customs and learning their language. Being provided with medicines, and skilled in the use of them, they soon get the Indians to trust more in their talismans for their cure than in their own. And the missionary becomes the Indian conjurer before he discloses his purpose. Their inquiry whence he had his talisman and its virtues naturally opens to him an occasion of discoursing to them of the supreme Being, whom they all have some notion of the *master of breath*, and of Christ Jesus the great Conjurer who cured all the world on the other side [of] the great water and would have come to the Indians if he had not been killed by bad people. He shows them a relic which he pretends cures all diseases and which his love for the Indians made him bring to them. So far from shocking their prejudices by preaching forgiveness of injuries or peace with their enemies, he points their enmity against his nation's enemies as those who had prevented the great Conjurer from coming to them. If by following his instructions they gain an advantage over their enemies or escape unhurt, they readily impute their good fortune to the virtues of his talisman and in their future expeditions submit to such discipline by way of preparation for a successful enterprise as he shall enjoin them. Thus are they baptized and made to believe in Christ without perceiving that they are become Christians, and their attachment to the missionary is such as to lead them to adopt implicitly any mode or custom he may think proper to institute. Such Christians do not indeed deserve to be called proselytes; for although they looked upon our Savior to have been a great benefactor to mankind, they neither know him for their redeemer nor conform to his doctrine or example. . . .

In this great undertaking government must lead the way. Instructions should be sent to the agents and governors to exhort the Indians to live in peace with each other. And to take away the motive of the young men to make war, the king's officers should be directed to distinguish those who were expert in hunting or cultivating the ground by presents, above the warriors. This would presently beget a civil means of becoming considerable. To induce them to leave their women and children always in their towns, which is the first step towards their civilization, they should be furnished with a variety of garden seeds and tools to plant them with. Neat[1] cattle would be acceptable presents and a great means of civilizing them, and poultry would oblige them to fence and enclose their habitations. Locks and hinges should be furnished them as a means of teaching them property, and no regard should ever be shown to those who made depredations upon others. Government having done so much, the Society might then begin. The missionary should be instructed in physic and be supplied with medicines. To give him consequence it would be proper that the superintendent gave him a deputation for the town or nation he resided in. He should be enabled to pay the Indians for building him a neat[2] house, and cultivating some ground as a garden. He should be furnished with cows and every means of subsistence which was intended to be introduced among the Indians. He might introduce the silk culture among them in the warm and temperate climates by planting the mulberry trees and paying the women and children for gathering the leaves. By such kindnesses they would be led to consider him as their best friend and would not oppose their children learning any song or rhyme he might pay them for getting by heart. The great Indian nations would never suffer their children to be taught our language; their policy is to keep as much from us as they can, so that whatever instruction is given them must be stolen upon them in their own language. As no real proselytes were ever made but those who sought to be converted, an illiterate people must first have a desire of knowledge excited in them before they can be taught. Curiosity must therefore first be excited in the Indians before their attention to any doctrine can be engaged, and when their attention is fixed, such things should only be proposed to them as their present state will admit of their receiving. It ought to be remembered that man was intended for polished society, and that the Christian dispensation is adapted to him in his best state. It was not till after the Greek and Roman civility had been spread over the world that Christianity was promulgated. While the Jews were an erratic[3] people, had settlements to purchase by the sword, hereditary antipathies against other nations to maintain, and were to pride themselves in customs which distinguished them from the rest of mankind, a less perfect system was thought better suited to their circumstances. The Indians have no sacrifices nor days of expiation, nor do they pay any sort of religious worship to anything in heaven or earth. It would therefore be impracticable in the beginning to make them comprehend the necessity for Christ's suffering or to convince them of the benefits derived to them through his blood. They could not possibly understand the prohibitions in either the

---

[1] [Ed. Clean.]
[2] [Ed. That is, a house free from embellishments.]
[3] [Ed. Nomadic.]

second or third commandment; and as all that they do is work of necessity, they would not be much edified by lectures upon the fourth.[4] Baptism should not be administered to children whose parents had not received it themselves or desired it for them.[5] I have said that the Indians are jealous of their independency, and if their children should be flattered to receive that sacrament, they would think something very different from its purpose was intended by it.

When the English traders come into the Indian nation, the missionary should then exercise his function. Their assembling on a Sunday would lead the Indians to inquire what was doing, and the missionary to oblige them might preach in the Indian language. His discourse should notwithstanding be directed entirely to the traders, but so framed as to make favorable impressions on the Indians and induce them to come again. On such occasions he should exhort the traders to look upon the Indians as brothers, all created by one common Father, the *Great Spirit*, and to deal justly and not to use their knowledge of trade to overreach the unsuspecting Indian. He should enlarge upon the great advantages they derived from having received their birth and education in a country where the will of Almighty God had been clearly revealed, and thence urge them to be more particularly careful in their conduct towards the Indians, who had no such advantages but were brought up in the wild forests without other instruction than their own natural sagacity furnished them with. He should represent it to be in an especial manner their duty to inform the Indians of anything which the *Great Spirit* had revealed if they desired to know it, and that as in another life they should be all one people, so they should now live together in the same manner. That they were to remember that in the other world, when they came to live again, they should be rewarded or punished according to what they had done here, for that the *Great Spirit* knew everything they did and saw them wherever they went. These are things the Indians could understand and would probably desire to hear again; and some would perhaps be led to wish for further instruction. . . . No point of controversy among Christians should ever be mentioned, not only to save the Indians the perplexity of discussing things with which they can have nothing to do but to engage the assistance of all denominations of Christians in the colonies who, if they were acquainted with the plan of our missionaries, would readily give their own the like catholic[6] instructions. Whatever be the method taken up, if any success be expected from it among the Indians, it must be founded on this principle—*that nothing is to be pressed upon them*; their own desires must move foremost, and those will always carry them to ask as much as they can receive.

TEXT: William Knox, "Of the Indians in the colonies," in *Three tracts respecting the conversion and instruction of the free Indians and Negroe [sic] slaves in the colonies*, new ed. (London: J. Debrett, 1789), 3–13.

4   [Ed. Knox refers to the Ten Commandments of Exod 20:1-17, including its prohibitions on idolatry (second), blasphemy (third), and Sabbath breaking (fourth). He alleges that since Native Americans *only* perform necessary work on the Sabbath, which Christian teaching allows, the fourth commandment has no relevance to their situation.]

5   [Ed. Knox's claim here is consistent with his overarching aversion to forced conversions.]

6   [Ed. Universal.]

WILLIAM CAREY
(1761–1834)
Missionary Call

"How then will they call on him in whom they have not believed? How will they believe in him whom they have not heard? And how will they hear without a preacher?" (Rom 10:14). These questions, first posed by the Apostle Paul, weighed on the minds of English Christians. In a time when the expansion of empire led to a new awareness that Christianity had only reached a portion of the world's population, some Christians found themselves willing to face the hardships of travel, the risk of illness and death, the need for language acquisition, the loss of commonplace comforts, and separation from family and loved ones so that the good news could be spread far and wide. The result was, in English Protestantism, the beginning of the modern missionary movement.

William Carey provided unparalleled leadership for the new movement. Carey was born in Paulerspury, south of Northampton, and educated under his schoolmaster father. After a brief time with Independent Congregationalists, Carey began attending a Baptist congregation, was baptized by John Ryland in 1783, and served as a Baptist pastor in Moulton. After publishing *An enquiry into the obligations of Christians, to use means for the conversion of heathens* (1792), Carey came into contact with Baptist ministers who shared his concern for missionary work and founded the Particular Baptist Society for Propagating the Gospel among the Heathen. The society (the first evangelical body of its kind) was also known as the Baptist Missionary Society and inspired the formation of many similar groups around the world.

Carey traveled with his wife and children to Bengal, India, in January 1793. He would never return to England. While working in an indigo factory in Malda and traveling to villages throughout the region, Carey learned Bengali and Hindi. By 1801 he had translated the Bible into Bengali. When the East India Company refused to grant non-Anglican missionaries permission to live in Bengal, Carey moved to Serampore where he and his colleagues developed a thriving missionary network throughout northern India. Finally, in December 1801 the group witnessed the first Hindu conversion. In the next two decades, they recorded 1,407 baptisms. Despite the loss of his wife (1807) and their son

(1794), Carey remained in India, and translated the entire Bible into six different Indian languages—including Bengali, Sanskrit, and Hindi—and portions of it into twenty-nine others. He also published numerous grammars, dictionaries, and other literary sources from Bengali literature (as in the collection of some 150 folk stories in *Itihasmala* [1812]). In 1829 Carey's strong social concern helped to abolish suttee, the practice of a widow committing suicide following her husband's death. He was buried in Serampore in 1834.

The year prior to leaving England, Carey published *An enquiry into the obligations of Christians, to use means for the conversion of the heathens.* The *Enquiry* begins with a consideration of the command of Jesus Christ to proclaim the good news to the nations of the world. In the following selection, Carey surveys the scope of the problem, challenges commonplace objections to the work, and emphasizes the need for workers. All people, in all places, need the gospel (England not excepted, he stresses). The task, he explains, would not be easy. Self-sacrifice would be required on the part of missionaries. Moreover, their work depended not on government support, but on the contributions of laity at home. The mission, however vast, could only be accomplished with hard work and divine grace.

><><

Sources: Donald Alban Jr., Robert H. Woods Jr., and Marsha Daigle-Williamson, "The writings of William Carey: journalism as mission in a modern age," *Mission Studies* 22, no. 1 (2005): 85–113; *BDE*; Rosalie Beck, "Baptist missions and the turn toward global responsibility: 1792," in *Turning points in Baptist history*, ed. Michael E. Williams, Sr. and Walter B. Shurden (Macon, Ga.: Mercer University Press, 2008), 102–13; *ODCC*; *ODNB*; Solomon Rongpi, ed., *Mission and the local congregations: essays in honour of William Carey's 250th birth anniversary* (Delhi: ISPCK/NCCI, 2011); George Smith, *The life of William Carey: shoemaker and missionary* (London: J. M. Dent, 1909).

WILLIAM CAREY

An enquiry into the obligations of Christians
1792

This, as nearly as I can obtain information, is the state of the world, though in many countries—as Turkey, Arabia, Great Tartary,[1] Africa, and America (except the United States), and most of the Asiatic Islands—we have no accounts of the number of inhabitants that can be relied on. I have therefore only calculated the extent and counted a certain number on an average upon a square mile—in some countries more, and in others less, according as circumstances determine. A few general remarks upon it will conclude this section.

First, the inhabitants of the world according to this calculation, amount to about seven hundred and thirty-one millions; four hundred and twenty millions of whom are still in pagan darkness; an hundred and thirty millions the followers of Mahomet; an hundred millions Catholics; forty-four millions Protestants; thirty millions of the Greek and Armenian churches, and perhaps seven millions of Jews.[2] It must undoubtedly strike every considerate mind what a vast proportion of the sons of Adam there are who yet remain in the most deplorable state of heathen darkness without any means of knowing the true God, except what are afforded them by the works of nature, and utterly destitute of the knowledge of the gospel of Christ or of any means of obtaining it. In many of these countries they have no written language, consequently no Bible, and are only led by the most childish customs and traditions. Such, for instance, are all the middle and back parts of North America, the inland parts of South America, the South-Sea Islands, New Holland, New Zealand, New Guinea; and I may add Great Tartary, Siberia, Samojedia, and the other parts of Asia contiguous to the frozen sea; the greatest part of Africa, the island of Madagascar, and many places beside. In many of these parts also they are cannibals,

---

[1]   [Ed. The region of northern and central Asia.]

[2]   [Ed. By comparison, the data for the year 2000 in the *World Christian encyclopedia* includes a total population of more than 6 billion people adhering to various religious traditions: 2 billion Christians, 1.2 billion Muslims, 811 million Hindus, 360 million Buddhists, 230 million ethno-religionists, 23 million Sikhs, and 14 million Jews. The emergence of some 770 million agnostics and 150 million atheists reveal a dramatic shift in the world's religious landscape (*World Christian encyclopedia*, ed. David B. Barrett, George T. Kurian, and Todd M. Johnson, 2 vols., 2nd ed. [Oxford: Oxford University Press, 2001], 2:3).]

feeding upon the flesh of their slain enemies, with the greatest brutality and eagerness. The truth of this was ascertained beyond a doubt by the late eminent navigator, Cooke,[3] of the New Zealanders and some of the inhabitants of the western coast of America. Human sacrifices are also very frequently offered, so that scarce a week elapses without instances of this kind. They are in general poor, barbarous, naked pagans, as destitute of civilization as they are of true religion.

Secondly, barbarous as these poor heathens are, they appear to be as capable of knowledge as we are; and in many places, at least, have discovered uncommon genius and tractableness; and I greatly question whether most of the barbarities practiced by them have not originated in some real or supposed affront and are therefore, more properly, acts of self-defense than proofs of inhuman and bloodthirsty dispositions.

Thirdly, in other parts where they have a written language, as in the East Indies, China, Japan, etc., they know nothing of the gospel. The Jesuits indeed once made many converts to popery among the Chinese, but their highest aim seemed to be to obtain their good opinion; for though the converts professed themselves Christians, yet they were allowed to honor the image of Confucius, their great lawgiver, and at length their ambitious intrigues brought upon them the displeasure of government, which terminated in the suppression of the mission and almost, if not entirely, of the Christian name.[4] It is also a melancholy fact that the vices of Europeans have been communicated wherever they themselves have been, so that the religious state of even heathens has been rendered worse by intercourse with them!

Fourthly, a very great proportion of Asia and Africa, with some part of Europe, are Mahometans; and those in Persia, who are of the sect of Hali,[5] are the most inveterate enemies to the Turks; and they in return abhor the Persians. The Africans are some of the most ignorant of all the Mahometans, especially the Arabs, who are scattered through all the northern parts of Africa and live upon the depredations which they are continually making upon their neighbors.

Fifthly, in respect to those who bear the Christian name, a very great degree of ignorance and immorality abounds amongst them. There are Christians, so called, of the Greek and Armenian churches in all the Mahometan countries; but they are, if possible, more ignorant and vicious than the Mahometans themselves. . . . Papists also are in general ignorant of divine things and very vicious. Nor do the bulk of the Church of England much exceed them either in knowledge or holiness; and many errors, and much looseness of conduct, are to be found amongst dissenters of all denominations. The Lutherans in Denmark are much on a par with the ecclesiastics in England; and the face of most Christian countries presents a dreadful scene of ignorance, hypocrisy, and profligacy. Various baneful and pernicious errors appear to gain ground in almost every part of Christendom;

[3]   [Ed. The travels of renowned navigator James Cooke (1728–1779) were a formative inspiration for William Carey.]

[4]   [Ed. Jesuit missionaries actively worked in China from the sixteenth century, but controversy over accommodation to Chinese religious culture led to sharp divisions not only among Christians but also with the Emperor.]

[5]   [Ed. Carey refers to Ali ibn Abi Talib (ca. 600–661), whom Shia Muslims regard as the first successor to Mohammed.]

the truths of the gospel, and even the gospel itself, are attacked, and every method that the enemy can invent is employed to undermine the kingdom of our Lord Jesus Christ.

All these things are loud calls to Christians, and especially to ministers, to exert themselves to the utmost in their several spheres of action and to try to enlarge them as much as possible. . . .

The impediments in the way of carrying the gospel among the heathen must arise, I think, from one or other of the following things: either their distance from us, their barbarous and savage manner of living, the danger of being killed by them, the difficulty of procuring the necessaries of life, or the unintelligibleness of their languages.

First, as to their distance from us, whatever objections might have been made on that account before the invention of the mariner's compass, nothing can be alleged for it with any color of plausibility in the present age. Men can now sail with as much certainty through the Great South Sea as they can through the Mediterranean or any lesser sea. Yea, and providence seems in a manner to invite us to the trial, as there are to our knowledge trading companies whose commerce lies in many of the places where these barbarians dwell. At one time or other ships are sent to visit places of more recent discovery and to explore parts the most unknown; and every fresh account of their ignorance, or cruelty, should call forth our pity and excite us to concur with providence in seeking their eternal good. . . .

Secondly, as to their uncivilized and barbarous way of living, this can be no objection to any except those whose love of ease renders them unwilling to expose themselves to inconveniencies for the good of others.

It was no objection to the apostles and their successors, who went among the barbarous Germans and Gauls and still more barbarous Britons! They did not wait for the ancient inhabitants of these countries to be civilized before they could be christianized, but went simply with the doctrine of the cross; and Tertullian could boast that "those parts of Britain which were proof against the Roman armies were conquered by the gospel of Christ."[6] It was no objection to an Elliot or a Brainerd in later times.[7] They went forth and encountered every difficulty of the kind, and found that a cordial reception of the gospel produced those happy effects which the longest intercourse with Europeans, without it, could never accomplish. It is no objection to commercial men. It only requires that we should have as much love to the souls of our fellow creatures, and fellow sinners, as they have for the profits arising from a few otter skins—and all these difficulties would be easily surmounted.

After all, the uncivilized state of the heathen, instead of affording an objection *against* preaching the gospel to them, ought to furnish an argument *for* it. Can we as men, or as Christians, hear that a great part of our fellow creatures—whose souls are as immortal as ours, and who are as capable as ourselves of adorning the gospel and contributing by their preaching, writings, or practices to the glory of our Redeemer's name and the good of his church—are enveloped in ignorance and barbarism? Can we hear that they are without the gospel—without government, without laws, and without arts and sciences—and not exert ourselves to introduce amongst them the sentiments of men and of Christians?

6   [Ed. Tertullian, *An answer to the Jews*, ch. 7.]
7   [Ed. Carey refers to John Eliot (1604–1690), the so-called Apostle to the Indians, and David Brainerd (1718–1747), who were known for their self-sacrificing work with Native Americans.]

Would not the spread of the gospel be the most effectual means of their civilization? Would not that make them useful members of society? We know that such effects did in a measure follow the aforementioned efforts of Elliot, Brainerd, and others amongst the American Indians; and if similar attempts were made in other parts of the world and succeeded with a divine blessing (which we have every reason to think they would), might we not expect to see able divines or read well-conducted treatises in defense of the truth even amongst those who at present seem to be scarcely human?

Thirdly, in respect to the danger of being killed by them, it is true that whoever does go must put his life in his hand and not consult with flesh and blood; but do not the goodness of the cause, the duties incumbent on us as the creatures of God and Christians, and the perishing state of our fellow men loudly call upon us to venture all and use every warrantable exertion for their benefit? Paul and Barnabas, who "hazarded their lives for the name of our Lord Jesus Christ" [Acts 15:26], were not blamed as being rash but commended for so doing, while John Mark, who through timidity of mind deserted them in their perilous undertaking, was branded with censure [Acts 15:39]. After all, as has been already observed, I greatly question whether most of the barbarities practiced by the savages upon those who have visited them have not originated in some real or supposed affront and were therefore, more properly, acts of self-defense than proofs of ferocious dispositions. . . . Nay, in general the heathen have showed a willingness to hear the word and have principally expressed their hatred of Christianity on account of the vices of nominal Christians.

Fourthly, as to the difficulty of procuring the necessaries of life, this would not be so great as may appear at first sight; for though we could not procure European food, yet we might procure such as the natives of those countries which we visit subsist upon themselves. And this would only be passing through what we have virtually engaged in by entering on the ministerial office. A Christian minister is a person who in a peculiar sense is "not his own" [cf. 1 Cor 6:19]; he is the servant of God and therefore ought to be wholly devoted to him. . . . He virtually bids farewell to friends, pleasures, and comforts, and stands in readiness to endure the greatest sufferings in the work of his Lord and Master. It is inconsistent for ministers to please themselves with thoughts of a numerous auditory, cordial friends, a civilized country, legal protection, affluence, splendor, of even a competency. The slights and hatred of men, and even pretended friends—gloomy prisons and tortures—the society of barbarians of uncouth speech—miserable accommodations in wretched wildernesses, hunger, and thirst, nakedness, weariness, and painfulness, hard work, and but little worldly encouragement—should rather be the objects of their expectation. Thus the apostles acted in the primitive times and endured hardness, as good soldiers of Jesus Christ; and though we, living in a civilized country where Christianity is protected by law, are not called to suffer these things while we continue here, yet I question whether all are justified in staying here while so many are perishing without means of grace in other lands. Sure I am that it is entirely contrary to the spirit of the gospel for its ministers to enter upon it from interested motives or with great worldly expectations. On the contrary, the commission is a sufficient call to them to venture all and, like the primitive Christians, go everywhere preaching the gospel.

It might be necessary, however, for two, at least, to go together, and in general I should think it best that they should be married men . . . two or more other persons, with their wives and families, might also accompany them, who should be wholly employed in providing for them. In most countries it would be necessary for them to cultivate a little spot of ground just for their support, which would be a resource to them whenever their supplies sailed. Not to mention the advantages they would reap from each other's company, it would take off the enormous expense which has always attended undertakings of this kind—the first expense being the whole; for though a large colony needs support for a considerable time, yet so small a number would, upon receiving the first crop, maintain themselves. They would have the advantage of choosing their situation, their wants would be few; the women, and even the children, would be necessary for domestic purposes; and a few articles of stock, as a cow or two . . . a very few utensils of husbandry, and some corn to sow their land would be sufficient. Those who attend the missionaries should understand husbandry, fishing, fowling, etc., and be provided with the necessary implements for these purposes. Indeed, a variety of methods may be thought of, and when once the work is undertaken many things will suggest themselves to us of which we at present can form no idea.

Fifthly, as to learning their languages, the same means would be found necessary here as in trade between different nations. In some cases interpreters might be obtained who might be employed for a time; and where these were not to be found, the missionaries must have patience and mingle with the people till they have learned so much of their language as to be able to communicate their ideas to them in it. It is well known to require no very extraordinary talents to learn in the space of a year, or two at most, the language of any people upon earth—so much of it at least as to be able to convey any sentiments we wish to their understandings.

The missionaries must be men of great piety, prudence, courage, and forbearance; of undoubted orthodoxy in their sentiments, and must enter with all their hearts into the spirit of their mission; they must be willing to leave all the comforts of life behind them and to encounter all the hardships of a torrid or a frigid climate, an uncomfortable manner of living, and every other inconvenience that can attend this undertaking. Clothing, a few knives, powder and shot, fishing tackle, and the articles of husbandry abovementioned must be provided for them; and when arrived at the place of their destination, their first business must be to gain some acquaintance with the language of the natives (for which purpose two would be better than one), and by all lawful means to endeavor to cultivate a friendship with them, and as soon as possible let them know the errand for which they were sent. They must endeavor to convince them that it was their good alone which induced them to forsake their friends and all the comforts of their native country. They must be very careful not to resent injuries which may be offered to them, nor to think highly of themselves, so as to despise the poor heathens and by those means lay a foundation for their resentment or rejection of the gospel. They must take every opportunity of doing them good, and laboring and traveling, night and day, they must instruct, exhort, and rebuke [2 Tim 4:2], with all long-suffering and anxious desire for them, and, above all, must be instant in prayer for the effusion of the Holy Spirit upon the people of their charge. Let but missionaries of the above description engage in the work, and we shall see that it is not impracticable.

⊁⌁⌁⌁

TEXT: William Carey, *An enquiry into the obligations of Christians, to use means for the conversion of the heathens* (Leicester: Ann Ireland, 1792), 62–76.

THOMAS COKE
(1747–1814)
Methodism in Africa

Widely known as the "Father of Methodist Missions," Thomas Coke shared John Wesley's passion for evangelism and emerged as the chief architect of Methodist missionary expansion around the world. Born in Brecon, Wales, where his father worked as an apothecary and later as a local government official, Coke served as an elected member of the common council (the town's administrative body) from 1769. He matriculated at Jesus College, Oxford in 1764, receiving a B.A. in 1768, M.A. in 1770, and Doctor of Civil Law in 1775. After a few years as a parish priest, in August 1776 Coke contacted John Wesley about joining the Methodist cause. Wesley discouraged Coke from hasty action. Despite Wesley's advice, Coke's embrace of open-air preaching and other Methodist practices led to conflict and departure from his curacy at South Petherton in 1777. Soon, Coke became one of Wesley's closest confidants. Some found the connection between the two ministers off-putting. Charles Wesley thought Coke insinuated himself into leadership roles. In 1784, when Wesley unilaterally acted on behalf of the American Methodists, Coke was set apart as superintendent (Charles quipped, "So easily are Bishops made / By man's or woman's whim? / W— his hands on C— hath laid, / But who laid hands on him?"). He traveled to Baltimore and ordained Francis Asbury as deacon, elder, and superintendent in quick succession. Coke and Asbury, now denominated "bishops" of the newly established Methodist Episcopal Church, never settled into peaceful coexistence. Asbury had long served in tireless self-sacrifice: he literally had no home, itinerating in the most rugged conditions, during decades of ministry exclusively in America. Coke, by contrast, served the Methodists by itinerating widely among churches in Britain, North America, and the West Indies. When John Wesley died in 1791, Coke rushed back to London, but the conference refused to elect him to the annual presidency until 1797 (he served again in 1805). Coke devoted his energies to preaching, publishing (most notably a six-volume *Commentary on the Bible* [1801–1807] and three-volume *History of the West Indies* [1808–1811]), and worldwide expansion of the movement. While

443

traveling to establish Methodist churches in India and Ceylon in May 1814, Coke died of an apparent stroke and was buried at sea.

Coke recognized the importance of overseas missions for the future of Christianity. In 1783, nearly a decade before William Carey's more famous appeal, Coke published *A plan of the society for the establishment of missions amongst the heathen.* The following selection, however, comes from *An interesting narrative of a mission, sent to Sierra Leone, in Africa, by the Methodists, in 1811* (1812), which tells the intertwined stories of the founding of Sierra Leone and the rise of Methodism in West Africa. Unlike some of his contemporaries, Coke recognized that black men and women were not only bearers of the divine image but also fully capable of Christian ministry. In the aftermath of the American Revolution, the British initially brought freed men and women of African descent north to Nova Scotia but soon thereafter offered to convey them to newly founded settlements in Sierra Leone. In this way, under the auspices of Methodists in England, former slaves from North America established thriving churches in West Africa.

Sources: *BDE*; Thomas Coke, *The journals of Dr. Thomas Coke*; ed. John A. Vickers (Nashville: Kingswood, 2005); idem, *The letters of Dr. Thomas Coke*; ed. John A. Vickers (Nashville: Kingswood, 2013); Kenneth Cracknell and Susan J. White, *An introduction to world Methodism* (Cambridge: Cambridge University Press, 2005); *ODCC*; *ODNB*; Stanley Sowton, *Thomas Coke* (Grand Rapids: Zondervan, 1956); Norman E. Thomas, "Methodist missions/missiology," in *T&T Clark companion to Methodism*, ed. Charles Yrigoyen, Jr. (London: T. and T. Clark, 2010), 112–32; Francis Bourne Upham, *Thomas Coke* (London: Robert Culley, 1910); John Vickers, *Thomas Coke: apostle of Methodism* (Nashville: Abingdon, 1969).

THOMAS COKE
An interesting narrative of a mission
1812

While Great Britain was engaged in a war with her American colonies, a vast number of Negroes forsook their masters and joined the British forces. These served with fidelity until hostilities were brought to a termination. But when the troops were about to be disbanded, it became a matter of considerable difficulty how to dispose of these consistently with the principles of justice, humanity, and honor. To abandon them in the United States was to expose them to the resentment of their ancient masters against whom they had fought and to reward them with slavery for their attachment to our cause.

To prevent these evils from taking place, great numbers were carried to Nova Scotia and declared free. But Nova Scotia was nothing more than a partial asylum. Many Blacks were incorporated with the British regiments and actually found their way to England. On being dismissed, the English soldiers repaired to their respective abodes, but the Blacks were left in a forlorn condition, without a home and without a friend in a foreign land. These men became, therefore, objects of genuine compassion.

It was well known at this time that Sierra Leone was but thinly inhabited, that the climate was more congenial to these fugitives than ours, and that whilst they remained they must either have been supported by charity or perish for want. It therefore occurred to some benevolent gentlemen in England to represent the case of these men to government, suggesting at the same time the propriety of sending them to this part of the continent and of purchasing from one of the native princes a tract of ground sufficient for their accommodation. . . . Accordingly, in 1786 about four hundred of these fugitives, attended by sixty white women of abandoned character who engaged to accompany them, left England for Sierra Leone at the public expense. . . . There was but little reason to imagine that a colony composed of disbanded Negro soldiers and abandoned white women—taken from brothels, stews, and dunghills of London—would ever become prosperous settlers. It was thought, however, that being urged by necessity and having a fruitful soil before them, they would in process of time become industrious and that industry would introduce order.

‡

... Among these Blacks, many had received serious impressions, and many had been savingly converted to God prior to their taking up arms. Most of these had received their serious impressions under the ministry of our preachers and had joined the Methodist societies in America. On this account, they felt an attachment to our doctrine and discipline, and cherished their partiality for both when they had no longer any connection with us.

As their bodies were preserved in the field of battle through a superintending providence, so their souls were preserved through divine grace in the midst of those dangers to which they were exposed. God, in this instance, has furnished us with a decisive proof that he can work without means as well as through their instrumentality. The field of battle, the sequestered plantation, or the edifice erected for public worship are alike to him. His angels are ministering spirits, sent forth to minister to the heirs of salvation [Heb 1:14], and every portion of the globe is alike accessible to them. They that trust in the Lord shall never be confounded [Ps 22:5]. When he has work for them to do, he will preserve them in the midst of surrounding difficulties and will not suffer anything to hurt them till all his purposes are fully answered. Both life and death are under the control of God [1 Sam 2:6].

On the arrival of these pious Blacks at Sierra Leone, they found the constitution of the colony congenial to their wishes, granting to all liberty to worship God agreeably to the dictates of their consciences while those in power encouraged the practice of every moral virtue. Thus circumstanced, they established the worship of God among themselves according to the plan of the Methodists—at the same time, earnestly inviting others to join them. Two or three, at this time, officiated as local preachers, and a few others bore the office of class leaders.[1] As their lives were exemplary and their preaching regular, their congregations soon increased and several others augmented the original number of the society. And so far was God pleased to bless their simple but sincere endeavors to promote his glory that from that time to the present hour they have been kept as lights in a benighted land.[2]

But though they were fixed in a distinct quarter of the globe, they never forgot that they had friends, both in England and America, whose spirits were congenial with their own. With these they opened a correspondence through the vessels which occasionally touched at the colony. It was by this means that we have heard of their welfare from time to time and have learned the progress which they were making in the divine life. In the progress of time, they contrived to erect a preaching-house, every way suited to the accommodation of their congregations. This preaching-house, we have lately learnt, is sufficiently large to contain four hundred persons.

During the intermediate years that have passed away, we have received many letters from them beseeching us to send a missionary to the colony, to second their own

---

[1]   [Ed. Under the leadership of John Wesley, local preachers were established among the Methodist laity to evangelize and exercise pastoral care to members of the community. Class leaders guided smaller groups of Methodists, typically ten to twelve members, in religious devotion and works of piety.]

[2]   [Ed. Coke draws the phrase "lights in a benighted land" from Charles Wesley's hymn "Come and Let Us Sweetly Join" (1740).]

exertions, and to instruct them more fully in the way of righteousness. But . . . we thought it useless to make any effort while the slave trade was suffered to continue, because we saw no prospect of success. It was hardly to be expected that the natives would embrace our religion while our countrymen visited their shores either to murder or enslave them. As soon, however, as this inhuman traffic was abolished by the legislature of our country, we turned our attention to the condition of the people at large and resolved, as soon as possible, to send some missionaries to the African shores.[3]

‡

As we had not heard from the society in this colony for some time prior to the sailing of these missionaries, we had estimated their number at fifty, and as such they stand in our minutes. But on the arrival of the missionaries, they were agreeably surprised to find no less than one hundred and ten persons, against whom nothing could be brought that could stigmatize them as unworthy members. These not only walk worthy of their vocation [Eph 4:1], but a considerable portion of them profess to enjoy the love of God in their hearts, and their lives afford a convincing evidence of the sincerity of their profession.

On the 22nd of Nov[ember], Moses Wilkins, a black man, preached.[4] Being unable to read, he delivered both his hymns and his text from memory, and, speaking from the fullness of his heart, was enabled to make many striking observations, well calculated to be highly useful to his equally unlearned audience. This, perhaps, in the ears of European philosophy, may have a singular sound. But we must not forget that God, in the wisdom of his providence, adapts his instruments to their work. In this, the divine goodness is as conspicuous as his wisdom. Religion is seated in the heart. And as nothing but infinite wisdom can find out the avenues which lead to it, so nothing but infinite goodness can prepare the instrument to affect it. Among the wise and learned of this world [Matt 11:25], many, no doubt, on such an occasion would be ready to exclaim, "What will this babbler say?" These men may draw what conclusions they please from their own cool calculations. But it is a fact which no reasoning can overturn that this man, in conjunction with his brethren, has been made instrumental in turning many to righteousness [Dan 12:3]. This is firm footing, and all in opposition to it is nothing more than visionary speculation.

‡

Within a week after the missionaries landed at Sierra Leone, they procured a house well accommodated to their wants and wishes. It is situated in an eligible place and is well adapted for the receiving of the sea breeze. This is a consideration of no small importance

---

[3] [Ed. Four missionaries, led by Rev. George Warren, sailed from Liverpool on September 21, 1811 to support the work at colony, foster educational opportunities, and learn the language of a nearby tribe: "every article of household furniture was provided for them prior to their departure, together with such books as were deemed necessary for the schools they intended to establish. To these I was enabled to add twenty-five Arabic Bibles, twenty-five English Bibles, and twenty-five Testaments, which I received as a present from the Bible Society. In addition to these, the benevolent inhabitants of Liverpool presented us, in all, with about two hundred Bibles and Testaments, in order to facilitate this great undertaking" (21).]

[4] [Ed. Coke refers to Moses "Daddy" Wilkinson, a former slave from Virginia who fled to freedom in 1776 and evacuated to Nova Scotia in 1783. Wilkinson, who had led a congregation in Nova Scotia, established the first Methodist church in Sierra Leone.]

in this burning climate. When our letters left the colony, which was about the 12th of December 1811, they had been on shore exactly one month and had not suffered any inconveniency from the change of climate which they had undergone. All were in good health, and, from the pleasing prospects which lay before them, their expectations were raised to an exalted pitch. We hope that nothing will happen to produce an unpleasant alteration in either.[5]

On the importance of carrying the gospel into Africa and the magnitude of the undertaking, it is needless to expatiate. It is not a solitary island nor even an archipelago which we are about to visit, but a continent peopled with nations of which we scarcely know the names. We have a promise that "Ethiopia shall stretch out her hands unto God" [Ps 68:31]. We cannot therefore but conclude that the sending of the gospel among its once favored but now benighted inhabitants is the most likely way to accomplish this great event. During a series of years we have compelled Africa to weep tears of blood; let us now endeavor to brighten her countenance with the smiles of joy as some compensation for the injuries we have done her. Already has the legislature of our country shown us the way by putting an end to the slave trade and by refusing to extort from her groaning children another pang. Let us follow the bright example thus set before us by applying the balm of Gilead to heal her wounds [Jer 8:22].

But future events are known only to God. We can use the means, but divine power is necessary to render them efficacious. We know that the promises of the gospel extend to the whole human race and that in due time these shall receive their full accomplishment. Already, the "Dayspring from on high" [Luke 1:78] has visited many barbarous parts of the earth, and we trust that the time is near at hand when the Sun of Righteousness shall rise upon the moral world with healing under his wings [Mal 4:2].

TEXT: Thomas Coke, *An interesting narrative of a mission, sent to Sierra Leone, in Africa, by the Methodists, in 1811* (London: Paris and Son, 1812), 5–6, 17–19, 30–31, 50–51.

---

5   [Ed. Rev. George Warren died only eight months into his residence in Sierra Leone. He was the first Methodist missionary to die in service to West Africa.]

WILLIAM CARUS WILSON
(1791–1859)
Heathen Cruelty

Encounters with foreigners abroad led some to compose chilling warnings against "heathen irreligion." Few writers combined pious children's literature and accounts of foreign depravity as memorably as William Carus Wilson. Raised on the Westmorland estate that his father inherited shortly after William's birth, Wilson matriculated at Trinity College, Cambridge in 1810 (B.A., 1815; M.A., 1818). Initially rejected as a candidate for ordination by the bishop of Chester due to Wilson's unwavering Calvinism, Wilson was finally ordained by the archbishop of York. Wilson served as rector at Tunstall and received a chaplaincy to the duke of Sussex (resulting, in part, from his father's influence as MP for Cockermouth). From 1825 he served as rector of Whittington, and from 1834 as perpetual curate of Casterton.

Wilson owes much of his lasting fame to his role as founder of charity schools for young women in Whittington and Lancashire. Although some pupils remembered Wilson as a kind and generous man, Charlotte Brontë's portrayal of Mr. Brocklehurst in *Jane Eyre* (1847) cast a long shadow over Wilson's reputation. Two of Brontë's sisters died of tuberculosis while students at Wilson's school, and some of Brontë's earliest biographers believed that Brocklehurst's repeated threats of damnation and miserable treatment of the Lowood Institute girls closely mirrored Wilson's own governance of the Clergy Daughter's School at Cowan Bridge. Recent scholarship has shown that Wilson's philanthropic work extended beyond the schools he supported in England. In particular, Wilson labored to evangelize and support soldiers living abroad: "During the Indian mutiny he distributed 1,500,000 Bibles and tracts to British soldiers, maintained a monthly correspondence with more than 200 of them, and established a soldiers' institute at Portsmouth, where he campaigned for temperance and reportedly caused a local brewer to retire from his business" (Barker, *ODNB*). Wilson's efforts were so highly regarded that noncommissioned officers and privates from the army erected a monument in his honor after his death.

Wilson's literary contribution came in the form of inexpensive devotional literature. Through monthly publications such as *The friendly visitor* (from 1819), *The children's friend* (from 1824), and *The teacher's friend* (from 1844), Wilson created highly moralistic tales for children. The tracts, which blend sentimental piety, anti-Catholicism, and combative judgment of sin, were so successful that, at their peak, Wilson produced three thousand copies of each for an eager reading public each month. The following selections from *The children's friend*, accompanied by vivid and sometimes horrific woodcuts, illustrate the way reports of foreign religious and cultural practices could be used as xenophobic fodder for a child's religious indoctrination.

‡

SOURCES: Jane M. Ewbank and William Carus Wilson, *The life and works of William Carus Wilson, 1791–1859*, second ed. (Kendal: Titus Wilson and Son, 1960); Jane Nardin, "A new look at William Carus Wilson," *Bronte Studies* 27, no.3 (2002): 211–18; *ODNB*.

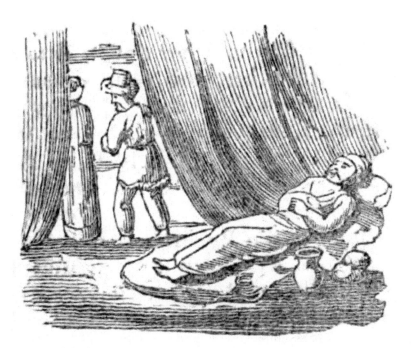

"Cruelty of heathen to parents" (Wilson, *The children's friend*, 105).

WILLIAM CARUS WILSON
The children's friend
1826

Cruelty of heathen to parents

"Without natural affection" [2 Tim 3:3] is indeed too just a picture of the poor heathen. Thus for instance the Tartars.[1] When their parents become very infirm through age, instead of the children watching over them with care and soothing their sufferings, they build a little hut, mostly by the side of some river, in which they place the poor sufferer with a small portion of food, not troubling themselves to look after him anymore. Of course the poor creature pines away and dies of disease and hunger in a slow, painful, and distressing manner.

In some parts of Africa, they are guilty of the same cruelty. Some Bushmen[2] left their aged mother, who was very ill, in the following manner. They took the hut to pieces and left her on the ground to the mercy of others. A converted heathen told her daughter to take care of her, but she refused, saying that her mother, being too old to get her living by labor, did not deserve to be taken care of or to have more food! This pious convert then took care of her till she died.

Others of the Bushmen put an end to the lives of old and infirm persons in a way equally cruel. Sometimes they put them into the bushes with only a little water. The Corannas[3] place them on a wild ox which is driven into the woods. Sometimes they drag them into the fields and leave them for a prey to the wolves!

Ah! What reader who loves his dear parents will not bless God for giving him birth in England and gladly give his money to send out missionaries who may teach the heathen to honor their father and mother!

[1]   [Ed. Inhabitants "of the region of central Asia extending eastward from the Caspian Sea" (*OED*); often associated with the Turks.]
[2]   [Ed. The aboriginal people of South Africa.]
[3]   [Ed. Wilson refers to members of the Khoekhoe people in southern Africa.]

Now may our hearts and voices raise
A grateful tribute to thy praise,
O God of love! for 'tis thy hand
Hath placed us in this Christian land.

We might have all received our birth
In the dark corners of the earth,
Where crimes and cruelties disgrace
An uninstructed heathen race.

But we are taught to know the truth,
To guide and guard us in our youth:
Then let it be our constant care
That others may this blessing share.[4]

‡

East Indies

A widow only sixteen years of age walked out of the town with crowds of people to select a spot on which to die. She held in her hand a naked dagger with which she drew a circle on the spot she fixed upon; and turning round, struck it three times in the ground, and returned to the town in the same manner she had come out. As soon as she retired, some men began digging a pit in the place marked out for the purpose. At about half past four o'clock in the evening, she came out to complete the dreadful sacrifice. The procession at times, and men with their bodies painted in the most hideous manner, danced before her, during which time she gave presents to those about her. She arrived at the fatal spot. She pressed the hand of her father for a second or two. It was a solemn moment—but it was only a moment. After taking off her jewels and ornaments, she descended into the pit by a foot path which had been cut slanting into it for the purpose, seated herself at the bottom of it, and had the corpse of her husband placed in the hole with his head upon her lap. The pit was now filled up with mud and earth so as to cover her shoulders. A cocoa-nut was placed under her chin, on which her head rested, inclining a little forward. A large basket, or hamper, full of fine dry river sand was placed on props opposite her head. These were intended to have been knocked suddenly away, when the mass of dry sand would have rushed forward, covered the head, and suffocated her. In this instance, however, the scene was still more horrible; for owing to the rottenness of the basket, the props were not so soon removed as they ought to have been, and the sand, therefore, fell but slowly on the head of this gasping, suffocating wretch—the victim of ignorance, superstition, and cruelty. At this moment, there was a general shout and clapping of hands set up by the assembled multitudes in whose faces joy and mirth alone were seen.

---

[4]   [Ed. The first two stanzas are the first and third of a hymn from John Buckworth, *Hymns for Sunday schools*, 5th ed. (London: James Willan, 1815), 8–9. Wilson wrote the final stanza, "But we are taught . . ."]

A better day, we hope, has now dawned on the females of India, and thousands of both sexes yet unborn will bless the memory of Miss Cooke, now Mrs. Wilson.[5] This lady, by her prudence and zeal, has in a great measure overcome the prejudices of the ignorant and bigoted Hindus. She has undertaken the care of the female schools and has now many hundred Hindu girls under instruction. The seed thus sown may yet produce an hundredfold.

‡

"Mexican worship" (Wilson, *The children's friend*, 208).

Mexican worship

In South America there is awful ignorance of the true God and Jesus Christ whom he hath sent. But there, as well as in other parts of the world, divine light is making its way; Bibles and Testaments are received with eagerness, and openings are making for much good.

In Mexico they worship the most ugly idols, and the chief part of their worship consists of human sacrifices! They often make war with their neighbors only to procure prisoners to fatten and slay on their altars in honor of their gods, and then themselves to devour their flesh.

The bloody rite is thus described: six priests were the chief actors. The victim was laid on his back on a large stone. Two priests held down his legs, two of them his arms, and another his head and neck, when the head priest, with a sharp flint, cut open his body

---

5   [Ed. Mary Ann Wilson (née Cooke) (1784–1868) was a member of the Anglican Church Missionary Society (CMS). She worked in India establishing schools for children and, following the death of her husband Isaac, founded an orphanage (Jocelyn Murray, "Wilson, Mary Ann [Cooke]," *Biographical dictionary of Christian missions*, ed. Gerald H. Anderson [New York: Macmillan, 1998], 743).]

and tore out the yet beating heart of the poor wretch and, holding it up towards the sun, offered the fume of it as an acceptable sacrifice!

Think, dear children, that it is from such horrid rites as these that we wish to free our fellow creatures by means of our missionaries and our Bibles!

‡

Japanese Christians

In 1613 eight Japanese Christians, having refused to become idolaters, were condemned to be burnt alive. Among them was a lady named Magdalen Mondo, with her son, a child of ten years old. These martyrs were fastened to posts of wood at some distance from each other. A few moments after they had been set on fire, the cords that bound the little boy gave way, and he instantly rushed through the flames which had already seized on his clothes. All present thought he was going to make his escape; but the child flew to the post where his mother was, and threw himself into her arms. Magdalen pressed him to her heart and, forgetting her own sufferings, seemed only to think of comforting and encouraging her son, who at last fell dead at her feet . . . in a few minutes after, she expired.

TEXT: William Carus Wilson, *The children's friend* (Kirkby Lonsdale: A. Foster, 1826), 3:105–6, 203–5, 208–9, 263–64.

REGINALD HEBER
(1783–1826)

Missions in India

Reginald Heber, bishop of Calcutta, was born in Malpas, Cheshire. His father was a rector and, having descended from a noted gentry family, inheritor of Yorkshire wealth and position. Heber attended grammar school at Whitchurch and proceeded to a boarding school outside London before matriculating at Brasenose College, Oxford in 1800. His early success in poetry, including authorship of the prize-winning poem *Palestine* (1803), set the standard for many of his later productions in prose and verse. In 1804 Heber was elected a fellow of All Souls, Oxford. The following year he traveled through Germany and central Europe into Hungary, Russia, and Scandinavia. Following ordination in 1807, Heber thrived in a series of positions, revealing his aptitude for church leadership. He received an appointment as prebendary of St. Asaph Cathedral and delivered the Bampton Lectures at Oxford on *The personality and the office of the Christian comforter asserted and explained* (1815). Heber also wrote a noted life of the seventeenth-century theologian Jeremy Taylor and, later, published what has remained the standard edition of his works (*The whole works of Jeremy Taylor*, 15 vols., 1822). Hymns, more than any other of his compositions, have preserved Heber's memory; though his only collection appeared posthumously as *Hymns, written and adapted to the weekly church service of the year* (1827), his compositions, including "Holy, Holy, Holy, Lord God Almighty" and "From Greenland's Icy Mountains," remain perennial favorites in congregations around the world. Heber's interest in the work of missionary societies led to his appointment as the second bishop of Calcutta in 1823. The reach of his episcopacy is mind-boggling today, extending throughout all of India, southern Africa, and Australia. Heber facilitated the first Anglican ordinations of Indians and established a college for training clergy.

Heber traveled extensively throughout India, and his *Narrative of a journey through the upper provinces of India* (1828) provided an influential account of the land, culture, and people. The work, edited and published by his widow, went through multiple editions and appeared in the pages of prominent publications such as the *Quarterly Review*: "Heber's interests encompassed the economy and administration, education and culture, and the predicament of Indian princes; he relished architecture of palaces and the grandeur of the mountains. He shared the usual contemporary British distaste for Hinduism but not the prejudice against its adherents, whose moral character he was at pains to vindicate; in his judgments on British rule, he was sometimes critical while also giving credit where he felt it was due" (Laird, *ODNB*). In the following selection, Heber describes religious and cultural practices in India. Like so many missionary ethnographies, Heber's narrative reveals a sense of cultural superiority, but one unmarked by racism; the iniquities he observes in India are traced to its religious and political institutions rather than the character of its inhabitants.

>

SOURCES: Geoffrey Cook, "'From India's coral strand': Reginald Heber and the missionary project," *International Journal of Hindu Studies* 5 (2001): 131–64; Derrick Hughes, *Bishop Sahib: a life of Reginald Heber* (Worthing: Churchman, 1986); M. A. Laird, *Bishop Heber in northern India: selections from Heber's journal* (London: Cambridge University Press, 1971); *ODCC*; *ODNB*; Dorothy J. Smith, "Bishop Heber as an Anglo-Indian churchman," *Historical Magazine of the Protestant Episcopal Church* 42 (1973): 367–401.

REGINALD HEBER
Narrative of a journey through the upper provinces of India
1828

Of the people of this country and the manner in which they are governed, I have, as yet, hardly seen enough to form an opinion. I have seen enough, however, to find that the customs, the habits, and prejudices of the former are much misunderstood in England. We have all heard, for instance, of the humanity of the Hindus towards brute creatures, their horror of animal food, etc.; and you may be perhaps as much surprised as I was to find that those who can afford it are hardly less carnivorous than ourselves—that even the purest Brahmins are allowed to eat mutton and venison, that fish is permitted to many castes and pork to many others, and that though they consider it as a grievous crime to kill a cow or bullock for the purpose of eating, yet they treat their draft oxen no less than their horses with a degree of barbarous severity which would turn an English hackney coachman sick. Nor have their religious prejudices and the unchangeableness of their habits been less exaggerated. Some of the best informed of their nation with whom I have conversed assure me that half their most remarkable customs of civil and domestic life are borrowed from their Mohammedan conquerors, and at present there is an obvious and increasing disposition to imitate the English in everything, which has already led to very remarkable changes and will probably [be] still more important. The wealthy natives now all affect to have their houses decorated with Corinthian pillars and filled with English furniture. They drive the best horses and the most dashing carriages in Calcutta. Many of them speak English fluently and are tolerably read in English literature; and the children of one of our friends I saw one day dressed in jackets and trousers with round hats, shoes, and stockings. In the Bengali newspapers, of which there are two or three, politics are canvassed with a bias, as I am told, inclining to Whiggism, and one of their leading men gave a great dinner not long since in honor of the Spanish Revolution. Among the lower orders the same feeling shows itself more beneficially in a growing neglect of caste—in not merely a willingness, but an anxiety to send their children to our schools and a desire to learn and speak English, which, if properly encouraged, might, I verily believe, in fifty years' time make our language what the *Oordoo*, or *court* and *camp* language of the country (the Hindustani), is at present. And though instances of actual conversion to Christianity are, as yet, very uncommon, yet the number of children, both male and female, who are now receiving a sort of Christian education—reading the New Testament, repeating the Lord's Prayer and Commandments, and all with the consent, or at least without the censure, of their parents or spiritual guides—have increased during the last two years to an amount which astonishes the old European residents, who were used to tremble at the name of a missionary and shrink from the common duties of Christianity, lest they should give offense to their heathen neighbors. So far from that being a consequence of the zeal which has been lately shown, many of the Brahmins[1] themselves express admiration of the morality of the gospel and profess to entertain a better opinion of the English, since they have found that they too have a religion and a Shaster.[2] All that seems necessary for the best effects to follow is to let things take their course, to make the missionaries discreet, to keep the government as it now is (strictly neuter), and to place our confidence in a general diffusion of knowledge and in making ourselves really useful to the temporal as well as spiritual interests of the people among whom we live.

‡

On the whole, they are a lively, intelligent, and interesting people. Of the upper classes, a very considerable proportion learn our language, read our books and our newspapers, and show a desire to court our society. The peasants are anxious to learn English and, though certainly very few of them have as yet embraced Christianity, I do not think their reluctance is more than might have been expected in any country where a system so entirely different from that previously professed was offered—and offered by those of whom, as their conquerors, they may well entertain considerable jealousy. Their own religion is indeed a horrible one, far more so than I had conceived; it gives them no moral precepts, it encourages them in vice by the style of its ceremonies and the character given of its deities, and by the institution of caste it hardens their hearts against each other to a degree which is often most revolting. A traveler falls down sick in the streets of a village (I am mentioning a fact which happened ten days ago); nobody knows what caste he is of, therefore nobody goes near him lest they should become polluted; he wastes to death before the eyes of a whole community unless the jackals take courage from his helpless state to finish him a little sooner and perhaps, as happened in the case to which I alluded, the children are allowed to pelt him with stones and mud. The man of whom I am speaking was found in this state and taken care of by a passing European, but if he had died his skeleton would have lain in the streets till the vultures carried it away or the magistrates ordered it to be thrown into the river.

A friend of mine some months ago found a miserable wretch, a groom out of employ, who had crept sick of a dysentery into his courtyard. He had there remained in a corner on the pavement two days and nights. Perhaps twenty servants had been eating their meals daily within six yards of him, yet none had relieved him, none had so much as carried him into the shelter of one of the outhouses, nor had any taken the trouble to tell their master. When reproved for this, their answer was "he was not our kinsman," "whose business was

[1]   [Ed. Members of the highest caste in Hinduism.]
[2]   [Ed. Hindu sacred writings (comparable to the authority of the Bible in Christianity).]

458

it?," "how did we know that the sahib[3] would like to be troubled?" I do not say that these are everyday instances: I hope and believe not, nor would I be understood as denying that alms are (to religious mendicants) given to a great amount in Bengal or that several of the wealthy inhabitants in what they consider good works—such as constructing public [water] tanks, making roads to places of pilgrimage, building pagodas and ghâts[4]—are liberal. I only mention these instances because none of those who heard them seemed to think them unusual or extraordinary, because in a Christian country I think they could not have happened, and because they naturally arise from the genius of the national religion which, by the distinction which it establishes, makes men worse than indifferent to each other. . . .

I need say nothing of the burning of widows, but it is not so generally known that persons now alive remember human sacrifices in the holy places near Calcutta; and that a very respectable man of my acquaintance, himself by accident and without the means of interfering, witnessed one of a boy of fourteen or fifteen, in which nothing was so terrible as the perfect indifference with which the tears, prayers, and caresses even which the poor victim lavished on his murderers were regarded. After this it is hardly worthwhile to go on to show that crimes of rapine and violence and theft are very common or that the tendency to lying is such that (as one of the judges here observed) "in a court of justice they cannot even tell a true story without spoiling it." But what I would chiefly urge is that for all these horrors, their system of religion is mainly answerable . . . [and] the direct tendency of their institutions is to evil. The national temper is decidedly good, gentle, and kind; they are sober, industrious, affectionate to their relations, generally speaking, faithful to their masters, easily attached by kindness and confidence, and, in the case of the military oath, are of admirable obedience, courage, and fidelity in life and death. But their morality does not extend beyond the reach of positive obligations; and, where these do not exist, they are oppressive, cruel, treacherous, and everything that is bad. We have heard much in England of their humanity to animals; I can only say that I have seen no tokens of it in Calcutta.

. . . Do not suppose that I am prejudiced against the Hindus. In my personal intercourse with them I have seen much to be pleased with, and all which I hear and believe as to what they might be with a better creed makes me the more earnest in stating the horrors for which their present creed, as I think, is answerable.

TEXT: Reginald Heber, *Narrative of a journey through the upper provinces of India, from Calcutta to Bombay, 1824–1825*, 3 vols., 2nd ed. (London: John Murray, 1828), 3:251–53, 261–65.

---

3   [Ed. A *sahib* often refers to an English or European man, but Heber uses the title in the broader sense of an Indian gentleman.]

4   [Ed. Landing places for a ferries or steps at the edge of a river.]

FRANCIS HENRY GOLDSMID
(1808–1878)
Jewish Emancipation

The Roman Catholic Relief Act of 1829 brought a once-despised minority a new freedom and status. Soon after, English Jews sought similar relief. Expelled from England in 1290, Jews gradually began returning during the mid-seventeenth century. By 1830 there were approximately eighteen thousand Jews living in London (represented by at least six synagogues) and around nine thousand more in other cities throughout Great Britain and Ireland. English Jews made important contributions to the nation and several intellectuals—including the political economist David Ricardo (1772–1823), the writer Isaac D'Israeli (1766–1848), and the Hebrew scholar Hyman Hurwitz (1770–1844)—published noted works that shaped the religious and cultural life of the Romantic period.

Sir Francis Henry Goldsmid, second baronet, was a Jewish lawyer born in London. His family, well-known for banking, fostered strong social and political connections through ties to leading London Utilitarians. Along with his father, Goldsmid provided leadership in the movement for Jewish emancipation. In January 1833 Goldsmid protested the custom of taking the barrister's oath on the Christian Scriptures; he was allowed to use the Hebrew Bible instead. He later served as the first English Jew selected to queen's council. In 1860 Goldsmid was elected to Parliament as a representative of Reading, providing a hitherto absent voice for English Jewry until the end of his life. His influence over domestic and international concerns can hardly be overstated: he founded the Jews' Infant School in London, served as solicitor general from 1871, contributed to British foreign policy in the Balkans, created the first Reformed Jewish congregation in Britain, helped found the Anglo-Jewish Association, and provided financial support for the nonsectarian University College, London (endowing a chair in mathematics and mechanics). Together with his wife Louisa, Goldsmid also campaigned for women's education.

Goldsmid's *Remarks on civil disabilities of the British Jews* (1830) capitalizes on the momentum of Roman Catholic emancipation (see Part IX). Goldsmid points out inherent contradictions in existing law—in particular, its failure to extend to Jews the privileges

460

granted dissenting Protestants and Roman Catholics. Goldsmid points out, for example, that Jews sit on juries, deciding the life and property of their neighbors, but remain disqualified for "the humblest corporate office" (16). In the following selection, Goldsmid offers three arguments for Jewish emancipation. First, he claims that the same reliefs that already apply to Unitarians (monotheists who reject the Trinity) should be afforded to other monotheist citizens. Second, he challenges longstanding prejudices related to moneylending and social standing by placing the blame squarely on disabilities imposed on Jews by Christians. Finally, Goldsmid assuages fears that emancipation will lead Jews to seek the conversion of their neighbors. Rather, he contends, Jews often feel compelled to convert for worldly advantages, but they have no interest in converting others. After nearly three decades of tireless political labor, barriers to parliamentary election finally were eliminated through the Jews Relief Act 1858.

<hr />

SOURCES: Todd M. Endelman, *The Jews of Britain, 1656 to 2000* (Berkeley: University of California Press, 2002); *ODNB*; Michael Ragussis, *Figures of conversion: "the Jewish question" and English national identity* (Durham: Duke University Press, 1995); Mark L. Schoenfield, "Abraham Goldsmid: money magician in the popular press," in *British Romanticism and the Jews*, ed. Sheila A. Spector (New York: Palgrave Macmillan, 2002), 37–60; Sheila A. Spector, ed., *The Jews and British Romanticism: politics, religion, culture* (New York: Palgrave Macmillan, 2005).

FRANCIS HENRY GOLDSMID
Remarks on civil disabilities of the British Jews
1830

Wherever the question of removing the disabilities under which the Jews now labor has been mooted, the friendly disposition evinced towards the measure has seemed so general among persons of all religious denominations that it was intended to have left its accomplishment to the spontaneous bounty of the Christian part of the community and not to have added a single line or document to the short statement published about two years ago.[1] But the Jews find that this silence is misconstrued, that the demeanor is ascribed to apathy in the cause of religious liberty, which has been dictated by sentiments of a very different nature. They feel, therefore, that they are compelled to depart from the course which they had intended to pursue, to protest against such interpretations of their conduct, and to enter at once upon an examination of the change which they desire. And in this examination enough surely will have been done if it be shown first that the welfare of the Jews will be promoted and secondly that the interest of the country will be in some respects perhaps advanced, and certainly in no possible way prejudiced by properly directing the energies of that long-neglected race. It is only by disproving one of these propositions that an adherence to the present system can be justified, and with reference to these alone, therefore, ought the subject to be discussed.

‡

Another question affecting the Jews has been less considered, and may be regarded as of a more dubious nature. It has been thought, I know, by some of those best qualified to decide on such matters, that the Jews are at this moment excluded from the protection of the Toleration Act.[2] That law . . . relieved nonconformists, with the exception of Papists *and such as denied the Trinity*, from certain grievous penalties to which all were previously

---

[1]   [Ed. Goldsmid refers to *Statement of the civil disabilities and privations affecting Jews in England* (1828).]

[2]   [Ed. As he goes on to explain, the Toleration Act (1688) granted freedom of worship to dissenters.]

liable who absented themselves from divine service in the churches. Originally, therefore, the Act of William and Mary certainly did not comprise the Jews.

But in the year 1813 a statute was passed which repealed in comprehensive terms the excepting clause in the last-mentioned Act as far as it related to persons denying the Trinity, and which, though obtained by the Unitarians, contained no words that can restrict its operation to that class of religionists.[3] Although, therefore, it may seem presumptuous in me even to whisper dissent from the high authorities to whom I have just alluded, yet I cannot refrain from saying that it appears to me at least somewhat dubious whether the law of 1813 did not extend to Jews, as well as to Unitarians, the benefits conferred by the Act of Toleration.

If, however, I err on this point, and it is still true that the nonattendance of Jews at the rites of a religion very different from their own may draw down upon them the severest fines and forfeitures, then assuredly that circumstance can only be considered as clearly showing how imperatively the laws of England, as they regard men of that persuasion, demand an immediate revisal.

‡

Among those who have expressed an opinion on the propriety of the enactment desired, none, I think, have predicted that any serious mischief is likely to result from it. Nor does it, for reasons to which I shall presently advert, seem probable that there will be found many such prophets of evil. Some men, however, may perhaps imagine that the change, though not likely to be injurious, is yet uncalled for, and that the Jews, if they obtain the full privileges of citizens, will be unqualified to exercise and enjoy them. We may be told that the followers of this religion have always been employed in trade, in money-getting, and are fit for no other occupation; that their minds are devoid of cultivation and that they are strangers to liberal pursuits. These, at least, are the exclamations which one age of prejudice has echoed after another and of which the sound has not even yet wholly died away from our ears.

And here, as elsewhere, the assertions of prejudice are not so much untrue as perversions and exaggerations of the truth. To the first article of the charge, indeed, the Jewish community must doubtless plead unqualifiedly guilty. In trade, the Jews have for ages past been almost exclusively employed. I am not, it is true, quite clear that this is a very heinous crime, and I am sure at all events that England is not the country in which it ought to be so accounted. But if it is a crime, the Jews are guilty. They have been prevented by the laws, and in some cases by the persecutions of Christian Europe, from obtaining power and not rarely even bread by other means, and they have obtained them by trade. The man who, as in Russia, may be driven from the country which he inhabits at the will of its sovereign, cannot be a cultivator. The man who, as in England, is unable to sit in Parliament or to accept an office under Government without submitting to a test inconsistent with his tenets, can neither be a legislator nor a servant of the state. In fine, you prevent the Jew from gaining subsistence unless by trade, or influence unless by acquiring wealth, and express surprise at his devoting himself to the acquisition of it with more zeal than

---

3   [Ed. In 1813 the benefits of the Toleration Act were extended to Unitarians through the exclusion of requirements related to the profession of the Trinity.]

other men, and consequently often with more success. You deprive our energies of almost all other objects, and are yet astonished that they should be directed strenuously towards this. You might as well turn six brooks into the channel of one and then wonder how it happened that the united current exceeded, in its depth and its strength, each separate streamlet.

The latter part of the accusation against the Jews, which charges them with deficiency in mental cultivation, is of a more serious nature. Yet of this also I must, I fear, admit the partial truth, whilst I at the same time maintain that this also is the result as well of the disabling laws as of the prejudices which have constantly prevailed against men of that religion. The ancestors of a great part of the present English Jews originally settled in this kingdom as traders somewhat less than two centuries ago. They came hither from countries in which they had been suffering under the most oppressive and degrading regulations. It could not therefore be expected that they should have reached the highest possible state of improvement. Here they were the objects of jealousy and contempt; they were necessarily shut out from places of public instruction; and lastly, the disabling statutes closed before them the paths which lead to all the higher functions of citizenship. The dislike against them which existed entirely prevented them from mixing with their more fortunate neighbors and thus deprived them of the most efficacious means of enlarging ideas and developing intellect—intercourse with various classes of men. Their exclusion from places of public instruction rendered it more difficult for them than it is for others to obtain superior education. Their exclusion from the careers, to success in which a superior education is most essential, removed from them the strongest motives for struggling with those difficulties, whilst all these causes combined to inspire every individual exposed to their action with a depressing sense of degradation which he would strive in vain to shake off—and to *cow* the spirit of the whole community.

‡

There is one plea usually urged in defense of restrictions on belief, on which it is somewhat difficult for a Jew to speak with propriety to Christians, but on which nevertheless I must venture a few words, because I am convinced that it is not only destitute of foundation but directly contrary to fact. We are told that such restrictions benefit the cause of true religion and keep alive a reverence for it in the hearts of men. These are the consequences ascribed to restrictions. What are their actual consequences?

If, among the followers of any other than the established faith, there be found individuals whose desire of worldly advantage is stronger than their love of the creed in which they have been bred, disabling laws hold out to them a direct encouragement to hypocrisy. They will know that they may at once avoid the inconveniences attendant on dissent by professing the religion of the country, even if their minds, though not attached, are yet inclined to that of their fathers. It is possible that such laws may in this manner produce some apparent but insincere conversions, and so secure to the predominant belief a support which every genuine friend of that belief would reject with disgust. But let us consider how far such laws are adapted to promote the *real* diffusion of truth, wherever truth is to be found? We have already seen how powerfully disabilities operate to retard, among the body of men subjected to their influence, the progress of education. We have already seen how the prejudices which they foster, by inspiring those who enjoy the full rights of citizens with a feeling of superiority often approaching to contempt, narrow (though they may not annihilate) freedom of intercourse between the privileged and the degraded classes. On the other hand, hardship endured has not, it is true, excited in the minds of the Jews any feeling approaching to dislike towards those who have inflicted it. Yet we cannot imagine that whilst the followers of the Jewish religion have been oppressed, the same warmth of affection towards their countrymen can have arisen in their minds which would otherwise have existed.

Now no one of these circumstances can be favorable to real conviction. The want of intercourse and of the highest cordiality prevents arguments from being listened to patiently and dispassionately, whilst the want of education incapacitates the mind from feeling their full force and value. How then, it will be said, do you, a Jew, mean to insinuate your persuasion that the abolition of restrictions on faith will facilitate the conversion of those who share your creed? No! I believe it not *because I am a Jew*, but I maintain that you, as Christians, must believe it—that you who doubt not that Christianity is synonymous with truth cannot reasonably doubt that it will be extended by all that contributes to destroy antipathies and diminish ignorance.

If those, therefore, who are anxious (from benevolent motives doubtless) that what they regard as spiritual blessings should be generally shared, think that mixing largely with our fellowmen nourishes prejudice or that knowledge increases error or that prejudice and error promote the interests of religion, then they will do wisely and well in resisting such changes as those here advocated. But if they believe the contrary of all this: if they believe that benevolence towards our neighbor, that an acquaintance with the works of nature and with the productions of highly gifted men, fit the mind for an acknowledgement of truth, and that the cause of truth is the cause of religion, then does it behoove them seriously to consider whether instead of opposing they ought not to further by every means in their power the removal of all restrictions upon conscience.

On the other hand, no Christian needs apprehend that he will diminish by a single individual the number of adherents to his faith if he promotes communication between them and the followers of the law of Moses.

Alarms of this description can scarcely, under any circumstances, be felt by a man thoroughly convinced that the correctness of his belief is clear and indisputable. But their existence is, I imagine, rendered impossible by the fact that the Jews never attempt to make a single convert. Nor is this line of conduct adopted from prudential motives; it is recommended by their religious opinions. The Jews have no idea[4] that it is incumbent on the whole human race to observe the ordinances of their inspired legislator; they conceive that this is *required* only of him whom birth has placed among the sons of Israel, and they hold that the stranger who declares himself a member of their community undertakes voluntarily, and perhaps somewhat presumptuously, a burthensome duty of which the strict fulfilment is indeed meritorious but the neglect thenceforward criminal. Their notions on this head are in fact forcibly, though perhaps rather strangely, expressed in a saying of the rabbis: "He who is not born in the law, needs not bind himself to perform the law; but he who *is* born in the law, must live in the law, and in the law he must die." These precepts

---

4   [Ed. That is, "it is no part of their system of belief."]

certainly inculcate that adherence to belief for which the Jews are remarkable, but can never produce a zeal for seeking proselytes.

><∙∙><

Text: Francis Henry Goldsmid, *Remarks on civil disabilities of the British Jews* (London: Henry Colburn and Richard Bentley, 1830), 1–2, 5–6, 17–26.

Printed in the USA
CPSIA information can be obtained
at www.ICGtesting.com
CBHW081037231124
17903CB00005B/78